Economic Growth and Change

in Bourbon Mexico

University of Florida
Social Sciences Monograph 80

Economic Growth and Change in Bourbon Mexico

Richard L. Garner

with Spiro E. Stefanou

University Press of Florida

Gainesville   Tallahassee   Tampa   Boca Raton
Pensacola   Orlando   Miami   Jacksonville

Library of Congress Cataloging-in-Publication Data

Garner, Richard L.
  Economic growth and change in Bourbon Mexico / Richard L. Garner
with Spiro E. Stefanou.
      p.   cm.—(University of Florida social sciences monograph;
80)
  Includes bibliographical references and index.
  ISBN 0–8130–1183–3
  1. Mexico—Economic conditions—1540–1810. 2. Agriculture—
Economic aspects—Mexico—History—18th century. I. Stefanou,
Spiro E.   II. Title.   III. Series: University of Florida monographs.
Social sciences; no. 80.
HC134.G37   1993   92–27064
338.972—dc20   CIP

The University Press of Florida is the scholarly publishing
agency for the State University System of Florida, comprised of
Florida A & M University, Florida Atlantic University, Florida
International University, Florida State University, University of
Central Florida, University of Florida, University of North
Florida, University of South Florida, and University of West
Florida.

University Press of Florida
15 Northwest 15th Street
Gainesville, FL 32611

For Kristin and Peter

and

Alexa and Andrew

with love

Contents

Figures and Maps

Tables

Preface

This project began about a decade ago, after I had finished working on a study of eighteenth-century Zacatecas. The idea grew out of a curiosity about the extent to which the findings for Zacatecas had relevance for the rest of the colony. My plan was to pursue archival research in those areas that the secondary literature did not cover satisfactorily and to rely on printed materials in those areas that had been thoroughly researched. As my research was ending I came to realize that the datasets that I had collected and constructed would benefit from more rigorous analysis than my own training would permit.

With this mind I asked Dr. Spiro Stefanou, associate professor of agricultural economics at Penn State University, to join the project, and he agreed. When he joined, I had already completed the first draft of the manuscript and was working on revisions. He read the entire manuscript, and we spent several months discussing it. Our discussions centered on the nature of the data, the statistical procedures best suited for analyzing the data, and the fit between my analysis of the data and the interpretations that I had drawn from that analysis. These discussions convinced both of us that the analytical focus had to be sharpened and expanded and that the argument I was making had to be strengthened. Consequently, many datasets were reanalyzed and substantial parts of the manuscript rewritten. As an agricultural economist Dr. Stefanou made important contributions to chapters 2 and 3, which are concerned with analysis and interpretation of colonial agricultural data.

The most important revision to come out of my discussions with Dr. Stefanou was in the argument itself. Growth did take place in Bourbon Mexico, and it can be observed in many economic activities and in most regional economies. What becomes important to an understanding of that growth is knowing how dynamic it was. Although often described as the "golden age," the eighteenth century must have seemed far from gilded to many of its inhabitants. Economic growth appears to have moved at a rate not much above the rate needed to sustain the population. Mexico's own material wealth, such as its precious metals, was not used to broaden or diversify its economic activities but rather to underwrite various imperial ventures that had little positive impact on the colony's economic growth. In the eighteenth century Mexico's population did grow by several million persons, and in response its economy by several tens of millions of pesos. But despite all that growth people may have been only marginally better off in a material sense at the end than at the beginning of the eighteenth century.

This collaboration is unusual in that Dr. Stefanou joined toward the end of the project. Thus the question of how to acknowledge his contribution arose. He is not, strictly speaking, a coauthor, but he was certainly more than a helpful colleague who agreed to read and comment upon the various drafts of the manuscript. In the end we agreed that his contribution should be acknowledged as shown on the title page. Of course, I bear full responsibility for any misrepresentations of the archival or secondary material. Dr. Stefanou could only apply his skills to the data that I provided him.

Many persons and institutions have assisted in this project. We would like to thank the staffs of the following libraries and archives: Archivo General de Indias, Seville; Biblioteca Nacional, Madrid; British Library, London; Archivo General de la Nación, Mexico City; Archivo Municipal de Zacatecas, Zacatecas, Mexico; Nettie Lee Benson Library, University of Texas; Bancroft Library, University of California, Berkeley; Clements Library, University of Michigan; Harlen Hatcher Graduate Library, University of Michigan; Sterling Library, Yale University; John Carter Brown Library, Brown University; New York Public Library, New York; Library of Congress, Washington, D.C.; Rosenbach Library, Philadelphia; and Pattee Library, Penn State University. Persons who have read sections of the manuscript, answered queries, sent data, advised on procedures and techniques, and otherwise provided aid and encouragement include Milton Hallberg, Penn State University; Eric Van Young, University of California, San Diego; John TePaske, Duke University; William Taylor, University of Virginia; John Coatsworth, University of Chicago; Murdo MacLeod, University of Florida; Woodrow Borah, University of California, Berkeley; Arij Ouweneel, Center for Latin American Research and Documentation, Amsterdam; Virginia García Acosta, Centro de Investigaciones y Estudios Superiores en Antropología Social, Mexico City; Gary Gallagher, Glenn Kreider, Jonathan Swaby, Jeff Rich, and Susan Shields, Penn State University. Funds for this project have been provided by the American Philosophical Society, the Council of Learned Societies, and the Institute of Arts and Humanistic Studies and the Office of the Associate Dean for Research, Penn State University. To all these institutions and offices we are deeply grateful. Finally, the staff at the University Press of Florida has made the task of turning a manuscript into a book both pleasant and painless. None of the aforementioned, of course, is responsible for any errors that might be contained in this manuscript. The principal author alone bears that responsibility.

Note to the Reader

In analyzing patterns and trends of several dozen datasets, we have been conscious of the need to apply conventional statistical tests before accepting or rejecting our findings. Except for occasional references in the text to confidence levels that fall below 99 percent, we have reported the results of the tests in the notes. In addition to the number of observations in any given series, we indicate the R^2 (coefficient of determination), the Student t value either in absolute terms or at the level of statistical significance, and correction for autocorrelation. The Student t values are derived from the slope coefficient. With respect to autocorrelation, we have not reported the Durbin-Watson statistic. Where the Durbin-Watson statistic fell in an acceptable range based on the number of observations in the series, we have assumed but not stated in the note that autocorrelation did not exist. Where it fell outside that range, we have indicated in the note a correction for autocorrelation. If a correction raised new doubts about the reliableness of a series, we have so indicated. Not surprisingly, some could not be corrected for autocorrelation. We have designated r as the symbol for the rate of change. When any correlation coefficients have been calculated (for which r could also be used), we have stated that these are correlations and not rates. The appendixes should be consulted for explanations of the statistical procedures and mathematical equations.

1

General Economic Trends
in Eighteenth-Century Mexico

By the late eighteenth or early nineteenth century a sense of economic crisis pervaded Mexico, Spain's richest and largest colony. It was presaged in a 1774 report from José Antonio Areche, *fiscal* (attorney) to Viceroy Antonio María Bucareli y Ursúa and nominee as *visitador* (royal investigator) to Peru. Areche found it more difficult to implement reforms and changes than to describe what stood in the path of change or reform.[1]

To begin with, Areche reasoned, Mexico's size and diversity often overwhelmed efforts to advance a coherent plan for developing its economy. Certainly the absence of an effective system of transportation and communication made such planning more complicated than ever. The cost and time of putting such a system into place was simply another drawback to reform and development, and without such a system, the creation of an integrated colonial market, which could encourage specialization and efficiency, would only be delayed. In addition, planning had to take into account the heterogeneity of Mexican life and culture. People with strong communal or local ties were especially suspicious of proposals that might compromise their interests.

Areche shrewdly observed, however, that in the second half of the eighteenth century much of Mexico was caught up in the same maelstrom—a backward economic system that could not be easily adjusted or changed at any level. The backwardness was pervasive and stemmed from structural and cultural processes. Areche ticked off a long list of ideas and practices that had to be modified or eliminated if Mexico was to rejuvenate and modernize its economy. As people deserted the countryside for the city, for example, the cities filled up with people who were unemployed and worse yet unemployable. With so many idle inhabitants, the burden of support fell disproportionately on fewer and fewer workers. Areche asked the obvious question: What was forcing people off the land?

The causes were numerous and complex but arose generally from an inefficient agriculture which the landowners themselves were largely responsible for perpetuating. Areche discounted soil as a major negative factor. Instead he stressed the prevalence of primitive tilling methods, heavily leveraged properties, and poor labor conditions as causes of low productivity and profitability in agriculture. He was especially irked by landowners who paid wages in merchandise rather than in cash, tyrannized workers instead of managing them, denied workers time off for festivals, concentrated on production of basic commodities, and refused to experiment with new products or explore new markets. He was also critical of Indian agriculturalists because they tended to produce only what was needed to sustain their households and to pay for drink and tribute. Reminiscent of the eighteenth-century physiocratic models, Areche asserted that without changes in agriculture, general economic improvement was unattainable. Even dietary and nutritional standards came under his scrutiny, and he concluded that morbidity levels were high because of the heavy consumption of maize, beans, and cheap bread.

Outside of agriculture Areche found much to criticize. Retail trade was hampered because too few workers were paid in cash and because too few small coins were in circulation. Moreover, merchants were so committed to maintaining the sale of merchandise through *repartimiento* (forced sales of merchandise) that they failed to see native communities for what they could be—vast potential markets for diverse consumer goods. Finally, Areche sharply condemned the small in-home weaving operations as an inadequate base from which to develop a manufacturing sector.

Other eighteenth-century reformers voiced similar criticisms and concerns, but Areche offered as frank and open an assessment as any late colonial public official. Although he unsparingly denounced the activities of merchants, landowners, manufacturers, and even native agriculturists, he did not adequately evaluate the role of the state as a contributor to the economic malaise and as an agent for change. Neither the fiscal nor his allies ever had the vision to see how an economic transformation could have been initiated. Indeed, given the failure of much twentieth-century developmental theory, reforming an eighteenth-century economy was probably beyond the capacity of even the most astute public servant or economic planner. The significance of the inquiries by Areche and other critics lay not in their accuracy, impartiality, or comprehension, for surely they failed to attain such loftiness, but rather in pinpointing the trouble spots and the general trends.

A quarter of a century later, as the colonial era was drawing to a close, many of the economic problems alluded to by Areche and others had simply grown more intractable. A report, based on a survey commissioned in 1806 by Mexico City's *Consulado* (association of import-export merchants), alleged that economic conditions had deteriorated further during the late eighteenth and early nineteenth centuries. The Consulado's report may be of special interest to twentieth-century scholars, who stress that the economic turmoil and the social unrest were being fed by an inflationary spiral.[2] What the survey turned up in its responses was the perception (if not the fact) that many households had experienced a steady loss in purchasing power since the 1780s—and perhaps before—because the prices of housing, food, clothing, and other necessities had been rising faster than incomes. According to the responses, predominantly from women, it was "now necessary to spend twice as much to maintain a household compared to twenty years before." The estimate was that the cost to maintain a well-to-do household had risen from three to six *pesos* (eight *reales* or 272 *maravedis* per peso) per day with the result that a salary of 2,000 pesos in 1806 actually had the purchasing power of 1,000 pesos twenty years earlier.

Although the survey did not make clear which prices had risen and by how much, it did attempt to explain why prices had risen and what the consequences were. Not surprisingly, the Consulado, which had opposed many of the commercial reforms of the Spanish Bourbons, traced the roots of the instability and disorder to the reforms themselves. But *hacendados* and ranchers, vendors and retailers came in for their share of blame as well. They operated with full knowledge that a rise in a population, even if it was an impoverished one, created a seller's market. By withholding grain, they inflated prices, but they also reduced quality in order to protect and enhance their profits. The colony had long known cycles of abundance and famine in the food supply, and during the late colonial years the swings grew more violent and the cycles more frequent. The power of the hacendado or the retailer to manipulate the urban grain market had become greater, in part because the agricultural sector now faced some intractable problems such as a shortage of easily accessible land, high transportation costs to move products overland from new agricultural centers to established urban centers, and limited financial and technological resources. These cycles did not mean that the colony was confronted with constant shortages, even in the late colonial period when so much economic uncertainty existed. Too often the long-standing problem of oversupply remained. Oversupply yielded low prices, and that situation discouraged a level and type of investment in agriculture that might have made it more efficient and profitable. By 1806 some large urban centers like the capital were faced with a twofold problem of managing an increasing population and an expanding supply network. This affected the wealthy as well as the poor and may have worked to the financial advantage of the commercial producer, even though the extent of that advantage remains more speculative than empirical. Greedy businessmen became an easy scapegoat at a time of economic dislocation and social upheaval.

One consequence of these mistaken policies and short-sighted changes, the Consulado observed, was a rise in the *inquilino* population. Inquilinos were those who did not own property and often lacked permanent jobs and residences. The Consulado said that it was ironic that the inquilinos had come to the capital in search of work only to find greater impoverishment. And their numbers could only increase because the rural economy, where they had found employment before, had ceased to expand and develop. Inquilinos had to live more by their wits than by the pesos in their pockets, and yet their presence in the capital only meant that more and more of the city's scarce resources had to be allocated to feeding, housing, and clothing them. Although often victims of demographic and economic circumstances beyond their control, they nonetheless posed a threat to the city's economic well-being because of their idleness and rootlessness. In short, they were a symbol of a rapidly disintegrating economic and social order.[3]

In another report written about 1806 the Consulado raised a related issue: not only had the government contributed to the economic stagnation through its reforms, but it had further burdened the economy with high taxes, heavy currency exports, and forced loans. The Consulado presented figures to support its assertion: between 1765 and 1791 the colony minted 456 million pesos but exported 424 million pesos to pay for goods bought in Europe and Asia (from which the Consulado benefited directly), to cover the transfers from the colonial treasury to other treasuries, and to account for contraband. In fact, declared the Consulado, probably the figures were too low and closer to 500 million pesos had been exported. The higher export figures meant a loss of 40 million pesos over and above what was minted. Such large currency exports, according to the Consulado, reduced the supply of coin in circulation, and that in turn raised the cost of doing business and slowed or checked the expansion necessary to meet the demand of a growing population. For every 10 million pesos' worth of trade, declared the Consulado, the government collected between 2 and 2.5 million pesos. Worse than the amount was the fact that almost no tax revenue was ever invested in the colony's capital stock. For example, at a time that goods had to be shipped longer distances at higher costs, the government played a limited role in the development of a more efficient transportation system.[4]

Surveys and reports from Mexico City's Consulado have some obvious drawbacks. Because of the Consulado's relentless opposition to the commercial reforms that moved Mexico closer to "free-trade" policies, its discussion of late colonial economic issues and problems must be viewed as having a self-serving quality. In particular, the Consulado feared that the reforms made it harder for merchants to control the supply and flow of bullion that was needed to pay their bills and balance their accounts.[5]

Behind the Consulado's shrill protests, however, was a perfectly legitimate question: After a century of reform, had impoverishment instead of improvement taken hold in the late colonial Mexican economy? Other individuals and groups made similar remonstrances: growth in output from mining, agriculture, and manufacturing had not visibly enhanced the material lot of the ordinary citizen. Growth in output alone could not insure a better life. As historians sort through the claims and counterclaims of what went right or what went wrong, economically speaking, they must consider not only why growth failed to unleash the basic economic changes that would have raised the standard of living in late colonial Mexico, but also whether royal policies so shaped and influenced the economic forces that reform itself may partially account for the failure. First, though, to understand more fully the impact of reform, we need to learn more about how the economy functioned and performed in the Bourbon era.

That is the task that we have undertaken: to analyze the performance of the eighteenth-century Mexican economy. Without a doubt the economy was able to expand in response to the rise in population. But the question of the colony's economic well-being is of another magnitude. Famines that caused tens of thousands of people to perish and many tens of thousands more to suffer resulted more from weather than from any Malthusian calculus in which the population had outstripped its resource base or the economy its productive capacity. At the same time it is true that whatever their causes, famines diminished temporarily the pressure from population growth on the economic system. To declare that economic expansion was generally sufficient to match the growth in the population does not mean, of course, that the growth applied uniformly or equally to all areas, groups, or individuals in the colony, or that expansion meant improvement. When other factors are analyzed, it appears that real economic growth could only have been modest at best. Technological advancements could have introduced important changes to spur real growth by raising productivity as well as output, but few such advancements can be documented. With few notable exceptions the pattern to boost output was to add more factors of production, such as land or labor, rather than to change the way in which they were applied.

Parallel to the expansion of the economy was the aggrandizement of the state. The crown's insatiable appetite for revenue increasingly diverted wealth from economic to fiscal activities. By 1800 the economy, like the state, was deeply in debt, and the expansion that was needed to accommodate population growth, especially migration from the countryside to the city, had itself become harder to maintain.

Framework of Study

Despite a number of publications on the economy in the eighteenth century, little has been published on patterns and rates of growth and how this growth affected the structure of the economy. Some historians have argued for substantial growth and others for modest growth, but few have had access to the data necessary to measure that growth.[6] In recent years the publication of long series for agricultural tithes and silver registrations means that we can now measure a part of the growth of the economy. For this study we have concentrated on the period 1700 to 1810 and the area bounded more or less by the cities of San Luis Potosí in the north, Guadalajara in the west, Oaxaca in the south, and Veracruz in the east.[7] Some of the statistical series, which are crucial to this study, cease to exist during or after independence or undergo such changes that they are inconsistent with the preindependence data. Moreover, to stress the linkage of the late colonial, independence, and early national periods does not necessarily negate the value of focusing on the eighteenth century or the late colonial period when Mexico was still a part of an old, established but revitalized empire and not yet a sovereign nation. Thus, given the documentation and the context, the eighteenth century constitutes a manageable and logical unit for the analysis of secular economic trends and the changes that flowed from them. In the seventeenth century, under a weak monarch, the colony gained a measure of economic autonomy within the imperial system; under the Bourbons, however, autonomy gave way to integration or, more precisely, to reintegration of the colony into the empire. Equally important is the fact that the eighteenth century was spared major political, economic, or social upheavals that characterized the nineteenth century and can complicate the analysis of secular trends. As we develop a clearer understanding of the economic background of the independence movement, we will be better able to examine the very serious problems that the new nation faced in the nineteenth century.

The geographic boundaries for this study conform to what can be described as the economic core of the colonial viceroyalty of Mexico.[8] Although less than half of the territory of the colony, it was the area in which the colonial population and the attendant economic activity were concentrated.[9] The core, however, consisted of various regional entities that were not always well defined, although discussions of these entities often proceed as if the boundaries and relationships are well understood.

The Valley of Mexico, for example, may be easier to comprehend as such an entity than Michoacán. The former was a compact basin 70 miles long and 45 miles wide.[10] The latter was an ecclesiastical jurisdiction that measured nearly 350 miles from the Pacific Ocean to San Luis Potosí and about 250 miles at its widest point in the southwest before narrowing to 60–100 miles in

Map 1. Section of Nuevo Mapa Geográfico de la América Septentrional Pertenenciente al Virreinato de México. Dedicado a los sabios miembros de la Academia Real de las Ciencias de Paris. Año de 1768. By José Antonio Alzate y Ramírez. Published in Paris by Dezauche in 1780[?]. From Harvard College Library (4370.1768A). Boundaries refer to ecclesiastical jurisdictions. Beginning at the lower right-hand corner, they are the Bishoprics of Oaxaca and Puebla, the Archbishopric of Mexico, and the Bishoprics of Valladolid, Guadalajara, and Durango. Map includes, in addition to major cities, many towns, villages, and topographical features such as rivers, mountains, and lakes.

the northeast. Encompassing several distinct regional entities, including the Bajío, Michoacán is also described geographically as "centro-occidental" or "centro-oeste."[11] In recent years another approach—to devise compact spatial units based on cities and their market areas—has gained in popularity and has been applied with success to urban centers like Puebla, Guadalajara, and Durango.[12] But historical statistics from which we create data bases do not always conform to spatial units that we might find intellectually desirable. A valuable tithe series exists for Michoacán. Although the series reflects activity in an ecclesiastical jurisdiction instead of a region bound together by common geographic or economic reference points, it can still be used to identify and analyze secular trends in Michoacán's agricultural sector during the eighteenth century, as well as to compare those trends with other regional and colonial economic indicators. Tithes are flawed. They reflected predominantly Spanish agricultural activity and did not capture all that was produced in a given area. Instead of discarding them, however, we should use them in ways that are consonant with what they are.

One finding underscored by city market studies is that an expanding urban population led to expanding demand for basic foodstuffs and agricultural commodities. Area producers generally responded by adding land and labor, but additional production did not necessarily result in substantial gains in productivity and profitability. Both low commodity prices and high transport costs limited how far the supply network could be extended. Moreover, the lack of information as well as the unfavorable ratio of prices to costs dampened any incentive for producers to seek and exploit opportunities in more distant markets. As undeveloped as interregional markets were, however, they did function for some classes of domestic manufactures, imported goods, and even farm products. How producers made the decisions to pursue business opportunities beyond their own immediate localities remains unclear, but that some did so can be gleaned from various economic studies.

In considering the role of markets in eighteenth-century Mexico, we confront a system of production and exchange that consisted of various layers that under some circumstances had a wholly local character and under other circumstances a regional, colonial, or even international character. Eric Van Young has applied the term *disarticulated* to describe an economy that consisted of overlapping local and regional exchange systems that constituted at best a weak integrated colonial market.[13]

One consequence of the Spanish mercantile system is that because the state had power to reach into every region and locality to impose taxes, regulate commerce, and settle disputes, it helped to erect market structures that linked producers, merchants, and consumers across natural or traditional boundaries. The power of the state to interpose itself in local or regional affairs, whether economic, administrative, or judicial, could be, as scholars have rightly pointed out, limited by circumstance, distance, and ineptness. But to assume that the colony's economic life operated only within the confines of local markets or at most on the larger regional scale is to miss the extent to which more complex structures were evolving in the late eighteenth century. As more data are collected, market structures will be easier to identify and analyze. For the time being, however, these series for broad administrative jurisdictions can be put to good use in an effort to arrive at some sense of how the economy performed at the various levels from local to colonywide in Mexico's Bourbon period.

Aggregated colonial series make up part of the data base that we use to describe and analyze the economy in Bourbon Mexico. Such series increase the risk of promoting the view of a more integrated colonial economy than in fact existed. Although we present "aggregated" series for sectoral production, prices and wages, and royal revenue, we do so with the full recognition of Joseph Schumpeter's warning that "aggregative thinking" with reference to how economic growth has been explained can lead to misinterpretation.[14] We do not accept either as an assumption or as a conclusion that the economic system was so localized or regionalized that any colonial series simply distorts the way in which the system operated. Intervention by the state is frequent and constant enough to compromise the autonomous character of the even the most remote areas.[15] All areas were influenced by similar forces of population growth, natural disasters, technological backwardness, and royal policies, and to no one's surprise, series for more discrete units, based upon geographic or economic constraints, tend to exhibit similar tendencies. The economy that evolved during the Bourbon era can be and must be analyzed from several different angles, including a colonywide angle. Regression techniques can be employed to examine how series from regions behave in relation to each other.

We can test several such series for Bourbon Mexico. Maize prices from Mexico City and the surrounding valley are correlated with a series from the Upper Bajío or, more precisely, from the area that served Guanajuato. In normal agricultural years during the eighteenth century very little maize could be shipped profitably from the Upper Bajío to Mexico City because the cost of transportation exceeded the price that could be expected. Even with low harvests or in famine years sellers still needed to consider the cost of transportation if they sought to realize the greatest return possible. Reflecting local rather than distant markets, the prices in the two series have an independent character. The aim in analyzing the series is to see how closely their movement matches up. We can also undertake the same analysis for two different tithe series, one from Oaxaca and one from Michoacán, for approximately the same period.

The results are that correlations between the two independent price series are strongly positive over the whole century, and between the two independent tithe series very strongly positive. It must be noted that the correlations of the two price series and the two tithe series are stronger in the second half of the eighteenth century than in the first half. On one level positive correlations between maize-price series or tithe-revenue series from different areas may be treated as indicators that local and regional trends were moving in similar directions because local and regional economies shared similar problems and underwent similar developments, especially after 1750. The rise in demand for agricultural goods because of population growth and rural-to-urban migration was experienced across the core of the colony and perhaps even on the periphery. Maize prices may be read as one indicator of how the agricultural sector responded to increasing demand for basic commodities from region to region. Producers had to decide what they could afford to sell and consumers what they could afford to buy irrespective of the locations of the markets. An intriguing question, though, is whether the activities of the markets in the capital, the Bajío, Oaxaca, or Michoacán had an influence or effect beyond their own boundaries.

On another level, then, these correlations may point to the dissolving of the autonomous or independent regional economies and the emerging of an incipient but inchoate colonial economy. The emphasis here must be on the process at work. There were too many obstacles both in terms of structure and policy to the creation of a fully integrated colonial market. One conclusion that emerges from the analysis of as many trends in as many sectors and areas as possible is that certain economic undercurrents at work in eighteenth-century Mexico did not necessarily recognize or respect local and regional boundaries.[16]

Although confined to Bourbon Mexico, we have not tried to write a history of Bourbon economic policy, how it originated, who implemented it, or what it encompassed. That history has been amply investigated in the last quarter century. We are concerned, however, with the impact of the policy on the economy, and discuss the policy to understand its impact. The Bourbons, despite their reformist outlook, remained firmly committed to the belief that state intervention was needed if the twin goals of economic growth and financial solvency were to be achieved. Intervention could take the form of direct ownership (i.e. the tobacco monopoly), but typically under the Bourbons it entailed regulations that were more stringently enforced and taxes that were arduously collected. By the end of the eighteenth century the main result of the Bourbon economic policy was the channelling of much of Mexico's wealth away from its own internal development and into state-sponsored projects designed to shore up a faltering empire.[17]

Estimates of Growth

In the past Bourbon Mexico—known as "siglo de oro"—has been described as if economic growth produced better times. There can be no doubt that eighteenth-century Mexico posted nominal growth—more maize, fabrics, silver, and other products—but nominal growth did not automatically equal real growth such as a gain in income per capita. If significant per-capita growth had occurred, then the average citizen would have been better off, but that does not appear to be the case. It is even possible that nominal growth not only slowed, but stagnated or declined. This changes the debate from how much the inhabitants may have gained to how much they may have lost.

Although economic growth probably kept pace with demographic growth for most of the eighteenth century, this may not have been the case by the end of the century.[18] To test this definitively we need better demographic and economic data than now exist. In the demographic area, based on census figures and modern estimates, the population probably reached 5 million or 5.5 million by 1800. Without a census from 1700, however, we cannot accurately calculate how much the population grew over the eighteenth century. If the population were between 2.5 million and 3 million in 1700, then it had doubled by 1800. This represents a growth per year of about 0.7 percent.[19]

For economic growth, either nominal or real, the picture is less clear. Several estimates exist for 1800, but none yet has been advanced for 1700. Trying to determine a rate of growth for the economy from 1700 to 1800 or 1810 has implications for nineteenth- and even twentieth-century economic history. If the size of the economy in 1800 is too small, then the growth needed in the nineteenth century to reach the level of output in 1900 may be higher than was plausible, given the political and economic developments of the nineteenth century. Similarly, though, too big an economy in 1800 could mean too steep a growth from 1700 to 1800. A total output estimate in 1800, therefore, must take into account both population growth (the population had to be fed, housed, and clothed) and the growth that Mexico's economy was capable of in the eighteenth century under Spain and in the nineteenth century after independence.

The estimated Gross Domestic Product (GDP) in current pesos for 1800 falls into a range of 100 million pesos to 250 million pesos. This is a substantial difference by any reckoning. If the colonial population were from 5 to 6 million in first decade of the nineteenth century, then per capita GDP (current pesos) could be as a low as 20 pesos and as a high as 50 pesos. A per capita GDP from 15 to 20 pesos in 1700 and from 20 to 25 pesos in 1800 would mean economic growth of 0.5 percent each year between 1700 and 1800. The closer the per capita figures in 1700 and 1800, the less the growth over the century. On the other hand, if per capita GDP were 20 pesos or below in 1700 and 50 or above in 1800, then yearly growth would be in excess of 1 percent. Looking ahead to 1900 we can compute that a per capita figure of only 20 to 25 pesos in 1800 would require a growth of 1.6 to 1.8 percent per year down to 1910, while a figure of 45 to 50 pesos in 1800 would require only 1 to 1.1 percent per year down to 1910.

It must be emphasized that these discussions about growth rates in the eighteenth and nineteenth centuries are strongly influenced by the fact that the best data are from the twentieth century. In effect we are trying to match up what we know from the twentieth century with what we can only estimate for the eighteenth century. Throughout this discussion we need to bear in mind that the faster the growth in the eighteenth century, the slower the growth in the nineteenth century, and conversely the slower the growth in the eighteenth century, the greater the growth in the nineteenth century.

In his research on total and per capita GDP in the nineteenth century John Coatsworth has began in 1800 with a figure for total GDP of 240 million (current) pesos and a per capita GDP of 40 pesos. At this level in 1800 the annual growth in total GDP to 1910 would rise at a rate of 2 percent and in per capita GDP at a rate of 1.2 percent. When converted to 1900 (or constant) pesos, the rate becomes slower: total GDP grew by 1.5 percent and per capita GDP by 0.6 percent.[20] If we assume that per capita GDP in 1700 was about half that in 1800, then its growth per year from 1700 to 1800 (based on 1900 pesos) would approximate that of the nineteenth century—actually 0.7 percent instead of 0.6 percent because of the slightly shorter time. At 28 pesos per person in 1700 the total GDP in 1900 pesos would work out to be from 56 million pesos with 2 million people to 70 million pesos with 2.5 million. For the whole century total GDP in 1900 pesos would grow between 1.4 and 1.8 percent per year, dependent upon the population figure chosen. Such growth rates for eighteenth-century Mexico, either in total GDP or per capita GDP in constant pesos, are high when compared to rates for more advanced economies, although such comparisons are not always valid.[21] The statistical evidence that Mexico's economy grew in 1900 pesos at such high rates does not yet exist over the long term of the eighteenth century.

Scholars have relied on two sources in assessing the size of the late colonial economy. First, Alexander von Humboldt compiled some sectoral data for mining, agriculture, and manufacturing that totaled about 60 million pesos. The second source, a compilation of what items Mexico produced and what each item cost on average, was the work of José María Quirós, the secretary of Veracruz's Consulado. Humboldt's estimates did not include government transfers or service jobs, while Quirós's figures could be inflated because raw materials and finished products—the value of the materials from which hats were made as well as the value of hats when they were sold—could both be counted. Researchers have tried to make these two sets of figures more usable by filling in Humboldt's gaps and eliminating Quirós's double-count-ing. The result has been that with revisions the GDP based on Humboldt's data ranges from 100 to 190 million pesos and the GDP based on Quirós's data from 220 to 250 million pesos. When we calculate growth rates in current pesos, we see that the range of 100 million pesos in 1810 to 2,179 million pesos in 1910 yields a rate of 2.9 percent per year over the whole century, while 250 million pesos yields a rate of 2.0 percent per year.

Another way to express the difference between these two rates is that with the higher rate GDP doubled every twenty-five years as opposed to every thirty-five years under the slower rate. GDP expressed in constant pesos has only been calculated for the higher figure, 250 million pesos, and that calculation based on 1900 prices shows that total GDP grew by 1.5 percent annually from 1800 to 1910. Part of the reason for the lower growth rate in constant pesos is that in the conversion to constant pesos the GDP for 1800 rose to 333 million pesos but for 1910 it fell to 1,600 million pesos. In general, though, growth rates in constant terms are lower than those in current terms.

Coatsworth has also refined these data in order to compare national income in Mexico with other nations. Converting the data to (1950) U.S. dollars, he has computed estimates of total national income and per capita national income for Mexico, Brazil, Great Britain, and the United States from 1800 and 1910.[22] These estimates show that if Mexico's national income is assumed to be high, above 200 million pesos in 1800, then Mexico registered the slowest growth (1.4 percent per year) among the four countries (nearly a full point behind Brazil) and the third slowest (0.5 percent per year) in per capita income. If the 1800 figures were halved to bring them in closer alignment with lower estimates of the level of the economy in 1800 and the figures for other countries remained unchanged, the growth in Mexico's total income to 1910 would be only a few tenths of a point behind Brazil. Its growth in per capita income, however, would be the second highest of the four, half of a point behind that of the United States.

Reducing Mexico's estimate for 1800 means faster growth in the nine-teenth century in order to reach the 1910 figure, and this in turn changes Mexico's position relative to the other countries. At 100 million pesos in 1800 Mexico's total national income during the nineteenth century would have grown faster than Brazil's and its per capita national income would have grown faster than Brazil's and Great Britain's. It seems unlikely that per capita national income grew faster in Mexico than in Great Britain during the nineteenth century. Unless some adjustment can be made in Great Britain's data, a national income figure higher than 100 million pesos for Mexico in 1800 would seem logical. How much higher remains the sticking point.

A consensus is emerging that total GDP or national income was probably higher, perhaps substantially higher, than what can be derived from Humboldt's unrevised data. Whatever figure is agreed upon for 1800 has an impact on how we view the eighteenth-century economy. If the 1800 figure were high rather than low, as proposed by Coatsworth, growth would slow down in the nineteenth century but speed up in the eighteenth century. Sharing an interest in how fast the nineteenth-century Mexican economy grew but using a different approach, Linda Salvucci and Richard Salvucci have tried to estimate a rate from 1750 to 1895. They found that per capita income in 1970 pesos from 1895 to 1940 rose at a rate of 0.82 percent per year. With 1895 as a benchmark they computed what per capita income would have to be in 1750 to grow by 0.82 percent annually to reach the 1895 figure (as stated in 1970 pesos): per capita income in 1970 pesos would be 747 pesos in 1750 and 1,124 pesos in 1800.

When Coatsworth's estimate of per capita income in 1800 is converted to 1970 pesos, it amounts to 1,869 pesos. The Salvuccis' 1800 figure, based on the assumed annual growth of 0.82 percent, is strikingly lower, only two-thirds of Coatsworth's figure.[23] Since we know that Coatsworth's figure for 1800 was approximately 40 pesos per person in current pesos, we can estimate that the Salvuccis' figure for 1800 was about 26 pesos. At that level, the growth in per capita income would be slower during the eighteenth century but faster during the nineteenth century than it would be if Coatsworth's 1800 estimate were accepted. On the other end, an assumed rate of 0.82 percent does not yield income per capita in 1910 that is as high as the recorded amount: 2,759 versus 3,103 in 1970 pesos.[24]

As intriguing as these explorations into the pre-1900 growth of national income or domestic product are, they leave us with a fuzzy picture. More research will certainly reduce some and perhaps all of the fuzziness. Based upon our analysis of existing series, economic growth appears to have followed a slow or modest upward path from 1700 to 1800. Such a path does not necessarily disprove the high-range numbers offered for 1800. If the path is slow or modest and the numbers high, however, then the task of explaining how they occurred is more complicated.

Population Growth

An estimate of the growth in population during the eighteenth century is needed in order to understand how much the economy had to grow to maintain the population. To date demographic patterns for a few cities and regions have been reconstructed and analyzed, but a colonywide rate for the eighteenth century remains unrealized. Three estimates can be used as benchmarks for determining population trends from 1650 to the end of the colonial period. In the middle of the seventeenth century, as a result of depopulation, the colony had approximately 1.5 million Spaniards, Indians, and mixed bloods.[25] In an informal census taken in the early 1740s and based on estimates of households, the count revealed a population in the range of 2.5–3 million persons, for an increase of at least 66 percent and perhaps as much as 100 percent since the middle of the seventeenth century.[26] The best, and yet a highly controversial, census was conducted in the viceregal administration of the Conde de Revillagigedo in the 1790s. According to Alexander von Humboldt, who studied the Revillagigedo census a decade later, the census counted about 4.5 million persons. Having uncovered numerical and methodological errors in the census, Humboldt concluded that the size of the population in the 1790s exceeded 5 million. By 1803, at the time of his visit, Humboldt believed that the population had reached 5.8 million.[27] Using Humboldt's estimates, some scholars have claimed the population surpassed 6 million in 1810 and then declined sharply due to the war.[28] This means that between 1740 and 1810 Mexico's population could have risen by as little as 50 percent and by as much as 150 percent. An annual growth rate based on the various figures from the census of the 1740s and the revised census of the 1790s ranges from 0.8 percent to 1.8 percent.[29]

For the region of western Central Mexico, which includes the modern-day states of Jalisco, Nayarit, Colima, and Aguascalientes and portions of the states of Zacatecas and Michoacán, Cook and Borah have calculated rates of population growth per year by decade. Those calculations indicate that the population dropped steadily until the middle of the seventeenth century and then reversed itself. The rates for the six decades from 1650 to 1710 ranged from a low of 0.1 percent per year from 1650 to 1660 to a high of 1.8 percent per year from 1700 to 1710. For each decade from 1710 to 1800 the rates fluctuated between 2 and 3 percent per year. For the decade from 1800 to 1810 the annual rate fell below 1 percent. For most of the eighteenth century annual rates by decades point to significant growth, although the annual rate over the whole century (rather than within decades) was probably equal to a doubling of that regional population every forty years. The high point was reached in the 1760s when the rate climbed to 2.7 percent per year. Even though it began to decline after that, the rate over the next two decades was still about 2.6 percent per year.

In explaining "this truly great expansion," Cook and Borah state that the causes can be traced to "a century of relative quiet and stability, with high birth rates, although accompanied by a high death rate. For the west-central region, there was also the impetus supplied by a heavy migration from Europe and from other parts of Mexico."[30] It cannot be automatically assumed that other regions or the colony as a whole duplicated these figures. A rate as high as 2 percent per year for the whole colony in the eighteenth century seems unlikely in light of the aforementioned censuses, but it cannot be completely ruled out either.[31] After examining birth-death ratios, based on the Revillagigedo census, Humboldt contended that "if the order of nature were not inverted from time to time by some extraordinary cause, the population . . . would double every 19 years." To double every nineteen years the annual rate would have to be in the vicinity of 3.5 percent, a rate that was certainly inconceivable over the long term.

When Humboldt corrected the Revillagigedo census and then extrapolated population growth from 1793 to 1803, he came up with a more conservative annual rate of 1 percent. But Humboldt remained dubious that a 1 percent rate was high enough to describe what was then happening or had been happening. "Yet well informed persons who have attentively observed the progress of agriculture, increase of villages and cities, and the augmentation of all the revenues of the crown . . . are tempted to believe that the population . . . has made a much more rapid progress." Over the long term, however, a 1 percent rate may not be unreasonable. At 1 percent the colony's population would double every seventy years and at a 2 percent rate the doubling would occur twice as fast, or every thirty-five years.

Higher mortality rates during famines and epidemics had the effect of slowing or reversing the rise temporarily. Rates could vary from time to time and region to region, and any estimated colonial rate will certainly not capture those variations. Some scholars believe that natural growth was faster in rural areas than in urban areas. When in-migration is added to their natural growth, urban areas could have experienced as much or more growth than the countryside. The in-migration had important economic implications for both the countryside and the city: it could benefit both economies if it matched up with structural changes in how goods were produced and distributed; it could also overwhelm these economies if such changes were too slow in coming or too narrow in scope. It is possible that after a century of population growth and migration the structural changes needed for economic expansion and development had failed to advance far enough to relieve the pressure that urban centers were being subjected to as they tried to maintain their ever-increasing populations.[32]

A series, based on counts and estimates of tributary population in central Mexico, exists for 1700 to 1810.[33] The counts were taken from "government registers" of those living in Indian pueblos scattered across fifty-one provinces in central Mexico. Methodological problems abound, but the compilers of this series appear to have exercised considerable care in analyzing the registers and assembling the statistics. What we most need is enough such data to compute long-term rates for individual pueblos as well as for the whole region. That is partially accomplished with this series. Overall the population rose. Around 1710 there were 200,000 tributaries (perhaps more than 1 million individuals), and a century later there were 300,000. The average for the whole period was 215,000, and the rate of increase was 0.7 percent per year.[34] Growth shows up less strongly in the first half of the eighteenth century then in the second half, when it may have increased by more than 1 percent per year.

Although the series can be faulted for having too many numbers that appear to be based on estimates rather than counts, it yields rates that correspond with other long-term demographic indicators that place Mexico's eighteenth-century growth above one-half of 1 percent but less than 1 percent per year. To be sure variations within Anáhuac should be noted because some pueblos lost population as others gained. Migration within Anáhuac as well as in or out of the region was an important factor in its eighteenth-century demographic history. And of course these calculations do not capture the growth in non-Indian groups. These data confirm a general impression that a secular population trend followed a moderately upward path with periodic variations that could be much more extreme.

How does a 1 percent annual rate (give or take a few tenths of a percent) for the whole colony compare to population growth in other societies? According to estimates collected by David Grigg, world population grew by 0.3 percent from 1700 to 1750 and 0.4 percent from 1750 to 1800. In Europe generally during the eighteenth century he calculates the annual rate to be 0.3 percent between 1700 and 1750 and 0.5 from 1750 to 1800. In specific European countries his rates range from 0.1 to 0.7 percent per year. Grigg concludes that population grew more slowly in the first half of the eighteenth century than in the second half, and that the rate of growth in the second half was "higher than . . . the preceding century." Until the eighteenth century European rural and urban populations rose at comparable rates, but after 1750 urban populations probably climb faster than rural populations.[35] What caused European populations to grow faster in the second half of the eigh-teenth century is a matter of dispute, although it was probably the result of a combination of factors from changing birth and death rates to improving dietary and medical conditions.

If Mexico's growth reached or exceeded 1 percent per year over the whole eighteenth century, then it was more robust than Europe's. Mexico's faster rate was explained in part by the fact that unlike Europe's eighteenth-century growth, Mexico's was part of a recovery, especially in the first half of the eighteenth century, which followed the end of the cycle of depopulation until 1650. Even though scholars are not yet in agreement about how much growth Mexico experienced in the eighteenth century or what factors caused that growth, they have provided a range of estimates that allow for consideration of economic growth against the backdrop of demographic change.

Growth in Production

Even without precise rates of growth in population for the eighteenth century we have enough information to suggest that the rate colonywide did not exceed 1 percent per year and it surely did not fall below 0.5 percent per year. An annual rate of 0.7 to 0.8 percent across the whole colony during the eighteenth century is estimated. Long-term rates could vary significantly from region to region and from time period to time period. Colonywide, long-term rates in the range of 0.5 to 1.0 means that the population doubled in no less than seventy years and no more than 140 years. To avoid shortages and crises caused by a population outstripping the resource base, the economy should grow at a rate comparable to that of the population. Although economic data are incomplete, enough exist to suggest that the economy was capable of growing to accommodate the rise in population. What is harder to determine is how much, if any, the economic growth exceeded what was needed to maintain the population. Anything above the rise in the population minus inflation could be treated as real economic growth.

An ecclesiastical tithe (10 percent), assessed mainly against Spanish landowners, was intended to raise money to support the clergy. Tithes were collected in kind—heads of cattle or sheaves of grain—and in cash. By the eighteenth century payment in cash was more common than in kind. If the tithe documents consistently listed the volume of output (in order to determine the value of the tithe), then we would have a most valuable record of agricultural and pastoral production. Only a few such series exist for eighteenth-century Mexico. What we generally have is a record of the receipts collected from the landowners to satisfy their obligations or from the sales of goods presented by them. The latter figures are a much less accurate reflection of what the landowners actually produced.[36] Although tithe series can pose difficult methodological problems, they remain the only available sources from which we can create production series for the agricultural sector. Money tithes are no more than a rough indicator of long-term output of the tithe-paying colonial landowners. Lacking a colonywide series, we have access to several regional series that can be analyzed individually and collectively for secular trends and growth rates.

The second series concerns mineral output. Colonywide data exist for silver from 1700 (and earlier) and for gold from 1733. Gold production amounted to less than 10 percent of the total output of gold and silver. For silver, several different series exist. Despite differing origins, they share common long-term characteristics.[37] The mineral sector differed from the agricultural sector in that its production curve had less of a direct link to demographic changes. The quantity of gold and silver produced depended on factors such as the grades of ore, accessibility to capital and labor, and the level of technology, although all these factors could be influenced by the pattern of growth and change in the population. Still, the determination of secular trends and growth rates for mineral production is necessary in order to develop a full picture of how all sectors of the economy were performing. An expanding mining industry obviously created an increase in demand for agricultural and manufactured goods as well as for labor and capital. It could also boost inflation because it increased the money supply.

The two longest tithe series are from the dioceses under the bishops of Michoacán and Oaxaca.[38] The length of the two series differs: for Michoacán 1680–1810 and for Oaxaca 1701–1800. The two regions had different demographic and economic characteristics, which must be taken into account in any analysis of regional trends. In combining the two series, as we have done here, we are only trying to show how a production curve for the agricultural sector might begin to look if we had data from all the ecclesiastical tithing districts. Although the shape of the curve and the rate of growth along the curve will change as more series are compiled and added to these two, this Michoacán-Oaxaca series probably accounts for one-quarter of the total tithe revenue. In absolute terms the value of agriculture in the two regions rose by 220.1 percent from 1.5 million pesos in 1701 to 4.8 million pesos in 1800. Colonywide this could translate into an agricultural sector worth 5–6 million pesos in 1700 and 20–30 million pesos in 1800.[39]

The growth rate for the combined tithe is 1.3 percent per year from 1701 to 1800.[40] At this rate the output of agriculture would double every fifty years. The secular curve (fig. 1-1) is impressive because the slope has a strong, upward appearance that reveals no major interruptions or reversals over the long term. Famines, epidemics, and other natural disruptions occurred, and perhaps with some regularity, but they were apparently manageable within the existing agricultural system. This condition began to change toward the end of the century in the aftermath of the famines of the 1780s as the pace of growth in the agricultural sector slowed, at least in comparison to earlier postfamine periods. While the agricultural crisis from 1784 through 1786 was particularly tragic in terms of human losses, it was also selective. Some parts of the colony were hit far harder than others, and that may help to explain why the impact on the tithe curve was so small.[41] A 1.3 percent rise in the agricultural curve would appear to be enough, although with little room to spare, to accommodate the estimated growth in population. If the population rate was close to 1 percent per year or, as some believe, slightly above 1 percent over the whole century, and the agricultural output grew at or above those rates, then a long-term demographic catastro-

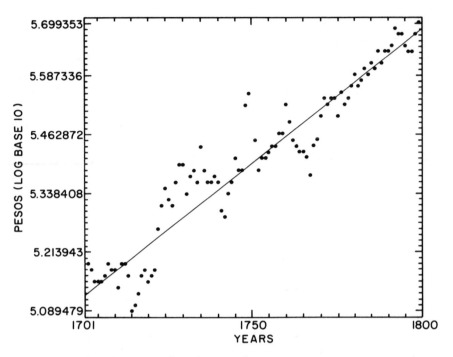

Fig. 1-1. Combined Oaxaca and Michoacán tithes, 1701–1800. *Sources:* For Michoacán, Claude Morin, *Michoacán en la Nueva España del siglo xviii. Crecimiento y desigualdad en una economía colonial;* for Oaxaca, Elías Trabulse, T. Pastor, L. Adelson, E. Berra, F. Hurtado, J. MacGregor, and G. Zermeño, *Fluctuaciones económicas en Oaxaca durante el siglo xviii. Statistics:* Growth rate = 1.3 percent per year, R^2 = 0.91, Student t = 11.90, corrected for autocorrelation.

phe could hardly have been unfolding, even though in the short run major famines had severe effects.[42]

When the Oaxaca–Michoacán series are disaggregated and analyzed, they reveal more clearly certain regional differences. The growth in agriculture in Michoacán at 1.5 percent per year from 1701 to 1800 was about twice the annual rate in Oaxaca at 0.7 percent. The Diocese of Michoacán included the area known as the Bajío, which D. A. Brading has described as "the pacemaker of the Mexican economy" in part because of its rich, fertile agricultural land.[43] That agricultural area supported a large and expanding population as well as a more diversified economy that included some large-scale manufacturing and mining. In addition, the Bajío and other areas in Michoacán became suppliers of foodstuffs to urban areas outside their own boundaries, no doubt a condition that helped to speed up whatever changes were necessary to increase agricultural production. Regional economic boundaries did not cease to exist in eighteenth-century Mexico, but they were becoming less pronounced where urban growth impinged on agricultural production. By comparison Oaxaca's less vigorous agricultural sector reflects slower overall demographic growth and economic change in the eighteenth century. The extent to which the local native population controlled the land supply, and thereby the agricultural economy, were factors in how much population growth and economic diversification were possible.[44] One could expect that inflation rates will differ with a higher rate in a more dynamic economy compared to a less dynamic one. In general one expects that the pace of growth and the pressure for change will be greater where demographic and economic forces are strong compared to those regions where they have a modest or moderate influence.

How much or how fast the Mexican economy grew did not depend entirely on the agricultural sector, as important as that sector was. It was the biggest sector and accounted for as much as half of the GDP in 1800; but despite its size it did not have as much clout in stimulating business or generating growth as mining, which accounted for between 10 and 20 percent of the total GDP. In agriculture wealth was accumulated slowly over time, but in mining it could be gained almost overnight. As quickly as mining could create wealth it could also lose it. Although the trend in mineral production was more or less independent of the trend in population, it could be a crucial gauge of how a major sector of the colonial economy was performing. The two datasets for gold and silver do not agree, even though they may have been drawn from the same accounts kept by treasury officials. The fact that gold is not counted until 1731 distorts the trends and rates calculated for the total of the two minerals because of the jump in the total both from any increase in silver production and from the addition of gold production. The curve may have a sharper upward slant than actually existed because we lack reliable gold data from 1700 to 1730 (fig. 1-2). The rate of growth for the two metals, even with the gap, was 1.4 percent from 1700 to 1810.[45] This may have been twice the growth in population and was slightly higher than the rise in output in agriculture. At 1.4 percent these precious metals, which were normally converted to coins, doubled in less than half of a century. In comparative terms, the growth in mining, as well as its impact, was probably more moderate than was previously assumed.

Silver was the most widely produced and closely watched mineral. When silver output is calculated from royal tax data, it climbs at an annual rate of 0.9 percent from 1700 to 1810. The total annual value of output of silver rose from 6.7 million pesos in 1700 to 13.3 million in 1810.[46] At an annual rate of less than 1 percent this silver series was close to the estimated population growth but lagged behind the probable growth in the agricultural sector.

The discrepancy between the silver tax series and the mint series cannot be fully explained but it is probably related to two factors: (1) some miners

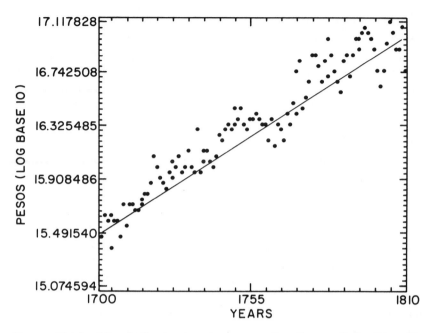

Fig. 1-2. Total gold and silver registrations, 1700–1810. *Source:* Pedro Pérez Herrero, *Plata y libranza. La articulación comercial del México borbónico. Statistics:*
Growth rate = 1.4 percent per year, R^2 = 0.92, Student t = 21.3, corrected for
autocorrelation.

were exempted from silver taxes and that could result in lower tax receipts; and
(2) periodically devaluations were announced and that could lead to an increase
in the volume of coins in circulation. Based on silver tax receipts, silver doubled
about every ninety years and on mint figures about every half century. The
difference is worth considering because the faster the rise in output of silver,
the greater the overall economic growth. Although neither series can account
for all the silver mined because a percentage—as low as 10 percent or as high as
20 percent—was never reported, the mint series may be a better gauge of the
growth of the mining sector because it counted silver that was mined and
processed in the camps and registered and marked at the treasuries.

In the extreme long term, from 1600 to 1810 silver production grew by 1
percent per year, a rate closer to the rate computed for silver tax receipts than
for the mint series. That is understandable in light of the fact that the
series for the very long term is drawn primarily from tax receipts. It is
possible, of course, that the rate from the discovery of silver in the sixteenth
century to the onset of independence in the nineteenth century was higher
than the treasury figures allow. According to tax data, the production of silver
grew fastest in the late sixteenth century and then slowed by about one-half

in the seventeenth century. It finally picked up again in the eighteenth century at a rate slightly below or comparable to that of the sixteenth century.

In Peru, on the other hand, silver output actually peaked in the early seventeenth century, after which it dropped continually until the early eighteenth century, when it turned upward again at a rate comparable to the rate of the second half of the sixteenth century. The most obvious and important distinction between Mexican and Andean silver mining was that Mexico escaped a prolonged contraction during its 250 years of silver mining. The temporary lapses in the silver curve during the eighteenth century stemmed from a variety of causes, such as famines, epidemics, labor disruptions, and mercury shortages. Even though the underlying structure was weak because of a limited capital and technological base, the industry succeeded in overcoming external and internal obstacles that could have stopped its expansion. More surprising than the disruptions, which could be expected in such a labor-intensive industry, were the quick recoveries. Without an expanding silver sector in the eighteenth century, overall economic growth would have been significantly slower.[47]

Trends in individual silver camps differed from each other and from the colonial pattern. A comparison of the silver tax receipts for two of the largest camps, Zacatecas and Guanajuato, offers a striking contrast of how they evolved in the eighteenth century. Although Zacatecas was Mexico's preeminent camp from the seventeenth into the eighteenth century, Guanajuato assumed that mantle in the eighteenth century. By the end of the eighteenth century both camps produced considerably more silver than at the start of the century. During the course of the century silver output at Guanajuato climbed steadily with no major interruptions or contractions. In Zacatecas, on the other hand, a prolonged contraction during the two middle quarters separated two periods of growth in output. The growth rates for the two camps—0.3 percent per year at Zacatecas and 1.8 percent per year at Guanajuato—from 1701 to 1800 illustrate how much variation there could be among the Mexican camps.

This brief comparison of silver production trends in these two important camps underscores a crucial feature of Mexico's eighteenth-century silver boom: Mexico escaped prolonged colonywide depressions in part because older camps like Zacatecas could still be rehabilitated even after a century or more of productivity. Mexico lacked a camp as rich and productive as Potosí, but it had other advantages in one-half dozen different camps where silver could be produced at a lower cost and a higher profit than in Peru. This meant that the silver mining industry not only consumed capital to pay for frequent and expensive renovations but it also generated capital and stimulated business in the economy at large.[48]

It is not yet possible to measure the impact of an expanding mining industry on the general performance of the eighteenth-century Mexican economy. Preliminary findings, recently published by the Salvuccis, on the relationship between mining and real total income in nineteenth-century Mexico show that a rise of 10 percent in output of silver yielded an increase of nearly 9 percent in income.[49] These data indicate that mining could make a significant difference in the level of income over time. For the eighteenth century we cannot yet test silver trends against income patterns.

A partial solution is to explore the relationship between tithe collections and silver registrations across Michoacán. Within the diocese there were important mining camps whose silver could be taxed in two Michoacán treasuries, Guanajuato and San Luis Potosí. Miners could register their silver at other treasuries and some probably did not register their silver at all, so that these registrations do not necessarily represent all of the silver mined in Michoacán or only silver from there. Our findings suggest that for every 10 percent rise in silver output the agricultural sector grew by about 7 percent. Although we do not know the value of the total agricultural output, since the tithe is an incomplete measurement, we do know that it is possible that the value of silver production could have exceeded or at least was comparable to the value of agricultural output. If we use only the silver registrations from Guanajuato, the diocese's principal silver camp and treasury office (a substantial part of San Luis Potosí's silver after 1770 came from outside the diocese), we find that mining had an even stronger relationship in which every 10 percent increase in silver yielded an 8 percent increase in the tithe. With these numbers mining could be a powerful force in determining the course of Michoacán's economy.[50]

Based on available data for eighteenth-century Mexico, we can assume that both agricultural and mineral output grew faster than the population. It is possible that there was a net gain in production over population, although not by very much. The long-term rates for Michoacán-Oaxaca tithes and for silver registrations fall about halfway between 1 and 1.5 percent per year. This may be an indication of how much total output grew under Bourbon rule, although as important data remain to be compiled and analyzed, this is only a first step in the determination of an eighteenth-century growth rate. If the rate were as high as or higher than 1 percent per year, it would compare favorably with more advanced economies in eighteenth-century Europe.[51] Such a rate was possible in a preindustrial economy like Mexico's as long as the basic resources to support that growth were available. When those resources grew scarce, then growth had to depend more directly on rising productivity levels. By adding land and labor, neither of which could be described as in short supply in eighteenth-century Mexico, the colony could for the most part sustain economic growth to accommodate demographic growth. In addition, the economic growth in general and the mining boom in particular provided the capital that had to be invested in order to utilize the land and labor. Toward the end of the eighteenth century, however, growth may have begun to sputter because those basic resources, especially capital, were more costly to add. Without fundamental changes in productivity levels, for which there is little direct evidence, the economy found itself stagnating.[52]

Growth in Treasury Revenue

Data for agriculture and mining represent the private sector of the colonial economy. There was also a large public sector that underwent rapid growth in the eighteenth century. Vast quantities of treasury statistics have been published in the past decade, and more no doubt will be published in the coming years.[53] The colonial treasury was one of the most visible and powerful public agencies, and during the eighteenth century the crown initiated reforms that only heightened the treasury's visibility and extended its power. One would expect the income of the treasury to grow along with the rise in the population and the expansion in the economy. Treasury income also grew because the crown assigned the treasury new taxes and monopolies and strengthened its administration during the eighteenth century. Treasury data can be used and have been used to measure growth in the general economy and in its specific sectors, but until we have a stronger consensus on how much the treasury collected during the eighteenth century we are limited in the application and linkage of those data to economic activities.[54]

At present three different series of the treasury's total income can be analyzed. The main issue concerns bookkeeping practices in the last quarter of the eighteenth century. Published figures for yearly totals of royal revenues skyrocket—from a range of 10–15 million pesos in the 1780s to 20–30 million in the 1790s and 40–60 million in the 1800s. Although most scholars believe that treasury income rose rapidly in the late eighteenth and early nineteenth centuries, many question whether these numbers are simply too large to be creditable, given the size and capacity of the late colonial economy. In spite of the disagreements, we can analyze the three series and establish a range of growth rates over the course of the century. We have designated the series as A, B, and C. Series A is by far the most conservative series and Series C is the most controversial because it includes the very large figures cited above. Series B is our revision that does not accept the high numbers in Series C but also does not scale back the numbers as far as Series A.[55]

The annual growth rates for all three series have a spread of less than 1 percent: Series A grew at 2.4 percent, Series B at 2.6 percent, and Series C at

3.2 percent.[56] The curves constructed from Series A and B exhibit somewhat steadier and less erratic behavior than the Series C curve, which contains the abnormally high figures for the late colonial period (fig. 1-3). Minimally the rise in receipts was the equivalent of a doubling every quarter century. That was about twice the rate estimated for the growth of the economy. There were some sharp but brief dips in the curves that coincided with well-documented natural disasters or economic crises. But the treasury overcame these disruptions with little apparent trouble, although some individual *ramos* may have suffered more than others. In short, the public sector's share was not just keeping up with an expanding economic pie, it was growing ever larger.

How the Crown spent the money that it collected or confiscated may be as important as the fact that it collected so much money. Part of it, certainly, was recycled through the economy in the form of payments for goods and services or for wages and salaries. Another and perhaps a larger part belonged to the Crown and was exported to Spain or to other colonies. The volume of treasury exports rose sharply during the second half of the eighteenth century, and the result was that more was being collected by the government and more being exported from the colony.[57]

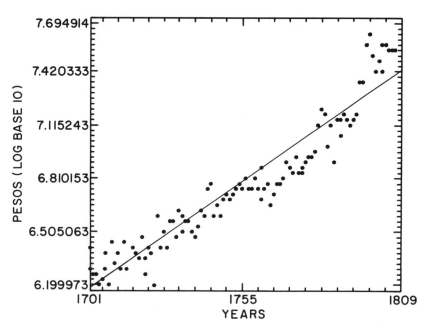

Fig. 1-3. Treasury receipts, series B, 1701–1809. *Source:* John TePaske with José and María Luz Hernández Palomo, *La Real Hacienda de Nueva España: La Real Caja de México (1576–1816)*, with revisions by Richard Garner as explained in chap. 1, note 55. *Statistics:* Growth rate = 2.6 percent per year, R^2 = 0.92, Student t = 35.1.

The role of the treasury in the eighteenth century is of interest to scholars. In the past scholars have found important links between the Bourbon Reforms and the improved economic performance. The revitalizing and streamlining of the treasury were major goals for the government reformers, and in general those goals were realized. These reforms had a double edge, however. The Crown granted concessions in the form of lower taxes or fewer regulations that scholars have correctly described as economic liberalization, but at the same time pursued diligently and successfully a policy of collecting more revenue. In both cases the efficacy of the treasury in the collection of the revenue was crucial. It became evident in the rising revenue curves.

In a recent essay Coatsworth has made the case that the colonial government became a highly effective agency in the extraction of revenue, at least in comparison with other colonial systems. But the capacity to extract money from the economy remained precisely that, to siphon money out of the economy into the treasury and not to circulate it through the economy. The state never became an instrument for economic transformation or modernization.[58] The estimated growth of the colonial economy pales in significance when compared to the growth in revenue collected by the treasury. Indeed, as the Consulado survey indicated, the economy may have reached its capacity to finance both economic growth and fiscal excess with the result that crises were both more frequent and more wrenching in the late eighteenth or early nineteenth centuries.

Inflation Factor

Another measure of what was happening in Mexico's economy during the Bourbon period was the movement of prices and wages. Colonial price data, though limited in many respects, have been collected more systematically than wage data. Long series of maize and wheat (or flour) prices from several regions have been compiled for the eighteenth century. Short series for other agricultural and household items have also been published. Wage data, by contrast, exist in a less organized and useful format, although as more and more are collected the data base will become more reliable. When we analyze prices and wages together, we usually have an interest in the determination of the impact of price levels or price changes on the consuming public. For now, however, we will focus on price trends, mainly grain prices, to learn about the behavior and performance of the economy.[59]

Of immediate concern in an expanding economy is how much inflation occurs. By definition, inflation means a rise in prices. It can also mean a reduction in consumer purchasing power as measured in a given unit of currency.[60] Although modern discussions about causes and consequences of inflation are elaborate and complex, historical explanations often revolve around an increase in the money supply as the result of mines being opened or currencies being devalued. This is widely treated as too much money chasing too few goods, or from another perspective, "demand driven." As more silver was being pumped into the economy even in the face of massive late colonial currency exports, conditions certainly existed to ignite an inflationary spiral. But there is another side to the inflation phenomenon. Even as both the volume and velocity of money expanded, the capacity to produce what the economy needed, especially foodstuffs, could lag behind both in the short and the long run.[61] In eighteenth-century Mexico agricultural capacity did expand, but after a century expansion may have become more and more difficult to maintain as land and capital-improvement costs increased over the course of the century. The lack of documentation, though, makes any effort to distinguish between demand-related and supply-related inflation very perilous. A comparison of food prices with other prices is one way to try to illuminate the difference. Demand-related inflation usually drives up prices in all categories, whereas supply-related inflation more often results from bottlenecks in food production and distribution. But since most of Mexico's eighteenth-century price data are for grains (maize and wheat), the opportunity to make such comparisons is limited. In late colonial Zacatecas a study of nearly two dozen commodities during the second half of the eighteenth century showed that some food prices were more volatile and tended to rise more quickly than other food and nonfood prices, but whether this is enough evidence to support supply-related inflation is problematical.[62] It is possible that both types fed whatever inflationary tendencies existed in eighteenth-century Mexico, or that one dominated for a time and then the other.

Given the quality of evidence, how inflationary does the eighteenth century appear to have been? Maize prices make up the longest and fullest series. Even with the inevitable gaps and inconsistencies the series is long enough to try to speculate on what the rate of growth in maize prices might have been over the very long term from 1525 to 1820. The calculation yields a rate of 0.4 percent per year.[63] Such a rate might be viewed as relatively modest because it required more than 175 years before the price doubled. Year-to-year changes in maize prices could be large, but if this rate has any validity, maize price levels only moved up slowly over the very long term. This suggests that long-term inflation, as measured by maize, was not much of a threat. In the short or intermediate term, of course, prices could be highly volatile in response to unexpected changes in supply (grain shortages) or demand (population shifts), but such volatility did not evidently translate into constantly rising price levels. Severe shortages that caused prices to skyrocket belonged to colonial Mexico's economic landscape, but at least until the late eighteenth or early nineteenth century supplies were probably ample rather than scarce. Indeed, it can be argued that over the long term prices were so low and supplies so ample that without making production more efficient a producer had trouble earning a big enough profit to justify or encourage investing further in grain or food production.

In the eighteenth century the rate of increase, based on maize prices, was twice as high at 0.8 percent per year (1700–1810) as the rate for the whole colonial period (fig. 1-4).[64] At that rate the price of maize doubled every eighty to ninety years. As the population rose, more maize was needed and more was produced. Despite this, the incentive to invest more heavily in maize farming could have diminished during the century because projected returns were insufficient to attract the capital needed for expansion. Without that expansion it became harder to manage maize price inflation. Maize prices customarily rose and fell, but an observable difference late in the eighteenth century was that prices not only rose to high levels but also remained there. That was the case after the crisis of the 1780s. Maize prices remained high through the 1790s and into the early 1800s instead of falling to usual postfamine lows.

The tendency for maize prices was to fall after a major shortage and then to move irregularly higher until the next major shortage. When we measure the rise in prices during these interfamine periods (major famines occurred in

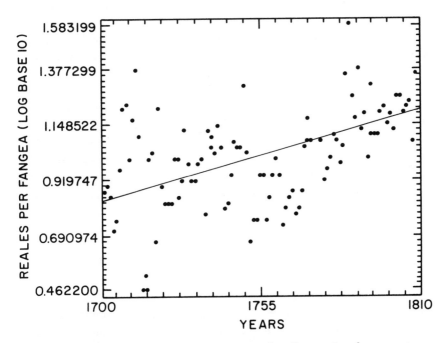

Fig. 1-4. Colonywide average maize prices, 1700–1810. *Source:* See chap. 1, note 59. *Statistics:* Growth rate = 0.8 percent per year, R² = 0.43, Student t = 3.44.

1714, 1750, and 1785) we find that the rate of increase was considerably higher than the rate for the century.[65] Since the most severe maize shortages and the attendant famines were weather-induced, the rise in prices during the interfamine periods was more likely caused by producers deciding to produce less, especially when prices were low. No doubt from time to time demand for maize outstripped supply, and the result was rising maize prices.

Quarter-by-quarter analysis is another approach to maize price movements. When we measure maize prices over the eighteenth century and on a quarterly basis without reference to famines, business cycles, or other possible intrusions, we find that the century-long rate was 0.6 percent per year and, equally significant, that it did not change from quarter to quarter during the century. However maize producers made their investment decisions, they could not have high expectations that prices would rise to more favorable levels.[66] What these quarter-century statistics illustrate is that despite their cyclical nature maize prices tended to rise slowly at a uniform rate across the whole century. The potential for recurring scarcities grew not only because of unpredictable weather conditions or high factor costs but also because price levels for basic staples like grain did not normally provide a high enough return.

We could build a stronger series with which to analyze price trends if we had monthly prices over long time periods. At this stage in price data collection, however, we are far from having such a data base. We can construct a partial series based on monthly averages of maize prices at Mexico City's *alhóndiga* (public granary) from 1763 to 1780. During this seventeen-year period, which ends several years before the severe scarcities of the middle 1780s, a price exists for every month, January through October. First, we compared growth rates for the colonywide series and for the Mexico City series from 1763 to 1780. The calculations indicate that the colonywide series rose faster than the Mexico City series by more than half as much per year. Such differences were possible and can be explained by the fact that the capital's price was regulated. Prices in Mexico City were already higher by the second half of the eighteenth century than prices in other cities and regions, and they tended to be less volatile and to rise more slowly as supplies began to shrink in the second half of the eighteenth century. Based on the statistical tests, however, the trends are not strong.

When we computed month-by-month averages, we found that prices were lower (11 pesos per fanega) in the late fall and winter months after the harvests and between 10 and 15 percent higher (12.5 pesos per *fanega of* 1.5 bushels) in the late spring and summer. Whether this represented a significant rise over the course of the harvest year depended on the consumer's economic status. Monthly trends, however, are difficult to verify. Monthly growth rates were as low as 1.6 percent per year in the winter months and as high as

2.6 percent in the summer months. This was to be expected. Prices tend to climb more rapidly in the months of low or dwindling supplies because at those times supplies are more vulnerable to whatever interruptions and fluctuations the economy experiences. Conversely, they climb somewhat less rapidly during the months of or after the harvests.

Monthly prices were higher from 1768 to 1776 than from 1763 to 1767. They fell in 1777 and 1778 to levels not quite as low as they had been in the middle 1760s. They rose again in 1779 and 1780 to levels nearly as high as those in the middle 1770s. Overall, prices were higher in the 1770s than the 1760s. We know, of course, that a major crisis loomed ahead (at least in some areas), and with that in mind we can postulate that the erratic, upward movement of maize prices during the two decades before the agricultural crises may well indicate that supplies were shrinking.[67]

Another grain series that can be examined is wheat (fig. 1-5). The output of wheat rose in the eighteenth century because the consumption of bread among the urban classes, mainly the poor, grew in the eighteenth century.[68] Although maize was cultivated widely, commercial maize production had to

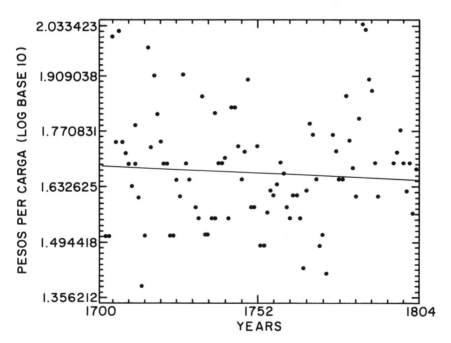

Fig. 1-5. Bajío average wheat prices, 1700–1804. *Sources:* Silvia Galicia, *Precios y producción en San Miguel el Grande, 1661–1803;* Flor de María Hurtado López, *Dolores Hidalgo, estudio económico, 1740–1790;* Cecilia Rabell Romero, *Los Diezmos de San Luis de la Paz. Economía en una región del Bajío en el siglo xviii. Statistics:* Growth rate = −0.1 percent per year, R^2 = −0.006, Student t = 0.63.

follow a fairly strict regimen to be profitable. For that reason it may have been more expensive to plant and harvest than wheat. Arij Ouweneel, who has reconstructed some important hacienda accounts, has determined that "maize-growing used a much more complicated, meticulous administrative schedule." It had a lower ratio of revenues to costs than wheat because it required more workers and more intensive cultivation than wheat.[69] It cannot be readily discerned from wheat price data that wheat represented a commercial advantage for the agricultural producer. When wheat prices from tithe sales in San Miguel el Grande, Dolores Hidalgo, and San Luis de la Paz—all of which were situated in the Upper Bajío near Guanajuato—are assembled and analyzed, they do not show much tendency to rise or fall over the eighteenth century. For the second half of the eighteenth century they show a slight upward movement at an annual rate of 0.9 percent (95 percent confidence level), a rate that requires eighty years for the price to double.[70] With slow or flat growth in prices profits could be earned only if wheat farmers could continually maintain or reduce their costs primarily through gains in productivity and efficiency. There is little evidence that wheat farmers ever realized such gains during the eighteenth century.

A wheat price series also exists for Mexico City, but we have not combined it with the Bajío series because we do not yet know how much of the capital's wheat supply originated in the Upper Bajío. We do not know, therefore, if the unit of wheat reported for the tithe in the Upper Bajío was the same unit of wheat sold later in Mexico City. Until the end of the colonial period a large part of its supply came from the Valley of Mexico. If the prices of "good" and "inferior" wheat, sold to Mexico City millers or bakers from 1741 to 1788, are combined into a single series and analyzed, they also fail to show any upward or downward movement. If we examine the series from 1754, a time of low wheat prices, to 1788, a time of high prices after the maize shortages, we find prices climbed at 1.2 percent per year.[71]

The Upper Bajío and Mexico City series have these common traits: if confined to the second half of the eighteenth century, the series exhibit growth in the range of 1 percent per year, and if longer than that they show little definite movement. What happened to prices between the agricultural crises of the 1780s and Hidalgo's Revolt is more difficult to discern in both wheat series. The Upper Bajío series peters out around 1800, and the Mexico City series contains prices only for "good" wheat. In both cases prices may have fallen briefly after the highs of 1785 and 1786 before establishing a range in which the average price was higher than it had been in the pre-1780 period. It is also possible, but not statistically verifiable, that wheat prices climbed slowly from 1790 to 1810, although fluctuation rather than growth was the more salient characteristic.

Prices of other commodities and products have not yet been systematically compiled and studied except for Zacatecas in the late eighteenth and early nineteenth centuries.[72] Although nearly two dozen different items were included in the price series with 1760 as the earliest date and 1820 the latest, some items were more fully represented than others. Among these were sugar, chili, lard, soap, and wool. All of these except wool rose in price at an annual rate of 1.0 to 1.5 percent. Wool rose at slightly below 1 percent. Even though the data for other items are too incomplete or inconsistent to be analyzed for trends, those available indicate that some could have risen more slowly or increased more rapidly than the items listed. To estimate the overall annual rate for all prices at 1 percent or slightly higher may be too conservative but is also reasonable in light of what we know about grain price series. In addition, it is probable that a rate of increase above 1 percent per year in the half century before the insurgency movement was higher than the rate for the first half of the eighteenth century and perhaps for the first two-thirds or three-quarters of the century.[73]

Even modest inflation in a preindustrial economy could have a disruptive effect on the consuming public. The Consulado survey implied that inflation was worse than modest, and whether it was or not, the perception was that rising prices among other things were causing a threat to the public order. We cannot corroborate, with the data that we have, that prices doubled between 1780 and 1805, as the Consulado reported, but we can say with some certainty that after the agricultural crises prices remained stuck at levels much higher than before.

For the well-to-do the inflation rates that we have calculated for various time periods probably had only a minor impact on their lives. Even though they complained about high prices along with other survey respondents, they were certainly more insulated from inflation than the less well off. For the average colonist, however, any rise in prices for a single year and certainly over several years had an immediate impact on what they could afford. Various estimates exist for how much money was needed to survive or to acquire a "decent living." A modern estimate places late colonial per capita personal income in the range of 20–30 pesos per year.[74] According to late colonial estimates, the breadwinner of a typical family in the lower class needed to earn 129–262 pesos each year or 2.8–5.7 reales each day of the year to be able to support that family. As Gabriel Haslip-Viera points out, however, not only was finding a job that paid several reales difficult but holding the job for more than a few days at a time was equally difficult. "As a rule, entire families had to work, with the men, women, and children alternately employed as day laborers, street peddlers, and servants."[75] An income of 300 pesos per year was set in 1813 as the minimum against which the government could levy any forced contributions, although that figure may only reflect the "decent living" of the petit bourgeoisie in Mexico City's economy.[76]

Although wage and salary data exist, they are not always readily converti-
ble into usable data series. Part of the problem is that cash payments, if made
at all, were often accompanied by payments in kind. There is evidence
during the eighteenth century that wages and salaries could rise and fall in
step with population growth and economic need. In some cases workers were
paid in cash, in others they were paid in kind, and in still others they were
paid with a combination of the two. Many categories of wages and salaries
were subject to regulation, although enforcement was often ineffective.
Wage and salary levels were not as static as the laws might indicate. When
labor was in short supply, the employer could be compelled to raise the cash
component of the wage package, and conversely when the supply was
abundant, he could be free to increase the ratio of merchandise to cash.
Translating merchandise into cash to determine the total wage package that
the worker received or that the employer computed is difficult because
information on what the merchandise was worth to the worker or to the
employer is not often available. It is possible that the more merchandise in
the package, the less value the package had for the worker. Unraveling all
these intricate variations presents a formidable if not impossible task.

Still, since wage and salary data exist, they can and should be examined for
whatever trends might be uncovered. The data base that we have compiled
includes wages and salaries for a wide variety of colonial occupations from
stonemasons to cowboys, from peons to mine supervisors. We have excluded
the obvious categories of the highly paid or the highly trained. The figures
are based on monthly wages as stated in cash, and although many categories—mostly among rural workers—qualified for rations, the figures include
only cash and disregard any payment in merchandise. An additional problem
is that data have not been found for all the years from 1700 to 1810, and yet
dozens of entries have been found for some years. If we establish the trend
based on all the data (about 200 items over about fifty years), we find that
wages and salaries did in fact rise at a rate of 0.8 percent per year. At this rate,
it can be argued, not only did wages and salaries respond to economic
changes, they also increased at a rate comparable to those for population and
price inflation. Another approach is to calculate an average monthly compensation from all the data for any given year. Under that approach the trend is
less pronounced with a growth of about 0.4 percent each year (94 percent
confidence level) or one-half the rate stated above (fig. 1-6).[77]

The data are too inconsistent and the R^2s too low to draw any firm
conclusions about colonial trends. It would be helpful, though not yet
possible, to create separate series for rural and urban workers. A preliminary
analysis of this dataset suggests that rural wages may have risen somewhat
faster than urban wages, but this is at best a most tentative conclusion. Nor is
it possible to break down the wage and salary series into shorter periods to

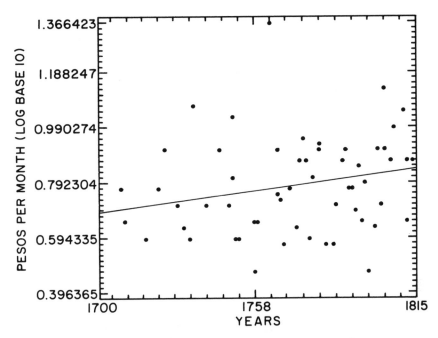

Fig. 1-6. Average urban and rural wages, 1700–1815. *Source:* See chap. 1, note 77. *Statistics:* For total wage data, growth rate = 0.8 percent per year, R^2 = 0.1, Student t = 4.68, insignificant autocorrelation; for average wage data, growth rate = 0.4 percent per year, R^2 = 0.0, Student t = 1.86.

determine if wage and salary trends differed over time. Thus, while eighteenth-century trends in wages and salaries kept pace with prices (one could also argue that the slow rise in compensation moderated the increase in prices), short-term rates cannot yet be calculated and compared. There is certainly no evidence to suggest that wages and salaries rose in the short or medium term at rates much higher than the century-long rate or at rates anywhere near the estimated rates for commodity prices. Whatever economic growth the eighteenth-century economy enjoyed, it was not accompanied by or concurrent with a significant boost in the society's living standards. If wages and salaries fell behind prices at times, that meant an erosion in living standards. And there is no evidence that wages and salaries ever grew faster than prices.

The long-term trends constitute only an outline of how the economy performed in eighteenth-century Mexico. Overall the economy's nominal growth probably was not much more than 1.3 percent annually. At that rate economic growth was able to keep pace with the growth in population (0.8 percent) and inflation (0.5 percent). Wages certainly did not advance any faster than prices. A more ominous comparison concerned the much faster growth in treasury receipts—three to four times the estimate just cited for the economy. But Mexico's eighteenth-century economy and the change that it underwent were more complex than the trends themselves suggest. An analysis of each component of the private sector (agriculture, mining, manufacturing, and commerce) and the public sector (treasury) will add the details that are necessary to understand the significance of the trends.

2

Trends in Agriculture

Bourbon Mexico was an agricultural society.[1] Agriculture generated the most income and employed the most people, and more people lived in the countryside than in the city. Agriculture underwent important structural changes in the eighteenth century that increased production, in some cases with greater economy and profitability. All regions probably underwent structural changes, but the pace and depth of change varied significantly from area to area. Regions with substantial urban growth experienced the most pressure to boost agricultural production. While the level of production for the colony as a whole and for separate regions rose sufficiently over time to meet the demand, it may have risen only enough to maintain a basic subsistence economy. The agricultural sector produced more by expanding the acreage under cultivation and in some places making it more productive, although the practice of husbandry changed only moderately over the course of the century.

A recent treatment of the late colonial agricultural economy explored its paradoxical character. In the second half of the eighteenth century—called a period of "Baroque splendor"—society was full of change and contradiction, no more apparent than in the agricultural economy. Agricultural production increased, but productivity stagnated; agricultural prices rose, but wages did not; estate owners grew richer, but rural workers grew poorer. Although growth was evident in absolute terms, it did not necessarily lead to development. "Capital investment in commercial agriculture" took the following forms: more acquisition of tillable land, land-use changes, and greater application of existing technology. With respect to the last of these, certain practices then being tried in Europe were seldom if ever found in Mexico or in Latin America in general. Although interregional trade grew in the eighteenth century, the less studied intraregional commerce around the large provincial cities may have been the major source of the expanded agricultural production. Small producers could find exploitable niches within the evolving market structure, although they could find it hard to compete with the commercial producers who might even be less efficient. In an agricultural economy that was probably growing more complex and hetero-geneous in the eighteenth century the return on capital was greater in the less populated and less developed areas of the "near-north and west" than in the more developed the regions of the center (Valley of Mexico), east (Puebla-Tlaxcala), and south (Oaxaca) where demographic and economic change had pushed agricultural expansion into more marginal and less productive land.[2]

Maize Production Trends

At the outset of this discussion of eighteenth-century agriculture, we must bear in mind that it showed considerable variation in terms of climate, soils, settlement patterns, and land tenure. Moreover, at the beginning of the eighteenth century, some areas had undergone more structural changes than other areas. For example, around 1700 the Anáhuac region, Mexico's tem-perate central plateau, still had a heavy concentration of indigenous peoples and a large crop-based village agriculture. The Bajío, however, because of its more arid climate and less dense population, had an agricultural system built upon ranching and large-scale landholdings. As the Bajío's population grew in the eighteenth century, expansion in crop cultivation, in particular cere-als, was accommodated within the system of large landed estates. The fact that village agriculture survived alongside *hacienda* agriculture in Anáhuac but that hacienda agriculture predominated in Bajío had an impact on how labor patterns evolved in the eighteenth century. The point is not that Anáhuac lacked haciendas and depended solely on village agriculture or conversely that Bajío had no small-plot farming and had only large-scale agriculture but rather that regional systems responded to changing economic needs in different ways to achieve similar goals. At issue is the extent to which all major regional economies, despite their structural differences, performed in terms of the pressures and forces at work in late colonial Mexico.

Analyzing the performance of the agricultural system without access to production data presents a formidable challenge. The best sources remain the ecclesiastical tithes, and only a half dozen such series now exist. No single tithe series for the whole colony in the eighteenth century yet exists, and some of the most important ecclesiastical jurisdictions have not yet been investigated. Also, as mentioned earlier, tithes reflect Spanish agriculture, even though Spanish producers served a much larger market than simply

Spanish consumers. Above all, methodological problems abound. In some cases tithe records can be used to analyze the volume of output in the agricultural sector. More often, though, the records contain the sales of tithed merchandise or the receipts of money in lieu of merchandise. The obvious question is whether these entries accurately reflect the value of the goods or the transactions of the marketplace. The other consideration is that the tithe covered only one-tenth of the value of the produce and that the remaining nine-tenths could be sold privately at quite different prices from what the tither, the collector, or the church reported.[3] Unfortunately, most of the recently published tithe series are stated in money collected rather than produce tithed. Their usefulness is diminished for that reason but not entirely lost. They still provide a base from which to measure long-term growth and to compare growth patterns of several regions.

Maize was often included in tithe calculations. It was important because it was a staple in the native diet and also was increasingly used as a food for work animals and as a substitute for cash wages. Maize could be grown almost anywhere in the colony. In normal or good years harvests could be very large, with the result that supplies rose and prices fell. For commercial producers serving major cities an abundance of maize could mean substantial losses. As noted earlier, commercial farmers could find maize operations costly because these large-scale operations required substantial labor inputs. The margin for error in commercial maize production was small. Planting, cultivating, and harvesting all had to fall within a prescribed calendar, compounded by unpredictable weather conditions. In addition, a harvest's marketability could never be fully anticipated. The ranks of commercial maize producers were thinned during the eighteenth century: some quit maize farming, others switched crops, and still others reduced the acreage devoted to maize. More and more, it appears, commercial farmers tried to preserve agricultural profits by controlling maize supplies. In short, they tried to turn the recurrent cycles of abundance and scarcity to their financial advantage. The extent to which they succeeded is hard to document, although public testimony indicated that from time to time they did. Large cities were obvious candidates for such market manipulation, especially in the late eighteenth century as Indian-grown maize had to be retained to feed rising native populations instead of being sold. Some commercial farmers built storage and warehouse facilities in order to influence the price and supply in the marketplace. A question remains whether with or without market manipulation maize prices could justify further investment in maize agriculture.[4]

Analysis of existing maize price series may clarify the discussion. A long series based on maize tithes for the parishes of León (1660–1768) and Silao (1660–1789) in the Upper Bajío can be studied for eighteenth-century trends.[5] It is important to note they do not agree chronologically: León's series ends when prices were low and harvests large, whereas Silao's series ends when opposite conditions—shortages and famines—prevailed. If these figures represent one-tenth of all the maize produced in the two parishes, then they suggest that the total volume in León was about 500,000 fanegas per year or around 5 million fanegas between 1660 and 1768 and in Silao about 700,000 fanegas per year and 7 million fanegas total from 1660 to 1789. These estimates appear to exceed what the local population could have consumed, and some maize was certainly exported to other parishes, mining camps, and cities. More than likely the volume of maize presented for the tithe was greater than one-tenth of the production of maize.

Growth rates have been calculated for both series: maize output grew by 1.0 percent per year at León (1660–1768) and by 1.6 percent each year at Silao (1660–1789). If we compare Silao with León for the period 1660–1768, we find that Silao's rate remains at 1.6 percent per annum. As such, Silao's rate was one and one-half times greater than León's from 1660 through 1768. In both León and Silao maize output slowed in the eighteenth century (1700–68 and 1700–89, respectively) compared to the growth rates from 1660 on.[6] Even though growth slowed in the eighteenth century, that does not mean that León and Silao faced constant maize shortages. Surely from time to time shortages occurred, but the eighteenth-century rates are in line with what we know about population growth in the two parishes. That the overall long-term rates (1660–1768 and 1660–1789) are higher than the rates in the eighteenth century may be partly a function of an expected faster growth in the late seventeenth century as maize production began to expand in response to rising populations in the two parishes and beyond. What the eighteenth-century growth rates may indicate is that maize trends were keeping pace with population trends but with little to spare. The longer Silao curve shows that about every quarter century output reached a new peak after which it fell back before it started climbing again. Over 130 years the peaks moved progressively higher from an output of 15,000 fanegas to 40,000, to 80,000, to 100,000, and finally to 200,000. For León, with its shorter series, the peaks and dips are not quite so sharply delineated, although output was about six times higher in the 1760s than in the 1660s.

The quantity produced was primarily a function of population growth but the additional production was a function of price. The prices from León's and Silao's tithes must be treated with caution because they do not necessarily represent market transactions. In addition, the statistical tests applied to the price series do not inspire much confidence in the trends and rates. In both parishes, it appears, the rise in prices lagged behind the growth in supplies over the long term. In the León parish, if a maize price trend existed (95 percent confidence level), it was nearly flat and perhaps even followed a slight downward tendency from 1660 to 1768, whereas in Silao they followed no apparent trend from 1660 to 1789 (if a trend existed it was up rather than down). If we compare the two series from 1660 to only 1768, we find that in Silao as in León the price of maize was flat (-0.3 to -0.4 percent per year with 95 percent confidence level in León and only 85 percent in Silao). For the eighteenth century maize prices in León were flat, and in Silao they rose by 0.8 percent per year. The difference may arise from the fact that the León series ends just as maize prices began to rise in the late 1760s and continued into the 1780s.

Although the statistical tests are not strong, from 1768 to 1789 the increase in prices could have been at a rate about three times faster than output. That in itself was an important departure from the aforementioned trends for prices and output. In terms of percentages, output may have grown by 0.7 percent per year and prices at 2.3 percent per year.[7] Given the reservations we have expressed concerning the statistical tests, all we can say is that at some point in the second half of the eighteenth century prices began to accelerate as output slowed. What was happening in León and Silao was becoming increasingly a dilemma throughout late colonial Mexico. Maize prices were edging up because supplies were drying up, not because more maize could not be produced, so that even with rising prices further investment in maize production was not very attractive.

Why did output grow from the middle of the seventeenth century to the middle of the eighteenth century even though the price that the farmer received was virtually stagnant? Stagnant prices imply no shift in demand, but evidence indicates that population and demand were growing. Two possible hypotheses can be advanced. First, supply and demand were increasing but the observed prices remained unchanged. Consider figure 2-1 in which D_0 is the initial demand, S_0 the initial supply, and P_0 the equilibrium price that can be observed. With an increase in demand (say, the result of changes in the level of population or income) the demand for maize shifts to P_1. However, if the supply of maize also increases (because of the expansion of cultivated land, technical changes, or more people having access to arable land), then the result would be a shift in supply to S_1. Thus the shifts in demand and supply do not lead to a change in the observed price, but they do lead to an increase in the observed consumption from Q_0 to Q_1. Given the technology of maize farming in the late seventeenth and early eighteenth centuries, the output price of P_0 could be the minimal price farmers must receive to make a profit. As demand increased over time, the initial adjustment would lead to the market price increasing to P_1. Profits would be higher so that more land would be brought under cultivation with the result that supply would then shift to S_1. The León-Silao data underscores this process of constant adjustment in the following manner: output gradually increasing

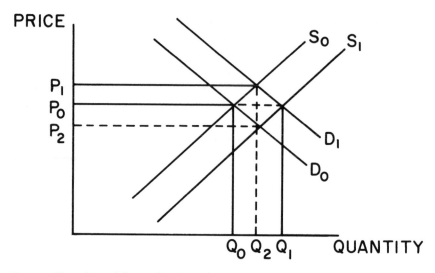

Fig. 2-1. Hypothetical demand and supply curves.

over time, and maize prices fluctuating about P_0 with no discernible upward or downward trend. The downward fluctuations could be the consequence of producers overcorrecting and increasing supply too much initially. Even a slight downward trend could result as more people gained access to farming and their action drove down what can be called excess profits.

A second hypothesis focuses on the household as a unit of production. Constant prices and increased production could suggest that the same amount of maize was being marketed but more was also being produced and consumed at home. While population growth should push up the demand for maize, a trend of more and more households producing maize for home consumption (say, because of better access to arable land) will serve to shrink the demand for maize in the marketplace. Thus the price of marketed maize would remain unchanged, but the output of maize (the marketplace plus the household) would increase.

Although these two hypotheses differ, they are not incompatible or inconsistent with each other. Some producers grew maize for the market-place and learned to adjust their supplies in accord with market behavior; some concentrated on production for the household; many may have oper-ated from time to time in both areas, producing for marketing and for consuming. That maize agriculture generated supplies that kept prices in check may suggest that costs did not rise to a consistently high level to discourage production. After 1760 or 1770, however, costs may have risen enough to act as a disincentive to adding or expanding maize cultivation.

The economist distinguishes between shifts in demand or supply curves and changes along the curves. How is that distinction made and how can it be applied to the maize market? Consumer demand is based on the assumption that the consumer, subject to certain budget constraints, will choose the commodities that will provide the greatest satisfaction or utility. The demand for commodity x will depend on the price of x, the prices of all other commodities that may influence the purchase of x, the consumer's income, and his tastes and preferences. When a demand curve for commodity x is constructed, it shows how the quantity of x demanded changes as the price of x changes. The curve must assume that the income of the consumer, the prices of other commodities, and tastes and preferences of the consumer remain constant. Under these conditions, then, the curve shows the response in quantity demanded for every change in the price. A shift in demand (moving the curve up or down) will occur if the consumer's income or preferences change or if the prices of other related commodities change. At the aggregate level, however, where national or regional demand may be analyzed, an increase in population alone can cause a shift (not just a change) in demand, even though consumer income, preferences, and other commodity prices may hold constant. Since consumer income apparently changed very little, tastes and preferences are hard to document, and prices of other commodities, in particular foodstuffs, often followed the lead of maize, the principal force coming to bear on demand was probably the increase in population.

On the supply side, where generally more information is available, we are dealing with the producer's desire to determine how to maximize his profits through the allocation of all the inputs within the context of the available technologies. In a perfectly competitive market the prices of both inputs and outputs are taken as givens. Consequently, the supply of commodity x depends on the price for the product in the marketplace and the prices of inputs, other factors of production such as land and equipment, and the available technologies. A supply curve for commodity x relates how the quantity supplied moves with changes in the market price of x. To assess the movement along the supply curve, prices of inputs, capital stock, and technologies are held constant. A shift in supply (or new supply curve) occurs when any of the foregoing variables changes. At the aggregate level where the total supply of commodity x is related to the market price of x, an increase in land under cultivation raises the supply and causes a downward shift (to the right) in the curve. Conversely, a decrease in land under cultivation lowers the supply and causes an upward shift. In eighteenth-century Mexico upward shifts in the demand curve almost solely resulted from growth in population, whereas downward shifts in the supply curve resulted primarily from adding more land (capital stock) and marginally from improving the cultivation of the land. Control involved decisions that producers could make about the amount and type of land to be added.

Not surprisingly, the supply of maize became inelastic in León and Silao during the eighteenth century. Elasticity measures the response of the producer or consumer of maize to a change in price. In modern times agricultural products tend to be inelastic in that most consumers will only spend so much income on food even if prices are falling. Food prices do decline from time to time, and yet food purchases as a proportion of the consumer's total income may not necessarily increase enough (if at all) to offer any inducement to food producers to raise their output. A surge in demand for food (with obvious implications for producers' profits) would not result simply because of lower-priced food. Under these conditions knowing how much to plant, given the expected demand, could be essential to the producer's profit margins. Without modern crop forecasts and market reports, an eighteenth-century producer who was serious about optimizing his profits probably used whatever information was available (even local gossip) to help him to decide how much to plant for his own use or for the commercial market.

One piece of information at hand was the pattern of maize prices in previous years: how much they had risen or fallen on the basis of how much he had planted. For León from 1660 to 1768 a measure of the elasticity of supply shows that a 10 percent change in price results in a 1.4 percent change in output; and in Silao for a longer period from 1660 to 1789 the ratio was 10 percent to 2 percent. When year-by-year elasticities are calculated from these ratios, they follow an downward path from the second half of the seventeenth century through the middle of the eighteenth century.[8] In León, up to the famine of 1714–15 (the first of several famines in the eighteenth century), a previous year's price could exert a strong enough pull to raise output by 4–6 percent; after those dates, though, the pull was in the range of 1–3 percent (fig. 2-2). The price of maize in León during the eighteenth century did not act as an incentive to raise the output of maize except in times of famine. In Silao for a somewhat longer period, the supply of maize based on the change in price also had greater elasticity in the seventeenth century than in the eighteenth century, although its eighteenth-century yearly data were in a higher range, 2–4 percent, than León's (fig. 2-3). Prices high enough to have an effect on production—even as Silao's eighteenth-century maize supply exhibited increasing inelasticity—occurred on several occasions (1730, 1750, 1772, and 1785). These changes, usually linked to shortages, amounted to 6 percent and above. On the other hand, in years between famines changes in output responsed to changes in price fluctuation by 1–3 percent yearly. Such wide swings meant that producing maize for sale in urban markets or outside rural estates was not financially attractive except in time of famine.

The capacity to produce maize had been slowly but steadily diminished.

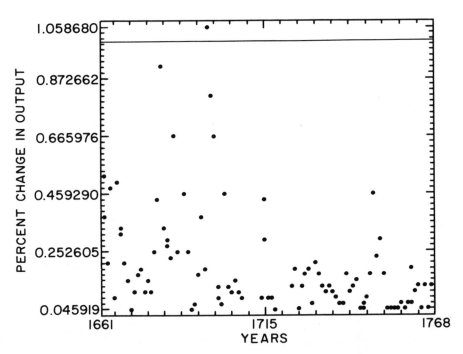

Fig. 2-2. Elasticity of maize output lagged to price: León, 1661–1768. *Source:* D. A. Brading, *Haciendas and Ranchos in the Mexican Bajío: León, 1700–1860.* *Statistics:* $R^2 = 0.37$, Student $t = 4.02$.

The level of output of maize in the Upper Bajío and other places may have fallen so low relative to demand that any shortage led to a crisis. John Tutino has calculated that during the famines of the 1780s Silao's death rate (86 per 1,000) was the second highest among a dozen rural parishes in Guanajuato's intendancy. This led him to conclude that while "[t]wo years of drought, combined with severe frosts" devastated the local agriculture, the "root of the catastrophe" lay in a fundamental transformation of the agrarian economy. As more and more maize farming was "relegated to marginal lands cultivated by poor tenants, production failed to keep pace with population growth."[9] In earlier times enough maize was produced to allow for some surplus that could be stored, but by the 1770s and 1780s that protection had vanished, not so much because of inefficiencies associated with marginal land operations but because as the elasticity data reveal over the long term, maize farming even on nonmarginal land did not provide any real incentive to expand or intensify maize agriculture.

The question of whether farmers were being forced more and more onto marginal land or whether they simply did not make good use of the existing arable land is almost impossible to answer with the documentation now

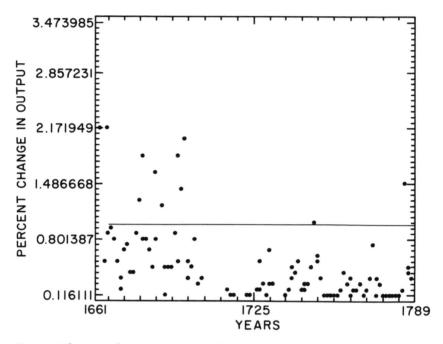

Fig. 2-3. Elasticity of maize output lagged to price: Silao, 1661–1789. *Source:* D. A. Brading, *Haciendas and Ranchos in the Mexican Bajío: León, 1700–1860. Statistics:* R^2 = 0.52, Student t = 3.81.

available. Apparently, Mexico was not well endowed with good soil. According to modern surveys only 13 percent of Mexico's total acreage can be classified as arable, and in colonial times the figure may have been even lower.[10] Although much of the land was too hilly, rocky, swampy, or arid to sustain crop cultivation, some such land was probably farmed, to the extent that this was possible, in densely populated or rapidly growing areas.[11] But precise information on the quantity and quality of land within the various categories (such as arable, pastoral, uncleared, and unusable) is so lacking that we are limited in what we can say about land use. From an economic perspective, marginal land brought under cultivation normally yielded lower output per unit of land than good land. Since the inputs (other than land) cost the same for both marginal or good land, the difference was that marginal land profits were lower and could easily turn into losses. Wide use of marginal land in late colonial Mexico, in particular to supply urban markets, could only occur if the price of food would provide a profit on land that was by its very nature more costly to cultivate. That is difficult to envision with maize, wheat, and other grains (and with foodstuffs in general) because the price of these products did not rise sufficiently or rapidly enough (except during a few severe famines) to assure those profits. The distinction that needs to be drawn more sharply is how much truly marginal land (with a population of several million people) was being pulled into cultivation versus how well the varying grades of arable land were being used for cultivation.

Maize remained the chief staple of the native population until the end of the colonial period. How much maize was needed to sustain this group and to accommodate its other uses is hard to estimate. The changing composition of the colonial population may have tempered the demand for maize from year to year, but it may also have reduced the availability of maize in times of crisis. In the middle of the seventeenth century Indians constituted about 80 percent of Mexico's population and during the next century and a half that figure dropped to about 60 percent. Still, as their share of the total population was declining, their actual numbers probably more than doubled.[12] At the beginning of the eighteenth century an Indian population of 2 million, given the estimated rates of consumption, may have needed 175,000 tons of maize per year; a century later with 3 million Indians the tonnage needed could have reached 265,000.[13] In addition, some Spaniards, mixed bloods, and blacks used maize as a staple, although their numbers were probably small. Finally, as the size of herds of horses, oxen, and mules used in plowing fields and operating machines grew during the eighteenth century, so too did the demand for maize to feed these working animals.

If maize output across the whole colony grew at rates comparable to the rates in León and Silao (between 0.8 and 1.2 percent per year), then the supply of maize could probably have met these needs, though with little to spare. Under these conditions building surpluses to protect against famines, which occurred in a minor form every decade and in a major form about every quarter to third of a century, undoubtedly became more difficult. As large producers, increasingly concerned with investments and returns, concentrated on controlling the flow of maize into the marketplace to prevent an oversupply from depressing prices, they were more inclined to limit rather than expand production.[14]

Tithes and Production Trends

Ecclesiastical tithes as indicators of agricultural production have long been controversial, and the colonial Mexican tithe is no exception. For some scholars tithes in cash cannot be used to measure output because they are badly flawed in two respects: they represent an inconsistent and ill-defined basket of agricultural commodities and the values recorded as tithes may not reflect actual market transactions.[15]

Most would agree that tithe series can lead historians astray, but not all would agree that because they can be troublesome they must be abandoned. Since the tithe was collected year after year, perhaps with more rigor in the eighteenth century than in prior centuries, and was based on an assessment of the Spanish landowner's agricultural activity, it can certainly serve as a gross measure of the agricultural output among the landowners who were liable to tithing. Since the goods against which the tithe was assessed could change from year to year and from landowner to landowner, it was not a measure of quantities of products but of values that may have been arbitrarily assigned to products. As with all such recorded transactions, problems as to what the values mean have to be solved. Little can be done about the fraud and misrepresentation that can enter such transactions.

Of greater concern to historians is the problem of price inflation. Since a convincing case for severe long-term price inflation has not yet been made for eighteenth-century Mexico, the possibility certainly exists that the tithe series, even though expressed in monetized values, captures a part of the underlying movement in production in the colony's agricultural sector over time. In the end, however, comparative analysis of the various regional series may represent the best approach by which to evaluate their reliability and usefulness.

Tithe series, based on landowners' declared values, exist for three dioceses: Puebla, Michoacán, and Oaxaca.[16] The Puebla series is longer but less complete than the other two. It covers the period from 1545 to 1794, although about eighty years are missing in segments as small as several years and as large as twenty. The Michoacán series covers 130 years from 1680 to 1810 with no years missing, and the Oaxaca series embraces a century from 1701 to 1800 with no missing years. Michoacán was the most northern of the three regions, and it was probably the most economically developed and the most ethnically diversified. Oaxaca was the most southern and the least developed, with a much larger Indian community than a Spanish community. Puebla fell somewhere between the other two, more diverse than Oaxaca but less developed than Michoacán.

All three series confirm that agricultural systems directly linked to Spanish landowners underwent an expansion in production during the eighteenth century. Inasmuch as Mexico did not then experience constant starvation, such an expansion can be safely assumed. The more relevant issues are identifying the rate of expansion across the colony and in specific regions and the periods of the greatest or the slowest expansion. In Puebla for the very long period from 1540 to 1795 the rate of increase in tithe revenues shows tithes doubling every forty years. That rate cannot be trusted in part because tithes rose steeply from a few hundred pesos to a hundred thousand pesos per year during the second half of the sixteenth century when the church implemented the tax. When the sharp rise of the sixteenth century is excluded, the growth from 1600 to 1794 is 0.3 percent per year, a reasonable rate over such a long term. In the seventeenth century Puebla's tithe grew by 0.3 percent each year, but in the eighteenth century (until 1794) it probably grew at a rate several times the seventeenth-century rate.[17]

The lack of data for the second quarter of the eighteenth century means that century-long rates cannot be computed with absolute precision. Our purpose in analyzing these three series is comparative. Even in the absence of second quarter data, how do the three series match up? For the period 1700–94 the calculations show that Oaxaca grew by 0.7 percent per annum, Puebla by 0.8 percent, and Michoacán by 1.6 percent. When combined, the growth of all three was 1.1 percent per year. Growth was slower in Oaxaca and Puebla than in Michoacán by as much as 50 percent or more. It has been argued that Michoacán, with the Bajío, was economically a dynamic region. These figures tend to confirm that it was growing faster than Puebla and Oaxaca and that Puebla was only growing slightly faster than Oaxaca.[18] Slow growth did not necessarily mean that a region was stagnating in comparison to a faster growing region. Rather, the varying rates simply confirm that although agricultural production, as measured by ecclesiastical tithes, was on the rise everywhere in Mexico during the century, that growth had certain regional accents.

These three dioceses may have accounted for as much as 40 percent of the total tithe in the eighteenth century.[19] For the colony as a whole, then, we can project an annual output of 7.5 million pesos in 1700, 11 million in 1750, and 19.5 million in 1800 for that part of the agricultural sector that paid the tithe. Given what escaped or was exempt from taxation, the total value of the agricultural sector (Spanish and Indian) was probably on average *several million* pesos higher for each of the years cited above.[20] A threefold increase spread over the eighteenth century would only require an annual growth of just over 1 percent. Based upon the calculations from these three dioceses, a colonywide rate on that scale was surely attainable.

In the second half of the eighteenth century (1751–94), comparing the rates reveals some interesting changes. Because we have excluded the second quarter, we have not tried to compare the first half of the century with the second half. For the second half the rates in Oaxaca and Puebla jumped to 1.3 percent per year as the rate in Michoacán dropped to 1.3 percent. Whatever the regional differences were that helped to create different secular rates, they became less apparent during the second half. The changes in Oaxaca and Puebla are impressive because after 1750 they represent a near doubling of the secular rate.[21] These regional differences are worth noting:

moderation or decline in the agricultural sector of Michoacán's economy, acknowledged to be generally more robust than Oaxaca's economy.

Since the tithes for Oaxaca and Michoacán are complete for the eighteenth century, these two series can be analyzed more intensively for regional variations than the three series. With every year accounted for (1701–1800) Oaxaca's tithes grew by 0.7 percent per year (compared to 0.8 above) and Michoacán's by 1.5 percent per year (1.6 above). The linear-spline, quarter-century approach highlights both continuity and variation in the secular rates.[22] What we find out about Oaxaca is that the burst in the growth of the tithe occurred in the last quarter. In each of the first three quarters in Oaxaca the rate was a constant 0.6 percent per year, but in the last quarter it more than doubled to 1.3 percent per year. In Michoacán, by contrast, with a rate of 1.5 percent over the long term as well as quarter by quarter, the rhythm of production as seen in the tithes remained constant.[23]

Since more is known about demographic change in Michoacán, the connection between the growth in tithe and the population can be studied more closely. Michoacán's population grew throughout the eighteenth century. Although the rate may have been as high as 2 percent a year in some parishes, such a rate could not be sustained across the whole diocese. A rate of 1.5 percent per year appears more reasonable (especially in light of tithe collection rates), but that is high for the eighteenth century.[24] It is also possible that the overall rate remained fairly robust during the century but that the rate slowed during the second half or during the late decades. In the parish of San Luis de la Paz (in the northeastern quadrant of the Michoacán diocese) Rabell Romero found that rate of growth in the local population was marginally higher in the first half: 1.01 percent per year, 1727–62; 0.85 percent, 1762–80; and 0.08 percent 1781–1810.[25] In the northwestern quadrant at León, Brading also found that the rate of increase slowed during the second half of the eighteenth century even though the rates themselves were perhaps twice as high as those in San Luis de la Paz.[26] If Michoacán's population rate slowed in the second half or the last quarter of the eighteenth century, that could help to explain the declining rate in the second half of the eighteenth century. The constant rates quarter by quarter suggest that large adjustments were not needed or were beyond the capacity of the sector to initiate. However, since population and agriculture moved along parallel lines over the long term, we may infer that the agricultural sector managed to produce what was needed to sustain a growing population.

In analyzing rates of growth in population and agriculture, one must also account for any price inflation in the ecclesiastical tithe. Héctor Lindo-Fuentes has proposed that, if inflation were taken into account, the Oaxacan tithe might show as much as a 2–2.5 percent decline per year in the last quarter of the eighteenth century.[27] To reverse the trend in Oxacan tithes at the rate suggested by Lindo-Fuentes would require a level of inflation far greater than any that we have yet uncovered. In the short or intermediate term, prices, especially for grains, could be pushed up quickly as a result of poor harvests and low surpluses. How quickly they rose depended on demographic pressures and agricultural capacities, but the upward spiral eventually slowed or reversed itself as supplies were restored. What we know about eighteenth-century grain price movements is that prices only edged up over time at rates of a few tenths of a percent per year. In modern times such a rate could hardly be called inflationary, but in the slower-growing eighteenth century such rates, where prices were half again as high at the end of the century as at the beginning, could have a disruptive impact, especially when combined with the oscillations in the prices. Based on grain prices and tithe receipts, both of which are incomplete measures, inflation (prices outrunning the value of production) may have been worse in the second half than the first half of the eighteenth century and more specifically from the middle of the 1760s through the middle of the 1780s.

In Michoacán we can analyze more closely what happened to tithe receipts and grain prices after 1750. For the second half of the eighteenth century tithes receipts grew faster than maize or wheat prices, although by only a few tenths of a percent. Those few tenths of a percent represent what was available to cover growth in population, and they were obviously smaller than what the population growth rates themselves indicate. From the early 1760s, when prices were low, to the middle 1780s, when the agricultural crises unfolded, maize or wheat prices rose two to three times faster than tithes. Under those conditions there was no room for future population growth and even less room for the population growth that had already taken place. But the measures are too imprecise to allow us to assert that these findings prove that agricultural production could not keep pace with population growth and thus that a wave of inflation ensued. The tithe did not account for all agricultural output, and maize and wheat prices were not the best predictors for all other food prices. Still, what must be considered as a possibility is that when population growth and agricultural production are analyzed as indicators they show that the margin of safety was relatively small and became smaller over time.[28]

The two curves highlight some other regional differences. In Michoacán output fell during the first decade until about 1715, and then in the middle 1720s it began to climb until the epidemics of the late 1730s. After declining in the early 1740s it rebounded in the late 1740s and reached a new high during the famine that began in 1749 and continued through 1750. Over the next fifteen to twenty years output alternately grew and shrunk until 1770, after which it moved irregularly but steadily higher to 1800. In Oaxaca, on the other hand, output moved irregularly in the first decade of the eighteenth century until the shortages of 1710 through 1715, when it first jumped and then dropped sharply. Over the next half century (1715–65) output advanced, although new peaks in tithe receipts were followed by several years of falling or fluctuating receipts. During the 1760s output leveled off at a point that was about 50 percent higher than at the start of the century. Around 1770 output began to climb with several brief lapses, the worst occurring during the 1780s agricultural crises.[29]

It can be seen from these century-long tithe series that while both series rose during the eighteenth century, they did not rise exactly in the same manner or at the same rate. This is also evident from the analysis of data from six tithing districts between 1770 and 1790. These statistics cover collections of tithes from the dioceses of Puebla, Michoacán (Valladolid), Oaxaca, Guadalajara, and Durango, and from the archdiocese of Mexico. These figures come as close to a colonywide tithe total as we will have in the near future. Whether they can be used in that way is open to debate. One problem is that the data for Oaxaca and Puebla do not agree with the data for the same period from the longer series. (For Michoacán they are identical.) Puebla's two series may differ because the 1770–90 set may be total receipts rather than receipts minus costs; and Oaxaca's two series may not match up because they do not cover the same geographic area. In addition, Brading raises the objection that the year-by-year entries for the 1770–90 dataset include balances carried over from one year to the next. If year-end balances were small and random, then their presence may not significantly disturb the trends.[30]

If the 1770–90 data by tithing districts are totaled to represent a colonywide figure for which a growth rate is calculated, the result is a rate of 2.5 percent per year. Growth rates for the short or intermediate term can be faster (or slower) than the long-term rate and cannot be used to estimate possible long-term rates. The long-term rate for the whole colony from 1700 to 1810 was probably in excess of 1 percent and may have reached 1.3 or 1.4 percent per year. Because we do not know the trend for the largest tithing district, the archdiocese of Mexico, we cannot be sure what the colonywide trend might be on the basis of the three dioceses previously discussed. The colonywide rate most likely did not replicate the archdiocesan rate, but because of its size the archdiocese would have influenced the slope of the curve. For the twenty-year period (1770–90) the inclusion of the archdiocese makes a difference.

The total tithe for 1770–90 amounted to 31.6 million pesos with almost a third (11.2 million pesos) from the archdiocese. Tithe income rose at varying rates in all districts from 1770 to 1790. As shown on table 2-1, the fastest growth occurred in the archdiocese of Mexico and the slowest in Durango, a sparsely populated region along the colony's northern tier. The patterns of

Table 2-1. Tithe Revenues for Six Districts, 1770–90 (in pesos)

Diocese	Annual average receipts	Rate per year	R^2	Student t	Autocorr. corrected
Mexico	548,358	4.9	0.94	6.1	Yes
Puebla	324,499	1.2	0.66	3.4	Yes
Michoacán	294,981	1.4	0.49	4.3	No
Guadalajara	220,802	2.7	0.44	3.8	No
Durango	100,775	0.9	0.41	3.6	No
Oaxaca	78,078	1.7	0.52	4.5	No
Total	1,567,459	2.5	0.95	5.7	Yes

Source: British Library, Egerton Collection, 520, fols. 199–205.
Note: Calculations are based on twenty-one observations.

the curves for the individual dioceses were similar in that tithes almost everywhere rose steadily during the 1770s and into the 1780s until the agricultural crises. The increases were greatest in the archdiocese followed by Guadalajara, both of which exceeded 2.5 percent per year. In Oaxaca, Michoacán, and Puebla tithes rose at more moderate rates between 1 and 2 percent per year, and in Durango they grew by less than 1 percent per year. Durango's tithe receipts peaked in 1780, several years before the crises, and Guadalajara's in 1783, a year before the crises. For the rest of the 1780s a mixed picture concerning the tithe emerges. Tithes fell off in all the ecclesiastical districts, in some more sharply than others, but in Guadalajara and Oaxaca and to a more limited extent in Michoacán tithes rebounded between 1785 and 1790. When the total tithes rather than each jurisdiction's total are studied, they reveal that receipts continued to rise until 1786 or 1787. The agricultural crises were a series of disruptions that began in some places as early as the 1784 harvest and continued across the colony until 1787 and perhaps 1788. Because the series ends in 1790, what happened in the aftermath of the disruptions cannot yet be ascertained.

It is doubtful that the population was growing at a rate comparable to the tithe; therefore, it can be asked how much of the expansion in the tithe was due to price inflation. The colonywide maize price series rose at an annual rate of 2.9 percent from 1770 to 1790, although the trend is weak. Prices rose in the early 1770s, declined and then stagnated for the rest of the decade, rose again in the early 1780s before skyrocketing during the mid-1780 famines, and finally retreated during the late 1780s. Because of the maize famines and their impact on prices in general, the rate of growth in the tithe series surely had an inflationary component. Comparisons of maize prices, wheat prices, and Zacatecas commodity prices reveal a mixed inflationary picture: more price inflation during and after the famines than before.[31]

The performance of the archdiocese is the most impressive of the six; it climbed at a hearty rate of 5 percent per year. Because Mexico City was the archdiocese and the capital of the colony, its tithe accounts may have contained receipts from other regions. However, agricultural output could be expected to grow more rapidly in Mexico's most densely populated region. Maize price trends (based on alhóndiga transactions) show a rise of about half that of the archdiocesan tithe. The difference between the two rates could be roughly interpreted as growth in population. Surely, though, such a rate (of 2.5 percent yearly) was higher than the agricultural base could possibly sustain. If the archdiocesan tithe rate were to be revised downward, then the gap between the growth in the tithe and the assumed inflation would shrink. If it were so revised, the colonywide rate would fall; if the colonywide rate fell, the gap between tithes and prices would widen and colonywide inflation would be worse than noted above. We are left with a riddle that cannot yet be solved. As inflation became more of a factor over the course of the second half of the eighteenth century, real growth in agricultural output was harder to preserve.[32]

Agricultural Supply, Risk, and Demographic Change

The market structure in eighteenth-century Mexico changed because supply lines in many urban areas had to be extended in order to feed and clothe their populations. Zacatecas, a large but remote mining center, had long imported many basic commodities, in particular maize and wheat, over distances sometimes in excess of 100 miles.[33] Similarly, eighteenth-century Guadalajara systematically expanded its supply network into the surrounding countryside along routes that were 50, 75, or 100 miles long.[34] There was a limit, of course, to the distance the lines could be extended because the prices of basic agricultural commodities never rose high enough to ensure profits after all production and transportation costs had been covered. Without higher prices than were normally reported for these goods, few producers could justify the investment in plant and equipment that was necessary to expand output.

Indeed, how producers, large or small, made decisions about what crops to raise, how much of each crop to plant, or whether to participate in local, regional, or any other market remains an unknown variable in any discussion about the changes in the agricultural sector. We can presume that they could estimate their own personal needs, but beyond that, to predict what the market needed, they were confronted with an array of ill-defined variables. Producers who decided to enter the marketplace had to try to manage the variables in order to minimize the risks and optimize their returns. There is an additional consideration, however. Producers may have had to enter the marketplace, irrespective of the risks, because they had few other economic opportunities to consider. No doubt, then as now when they entered the marketplace, they tried to glean as much information as possible from past and current performance of commodity prices—their level, direction, and variation. In modern times producers who have a considerable amount of information at hand to minimize the risk may not have to rely so heavily on prices. The situation in eighteenth-century Mexico was quite different.

Although eighteenth-century prices did not often follow a pronounced upward or downward trend over time, they did, as discussed earlier, exhibit considerable variation. Such variation in price meant that the producer faced a risky economic environment. How, then, did agricultural supply respond to prices that could not be reliably predicted from one growing season to the next? One can hypothesize that producers had to take into account both the level and the variation in prices. Production decisions made in response to price variations can be viewed as the producer's response to risk.[35]

Since both tithe and price series exist for Michoacán for the second half of the eighteenth century, we have used them to create an econometric model to assess how producers in that region might have responded to the variations in price and the risks that those variations imposed.[36] For the purposes of the model we have assumed that church tithes represent agricultural supplies and maize prices serve as a general index of agricultural prices. In addition we use colonywide maize prices as a gauge of interregional marketing conditions. These can be heatedly debated assumptions, of course, and the value of our findings must depend on the acceptability of the assumptions. By comparing Michoacán maize prices and colonywide maize prices from 1748 to 1799, we can see that colonywide prices display more variation (fig. 2-4). The risks as reflected in the oscillations appear to be the most severe in the 1750s, a period of contraction and consolidation for some commercial haciendas. During the famines of the 1780s price variation was also severe but less so than in the 1750s. On a strictly hypothetical level producers encountered more risks in trying to anticipate the supplies of interregional markets than nearby markets (table 2-2).

Price oscillations obviously complicated producers' decision making as to what and how much to plant, irrespective of the locations of the markets. Price information from which to determine the "expected" price existed in two other forms. First, there were current prices, that is, the prevailing prices from which expected prices could be estimated. Current prices required producers to act quickly, and to act quickly producers probably needed more foresight and knowledge than they had in the eighteenth century. A second and perhaps more realistic approach was to estimate prices not by using current prices but past prices—such as the average price over the past few years. Here again the producer needed knowledge that was a mix of current information and past experience. More likely than not what

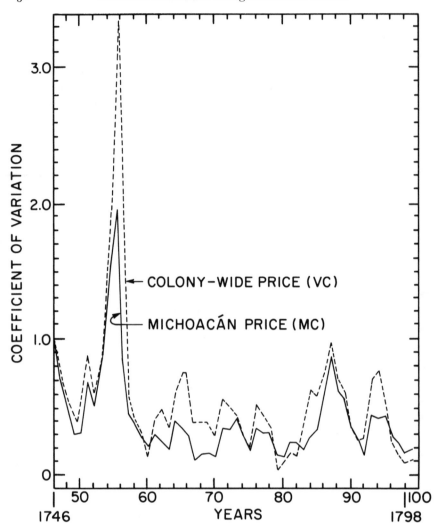

Fig. 2-4. Variation in maize prices, colony versus Michoacán, 1746–98. *Source:* See chap 1, note 59. *Statistics:* See table 2-2.

this entailed for the average producer was to carry around such information in his memory. It should be pointed out, however, that when a producer tried to calculate the expected price from past rather than current transactions, he was relying on price levels and downplaying price fluctuations.

When we analyze (with the model) how Michoacán producers might have adjusted supplies in response to changes in prices, we find that to rely on mean prices involved less risk than reliance on current prices. The model shows that a positive correlation (although not statistically significant) exists between expected prices and agricultural supplies when the mean price is

Table 2-2. Estimated Coefficients for Agricultural Supply Response in Michoacán

Variable	Current price model	Expected price model
Constant	5177300.0	3419900.0
	(3.28)	(2.22)
P_m (Price Michoacán)	−3582.8	6930.0
	(1.55)	(1.00)
P_c (Price Colony)	5299.6	−9883.4
	(2.03)	(1.29)
V_m(Supply Michoacán)	97446.0	99682.0
	(3.70)	(2.98)
V_c(Supply Colony)	−162640.0	−167340.0
	(3.62)	(2.98)
t (Time Trend)	−2907.6	−1872.6
	(3.26)	(2.14)
R^2	.77	.75

Note: Figures in parentheses are absolute values of Student t's. For source and methodology, see chap. 2, note 36, and appendix 1. Expected price is based on a moving average.

used, but a negative correlation (also not statistically significant) exists when the current price is used. In both cases (current and mean prices) agricultural supply reacted positively to price variation in Michoacán but negatively for the colony as a whole. Quite naturally, Michoacán producers could best understand their own local market because that market was more manageable in terms of risk, especially in terms of estimating prices and forecasting supplies, than distant markets. These decisions concerned how great the risk was to service a market outside the region.

The negative supply response to variation in colonywide prices is consistent with risk-adverse production decision making. Such a response can be interpreted as an income security effect because it was not in the producers' financial interests to exploit distant markets. The positive supply response to increased variation in Michoacán prices was an appropriate reaction by producers who preferred to protect household stores and to service local markets. This can be interpreted as a food security effect. Michoacán producers may have been aware of the risks in both local and distant markets and may have moved in and out of both markets as conditions dictated. What a model such as this suggests is that even in the absence of a well-developed marketing structure, producers could make choices based on the level of and variation in prices. And the prices that producers could expect did not encourage them to exploit distant markets at the expense of local markets.[37]

From the statistical evidence we can infer that demographic and agricultural growth proceeded at roughly comparable rates over the long term of the eighteenth century. This does not mean, of course, that growth was uniform throughout the century or the colony. As a result agricultural supplies could be temporarily inadequate in a given place or at a given time. Some interregional trade had grown up between areas with agricultural surpluses and agricultural shortages, but that trade was limited because of the risks and costs involved for the producers.

As the population increased, especially in urban areas, the pressure on the agricultural system to expand could have exceeded its capacity to do so. Major famines (and epidemics) did occur every thirty to forty years (1713–14, 1749–50, 1784–85) and caused the deaths of tens of thousands of people, although mortality rates differed significantly from region to region and from city to city. These famines usually resulted from unpredictable weather patterns, but because more and more people were flowing into urban centers, the severity of weather-induced famines was simply made worse. Within the Malthusian calculus a steadily rising population could eventually outstrip an "inherently inelastic" agriculture with the result that "output per head [would] decline." Thus, to complete the Malthusian argument, as "income per head and material well-being deteriorated, so mortality rose, until population growth came to a halt." An increasing mortality rate cut off growth in population and restored, at least theoretically, a balance between population and agriculture.

Although the three major famines and attendant epidemics were related to weather and not overpopulation, they also helped to reduce pressure from population growth on agricultural capacity. Mortality rates in eighteenth-century Mexico were normally high, as they were in most preindustrial societies, and these famines and epidemics (David Grigg's "crisis mortality") temporarily pushed the rates higher. Without periodic famines or epidemics, one can ask, Would Mexico have eventually attained a level of overpopulation that would have triggered the Malthusian reaction? Because of natural disasters and other society-induced disruptions that in effect controlled population growth in preindustrial societies, the issue of whether that growth ever so overwhelmed the agricultural base as to cause a demographic catastrophe is not easily resolved. There is no doubt that population pressure could induce land shortages that could result in various structural changes all the way from the most beneficial, in the form of higher yields and greater specialization, to the least beneficial, of poorer diets and higher vagrancy. Quite clearly, Malthus misjudged how much the economic structure could change, as the nineteenth century proved, and he may have misunderstood how it had changed in the eighteenth century as well.[38]

To modern scholars like Ester Boserup, Malthus's formula was too rigid. The food supply was often more elastic than Malthus described it, for as the population grew, producers responded to the increases in demand in various ways: introduction of new methods, changes in land-tenure systems, and an abandonment of old techniques. This rearrangement made the food supply more dependent on population growth because without that growth the agricultural sector had no need to modify the system.[39] Further research on preindustrial agricultural societies has turned up another variation in how the agricultural system interacted with demographic change. In some societies significant horticultural changes, especially in regard to improved productivity, came about in times of a lull in population growth (as producers presumably tried to reduce their costs to maintain their profits) and conversely less significant changes came about in times of a surge in that growth (as producers could expect high prices to cover their costs and preserve their profits).[40]

The extent to which these and other theories may apply to colonial Mexico has not been systematically investigated. Mortality rates could soar during famines and epidemics, but in the aftermath of such major crises recovery in the agricultural sector (in terms of both tithes and prices) was fairly rapid. It is possible, though, that as urban densities rose over the course of the eighteenth century, the severity of these crises intensified and the recovery from them lagged. Higher-than-usual maize prices after the crises of the 1780s may have been symptomatic of a widening imbalance between agricultural production and urban demand. Even so, it is not yet clear that the imbalance had evolved into a permanent condition. It is possible that in terms of maximum agricultural capacity Mexico had a general condition of underpopulation rather than overpopulation in the eighteenth century. Except during famines and epidemics, which did not necessarily stem from overpopulation, growth in population led to a rise in output. From an economic standpoint an increase in output could signal that producers foresaw the possibility of higher returns from their inputs of labor (primarily for small producers) and capital (plus labor for larger producers.) But, if or when the agricultural sector began to reach its optimal level and output began to slow or reverse, the threat of overpopulation could become quite real. Overpopulation might be avoided by basic technological innovations or by periodic mortality crises; the latter was more evident in Mexico than the former.[41]

Increasing agricultural output, even to accommodate population growth, can be more complicated than adding more factors of production (land, labor, capital management) or introducing a technological breakthrough. Thomas Charlton's work on the Otumba region in the Teotihuacan valley found that in two Indian communities—Oxtotipec and Cuauhtlacingo—land that might have been used for basic agricultural production, mainly the production of maize, was not being farmed, rented, or otherwise exploited in the 1790s. (Income from rented land could be spent on the purchase of food.) Perhaps as much as 100 hectares in Oxtotipec and 200 hectares in Cuauhtlacingo were left idle. In Oxtotipec, with 238 families, the land assigned to household and community maize production under the best conditions would yield about 10 fanegas per family when 15 to 20 fanegas per family were needed. In Cuauhtlacingo, with 130 families, the land assigned to maize farming may have yielded less than 10 fanegas per family. More research must be done on why these communities did not use all their land. Large parcels may have been permanently alienated and therefore beyond the control of the communities. In any event, this is an example of how agricultural expansion did not automatically proceed even when arable land was available and how it could become bogged down in noneconomic issues.[42]

What needs to be studied more thoroughly (in addition to general population levels and rates) is the character and impact of the urban population growth. Colonial Mexico is often described in terms of its urban character, but in fact we know little about its scope or scale. At the end of the eighteenth century perhaps less than 10 percent of the population lived in the largest cities and towns. Some urban populations may have increased more rapidly in the late eighteenth century than the agricultural economies surrounding these urban centers could always support. That of course could create lower supplies, higher prices, greater unemployment, and even more tragic results such as periodic famines. But we are still in the dark on how often these problems arose and how severe they were both in the long and short term. In an agricultural sector that was still heavily pastoral in Mexico in the first half of the eighteenth century, it entailed at the most basic level turning from raising animals to tilling crops. In the Valley of Mexico, although statistics are lacking, that process had surely gone as far as making crop production bigger than livestock production. From the center to the periphery the process was in various stages of development and completion. On the periphery and beyond it had barely begun.

How the process worked can be seen in the parish of Dolores Hidalgo, a few miles northeast of the burgeoning mining center of Guanajuato. The majority of the 12,000–13,000 people counted in the 1792 census lived on or near three dozen different haciendas and ranches, and more than half of the population was classified as Indian.[43] The principal business was agriculture. Flor de María Hurtado López, by carefully analyzing tithe data, constructs a picture of how this rural economy was organized. In the data provided by Hurtado López the ratio of pastoral activity to crop agriculture from 1740 to 1757 was about 60 percent to 40 percent. From 1758 to 1790, however, each accounted for about 50 percent.[44] The total volume of all tithed crops—maize, wheat, barley, beans, chilies, and grapes—grew 144 percent between the 1740–57 and 1758–90. In contrast, the volume of livestock grew only 38.9 percent between the two periods. Since what was being reported was the value of the crop or livestock, a part of that increase was due to inflation. Another part of the increase of crops compared to animals was attributable to the price of crops being more inflationary than the price of animals. Inflation notwithstanding, the rise in the value of farming versus ranching is an indication that landowners understood the need and opportunity for change, and that they could carry through.

In addition, the mix within the general categories of farming and ranching was changing. Maize was still the principal crop, but its share of the total tithes dropped from 73.8 percent in 1740–57 to 68.3 percent in 1758–89, whereas chilies climbed from 1.8 percent to 7.2 percent. The mix of livestock did not change as much, although the proportion of sheep and horses fell as the proportion of cattle and mules rose.[45] No doubt Dolores Hidalgo's proximity to Guanajuato, a city of several tens of thousands, accounted for these shifts in the parish's rural economy. It was possible that land still being used for animal herds, especially for sheep, could have been converted to crop cultivation to satisfy any additional demand from the urban market, but the change was small as the ratio between ranching and farming activities had only changed about 10 percent during the second half of the eighteenth century. Half of the region's agricultural activity was still pastoral. The absence of a greater change may indicate two alternative conditions: the cost of converting more land was too high or the demand for converting more was basically satisfied.

In the early nineteenth century two reports prepared for Veracruz's new Consulado on the economic potential of the Guadalajara region illustrate how far the reordering in Guadalajara had advanced by the early nineteenth century.[46] Long dominated by the pastoral industry, Guadalajara was becoming more diversified agriculturally. The Intendancy of Guadalajara was a vast area of just under 100,000 square miles on the Pacific side of the Mexican viceroyalty. It had a widely scattered population of a half million, with the largest concentration of people around the capital of Guadalajara, which was more than 300 miles from Mexico City and twice that far from Veracruz.

Two sets of figures that might be loosely described as representing the "gross regional product" in 1802 and 1803 resulted from these inquiries. Total production (excluding imports and exports) rose about 2 percent from 1802 to 1803, that is, from 8,560,000 pesos to 8,730,000 pesos. Not surprisingly, most of its economic life was built around agriculture. Guadalajara had some manufacturing (cloth) and mining (silver), but 72.4 percent of its total output in 1802 came from farming and ranching operations and 80.1 percent in 1803. Without attaching too much importance to percentage changes in just a two-year interval, we can still observe that farming operations rose by 17.4 percent from 1802 to 1803 but ranching operations (mostly livestock) fell by 29.4 percent. Two other categories—*industrios* and *curtidos*—also basically concerned farming and ranching: the first included such items as cheese, fish, oil, salt, and ordinary household goods, whereas the second included primarily merchandise of leather. If we organized the categories as farm-based versus ranch-based, we find that during these two years the former accounted for nearly half of the regional product and the latter for just under a third. Although those figures may be cited to demonstrate that farming had overtaken ranching as the region's chief activity, the spread between the two percentages must be treated with caution because of the way in which the items were categorized. The category "processing" included both farm and ranch products. Of particular interest is the size of the figure for the net export (exports minus imports) of farm and ranch products, a figure that equaled about a sixth of the total production in 1802 and 1803. Net exports of farm goods were two to three times higher than those of pastoral goods (1.2 million pesos versus 0.3 million pesos). Not only had Guadalajara's economy, once heavily dependent on ranching, broadened its base, but it had also expanded its commercial links with other regions.

The 1803 report presented a fairly detailed picture of Guadalajara's economy and particularly its agricultural sector (table 2-3). While agricultural and pastoral activities involved 100 different crops and products, about two dozen of these items each generated income in excess of 100,000 pesos in 1803. More than two-thirds of the value of all agricultural and pastoral goods (6.1 million pesos) derived from seven products: maize, 30.4 percent; live cattle, 11.8 percent; salt, 8.2 percent; wheat, 5.3 percent; suet, 4.7 percent; soap, 4.5 percent; and live horses, 3.4 percent. The two grains contributed twice as much (35.7 percent) as processed goods (17.4 percent) and live animals (15.2 percent) to the total of the agricultural and pastoral categories. Although in 1803 it still had a huge livestock industry with more than 750,000 heads, the region had developed a more intensive farming sector to support the growth of the city of Guadalajara.[47]

But not all agricultural and pastoral production was destined for the city. One-quarter of the two grains and almost 60 percent of the salt, suet, and soap was exported, but only about 12 percent of the livestock was exported. In a region that still had a large ranching industry exports of by-products such as suet and soap were not unusual. A few exports consisted of products that were imported in quantities as great as or almost as great as what was raised locally. Exporting nearly 10,000 pounds of rice, Guadalajara only produced (at least in 1803) 3,000 pounds and it imported more than 95,000 pounds. Because the prices of the products whether produced in Guadalajara, exported, or imported are always the same, they cannot be used to ascertain if goods being imported were being processed for reexport. Such businesses could be expected to develop as a part of the changing agricultural sector. In most cases, however, Guadalajara's exports were regional goods that had to

Table 2-3. Summaries of Values of Products from Guadalajara, 1802 and 1803 (in pesos and thousands)

Sector	Product	Percent	Imports	Percent	Exports	Percent
			1802			
Farming	2,599	30.4	123	5.5	631	23.7
Ranching	1,898	22.2			231	8.7
Processing	1,282	15.0	59	2.6	590	22.1
Tanning	419	4.9	124	5.4	168	6.3
Textile	1,601	18.7	191	8.5	291	10.9
Commerce			1,749	77.3		
Metal	760	8.9	15	0.6	755	28.3
Total	8,560		2,261		2,666	
			1803			
Farming	3,051	35.0	151	5.5	904	28.4
Ranching	1,341	15.4			261	8.9
Processing	1,321	15.1	69	2.5	624	19.6
Tanning	407	4.7	129	4.7	199	6.3
Textile	1,620	18.6	136	5.0	308	9.7
Commerce			2,241	81.9		
Metal	990	11.3	12	0.5	885	27.8
Total	8,730		2,738		3,180	

Source: AGN = AHH, Consulado leg. 917, exp. 1.

be sold to reduce surpluses or were produced for export markets. A net balance in agricultural and pastoral products helped to pay for a large share of the imported manufactures. Guadalajara registered a favorable trade balance of 500,000 to 600,000 pesos in each of the two years and the agricultural sector made an important contribution to that figure.

Did a more diversified economy create a more dynamic one? Van Young has analyzed the same figures and has concluded that the trade balance figures are relatively small for a truly dynamic economy. Although the agricultural sector had become more diversified during the second half of the eighteenth century, it served primarily, as in the past, a regional rather than an interregional market.[48] But there is a further indication that structural changes were coming slowly at best. In 1803 a quarter of the economy was still tied to ranching or related businesses. Guadalajara still produced more than 750,000 heads of livestock and hundreds of thousands of pieces of leather plus a huge volume of other by-products. Livestock sold for as little as 1 peso and as much as 5 pesos per head; most by-products including tanned leather sold for a fraction of a peso per pound or piece. At these prices the margin of profit and the return on capital, if they could be accurately calculated, would probably be very small. In one set of accounts for several eighteenth-century cattle drives, Van Young found that about 1,600 heads of cattle (driven to Mexico City and sold for 6–7 pesos per head) showed a gross profit of slightly more than 1.5 pesos per head. That profit margin might be even smaller if all the actual costs of the ranching operations were accounted for.[49] Most of the livestock raised in Guadalajara was sold there. While the transportation costs would be lower, so too would be the per-head prices. In either case, profit margins were probably very similar.

On the periphery the pastoral industry remained deeply entrenched. In the Intendancy of Durango, with more area and less population than its southern neighbor, Guadalajara, sheep-raising was the chief pastoral activity. Sheep were preferred to other livestock because wool was easier and cheaper to ship than live or slaughtered animals. Wool sold for only one-eighth to one-fourth of a peso per pound and was so seldom in short supply that the price was fairly consistent during the late colonial period.[50] Even with a large animal population (more than 1 million) the gross value of Durango's ranching business was probably not much greater than Guadalajara's, and the total output of Durango's economy was probably one-tenth to one-fifth of Guadalajara's. Ranching was not the kind of business that promoted the intensive economic activity or the rapid capital accumulation that generally preceded the restructuring of the economy. Grazing, which at times allotted an acre per animal, was hardly based on the efficient and careful exploitation of land. That same acre, if planted in maize, might yield ten times as much revenue even at the low price of one peso per fanega.

Productivity and Land Use

There is little in the published research to indicate that the changing demographic character was so profound and persistent that agricultural producers had to alter radically the way in which they used the land. Van Young believes that existing technologies were simply applied more intensively to land that was added to production or was converted from one crop to another. He finds no evidence of the introduction of new strategies such as rotating crops or using fertilizers on a scale large enough to produce much higher yields per unit of land cultivated.[51] By adding or converting land, installing irrigation systems, or building storage facilities, agriculturalists were taking relatively small steps to raise yields enough to satisfy demand. In general, producing more food often entailed adding more workers to clear the lands, prepare the fields, and harvest the crops, and since labor was relatively abundant and cheap, adding workers was preferable to other approaches.

Productivity varied from region to region and from crop to crop. Some land was naturally productive, and some had been improved over time.[52]

Improvements in yields were only selective during the eighteenth century. Alexander von Humboldt treated productivity as a part of a general discussion of eighteenth-century agriculture that ranged from soil types to rainfall amounts, from plant varieties to government policies. In sorting out these various factors, some of which were easier to remedy with an enlightened agricultural program than others, Humboldt adopted a position (which some twentieth-century scholars, following his lead, have also adopted) that a continuing major obstacle to improved productivity was the high ratio of land to people, which made intensive cultivation less an imperative in Mexico than in Europe.[53] He was impressed with the fertile land and the agricultural engineering that he found in Querétaro and León in the Bajío and observed that the use of water in the production of wheat had raised yields to levels higher than those recorded in France, despite the fact that farmers in Mexico as in Europe probably could have done even better if they had refrained from planting the seeds so close together that they choked each other off.[54] Around Guadalajara Van Young found that enlightened use of fertilizer, topsoil, and water can be documented on a limited basis in the production of maize, wheat, fruits, and vegetables. The utilization and management of the water supply in Guadalajara (and in other places as well) was probably the most widespread advance in farming techniques.[55]

Current research into small-scale, labor-intensive plots in traditional agricultural communities reveals how productive some can be, although it shows up most clearly through the analysis of the scale and technology of specific crops in specific locations. The expectation of higher income may cause traditional farmers to try to boost their yields, but obstacles not directly related to productivity may frustrate those expectations.[56] How to apply these contemporary findings to eighteenth-century Mexico remains a puzzle. What these studies suggest, though, is that even when the financial incentives existed—and that remains to be examined more systematically for eighteenth-century Mexico—the producer may have confronted an array of problems (particularly how to deal with distribution bottlenecks) that could not be solved strictly in terms of yield-revenue ratios.

Even with maize, the most important staple, yields varied widely. Estimates generally ranged "from 70 to 125 fanegas" harvested for each "fanega sown." There were reports of ratios of 200 to 1 and even 800 to 1. Within a single area, such as the Valley of Mexico, the range of ratios could be extensive: in the northeast at Axapusco on inferior acreage yields were 40 fanegas for each planted, while in the southeast on better land they were 133 to 1. The quality of the land was not the only factor. Indian cultivators continued to use the coa or digging stick to plant the maize, although some communities employed Spanish methods with plows and work animals. Irrigation, which Indians had used before conquest, was largely taken over

by the Spanish farmers for their wheat production.[57] Humboldt's observation
of Querétaro haciendas having 400 to 1 yields can almost certainly be
discounted. León and Silao with enough rain could apparently reach 150 to 1.
Some other reports from the Upper Bajío quoted figures of 80–100 to 1.
Brading's research reveals another problem, however. Year-to-year yields on
the same hacienda could be highly variable. On one estate (Duarte) during
the eighteenth century they fluctuated between 40 to 1 and 100 to 1.[58] Even
with maize eighteenth-century cultivators had not yet attained a level of
control that allowed for consistency from one year to the next, without which
any improvement was slow in coming. In Guadalajara, where maize cultivation was growing in importance, the ratio stood at 100 to 1, even though some
producers did better than that.[59] To consider 100 to 1 to be the colonial
average would be in line with these various estimates and reports, an average
that worked out to about 11 fanegas or 17 bushels per acre. The range of ratios
suggests that maize productivity in some regions could have been boosted to
and sustained at levels higher than 100 to 1. That this did not occur may be an
indication of the uncertain economic stature of maize farming in both the
Indian and the Spanish agricultural sectors during the late colonial period.

Wheat was the grain of choice for some eighteenth-century Mexican
agriculturists and yet the ratios of wheat harvested to wheat sown were as
disparate as those for maize. Brading reports that planting wheat in León was
a gamble unless it was planted near the León River. He dismisses a ratio of 15
to 1 as untrustworthy (from twentieth-century sources) because it did not
distinguish properly between the yields from irrigated and nonirrigated land.
Still, if the two land types were combined, the ratio would probably be quite
low because without access to water wheat yields fell off sharply. Again,
Humboldt found higher yields of 35 to 40 *cargas* of wheat (approximately 300
pounds each) for each carga sown around Querétaro, which generally had a
better water supply. For irrigated land, at least, Brading was inclined to
accept Humboldt's estimate. In Guadalajara, on the other hand, the ratio of
wheat harvested to wheat sown may have only reached 4 or 5 to 1, one-tenth
to one-fourth the yields in the Bajío. Guadalajara may have been particularly
unsuited to wheat cultivation because of its "mediocre, sandy soils" that
could be easily damaged by careless tillage or heavy rain. The periodic heavy
rains did not obviate the need to install irrigation or to manage water; rather
they compounded the problem in the sense that erosion in the rainy season
had to be controlled even as water had to be husbanded for the dry season.[60]
No doubt in some wheat-farming areas Mexican wheat farmers had yields
comparable to the English wheat growers, but in other areas they were far
from achieving or maintaining these ratios. It is likely that as water management improved so too did wheat yields during the eighteenth century,
although by how much remains speculation. The reason for planting wheat

and risking the investment in irrigation was that the return could be greater than other crops including maize. The expansion of wheat cultivation in the eighteenth century testifies to both the expectation and the realization that, whatever the risks, wheat was an investment worth making. Given the range of ratios of plantings to yields, however, wheat farming had not yet evolved to the point where uniformly high productivity scales could be achieved and maintained.

In the final analysis, however, the absence of discussion about techniques that could lead to higher yields, lower costs, and higher profits in the agricultural literature may be the most telling example of how little attention was paid to the agricultural sector or how little progress could be expected.[61] Irrigation, for example, was a key to progress in Mexico. Yet little was written about how to manage or, more important, how to finance such water systems. Certainly, inertia toward innovation and modernization in agriculture (as well as in other economic sectors) was deeply rooted in colonial society and was hard to overcome. The expanding market for crops as a result of dual demographic pressures of general population growth and urban population growth had only a marginal impact on how the agricultural community viewed its opportunities. The explanation for this may lie beyond the economic analysis that can be brought to bear on the quantifiable evidence. Humboldt's observation (which Van Young has refurbished and expanded) that the colony did not reach that critical mass in terms of growth in population and availability of land necessary to force profound changes in the agricultural sector represents one point of departure for further research and analysis. On a grander scale one might consider Coatsworth's observation that overhauling a sector of the economy, such as agriculture, entailed a much larger task of reordering the relations between the state and the economy.[62]

The common response (as opposed to raising productivity) was to add new land to the tillable stock or to convert land from one use to another. Land that had lain idle or had been used for less intensive activities like pasture and forage could be converted to cultivation as changing market conditions required. There were limits to how much land could be added or converted to cultivation. Not all land was arable, and the amount available during the eighteenth century, as noted earlier, remains a matter of debate. Today Mexico has about 700,000 square miles of land of which 100,000 square miles, or more than 60 million square acres, are arable. Mexico probably did not have that many square acres of arable land in the eighteenth century, but it may well have had more than 10 million. To produce 5 million fanegas of maize the colony needed up to 0.5 million square acres or 5 percent of the total. The problem with such gross calculations is that they do not distinguish among regions.

In some densely populated areas most arable land was under tillage, or the cost of creating more such land was greater than the expected return from the use of that land. That raises the second issue: converting virgin or idle land or less intensely exploited land to cultivation could be more costly than the owner could afford or than the return could warrant. The extent to which eighteenth-century Mexico had a shortage of arable land in the face of mounting demand depended more on location and cost rather than on the absolute supply of arable land itself. Against the total supply of arable land in Mexico with a population of 3–6 million in the eighteenth century, a shortage of land for cultivation cannot be automatically assumed. In certain regions, however, arable land may have fallen short of need.[63] Low agricultural prices combined with high transportation costs made it difficult to balance the scarcity in one region with the abundance in another region.[64]

Hacienda scholars have found numerous examples of how land-use patterns changed over the eighteenth century in response to the rising demand. Without doubt Mexico (especially the core) had more land under plow at the end of the eighteenth century than at the beginning because owners were willing to invest in clearing, irrigating, and improving land that heretofore had lain idle or had been used for less intensive agriculture. In 1700 most of the land in the immediate vicinity of León, located in the Upper Bajío, had been cleared, for example, but by 1750 most of the land twenty to thirty miles from the city had also been cleared, although all of the cleared land was not necessarily tilled.[65] On one large León hacienda studied by Brading, however, crop land rose from 1,200 acres to 10,000 acres, almost a tenfold increase, between 1746 and 1790.[66] Another reflection of land-use changes was investment in facilities to support cultivation. At an hacienda near Oaxaca (Antequera) an irrigation ditch about 4,300 yards long was constructed to water about 1,000 acres of arable land.[67]

It has been argued, of course, that one consequence of the shift to more arable land was a rise in land prices. "[A]ll land," writes Brading, "no matter what its quality, increased in value"; when "viewed from the perspective of assessment, the greatest rise came from clearance and irrigation."[68] Brading provides a series of land prices, some of which were estimates rather than actual transactions, around León. On average during the eighteenth century rural land sold for about 250 pesos per caballería (approximately 106 acres), or just above 2 pesos per acre. If we lump together all the estimated and declared land values, we find that the value of León's rural land rose at just under 1 percent per year.[69] That meant that a caballería of land, regardless of its condition or use, could have doubled about every seventy years. This can only be described as modest growth. Moreover, when the data are broken down into their several categories, the price of prime land—cleared or irrigated—did not rise as fast as the price of uncleared or pasture land. Under the pressure to develop more arable land, less desirable land that had previously sold for low prices may have increased in value faster than the tillable land that had always been more highly priced. Irrigated land was the highest priced with a range of 350 to 900 pesos per caballería, whereas arable land fell into a slightly lower range. Pasture land sold from 40 to 150 pesos per caballería and uncleared land from 20 to 300 pesos per caballería. Pasture land close to farm land could still be in demand because crop cultivation required acreage for work animals, such as oxen. In any event, not too much can be made of these trends because of the inconsistency and incompleteness of the data.

It should be noted, however, that some estates continued to report large holdings of nonarable lands and some even added to those holdings. Not all land could be converted, of course, and estates varied in the amount of land that could be upgraded or converted. In León, for example, the Otates estate with more than 15,000 acres had only about 10 percent in cultivation at the end of the eighteenth century.[70] In and around the Valley of Mexico where the Jesuits had created a huge (unconnected) hacienda known as Santa Lucía, they acquired new lands both for raising crops and pasturing animals. Figures on harvests of crops at Santa Lucía show that production grew in the first half of the eighteenth century (unfortunately the data end with the expulsion of the Jesuits in 1766). Between 1713 and 1766 maize harvests more than doubled while barley harvests rose by slightly more than half. Growth could not always be guaranteed; between the famines of 1714–15 and an epidemic in 1737–38 the output of maize and barley grew but that of chickpeas and beans fell. Herman Konrad's extended analysis of Santa Lucía's operations led him to conclude that despite new opportunities associated with crop ventures the long-term picture showed an "inconsistency of returns from farming endeavors." In the eighteenth century Santa Lucía still had a sheep herd that numbered around 100,000, for which tens of thousands of acres of pastures were needed. In the eighteenth century Santa Lucía acquired nearly 400,000 acres, of which less than 1 percent can be definitely identified as farm land. Over 75 percent was described as *sitios de ganado mayor* and the remaining 24 percent as *sitios de ganado menor* (ranches for large and small animals). In spite of the shift from farming to ranching more pastures had to be added not only because some land had become too arid for any animal except goats but also because the herds (sheep, goats, horses, and mules) were being enlarged.[71] Other studies of estate operations after the expulsion of the Jesuits in 1766 reveal that while farming had grown in importance, ranching still accounted for almost half of the total receipts from the business operations.[72]

Changing land-use patterns could have a devastating impact on small independent farmers (in contrast to Spanish hacendados and Indian communities). The size of these holdings could vary from several hundred acres to more than a thousand. Called *ranchos* and *labores* (ranches and farms), they could be owned or leased by their occupants. Often in dispute over land these owners or renters had much less economic or legal clout than the hacendados or communities. Unlike the large estates, which often combined farming and ranching activities with an increasing emphasis on the former, these small landholdings specialized in ranching or farming. Both were subject to alienation as the pressure on land grew, but the loss of the food-producing small farms may have been more costly for the economy than the loss of small ranches.[73]

The analysis of some large and small operations point to the possibility that labores were more efficient than large estates. In the Upper Bajío Brading described the first half of the eighteenth century as a "golden age" for these small proprietary farmers before the land-use patterns tilted toward a dual development of the less efficient "latifundia" and "minifundia" that virtually ended the role of small farmers.[74] The "small-scale agriculturalists" in Morelos were more often renters than owners, but they lost their independence as their water rights were suspended or their land rents were raised.[75] In the Valley of Mexico by the late seventeenth century, the haciendas supplied most of the wheat, maize, and other grains to the towns and cities, and over the course of the next century they expanded their control and power at the expense of the small producers.[76] The contribution of small-scale agriculture to the development of the economy as well as its loss is hard to assess. As Gibson has observed with respect to the Valley of Mexico, holding land for prestige alone without concern for profit and loss was not feasible any longer under the new and changing economic order.[77]

Agricultural trends indicate that over the long term of the eighteenth century production grew fast enough to accommodate demand. Regional differences could be significant, although they probably only reflected the peculiar growth of the population in the region. In the short run, of course, demand could outrun supply, especially with maize. But the agricultural sector could and did recover from shortages and famines rather quickly, even the worst of the famines in the middle 1780s. Another indication that the supply of agricultural goods was generally sufficient over the long term is the performance of agricultural prices. Some long-term inflation can be detected. Between major famines every twenty to thirty years prices rose faster than the long-term rate. But the short-term rise was due in part to the fact that prices usually fell sharply after famines and remained low for one-third to one-half of the time from the end of one famine to the start of the next famine. Low prices of agricultural goods, even wheat, discouraged producers from expanding their production too much out of fear that the yield would not cover the investment. Agricultural production, especially on the heavily leveraged estates, became tied not to a change in technology that might have lowered per-unit costs and improved the rate of return, but rather to the cycle of famine. Withholding agricultural produce from the urban markets became a way of regulating prices by hastening shortages.

3

Estate Operations
and Urban Markets

As urban centers grew in the eighteenth century, they came to depend more heavily on the surrounding rural areas to supply their markets with comestibles and other processed goods. Much of what was produced and processed in rural areas for urban markets originated on Spanish estates and ranches. Although some Indian communities and family farms raised corn, fruits, vegetables, and barnyard animals to be sold in nearby towns and cities, dependence on Spanish agricultural production intensified because population growth in native communities reduced their surpluses and raised costs for land acquisition and improvements. This made some small-plot farming less financially feasible. In addition, long-standing conflicts over boundary lines and water rights usually between Spanish estates and Indian villages could temporarily turn violent and disrupt production, although the long-term economic effect was probably not significant. In general the view held by some scholars is that as urban markets extended their supply lines, estate agriculture assumed greater control over the flow of goods from the countryside to the city.

The proprietors of the estates came to realize that periodic scarcities, even if mainly weather-induced, could be made to serve their financial interests. By holding back supplies until prices had risen, they could boost their own incomes. Scarcity was unpredictable, however, and so was their control over the market. In addition, given the indebtedness that many estates had acquired by the second half of the eighteenth century, pursuing the economics of scarcity may not have helped them to balance their books or to redirect their operations. The relationship between commercial estates and urban markets is not easy to understand in part because the data that we need to analyze prices, costs, and profits are not readily available. There can be no doubt that market conditions influenced the decisions about what to plant and when to sell, but market conditions did not always favor commercial agriculture. Even when practicing the economics of scarcity, commercial agriculture still had to confront its own undercapitalized condition. That meant that while scarcity temporarily and marginally pushed up income on what was normally produced, it did not provide much incentive or opportunity to establish more efficient or profitable operations.

There was another side to the linkage between estates and markets. We know more about how haciendas operated than how urban markets functioned. Part of the problem is demographic. We do not yet have precise figures on the size and composition of urban populations except for a few scattered years. Numerous reports, such as the Consulado survey discussed in chapter 1, leave the impression that urban population growth by the late eighteenth century was dangerously high because it entailed so much migration from the countryside to the city. But we have few investigations on how or where this migration occurred and the rate of increase for selected cities or across the colony.

Even with such incomplete knowledge about urban demographic changes we have other problems to be considered. Urban markets included both private and public sectors, although the private sector was subject to heavy regulation. The public sector generally involved the sale and distribution of grain, mainly maize but also wheat or flour, through municipal granaries or licensed shops. The purpose was to maintain adequate supplies of staples at reasonable prices, especially for the poor. Whether the system ever worked efficiently is problematical, but over the course of the eighteenth century it proved itself to be incapable of accommodating the changes taking place in the population or economy. Even if these public agencies could have adapted to changing conditions, they were often poorly administered, especially in times of crises when certain urban constituencies were in need of help. Although difficult to demonstrate empirically because we lack proper data, these agencies may have caused serious dislocations in the supply systems that they were supposed to help maintain for the benefit of the consuming public. At the very least how these agencies affected the urban marketplace and the agricultural sector needs to be explored.

Financial Health of Rural Estates

The process of adding or upgrading land had an essential financial component. Landowners had to raise capital to buy or improve the land. To stay in business they had to earn returns that justified their investments. Large landowners may have been better positioned to raise money, but that did not necessarily mean that they were also skilled managers. In theory, at least, those who converted land from pastures to crops could earn more income because farming made each unit of land more efficient and profitable. Some individual estates engaged in large-scale agriculture were moving precisely in that direction in the eighteenth century. That a more efficient and profitable agricultural sector developed is far less certain.

A series composed of "net revenues" (also "annual profits"), or operating surpluses, exists for the Jesuits' Santa Lucía for sixty years between 1582 and 1773. The surpluses, totaling more than a million pesos or about 20,000 pesos per year, rose at an annual rate of 0.5 percent over the sixty-year period. For the eighteenth century (1724–73) surpluses in slightly more than half the years totaled nearly 700,000 pesos or 24,000 per year. The annual growth rate was 1.5 percent (94 percent confidence level).[1] It is likely that Santa Lucía's surpluses did grow over time, but it is unclear, because of large gaps in the dataset, that these rates capture the actual growth in the surpluses. Moreover, how to interpret these figures without more information on costs of land acquisitions and capital improvements is unclear. Given the fact that Santa Lucía owned tens of thousands of acres, the surpluses appear to be modest. Santa Lucía inherited and purchased land. How the former was accounted for in the overall financial statement is not known. The growth rate meant that surpluses doubled about every third of a century, a moderately impressive accomplishment but no greater than other series that we have examined.

Other former Jesuit properties reported surpluses for a brief period from 1767 to 1771. The figures ranged from a few thousand pesos to 50,000 pesos per year, with one-fifth of the properties reporting from 10,000 to 50,000 pesos. In general, the estates (such as Santa Lucía) that combined farming and ranching had the highest annual surpluses.[2] If the agricultural sector was capable of making money for its owners and investors, then that should show up in rising values of rural properties. Little data for long-term analysis of rural property values now exist. Data exist for Guadalajara where values follow a rising curve in the eighteenth century. According to those who have studied Guadalajara's rural economy, speculating in land to take advantage of rising property values did not appear to be widely practiced.[3] Investment for the purpose of making an estate more efficient and productive can be documented in Guadalajara and elsewhere. One example in Guadalajara is Potrero, which Raphael Hernández y Chacón bought for 4,000 pesos (not stated if a loan). He then borrowed 4,000 pesos to prepare about thirty-three acres for planting in wheat. The land itself constituted a small part of the estate's total value. The value of the estate rose from 4,000 pesos in 1800 to 10,050 pesos in 1805 to 17,000 pesos in 1821 largely because the owner invested in improvement of land and facilities.[4] We can estimate that if only 8,000 pesos were invested (for purchase and improvement) between 1800 and 1821 that investment grew by just under 4 percent per year. Simply in terms of the value of the estate, the investment had more than doubled in just two decades.

Potrero may not have been typical of the average rural estate in the Guadalajaran district. When all the sales and appraisals are aggregated, the rise in the value of these properties was 2 percent per year, or a doubling in their value every thirty-five to forty years.[5] Among the economic indicators that we have analyzed, the property value series is higher than most; only several treasury series are higher. Without other series based on property values the growth cannot be considered within a larger context. For property to need more than a third of century to double in value is not a stellar performance, but for eighteenth-century Mexico it may be a better-than-average performance.

Wealth accumulation through property investment was a long-term venture. The average transaction (sale or appraisal) was 36,000 pesos. Some estates were located in Toluquilla Valley, a few miles from Guadalajara and virtually fully developed, and some were located farther away in less-developed areas. Several highly valued but huge estates were in the outer ring of the agricultural network that served Guadalajara. Van Young's research has uncovered that "the increase in estate values was less spectacular in those areas, such as the Toluquilla Valley, which were already well-developed by the mid-eighteenth century." One might expect that those closer to Guadalajara would experience a sharper rise in value than those farther out on the basis that proximity would offer certain advantages (especially in transportation) to their owners. The disadvantage could be that "well-developed" meant more investment would be necessary to raise crop productivity in order to exploit the Guadalajaran market than was required in less-developed areas that still had virgin cropland. If we could determine per-acre values, we may find, as Van Young suggests, that the sprawling estates on the outer fringes only had larger sale or appraisal figures because they included so much more acreage.[6] In any event, the rise of the eighteenth-century Guadalajara market not only expanded the countryside that served the city but also made rural property a potentially valuable investment. How valuable depended in part on other investment opportunities in the eighteenth century, although the range of such opportunities must have remained relatively narrow.

The rise in real estate values may have had some unintended results. With their estates worth more money, rural landowners could borrow more money to pursue a variety of personal and business projects, including loans to purchase and improve the estates. It had become customary for businessmen and landowners in particular to tap the wealth of the church to underwrite the expansion of the eighteenth century. In the area served by the Diocese of Guadalajara the church was the major player in the credit market. In her study of the credit market of Nueva Galicia, a jurisdiction that was larger than that defined by Van Young and others as the Guadalajara region, Linda Greenow has shown that hundreds of rural properties carried liens in amounts from a few thousand to tens of thousands of pesos during the eighteenth century. Not only did the number of loans for which estates were used as collateral grow over the course of the century, but so did their amount. Some estates were in debt with loans that were equal to as much as 80, 90, or 100 percent of their assumed value. Landowners not only had many reasons to borrow money but also had many opportunities to do so because of the rising value of their "mortgageable property." Consequently, they borrowed so heavily that many could probably "never return to financial solvency."[7]

In a more concentrated region known as *caxcana*, in the southern part of the modern state of Zacatecas, the volume of agricultural loans made by various religious foundations rose steadily from 1700 to 1790 (with a dip in the 1760s), after which they fell until 1810. Demand for agricultural loans may have fallen off after 1790 because some haciendas had indebtedness that amounted to one-half or more of the estate's assessed value.[8]

Debt in and of itself is not a sign of a weak or ill economy; rather the ratio of debt to other variables such as income, profit, or return can be a more crucial indicator of the impact of any encumbrance on the operations. These are the most elusive pieces of historical statistical data. The more business-oriented the operation, the more likely the owner was to incorporate his indebtedness into his calculations and expectations. Van Young is more sanguine about the role and magnitude of the agricultural debt in Guadalajara, certainly by the end of the century. It is difficult, he warns, to sort out loans for religious purposes from those for agricultural purposes. The purpose of the loan did not have to be declared, nor did the decision for making the loan have to follow strict credit-worthiness procedures. Agricultural loans totaling slightly under 500,000 pesos were recorded for the period between 1787 and 1794. In 1787, after the agricultural crises of the middle 1780s had subsided, only 14,000 pesos in borrowings were approved. This suggests that few agriculturalists were compelled, as a result of these crises, to enter the credit market. On the other hand, since we know very little about the supply of credit in times of crisis, this may also suggest that the credit market was temporarily incapacitated. From 1788 to 1791, however, lending activity picked up in that about 100,000 pesos' worth of loans were extended each year, although the majority of the borrowers came from outside the Guadalajara market region. Whether that was a positive or negative sign for the Guadalajara economy is not immediately apparent from the documentary record. Van Young observes some additional positive signs. There was the usual number of bankruptcies and disputes, and yet both the lender (the church) and the borrower (the agriculturalist) seemed to take their respective financial responsibilities seriously enough: the former insisted on prompt repayments and the latter invested mostly in capital improvements. Furthermore, the possibility that estate bankruptcies were declining and property transfers were stabilizing could mean that the credit market was functioning well because the local economy was generally prosperous.[9]

In the end what counted was not so much the size of the debt or the rate of turnover in ownership but rather, given the costs (capital as well as operational), whether the landowner could expect a reasonable return on his investment. Some estimates of annual returns can be calculated from the inventories and ledgers kept by estate managers and owners, and they show returns on average of 4–5 percent.[10] The sample is so small that we do not know how valid these rates were for the range of estates from the smallest to the largest. Some estates not only made money almost every year but also met their annual interest payments and repaid their loans. Others seldom made money and carried large debts with both interest and principal payments in arrears. But the majority of the estates probably fell somewhere between these two extremes.

A set of accounts from the Hacienda de San Agustín de los Amoles, comprising a half dozen ranches and farms scattered across western Mexico, reveals in some detail for one year, 1803, how its business had evolved by the end of the colonial period. In the case of San Agustín, which probably belonged to the Augustinians, we cannot calculate a rate of return in 1803 (its properties could have been inherited rather than purchased), but we can analyze the cash flow. Although the total acreage was not stated, its herds, numbering in the tens of thousands, needed many thousands of acres for grazing. It had several hundred acres, a fraction of its total, in cropland. San Agustín encompassed two large properties that combined farming and ranching, with the latter occupying far more acreage and several small specialized operations. In a consolidated balance sheet that showed no operating surplus, the hacienda's income from selling its products in the outside market was less than 15 percent of its total revenues. Most of its income-producing activity (for bookkeeping purposes at least) involved internal operations: buying and selling among the various operations and, in particular, transactions between workers and administrators. What the hacienda had to sell was livestock, soap, leather, sugar, meat, and water, none of which was sold in large quantities or at high prices. One of its major products, *piloncillo* (brown sugar loaf), may have had more sales among the hacienda's various units than outside the estate. Under these conditions the return on investment or capital had to be small and may not have mattered at all. It is not that San Agustín cut itself off from the external market, for it bought maize, cloth, and household items to sell to its workers, but that it was organizing less and less of its business life around that market.[11]

Having to commit more of their resources to internal operations could be a sign that haciendas were faced with a deteriorating financial condition. On the basis of published hacienda accounts the large estates with more access to capital and more interest in diversification had a better chance to attain higher returns than smaller landholdings. In a few cases returns as high as 10 percent have been calculated. Some small estates and perhaps some family holdings were as efficient and profitable as the larger operations, although such efficiency or profitability did not mean that returns on investments were sufficient over the long term to continue to upgrade or to expand their operations.[12]

It is worth noting that a rate of return between 4 and 5 percent or higher was unusual in eighteenth-century England, where horticultural change was as far-reaching as in any western agricultural system.[13] English agricultural-ists raised productivity by introducing labor-saving techniques, improving yields, and becoming skilled managers. Such changes are harder to account for across the agricultural sector in eighteenth-century Mexico. Without such basic changes productivity stagnated, income fell, and indebtedness grew. More borrowing had an economic cost. Unless the landowners could sell more goods or charge higher prices, they only found themselves saddled with greater fixed costs and lower profit margins. Rates below 5 percent per year meant that agriculturalists had to try to make their operations more productive and efficient in order to cover their costs, reduce their debts, and protect their investments. Individually some Mexican agriculturalists imple-mented the necessary changes and realized the rewards that such changes brought. In the aggregate, however, Mexican agriculture saw indebtedness rise but not profitability.

Two other developments in eighteenth-century Mexico signaled trouble for the agricultural economy. One was an increasing amount of acreage rented or leased by the owners of the estates; the other was the relatively static wage levels of the rural workers. On the surface the decision not to work the land directly could save the landowner the cost of developing and maintaining the land as well as the cost of planting and harvesting the crop. Arrangements varied from owner to owner. Some owners did undertake the cost of preparing the land or buying the seed. Even if the owners provided some services, these arrangements allowed them to divorce themselves from the financial commitments of day-to-day operations of their own estates and to live off the rents or shares of their tenants. They could maintain a flow of revenue without assuming any more indebtedness for land acquisition or capital improvement. In theory the landowner could raise his rents or shares as needed to cover his costs and to preserve his profits. Without tenants, of course, the land lay idle and the owner's income ceased.

Landowners surely understood that they could not exact more from their tenants than the tenants could afford to pay, and yet landowners, under pressure to meet their own financial obligations, may have ignored this basic economic principle. It is an open question as to how productive or efficient such leased plots were. Some modern studies have found that small-plot or family-plot farming not only survives in Latin America but also shows itself at times to be remarkably entrepreneurial. Whether this applies to the rental rather than the ownership of land is debatable.[14] In addition, though, many eighteenth-century renters lacked knowledge about resources and techniques that would have made it possible to convert their plots into profitable operations. How widespread leasing and renting had become in late colonial Mexico is not known, but most hacienda accounts that have surfaced have a rental revenue category.

At the Hacienda de San Agustín in 1803 rental revenue provided at least 36 percent of the total revenue, and it could have been higher because some accounts for the smaller holdings were consolidated rather than itemized. Rents were collected in the spring, although a few were paid as late as December (1803), on the basis of the quantity and perhaps the location of land. On the lists compiled by the administrators 130 rentals were identified, for an average rental of 36.9 pesos. In a few instances a renter's name appeared more than once: for example, Pablo Ortiz paid rents on two different plots. In other instances several renters with the same surname from the same locality appear on the lists; without more evidence one can only assume that they were related. In fact, the per capita average given above may be misleading because four persons (who carry the title *don*) paid more than two-thirds all the rents for an average of 825 pesos! What has not been determined is whether they were actual renters (perhaps small ranchers or farmers) or rent collectors at other sites. It is evident that they should be distinguished from small-plot renters. The remaining 126 renters paid an average rent of only 11.9 pesos. The lowest rents were 1 peso and the highest (excluding the four above) were several hundred pesos. The frequency of rents by categories for all renters has the following distribution: 1–5 pesos, 58 percent; 6–10 pesos, 27.1 percent; 11–15 pesos, 8.5 percent; 16–20 pesos, 5.4 percent; 21–25 pesos, 0 percent; 26–30 pesos, 2.3 percent; and above 30 pesos, 11.6 percent. The last group includes the four highest of 600 to 1,400 pesos. More than 90 percent paid less than 10 pesos, and that means that if the rents were indicative of size, the vast majority had small holdings. The site within San Agustín known as *tierras nuevas* (possibly just newly added land) had among the lowest rentals, but it also had a large number of above-average rentals. The site with the lowest rentals per capita was called Dolores. Presumably the product of the rented land was used to provide for the renter's household and to pay the rent. How surpluses from rented lands, if any existed, were disposed cannot be traced. Although details about plot sizes and rental terms are missing, what is known points to the maintenance of an economy based on subsistence rather than opportunity for the worker's household.[15]

Whether the rented land was used for crops or pastures is not indicated, and perhaps from the estate's viewpoint that did not matter. As a general rule owners turned to rentals when their own efforts with the more costly croplands did not have a sufficient return to justify further investment or attention. Those who expressed a preference for renters, tenants, or share-croppers have often been described as the "laggards" (as opposed to "innova-tors") in the history of change in agriculture. An agricultural system that involved dividing up estates or farms into ever-smaller units, of separating ownership from operation, and of negotiating short-term contracts subject to frequent modifications (such as the amount of rent) is viewed as less efficient and productive than the system where management and operation were the business of the owner. Preserving income was a stronger motive than maximizing profit for the laggards. Hence the holder of the contract had more control over the rate of change in agriculture than the cultivator of the land.[16]

The profit-and-loss statements for various Jesuit estates also show that by the second half of the eighteenth century rent from land had become a sizable revenue item. Tetillas, estimated to be worth 281,363 pesos in 1767, received 25 percent of its revenue from sheep sales and 75 percent from rents and sales of some other animals and products, although the latter category was not further broken down.[17] At Santa Lucía a rental strategy was developed early in the second half of the seventeenth century. Lands held by the Jesuits under *mayorazgos* could not be sold but could be rented. Jesuit administrators approved rental contracts on donated lands during the late seventeenth century and throughout the eighteenth century up to the expulsion, with the duration of the contract from two to nine years. By 1743 sections of Santa Lucía had been rented to more than 600 renters for a variety of reasons, from ending disputes with their neighbors over land incursions to increasing revenue. Renters produced a variety of products: maize, barley, sugar, beans, pulque, firewood, charcoal, and livestock, some of which the estates consumed and some of which were sold to the public. These 600 renters paid 5,700 pesos or 9.5 pesos per renter per year, a figure that was 2 pesos less than the annual average rents at San Agustín (excluding the four largest renters). That rents were important to Santa Lucía as early as the 1740s is evident in that they accounted for one-quarter of the estate's total revenue.[18] Without reading too much into these scattered figures, we find that they pose some interesting questions about how much a fairly static rent structure contributed to the agricultural sector's overall ability to boost its revenues and to trim its encumbrances.

Similar trends can be observed in Bajío and Guadalajara. By the end of the eighteenth century, according to Brading, raising maize or livestock to sell for profit entailed greater financial risks at some estates than living off the income from a system of leases and tenants.[19] Agreements were often "verbal or informal" and could be extended from year to year. At Otates in 1814 the arrangement was spelled more precisely in that it cost 10 pesos to lease a *fanega de sembradura* (about 9 acres). If similar terms existed at San Agustín, where we know about rent levels but not about plot sizes, more than half of the renters occupied five acres or fewer. Even a half century before the insurgency period one-third of all Otates's maize was produced by tenants.[20]

Brading does not view the preference for leasing as necessarily a positive or desirable development because it was accompanied by a growth in the size of the hacienda and diminution in the number of small proprietary farms and ranches. It could have laid the foundation for the expansion of the nine-teenth-century sharecropping system, and that, according to some studies, retarded agricultural progress.[21] In the Guadalajaran region there was con-siderable variation from estate to estate in the amount of land under lease. For some landowners renting or leasing land was not yet as attractive a financial alternative as raising and selling their own products. At the end of the century Toluquilla, with a value of 97,000 pesos, had livestock sales of 48 percent of the total income and cereal sales, 41 percent. Rental revenue provided only 3 percent. In contrast to Toluquilla, Sauceda—valued at 150,000 pesos—over three years (1807–9) derived 38.5 percent of its revenue from livestock sales, a possible 25.6 percent from cereal sales, and 15.8 percent from land rentals. La Barca rented nearly all of its 100,000 acres, and El Carmen almost none. Sharecropping existed in late colonial Guadalajara on a limited basis, and it was more prevalent in maize production than in other agricultural operations.[22]

More people lived and worked in the countryside than in the cities, and how as well as how much they were paid had an impact on economic growth and change.[23] The impact of the eighteenth-century demographic changes varied by region and by decade, but in general as the population grew in the countryside so did the supply of labor. It is also true that at times employers complained of shortages because they were forced to pay higher wages to attract workers. Some shortages were severe enough to persuade the crown to approve labor drafts, although they were the exception rather than the rule.[24] Since skilled laborers were often in short supply, they could more easily earn higher salaries or win quicker promotions than could the un-skilled. On the whole, however, whatever advantage some workers may have had at various times or at different places, the growth in population combined with a slowly changing economic structure left the average worker with few employment opportunities from which to choose.

In the absence of any major technological breakthrough the more intensive use of land came about with the more intensive application of labor.
Labor was needed to build fences, irrigation systems, and sheds as well as for
planting seeds, weeding fields, and harvesting crops.[25] Thus in accounts for
estates that combined farming and ranching labor probably constituted about
half the costs in the total operating budget. Unfortunately, the data are too
imprecise and incomplete to reach any firm conclusions about what was
happening to the ratio between labor costs and total costs. If, for example,
adding fertilizer were cheaper than hiring more labor to increase output, the
ratio of labor to total costs would decline. But since we have no evidence yet
that the rise in agricultural output resulted from important changes in
agricultural methods, we assume that the increase stemmed from adding
labor, not from altering technology. Under these conditions, if more workers
were needed to raise more crops, the share of labor costs to total cost would
increase. If more workers were hired but total wages to total costs declined,
even just slightly, wages paid workers would be declining.[26] In other words,
more workers at lower wages meant that total wages as a percentage of total
costs did not rise much but remained about constant.

One serious drawback in trying to analyze the rural wage question is that
workers were paid in several different ways. Rural wages for both farming
and ranching ventures included payments in cash (when money was available), in kind, and in a combination of the two so that the true value of the
rural wage may never be known. When we examine the data for compensation in cash, we find that from 1700 to 1810 the trend was flat. This agrees
with the findings of Brading, Van Young, and others that rural wages (about 5
pesos per month) changed little during the century.[27] There were periodic
fluctuations in some occupational categories, but neither the upward nor
downward movement was more than a short-term phenomenon. If wages
were as static as these trends indicate, then one could argue that producers
did not face a disproportionate rise in the labor component of the total costs
that could result from hiring new workers. In the absence of such a rise there
was no pressure to experiment with more productive and efficient methods of
farming (or ranching) in order to lower operating costs and preserve profit
margins. It is possible, of course, that a flat or at most a modestly rising wage
curve helped to keep inflation in check during the eighteenth century.
Shortages of goods, in particular foodstuffs, caused prices to rise in the
eighteenth century. Wage levels, on the other hand, were too static to cause
much price inflation as the result of higher consumer spending.

At Hacienda de San Agustín a complex labor system of full- and part-time
workers paid in cash and in merchandise was evolving. From *mayordomos* to
peones about 500 people appeared on the wage roster in 1803. They earned
nearly 13,000 pesos in wages, but the portion paid in cash may have been no

more than several thousand pesos. San Agustín, the largest ranch within the hacienda, had fifty-five permanent pastoral workers, and Buenavista, the adjacent and largest farm, had thirty-four permanent agricultural laborers, for a total of eighty-nine. The two groups received about the same annual wages: 26 pesos for ranching employees and 24 pesos for farming employees. The former received 77.1 percent of their wages in merchandise and the latter 56.1 percent. The highest paid were ranch captain, at 60 pesos per year, and farm foreman, at 96 pesos per year. Some or all of these workers may have received lodging and grain rations in addition to their wages. For ranch hands the average debt of 24 pesos was almost equal to the average wage, and for farm hands the average debt of 19.1 pesos was notably lower than the average wage. It appears that what the workers on these two units, as well as other units, actually earned was based on the number of days worked. The stated wage for a month or a year (when given) was not a guaranteed compensation. In addition to permanent workers, temporary day laborers were hired from surrounding villages for a week to six months at rates slightly below those for the permanent workers. In analyzing rural wages we want to emphasize that not only is the rate important but also the length of employment and the form of payment. These data show that rural wage earners had limited means by which to enter the consumer economy. In larger terms the potential for economic growth and transformation through the participation of rural wage earners was minimal.

These findings conform to those published by other scholars of rural labor systems in eighteenth-century Mexico, and they reinforce the view of the bleak prospects for the rural workers in particular and for the rural economy in general. For the worker it was not only low wages, but it was also low wages combined with short work periods. In the case of the San Agustín workers, their monthly wage rate was probably two to three times higher than the figures cited above, but their actual monthly payment was one-third to one-half less than the rate. Even though wage rates remained constant, employers, who may well have faced rising costs in other areas, such as debt service, tried various strategies to keep wage costs as low as possible. With a larger population pool owners could employ day laborers for the seasonal jobs instead of adding to the permanent work force. Day workers cost less than permanent laborers. They were only paid for the days that they worked and they received few if any allowances (except possibly a grain allotment), since they resided not on the estates but in nearby villages.

Owners could enjoy further savings on wage bills by increasing payments of rations and lowering payments in coins, which were often in short supply anyway. How these arrangements were modified and implemented depended on the balance between the demand for and supply of labor in a given region. On the periphery in the north and in the south the supply of labor may have been tight enough to support a labor system based in part on debt peonage.[28] Peonage, a mechanism by which landowners in need of resident workers used advances of cash or merchandise to gather up resident laborers, functioned all across the colony in the eighteenth century, although it certainly lost its economic appeal as rural labor became more and more plentiful.[29] It is becoming evident that population growth stimulated agrarian expansion but not necessarily agrarian development, with the result that colonial rural life experienced rising impoverishment.[30] After nearly a century of growth in output during which land tenure and land use underwent major changes, many landowners, including some of the colony's largest hacendados, headed only marginal agricultural enterprises and most workers found themselves with declining living standards.

There may also have been some cost for the producer as rural labor systems underwent these and other changes. In some estates where labor records survive, there is ample evidence of worker mischief and personnel turnover. The increasing use of day labor and the substitution of in-kind payment for cash eroded the loyalty of the worker to the employer and reduced whatever pool of knowledge and skill about a particular estate the permanent work force might have represented.

Urban Markets and Food Supplies

As the urban population increased (perhaps faster than the general population) the link between the city, as the consumer of agricultural goods, and the countryside, as the producer, became more pervasive.[31] Although agricultural capacity may have been sufficient to meet overall demand, it did not provide total protection against periodic famines. In some urban areas growth in population exceeded the capacity of the surrounding agricultural region to sustain that growth, with the result that food scarcities were frequent, living standards declined, and impoverished conditions became permanent. Severe famines, however, were still mainly a function of weather. Other agricultural regions may have produced or could have produced surpluses, but the cost of transporting agricultural goods from one region to another region were high enough to make such transfers uneconomical except in times of severe shortages and high prices.

Although public policies were less concerned with food production than its distribution, they could affect how the rural economies responded to urban needs. If public policies reduced the incentive to invest in agriculture, the impact on urban markets would be lower supplies and greater shortages. Although the regulations and how they were enforced could vary from municipality to municipality, the standard model was that city councils had the power to force grain and meat producers to do business with the municipal agencies charged with providing for the population. In addition, city councils could enact regulations concerning retail operations from establishing weights and measures to preventing fraud and dishonesty.[32] Even in regulated markets some incentive to produce and to invest in expansion had to exist before production or investment would grow in step with demand. Public policies governing urban markets may well have distorted that relationship.

In the late sixteenth and early seventeenth centuries when native depopulation severely reduced the agricultural work force, municipal governments introduced policies and established agencies that were designed to protect against urban famines and exorbitant prices. These included alhóndigas and *pósitos* (grain markets), price schedules, and licensed retail outlets. Many municipal governments, despite an erosion in power and influence after the sixteenth century, remained involved in the regulation of the marketplace, most directly with foodstuffs. Why were such agencies maintained in a colony that could probably grow enough food to feed its population, certainly after 1650? Part of the explanation (besides simple inertia) might have been to build up the surpluses that were needed for future famines (except that these surpluses seldom materialized). Another, more persuasive reason may have been that personal income (except among the wealthy) changed so little over the last half of the colonial period (especially since wage rates were technically regulated) that municipal intervention to set prices or influence the marketplace was deemed necessary to protect the poor, the unemployed, and even the average worker.

It is not yet clear what the long-term economic benefits from municipal intervention were, even in the most severe agricultural crises. Prices rose and fell in response to changing conditions, and mechanisms for regulating prices may have made it more difficult for both producers and consumers to adapt to those changes. In any event, the rise in demand for food that accompanied the surge in growth of cities during the second half of the eighteenth century again focused attention on the municipality's role in the urban marketplace. In general, it appears that policies and agencies based on earlier models were revived or strengthened, mainly in response to the rising number of urban poor.

In his study of late eighteenth- and early nineteenth-century Puebla, Guy Thomson argues that "[t]he importance of keeping a large city, composed mainly of poor people, fed at fair and acceptable prices accounts for why the ordinances regulating food supply were the most important and consistently applied set of regulations."[33] It can be debated whether or not this was appropriate action. Setting prices could be counterproductive because producers and dealers could try to withhold supplies until prices were forced higher. But it may have been necessary because, given the economic system, more than removing controls over sales of staples was needed to reform the urban marketplace. The fact that municipal food supply programs were mismanaged and underfinanced only compounded the problem of trying to serve the urban population.

Many municipalities had long tried to regulate the supply of meat within their jurisdictions. The rationale for this was somewhat clearer in the sixteenth century before the development of the ranching industry than in the eighteenth century. Cities in areas where ranching was receding because it was no longer profitable or because land was being converted from grazing to farming viewed monopolies as necessary in order to maintain meat supplies at reasonable prices. But the meat monopoly survived in places like Zacatecas and Guadalajara, where ranching operations were extensive. In Zacatecas the contract usually called for a few thousand head (cattle and sheep) to be sold to the local butcher shop at about one peso per head. Few ranchers or merchants ever showed much interest in bidding for the contracts, and the contracts were often held by the same person or family for years and even decades. In 1816, when the meat contract system was officially abolished, the city's *cabildo* was much less concerned over meat supplies than over the loss of another municipal prerogative.[34]

Land-use changes in late colonial Guadalajara could have caused a reduction in the supply of meat and a rise in its price. Records indicate that the number of sheep slaughtered declined slightly, whereas the number of cattle slaughtered remained nearly steady. But "the level of meat consumption," writes Van Young, "remained roughly stable, or perhaps increased slightly, during the latter half of the eighteenth century." For most of the century the contract price of lamb was two to three times higher than beef, but in the last quarter the gap between them narrowed as the price of beef rose more rapidly than lamb. The displacement of ranching by farming close to the city helped to push up meat prices because of higher transportation costs. It is questionable whether those at the low end of the economic scale could afford meat even at the regulated price.[35]

In Puebla, Manuel Flon, the intendant, actually ended the meat monopoly around 1800 because it was not working efficiently. During the late eighteenth century, as contractors bought more and more meat from outside the Puebla region, in the northern ranching areas quality declined, deliveries became sporadic, and prices rose. By ending the monopoly Flon counted on local producers, who had quit ranching, to become once again the source of supply for Puebla. That was what happened, although efforts to reimpose the monopoly, beginning in 1805, make it difficult to evaluate the impact. Given the new opportunities, local producers apparently responded by enlarging their herds. The details of how these changes were made and what their impact was on the producer, the butcher, and the public remain obscure. As Thomson points out, because meat was a "luxury and not an item

consumed by the poor or by the city's large Indian population," the controversy surrounding the meat monopoly—whether to abolish or restore it—did
not entail as much "political" risk as might have been the case with other
public functions.[36]

For the city of Cuernavaca meat contract prices for beef and mutton have
been collected and analyzed over a period of about 180 years, from 1630 to
1810. Its eighteenth-century curve is similar to Guadalajara's curve. The
meat contract prices were volatile but the trend was flat until the last quarter
of century, when they turned sharply higher.[37] Like other contracts the price
of beef and mutton sold to the city were fixed for the life of the contract (up to
five years), and such a series does not readily admit to trend analysis. It is
worth pointing out that the Cuernavaca curve exhibited two other characteristics that showed up in the colonywide maize curve: first, the sharp rise in
meat contract prices began in the late third quarter and continued until the
middle or late 1780s at rates notably higher than for the century as a whole;
and second, the rise was followed not by a decline, but by a leveling off that
kept prices higher than they had been for most of the century.[38]

The meat-consuming public was a small part of the urban population, and
it had to pay higher prices for monopoly-supplied meat for reasons that
related to demand, weather, transportation, and mismanagement. Meat
consumers had more choices than beef and mutton. From Zacatecas's *alcabalas* records we discover that various kinds of fish, poultry, and game were
sold by butchers, grocers, and peddlers. The quantities were not large, and
the prices, where several years can be strung together, could fluctuate but
showed little tendency to rise in the second half of the eighteenth century.[39]
Alexander von Humboldt's figures on meat consumed in Mexico City have
often been cited because they include large quantities as well as variety: fowl,
1,255,340; sheep, 278,923; turkey, 205,000; partridge, 140,000; duck,
125,000; pigeon, 65,300; pig, 50,676; kid and rabbit, 24,000; cattle, 16,300;
and calf, 450. What Humboldt wanted to underscore was that per capita meat
consumption in Mexico City, estimated to be 189 pounds per individual (in
1791), was higher than Paris's consumption of 163 pounds per person. Since
one-fifth of the population were Indians, who ate almost no meat, the per
capita consumption, based on those who could be expected to buy meat, was
in the range of 250 pounds per person.[40] But Humboldt's list is interesting for
other reasons. More than 2 million animals on Humboldt's list could be
classified as barnyard and wild birds, another 0.25–0.5 million as hoofed
animals. Although 2 million is a very large number, it works out to no more
than two dozen per year per person among those who consumed meat. Fowl
could have been so numerous because feathered animals, compared to other
animals, were cheaper to hunt or raise and to ship to the capital. Since
Mexico City was more heavily hispanized, people there probably consumed

more meat and more varieties of meat than in any other urban center.[41] In addition, hoofed animals were still sold under a monopoly. The contract for beef and mutton was held by an individual, who earned a fee from each animal slaughtered, although he was not obligated to provide the livestock nor was he successful in establishing a complete monopoly over meat transactions. All the other items were provided through the supply network that had grown up to serve the city in the late eighteenth century. In many cases owners of slaughterhouses had been or continued to be in the retail trade, usually with no direct affiliation to a rural estate.[42] Not much is known about the public or private meat trade in the capital, how far the supply network had reached, or how much prices had changed. It can be assumed that the demographic pressure was such that land around the capital was more profitably used for farming than ranching, and that most of the hoofed animals were imported from regions beyond the Valley of Mexico.

Municipalities were more deeply committed to regulating grain supplies than meat supplies because grain was the important staple of the urban diet. In Puebla Thomson describes the procedure for the regulation of maize that was in effect from 1666 to 1843:[43]

Maize farmers of substance (labradores) deposited their maize under cover in storage rooms (tojes), known as "adentro," where it was held until they instructed alhóndiga officials to sell it. This had to be within a maximum of twenty days of being brought into the city. If the public was unsupplied, granary officials did not have to await permission from labradores before selling, and could sell at their discretion. The alhóndiga offered this storage service to labradores because most of Puebla's maize came from estates at a considerable distance (. . . San Juan de los Llanos and Tepeaca) and in such quantities that it would often not be sold on the day of arrival. Small farmers (perujaleros) and muleteers (arrieros), who transported maize from Indian villages on their own account, sold the grain directly from the patio of the building, known as "afuera", on the day it was brought in. . . . Wealthier maize farmers, selling large quantities of maize in the city, qualified for . . . the trojes while peasants, small farmers and petty merchants and muleteers were confined to the exposed patio. Grain was sold from 10 A.M. to 5 P.M. at a price fixed at the level of the first free sales of the day.

Variations of this government-operated public agency probably existed across most of the colony's large cities, although in Zacatecas during the first half of the eighteenth century the alhóndiga/pósito operations were farmed out to the highest bidder, usually a merchant.[44] Fees and taxes were assessed against grain deliveries and sales in order to support the alhóndigas and pósitos as well as other municipal functions. In Mexico City, like Puebla, the granary set a price daily for the sale of maize but on the basis of the local market price of the previous day. In Zacatecas and Guadalajara the granary did not fix the price but served as a place where buyer and seller could negotiate a sale.[45]

Municipal alhóndigas and pósitos had to accommodate an ever-increasing demand in the late eighteenth and early nineteenth centuries, as urban populations grew. In Guadalajara, for example, maize deliveries to these agencies rose at an annual rate of just under 1 percent between 1748 and 1820.[46] From 1780 on they probably rose faster than the seventy-year average. In Zacatecas both alhóndiga deliveries and prices rose in the second half of the eighteenth century, but as deliveries tailed off after 1800, prices may have risen more sharply.[47] In Puebla the long-term trends up to 1800 are less clear, but from 1800 to 1830–40 both supply and price declined. In the decade from 1800 to 1810 deliveries to and sales from the granary appear to have risen and then fallen while prices moved in the opposite direction.[48]

The experience in late colonial Puebla, while not typical of all the cities, underscored the problem that many cities began to face in 1790s. In short, the granary system was breaking down. The crisis, it appears, arose because suppliers (mainly Puebla's grain farmers) were becoming more successful at controlling the flow of grain to the city—reducing supplies and boosting prices—with the result that granary's supply was perennially uncertain. Mismanagement at the granary only made the situation worse. The result was a steady growth in sales of maize in the streets and plazas away from the alhóndiga with little regard for the official prices. Even when droughts reduced the harvests and famine and disease were spreading from 1808 to 1810, the old monopolistic grain practices could not be restored. Thomson could only conclude that the "limits of corporate institutions in mitigating the cruel workings of the urban maize market" had been reached.[49]

Despite Thomson's detailed recounting of events in Puebla from 1800 to 1810, the exact relationship between supplies and prices cannot be calculated. His graphs suggest that, in terms of official deliveries and prices, the trend for supplies was downward and for prices was upward in the first decade of the nineteenth century. But we can only speculate about the state of the overall maize market because we lack data on street and plaza sales. Notwithstanding the inherent failure of the granary system to perform as it was designed, the underlying economic issue was the inelasticity in the supply of maize. Was there enough economic incentive even among marginal producers, who could temporarily benefit from the current crisis, to invest either to improve or expand maize agriculture?

At another level of municipal intervention was the institution known as the pósito. Technically, this was a fund established and managed by the local municipality to purchase grain (mainly maize) for resale to the public in general, but to the poor in particular. By the end of the eighteenth century a *junta* (agency) separate from the *ayuntamiento* (city council) was responsible for the pósito. In theory the pósito bought maize in times of abundant harvests when prices were low in order to sell in times of scarce harvests when prices were high. Government officials were not very adept at predicting the movement of the maize cycle, and even when they did, they lacked the financial resources to purchase enough maize to make much difference. Zacatecas's pósito at the onset of the scarcity in maize in 1797, after several years of ample supplies at moderate prices, could only acquire a couple thousand fanegas at prices almost as high as the local market prices. Even if the poor could afford the maize, the pósito only had on hand enough to feed about a dozen families for a single year.[50]

The damage that the pósito could do to the grain market was apparently understood in Guadalajara, where officials tried not "to undersell private suppliers" because that would simply force producers to withhold grain until the price rose or until the grain rotted. Rather, their policy was to set a price that encouraged farmers to release their supplies at a price, no doubt, that few poor could pay. The supply of maize relative to the demand in Guadalajara continued to shrink with the result that prices continued to climb. The city fathers were forced to buy maize on contract under terms that were more favorable to the producers. Although the municipality passed legislation to protect the citizenry and to strengthen the pósito, it could not make maize producers produce more or grain speculators speculate less.[51] Government policy could not overcome and may well have been at odds with the long-term trends that made for an increasingly inelastic supply of maize.

The second main staple subject to regulation was flour. We have already discussed how wheat production increased during the eighteenth century because a rise in demand for bread made wheat a more profitable investment than maize, at least in some regions. Like maize, however, the production of wheat may have grown to the point that it no longer offered a return much greater than maize. The late third and early fourth quarters may have witnessed the fastest growth in wheat production after which it leveled off. In Puebla, where bread consumption had probably always been large, flour consumption in 1802 was nearly 53,000 cargas compared to nearly 30,500 cargas in 1698, a rise of 77 percent. But single-year comparisons are not very useful for the determination of any trend.[52] In Guadalajara, on the other hand, a series based on wheat and flour deliveries shows that between 1750 and 1810 the volume rose from about 1,000 cargas in 1753 to about 10,000 in 1781, fell to less than 5,000 in 1796, and finally rose again to nearly 17,000 in 1809.[53]

The controls that municipalities tried to impose covered the sale of bread rather than the production of wheat or the delivery of flour, although periodic inspections of wheat farms and flour mills were not uncommon. In addition, public officials discussed the establishment of wheat or flour granaries that would operate on the same principle as maize granaries. In Guadalajara both approaches were considered. Although bakeries were supposed to be licensed shops and to charge official prices, so many establishments were engaged in making and selling bakery goods that "the trade was impossible to regulate." The abuses were numerous, from overcharging the poor to substituting rotten for good flour, and even when they were acknowledged, the abuses were hard to eradicate. The municipal government's specific responses involved the creation of a wheat granary and a bakers' guild, which formulated an "elaborately detailed ordinance for the production and sale of bread" (1786) through the use of a *calicata*, "a sliding scale which pegged the price of bread to the price of wheat in a fixed ratio." The procedure for enforcing the calicata, first tried in 1701, required that all costs from ingredients to salaries be calculated and periodically revised. Problems arose not just because of periodic lax enforcement but also because of widespread public disregard. The granary was probably the most conspicuous failure. After plans were drawn up twice, the idea of building a granary was apparently abandoned. In a final appraisal of why the city's effort to regulate the distribution and sale of bread was so glaringly ineffective, Van Young states that landowners, the dominant voice in the municipal government, knew that they stood to gain from higher bread prices.[54]

Maize and Flour Markets in Mexico City

Mexico City had the largest urban population and maintained as elaborate a system of regulation as any municipality in the colony. Moreover, because of its size and importance, the regulatory system which Mexico City erected had an impact on the economy of the Valley of Mexico and beyond. The population was growing in both the valley and the city, but because of in-migration the rate of growth was probably higher in the city than the rate across the valley. Population growth placed the valley's agriculture under heavy pressure, and by the end of the eighteenth century without changes in the system of production and distribution the capacity of the valley to supply both the valley and the city may have been reached or exceeded. How far beyond the valley and into the interior the supply network reached depended partly on transportation costs. But additional problems in supplying the city with staples arose because of the way in which the city's marketplace was organized and regulated. If urban populations like Mexico City's became increasingly impoverished during the eighteenth century, how urban markets functioned must be taken into account in any explanation of that impoverishment.

An alhóndiga and pósito were established in Mexico City in the 1580s to help alleviate shortages and moderate the prices of grain.[55] Down to the eighteenth century the particular regulations changed but the basic obligation remained in place—to provide the city with a supply of essential grains at affordable prices. The alhóndiga and pósito came to be used exclusively for the sale and distribution of maize. In Mexico City the price of the maize sold in the granary was set daily. The officials calculated the price for each grade on the basis of a crude measure of the local supply and demand. At the end of the business day the *alcalde* (magistrate) asked the producers what they intended to charge the next day; if the alcalde was satisfied with their information, he would then announce the various prices when the alhóndiga opened the next day. If he was not satisfied or if the producers disagreed, he would announce his own price. Through experience the two parties learned that agreeing was advantageous to both. The rules governing operations and sales—time for opening or closing the granary or procedure for disposing of old grain—were elaborate, although they may not have always been strictly enforced.

Despite these elaborate rules and procedures maize was still sold through private retailers. The volume of maize sold by private retailers in the late colonial period may have reached 50,000 fanegas a year, an amount that was almost equal to what entered the granary.[56] Maize price trends at the alhóndiga are better understood than maize supply trends, although it can be safely assumed that rising prices or high price levels indicate that demand was exceeding supply. Although alhóndiga maize prices were regulated, they could still move in an irregular fashion. The long-term rate in Mexico City was comparable if not slightly slower than the colonywide rate of 0.7 percent per year, but like the colonywide rate the Mexico City rate moved up more aggressively, by two or three times the secular rate, in the last half of the eighteenth century. Although such rates do not represent unmanageable inflation, they do suggest, especially for the last half of the eighteenth century, that the lag in supply was getting progressively more serious. Alhóndiga prices tended to be higher than other maize series, but the rate of increase does not vary much from series to series (see table 3-1). A few scattered statistics lend support to the observation that granary prices rose after 1750–60, not only because total demand for maize rose, but also because alhóndiga deliveries fell, by perhaps as much as one-half between the 1740s and the 1780s.[57] The unknown factor is whether a decline in alhóndiga supplies was being offset by an increase in private supplies sold through local retailers. Since granary prices were partially based on market transactions, supplies must have been falling behind demand.

Although linked to the granary, Mexico City's pósito had a different role: to sell grain to the poor at reasonable prices when declining supplies pushed up market prices. Predicting the market from one year to the next was

Table 3-1. Comparative Maize Prices, Mexico City, 1768–89 (in reales per fanegas)

	Pósito bought	Pósito sold	Granary price	Colonywide price
1768	12.0	11.3	10.9	6.4
1769	0.0	8.6	10.4	7.6
1770	9.7	12.5	12.5	11.7
1771	12.8	13.3	12.6	12.3
1772	15.9	21.6	19.9	15.1
1773	15.2	16.7	17.5	12.0
1774	14.0	15.4	15.4	10.2
1775	9.6	11.7	12.4	8.0
1776	12.5	14.3	15.3	12.2
1777	7.5	9.6	10.0	8.3
1778	9.1	9.2	9.1	9.0
1779	7.5	11.1	11.2	10.5
1780	0.0	13.5	14.4	12.6
1781	19.4	21.0	20.1	11.9
1782	14.0	13.9	20.0	10.0
1783	0.0	11.2	0.0	7.8
1784	0.0	10.1	11.1	11.3
1785	16.1	24.1	23.3	22.8
1786	0.0	32.2	40.1	36.9
1787	0.0	0.0	27.6	17.9
1788	12.0	11.0	0.0	14.7
1789	0.0	0.0	0.0	23.9
Average	12.5	14.6	16.5	13.3

Source: Pósito prices from British Library, Additions 17561; colonywide prices from chap. 1.

difficult enough for both producers and officials and was nearly impossible beyond that year. In addition, facilities for storing maize were often unsatisfactory. Although the alhóndiga and the pósito were related in that they shared facilities and duties, they could be administered (as they were in Zacatecas) as separate functions. It is unclear whether the financial administrations of the Mexico City alhóndiga and pósito were entirely distinct. The receipts from fees and sales at the pósito may have been used to pay salaries of the employees and repairs of the facilities of the alhóndiga. One thing that the pósito needed was capital to buy the grain before it was sold. Whether linked directly to the alhóndiga, the pósito's role is fairly well documented for a brief but crucial period from 1768 to 1789.[58] Accounts show not only how complicated the business of buying and selling maize was but how vulnerable public agencies like the pósito were to being raided for their funds.

On tables 3-2 and 3-3 the revenues and costs are presented year by year from 1768 through 1789. Receipts consisted of two basic sources: fees

Table 3-2. Revenues and Balances, Mexico City Pósito, 1768–89 (in pesos)

Year	Taxes	Sales	Total revenues	Yearly balances	Cumulative balances
1768	00	4,842	4,842	(20,221)	(20,221)
1769	00	3,387	3,387	(10,755)	(30,976)
1770	00	16,201	16,201	(18,492)	(49,468)
1771	8,825	20,602	29,427	11,014	(38,454)
1772	14,152	97,030	111,182	19,170	(19,284)
1773	12,261	29,412	41,673	(29,077)	(48,361)
1774	11,684	39,218	50,902	6,672	(41,689)
1775	12,435	12,496	24,931	(30,647)	(72,336)
1776	13,088	38,933	52,021	22,777	(49,559)
1777	13,042	9,802	22,844	(3,002)	(52,361)
1778	12,721	16,938	29,659	(11,390)	(63,751)
1779	12,110	6,105	18,215	1,340	(62,411)
1780	10,544	16,303	26,847	17,088	(45,323)
1781	10,735	12,163	22,898	5,173	(40,150)
1782	11,081	8,930	20,011	(21,023)	(61,173)
1783	11,101	10,378	21,479	11,209	(49,964)
1784	10,838	731	11,569	4,543	(45,421)
1785	10,039	23,517	33,556	15,253	(30,168)
1786	13,252	15,060	28,312	20,631	(9,537)
1787	10,925	00	10,925	1,834	(7,703)
1788	10,336	688	11,024	4,253	(3,450)
1789	11,306	00	11,306	2,777	(673)
Total	220,475	382,736	603,211		

Source: British Library, Additions 17561.
Note: The carryover of 58,840 pesos from 1767 is not included in the cumulative balance. Balances are calculated by subtracting total expenses shown in table 3-3 from total revenues. Parentheses indicate losses.

assessed against all maize and flour (wheat and barley) deliveries to the city and sales of maize. The fees amounted to three-quarters of a real for each carga of flour shipped into the city and one-half of a real for each carga of maize. Those fees totaled more than 220,000 pesos or just over 10,000 per year, while sales of nearly 383,000 pesos averaged nearly 17,500 annually. By the 1780s sales had fallen off so precipitously that the fees came to be the principal revenue. Declining sales could mean that maize was so readily available that the pósito was not needed; it could also mean that regardless of the supply of maize pósito operations were being curtailed, ignored, or abandoned. The price of maize at the alhóndiga and the pósito during the 1770s and into the 1780s does not indicate a surplus at hand in that maize was selling at a price above the eighteenth-century average (11.6 pesos per fanega). Rather, the pósito had spent tens of thousands of pesos on various

Table 3-3. Operating Expenses, Mexico City Pósito, 1768–89 (in pesos)

Year	Purchases	Freight	Salaries	Expenses	Totals
1768	24,041	00	1,022	00	25,063
1769	00	2,000	650	11,492	14,142
1770	28,081	3,440	2,666	506	34,693
1771	5,075	9,237	543	3,558	18,413
1772	63,730	21,000	1,627	5,655	92,012
1773	59,463	5,286	135	5,866	70,750
1774	28,538	4,313	5,490	5,889	44,230
1775	44,811	1,500	00	9,267	55,578
1776	11,531	9,925	1,650	6,138	29,244
1777	12,332	872	2,900	9,742	25,846
1778	27,863	6,000	1,350	5,836	41,049
1779	9,375	00	1,350	6,150	16,875
1780	00	2,000	1,488	6,271	9,759
1781	3,450	2,000	1,350	10,925	17,725
1782	21,000	1,000	1,250	17,782	41,034
1783	00	1,000	1,350	7,920	10,270
1784	00	00	1,250	5,776	7,026
1785	10,063	00	2,433	5,807	18,303
1786	00	632	1,350	5,699	7,681
1787	00	00	1,250	7,841	9,091
1788	750	00	100	5,921	6,771
1789	00	00	2,500	6,029	8,529
Total	350,103	70,205	33,704	150,072	603,884

Source: British Library, Additions 17561.
Note: Expenses include cost of administration and maintenance. Yearly totals have
  been substracted from total revenues for yearly and cumulative balances shown in
  table 3-2.

projects from rebuilding satellite operations to assisting public charities. In
addition to having less money to spend on purchases of maize, it had less
maize than it expected because producers had reneged on contracts that they
had signed for delivery of maize to the pósito. By the middle 1780s, just as
disaster struck, the pósito had squandered a surplus of nearly 60,000 pesos
from 1768 on projects that had little to do with maize purchases and was
operating in the red. Only by using borrowed funds could it make maize
purchases during the agricultural crises.

Viewed strictly from the standpoint of what operating costs were, the
pósito posted surpluses, totaling 20,000 pesos, in fourteen of twenty-two
years. When losses occurred, however, they often exceeded 20,000 pesos
per year, and when the cumulative gains and losses are tallied, they show
that the pósito was in debt by almost 700 pesos in 1789. In 1778 the
cumulative loss was more than 63,000 pesos, and during the next decade the

loss was cut to under 1,000 pesos largely by reducing or suspending sales and in effect by using the fee to cover the expenses and balance the books. In short, the surplus from 1767 would have remained virtually intact by 1789 except that other nonoperating expenses, such as nearly 60,000 pesos for public aid during the epidemics of 1768, 1773, and 1779, were charged against the pósito.

Between 1768 and 1789 the pósito purchased more than 233,000 fanegas of maize at an average price of 12.0 reales per fanega. Of that amount about 197,000 was delivered and sold at an average price of 14.5 reales per fanega, which was two reales less than the average price of the maize sold through the alhóndiga. The price charged for the maize from the pósito did not cover all the costs for purchases, freight, employees, and maintenance. To have covered all these costs the price would have had to be set at almost 24 reales per fanega. The taxes on maize and flour shipments amounted, therefore, to a subsidy of about 10 reales per fanega sold.

During this period the pósito contracted to buy more than 233,000 fanegas but only received about 197,000 fanegas. Those who failed to live up to their contracts (unless there were extenuating circumstances) were usually charged an 8-real penalty per fanega regardless of the price that the contract called for. It is possible that some producers decided that even with the penalty (which was not always collected) they could still make money by breaking the contract and selling elsewhere. Purchases and sales of maize were reported for all the years in the 1770s. During the 1780s, however, only four years had both purchases and sales. In 1772 and 1773 the pósito bought more than 63,000 fanegas and sold about 50,000 fanegas; a decade later (1782–83), just prior to the famines, the pósito only handled about 12,000 fanegas. For whatever reason—shortage of money or maize, inept management, or change of policy—after the 1770s in which purchases and sales averaged 15,000–20,000 fanegas annually, the pósito assumed a lower profile with transactions of a few thousand fanegas yearly. Most notably, it was ill-prepared for the loss of the harvest in 1784.

The pósito accounts provide an opportunity to expand the discussion from the state of the pósito's financial management to the state of the city's grain market. The fee on maize and flour was supposed to be collected on all such grain that entered the city, although in reality it included only the grain that was delivered or reported to the granary. The amount of maize purchased by the pósito declined between 1768 and 1789 at a substantial rate of 12.9 percent annually.[59] The trend for the city's maize market cannot be precisely extrapolated from the trend at the pósito. By analyzing the fee that maize shippers paid to the public granary, we can estimate that the volume of maize (including what the pósito bought) delivered to the capital from 1771 through 1789 declined at an annual rate of about 1 percent.[60] Officials knew that only part of the maize delivered to the city was entering the granary, and they estimated that 50,000 fanegas escaped taxation (at least when they compiled the report in the late 1780s).[61] The city may have received delivery of 2.6 million fanegas between 1768 and 1789, or an annual average of 120,000 fanegas, three-fifths of which entered the granary and two-fifths of which did not. During that period, however, the volume of maize entering the city probably did not grow significantly; it could also have declined slightly through the early 1780s, after which it may have started to rise again through the 1790s.

Was there enough maize before or after the famines of the 1780s to sustain the maize-consuming population? Some have estimated that the city had 30,000–35,000 Indians during this period. If they were the principal maize consumers, on an annual basis of 3.5 fanegas per person they needed 105,000–123,000 fanegas per year. On average, it appears, for the major maize-consuming group, the supply (combined public and private markets) was adequate during the late third and early fourth quarters. It was not bountiful, however, and over time the growth in supply may have slowed. Thus the rise in the price of Mexico City maize during the late third and early fourth quarters probably resulted from a growing imbalance between supply and demand.

The impact of shrinking or slowly growing maize supplies may have been lessened by the fact that Mexico City consumers had another choice, namely bread. Mexico City residents may have consumed as much bread as European urban populations. One estimate made in 1792 declared that per person 1.4 more pounds of wheat (which was used primarily for bread) was consumed than maize, that is, 42.3 million pounds of wheat versus 30.0 million pounds of maize.[62] How consumers, the poor in particular, allocated their income in the purchase of maize, flour, and food in general remains to be studied. Whether the poor bought bread or tortillas probably depended more on cost than on quality, for neither item was necessarily prepared with uncontaminated ingredients or under ideal conditions. Although direct proof is lacking, the rise in flour shipments would suggest that bread was viewed as an alternative to tortillas.

Wheat and flour were not sold through an alhóndiga. Plans were discussed but never implemented for a wheat granary. By the middle of the seventeenth century many small wheat farmers had quit business because they could not compete with the large haciendas. The system for producing wheat and selling bread was tripartite—grower, miller, and baker—but entailed more regulation (and taxation) for the baker than the other parties. In this system, instead of government-controlled warehouses and markets as with maize, the mill became the place where much of the wheat and flour business was conducted. This was in part because mills had storage. The system may have worked most of the time to provide Mexico City with its daily bread, although the suitability of central Mexico's climate to wheat production may have assured that supplies were adequate.[63]

The adequacy of wheat or flour supplies can be observed in long-term prices. Wheat prices from tithe studies for San Miguel el Grande, Dolores Hidalgo, and San Luis de la Paz in the Upper Bajío, as explained earlier, were virtually flat over the whole eighteenth century (fig. 1-5). During the second half of the eighteenth century wheat prices rose irregularly between 1750 and 1786, after which they plummeted, unlike maize prices which fell only moderately and then leveled off at higher-than-normal levels. Some price inflation showed up during the late third and early fourth quarters, but outside of those years it was modest. Some data on wheat sales to Mexico City millers during the second half of the eighteenth century or into the early nineteenth century also yield relatively low yearly rates, in the range of 0.5 percent. As noted earlier, while the rate of increase in wheat prices was relatively flat across the whole century, wheat prices probably rose at a rate in excess of 1 percent annually, and perhaps as much as 1.2–1.3 percent during part of the third and fourth quarters of the century. This is a figure that is slightly above the rate for wheat during the same period in the Upper Bajío and slightly below the rate for maize during the same period in Mexico City.

Wheat was classified as good and inferior and by harvest year and calendar year. Good wheat was preferable to inferior wheat and, not surprisingly, carried a higher price that rose faster over time. Naturally flour deliveries and prices, including a surge in prices during the late third and early fourth quarters, moved in step with wheat during the eighteenth century.[64] Deliveries peaked in 1772 at 127,000 cargas after which they slid to 95,000 cargas in 1780, and then leveled off with considerable irregularity. Prices followed an opposite course: they fell in the first half of the 1770s when supplies were large, they rose in the second half through 1780 as supplies became less plentiful, and they dropped again as supplies rose before stabilizing at a somewhat higher plateau than in the early 1770s. Prices were higher in the 1780s, not because flour supplies had fallen to such low levels but rather because the shortage of maize had boosted the demand for flour. Had a great imbalance between the supply of wheat and the demand for flour appeared, surely flour prices would have risen much faster than they did.[65]

Shortages did occur periodically, in large part because of drought or disease, and one of the worst to affect Mexico City was during the early 1770s. What concerned public officials was not the weather-related shortage, which they could do little about, but the attempt by farmers, brokers, millers, and bakers to exploit the crisis to their economic advantage. When wheat supplies were scarce, as when maize supplies were scarce, an opportunity opened for producers and processors to make more money in a business that generally operated with an oversupply of grain on one end and price regulation on the other end.

José de Gálvez, who had been serving as the Crown's special envoy on financial affairs since 1765, presented a report (12 November 1770) on the crisis.[66] Gálvez's recommendations, which were ultimately rejected, included organizing a guild of bakers, reducing the number of bakeries, building a pósito with funds from taxes on bakeries, and curtailing the constant and expensive litigation involving bakeries.[67] Building a pósito to deal in wheat or flour or curtailing litigation probably had little chance of immediate implementation. Organizing a guild of bakers and reducing the number of bakeries could have been accomplished more quickly except that important groups and individuals—consulado, archbishop, ayuntamiento—spoke out in opposition to the Gálvez plan. Twice in 1773 the monarch prohibited enactment of Gálvez's plan. Gálvez's plan was born in a time of scarcity (1770), and when the scarcity returned in 1780 the plan was revived, although again it was not enacted. Gálvez's response to the flour shortages in 1770 and 1771 fit the pattern, established during his official visit to Mexico, of preserving but streamlining the state's role in controlling the sale of bread. Under his plan the number of bakeries would be reduced from seventy to thirty-six and then to thirty. In his opinion a smaller pool of bakeries would not only be easier to regulate but would also be stronger financially inasmuch as each bakery could command a larger share of the local market. It was precisely the latter point that worried some opponents: the plan when combined with the establishment of the guild simply made the bread business more concentrated than before.

The flour mill was a crucial link in the chain from the producer to the baker. In addition to its milling operations, it was also the place where producers, millers, and bakers negotiated their sales and where wheat and flour were stored until sold or needed. What the miller could charge for processing the flour was fixed at 12 reales per carga, which was added to the price of the wheat now converted to flour. Wheat prices were not fixed. They changed in response to varying market factors—supply, demand, quality, and transportation. Wheat sold in April 1770 to Mexico City bakers from supplies held by local mills for various producers differed by as much as 50 percent per carga. For example, Vicente Arrieta from Tepetitlan, twenty-five miles northeast of the capital, was paid 396 pesos for 36 cargas, or 88 reales per carga, whereas Francisco Xavier Martínez from Texcoco, fifteen miles from Mexico City, with 396 cargas was paid 3,069 pesos, or 62 reales per carga.[68]

Official inquiries were undertaken when shortages occurred because the supply of flour was important to the city and the mill was central to how the system worked. In the aftermath of shortages in 1770 and 1780 officials required mills to install better accounting procedures that would allow the government to make an accurate and rapid assessment of the current state of the flour supply. But accounting rules alone could not temper shortages. Unfavorable weather conditions could create almost instant shortages not only because of reduced harvests but also because of inadequate storage facilities.

An inquiry in the fall of 1770, after a mediocre harvest in 1769 and a less than promising harvest in 1770, found that nine mills had only 12,000 cargas of wheat on hand for an urban market that could easily consume that amount in two months. What the inquiry turned up was that producers, some of whom were also bakers, perhaps in cooperation with the millers, had not released as much wheat as they could in hopes that the shortage would boost prices. Belem held the largest quantity of 3,000 cargas, followed by Santa Mónica, Santo Domingo, El Conde, and Blanco with amounts in the range from 2,700 down to 1,100 cargas. Some producers had anticipated that prices for all grades would rise. At Valdes with 674 cargas (30 of which had not been bought by bakeries) the administrator reported that Agustín Peña had bought 140 cargas of bad wheat at about one-half the normal price because even when spoiled it commanded a high price during shortages. At Del Rey with 483 cargas, 248.5 cargas were still held in the name of labradores while the remainder was assigned to bakers. Labradores had left instructions to sell their wheat at the high end (112–20 reales per carga) of the price schedule, in apparent violation of the law. Similarly at Prieto, more wheat was unsold than sold, although the differential between what the labrador wanted and what the baker was willing to pay was narrower. And at Santa Mónica with 2,677 cargas only 354 cargas had been sold to bakers at prices in the range of 80–120 reales per carga. Finally, at Río Hondo there was some confusion as to how to proceed with the sale of 200 of the 400 cargas on hand because the labradores to whom the wheat belonged had not left instructions about the prices that they would accept, although producers of another 60 cargas were asking for 120 reales per carga.[69]

The shortage of 1780 was probably less severe than that of 1770. The official inquiry listed forty-six bakers who claimed 16,503 cargas of wheat at the mills. More than that may have been stored at the mills by growers or millers; the amount owned by the bakers at the time of the shortage was twice as much as they had on hand in the fall of 1770. Still, if the shortfall persisted into the fall of 1780, the supply of wheat held at the mills could soon be exhausted. Averaged among the forty-six listed bakers the amount of wheat per baker was 358.7 cargas. Since fewer than three dozen claimed to own wheat, the amount averaged out to 515.7 cargas each.

According to Virginia García Acosta, José de Lara, an active baker from

1770 to 1811, owned two bakeries, administered a hacienda molino (Socorro), and served as an officer in the local bakery guild several times. Lara owned the most wheat—1,761 cargas or 10.7 percent of the total, followed by three bakers who owned 1,574 cargas (9.5 percent), 1,570 cargas (9.5 percent), and 1,408 cargas (8.5 percent), respectively.[70] These four, one-eighth of the bakers, held 38 percent of the supply. Bakers held wheat at more than one mill. The bulk (1,348 cargas) of Lara's wheat was stored at Santa Mónica, with smaller amounts stored at Del Moral (241 cargas), Fomacoco(?) (100), and Del Rey (40). At Socorro, where he was listed as the administrator, he stored only 32 cargas. In addition to wheat, however, the inquiry uncovered that bakers had claims on 608 bags of flour ready to be shipped to the bakeries. That averaged out to 13.2 sacks per baker. Again Lara also had the highest number of bags with 32 (5.3 percent), but the distribution of bags of flour (ready to be shipped) was more broadly held among the bakers than cargas of flour. Fourteen who owned bags of flour did not claim to own any cargas of wheat, although some could only claim a couple of bags of flour.

Since the public inquiries were undertaken in years of scarcity and not years of abundance, they may distort the actual long-term picture. There can be no doubt that weather and disease combined with an inefficient distribution system could result in periodic shortages. When we analyze flour delivery and price trends for Mexico City in the second half of the eighteenth century, we do not find much evidence for a persistent underlying shortage. We agree with García Acosta that the bakery business in the capital underwent a restructuring that favored the large bakers as well as the large grocers, who were becoming more involved in the bread trade. This showed up in the public inquiries (as Gálvez had anticipated) because more than a dozen bakeries, many of them small, had closed their doors between 1770 and 1780, unable to compete with the largest bakeries.[71]

Wheat growers, including the large commercial haciendas, faced the same problems as the maize growers: wheat price trends, except in the short run, did not justify continuing investment in wheat farming. Demand for wheat or flour surely rose during the century but not with such force or persistence as to boost the price of wheat much. It was still possible, of course, that converting from another crop or activity to wheat was a sound financial choice from the producer's view within the existing economic climate, although such conversions did not have an unlimited future. Unless producers made a technological breakthrough, found new markets, created new products, or confronted a demographic explosion, returns on investments in wheat would eventually grow less attractive. In other parts of the colony, where large-scale wheat production was just beginning to develop, the inelastic character of the supply curve for most other staples may not yet have taken hold. In the more developed agricultural regions, however, periodic weather-induced crises offered to producers an opportunity to enhance their returns if they had the foresight or capital to prepare for just such eventualities.

As the shortages grew more widespread in 1770, the official inquiry tried to determine not only how much wheat or flour was in reserve, but in December 1770 and January 1771 also how much had been harvested and shipped and how much was to be planted next season. Unfortunately, not all of the officials maintained their records as the ordinances specified, but enough did to give us more than a glimpse of what they had found out about wheat farming around Mexico City. They could not have been encouraged. In the major wheat areas of Chalco, Texcoco, Cuauhtitlan, and Toluca (and some adjacent areas), according to the officials' compilations, after the 1770 fall harvest only 25,000 to 30,000 cargas were available to be shipped (or in a few cases had been shipped) to the mills in January 1771. This represented only one-fifth of what was needed in the next nine months. Although the officials had been instructed to examine closely the books of the labradores, small farmers whose output was less easily monitored, they did not figure prominently in that year's harvest. In Cuauhtitlan, twenty to thirty miles northwest of Mexico City, the labradores, for example, controlled no more than 650 cargas of wheat ready to be shipped. At a minimum, the number of places visited in search of wheat was sixty haciendas, twelve ranchos, and three *pueblos* (native towns). Surely, the number of visits was higher than that because the figures presented by the officials did not list individual units for Chalco and several other minor jurisdictions. Of this total the ranchos and pueblos accounted for only a few hundred cargas. Not surprisingly, most of the wheat was stored at haciendas. In part, the aim of the inquiry was to speed up wheat deliveries not only to moderate the growing scarcity but also to neutralize the power of the producers (mainly the large commercial ones) to use the scarcity to negotiate ever higher prices. The best that the officials could do, however, was to order producers to ship their supplies immediately; they could not create more wheat, nor could they be certain, unless they actually accompanied the wagons, that the wheat was ever shipped. Joseph Parada, owner of the Hacienda del Santa María Pilar near Toluca, was ordered to deliver 400 cargas, 80 to Belem and 320 to Prieto. At the Hacienda de San Nicolás del Monte in the nearby town of Ixtahuacan (just a few miles southeast of Mexico City), the owner, Joseph Hurtado, was asked to explain why his wheat was not being shipped to the mills that served the capital. Many of those interviewed agreed to make their deliveries "promptly," although what assurances they gave or the officials demanded were not revealed. The visiting officials were not completely powerless. The labradores of Cuauhtitlan, for example, were given fifteen days to make their deliveries and, in addition, were fined (apparently to be paid in wheat) 200 pesos for having not already done so. Not all the wheat found could be claimed for the capital. Some wheat was of such inferior quality that it could not be used, and some had to be held back for next year's planting. In the case of the Texcocan visit the officials asked for the amount of the wheat harvested as well as the amount planted. The documentation is not clear that the wheat just harvested was the source of seeds for the wheat to be planted for the next harvest, although that normally was the practice. If that were the case, then for each carga planted only 3–5 cargas were harvested. That was considerably less than what some scholars have reported for other regions.[72] In any event, some wheat, perhaps as much as one-quarter or as little as one-eighth, had to be held back for seed.[73]

Mexico City also had to compete for wheat with nearby towns. In the region of Toluca, which reported 11,712 cargas and was by far the largest of any of the jurisdictions, a total of 1,700 cargas or about 15 percent was needed for the Tolucan region (1,300 cargas) and for the mines at Temazcaltepec and Sultepec (400 cargas), some miles southeast of the town of Toluca.[74] Manuel Cisneros, who owned the Hacienda de la Huerta near Metepec just south of Toluca, reported that of the 600 cargas he had, a small part (perhaps no more than 12 cargas) had been sold to a baker in Toluca and the rest to Juan Huerta, one of capital's largest bakers. The officials ordered Cisneros to ship his supply to the mill immediately without specifying, unfortunately, whether that included the quantity sold in Toluca or whether both prior sales had been voided. In other entries, though, wheat farmers were ordered to ship wheat promised bakers in nearby towns directly to the capital.[75]

Another part of the harvest on many farms had been set aside for the tithe, and in recognizing that this was protected from confiscation or assignment the officials would order that it be deducted from the total amount. The quantity was not necessarily large, though. Of the wheat stored in the Chalco mills, only a fraction (30 cargas) of the 4,800 cargas was exempt because of the tithe. The bulk of the wheat stored in the Chalco bakeries had already been sold to various nearby bakeries and could only be claimed for Mexico City by confiscation, a risky remedy.[76]

While orders or penalties could be imposed against wheat producers and flour millers, the most direct controls were imposed at the bakeries. Regulations issued in 1724 and again in 1754 elaborately specified size and price of each loaf based on availability and price of flour. Bread price schedules were common in Western European cities, although in the eighteenth century they were being abandoned or modified. A case could certainly be made for establishing government codes to prevent the use of contaminated ingredients in or the misrepresentation of the contents or weights of the loaves. The rationale for the establishment of bread price schedules was clear—to protect bread consumers, many of whom were poor, from price gouging. On paper such controls over quality or price must have appeared to be enlightened, but in reality they were so difficult to enforce in any systematic way that the quality of bread may have declined and the consumer price of bread, based in part on quality, may have risen.

Although flour prices did not change much over time, they could change from year to year, and in those fluctuations producers might find ways (some illegal, no doubt) to generate more profits. Between 1748 and 1810, while the average flour price was 72 reales per carga, year-to-year prices moved from a low of 50 to a high of 100 reales per carga. Such fluctuations, as pointed out earlier, posed certain risks, but they also entailed certain opportunities. By contrast bakery profits were virtually fixed regardless of weather or market conditions, and in response bakery owners sought to enhance their profits by tampering with the size or content of a loaf of bread.

The regulations granted the baker a profit of 14 reales on each carga of flour regardless of the demand, supply, or any other factor (table 3-4). A carga of flour ideally weighed 262.5 pounds or 4,200 ounces. If a carga sold for 40 reales, an abnormally low price, then the bakery was expected to make 140 loaves of 30 ounces each; however, if it sold for 248 reales, far higher than any recorded price to date, then the bakery was allowed to make 600 loaves of 7 ounces each. The theory behind this was that because of a shortage of flour more loaves had to be made from each carga. A person would have to eat 4.2 times as many loaves at the high price as at the low price to get the same value, an improbability, we can assume, because the shortage of wheat had driven up the price. At either extreme, a loaf of bread was supposed to sell at one-half of a real (*medio real*) or 6 *granos*, although according to the published computations it would have to sell for slightly more than 6 granos (about 6.3 granos). Although the average flour price of 72 reales (1748–1810) was not listed, it fell between 64 and 76 reales per carga and was closer to the latter than the former. At 76 reales the bakeries were expected to make 221 loaves of 19 ounces each from each carga with one ounce unused; but at 64 reales they were expected to produce 195 loaves of 21.2 ounces each with 66 ounces unused, enough for 3.5 more loaves.

At several prices the baker could make more loaves than the schedule stipulated and could make (theoretically) one-third of a real more in profit. At 115 reales the baker could make 7.2 loaves more for an even higher profit, although the price of flour seldom reached that level. In addition, the baker could squeeze out a fraction of a real of profit per carga simply because of the way in which the numbers were computed and then summed. For example, at a price of 52 reales per carga the computations worked out in such a way that the baker could realize a profit of one-half of a real per carga. At 61 reales, however, they would confront a loss of one-third of a real per carga. In fact, though, the baker was not unilaterally free to alter the weight of a loaf of

Table 3-4. Bread Price Schedule, Mexico City Bakeries, 1724, 1754 (in reales)

[1]	[2]	[3]	[4]	[5]	[6]	[7]	[8]
40	30	140	74.75	12	8.75	14	0.25
52	25	168	94.00	12	10.50	14	0.50
61	22	186	98.58	12	11.50	14	(0.25)
64	21	195	104.17	12	12.17	14	0.00
76	19	221	115.50	12	13.50	14	0.00
84	17	240	125.00	12	15.00	14	0.00
94	16	262	135.33	12	16.33	14	0.67
101	15	280	144.50	12	17.50	14	0.75
115	13	311	160.50	12	19.50	14	0.00
132	12	350	178.00	17	11.00	20	0.00
248	7	600	303.75	17	18.75	20	1.25

Source: AGI, México, leg. 2779.
1, Flour per carga; 2, ounces per loaf; 3, loaves per carga; 4, actual cost; 5, milling cost;
6, retail guarantee; 7, bakery profit; 8, gain (loss)
Note: The entire table has not been reproduced. By adding columns 1, 5, 6, and 7 and
by subtracting that number from column 4, we can estimate the bakery's expenses.
A gain (or loss) was computed by subtracting the actual costs from the estimated
costs, which were shown on the original table but not reproduced here.

bread on the basis of the price that he paid for his flour. As frequently as
every three months and at least once a year, the city government issued a
postura, the weight in ounces of a loaf of bread based on its calculation of
current flour prices. Whatever changes occurred in the price of wheat or
flour that the baker paid in the intervening period could not be incorporated
into his own financial calculations until the next postura.[77] Since the baker
was legally limited in terms of price and profit levels, he might well be
disposed, despite the risk of inspections and inquiries, to alter the size or the
content of bread if that could enhance his economic prospects.

Bakers were only entitled to 14 reales in profit regardless of the cost per
carga or the number of loaves produced per carga. With reference to table
3-4, column 7 showed 14 reales profit whether the baker made 140 loaves
from a carga of flour, 221, or 311. At 140 the profit per loaf was 1.2 granos or
one-eighth of a real, at 221 it was three-quarters of a grano or one-fifteenth of
a real, and at 311 it was one-twenty-fifth of a real. As noted, there were other
ways, some notably dishonest, to raise bakery profits. But the bakers, to the
extent that they conformed to this chart, had no incentive to become more
efficient—to earn more by producing more. In short, it would be more
profitable to handle fewer loaves.

Column 6 on the bread price schedule (table 3-4) refers to a guarantee for
the store where the bread was sold based on the number of loaves. At 240
loaves, for example, it was 15 reales, an amount that exceeded the baker's

profits and continued to rise until it reached 19.5 reales. Presumably, this was to compensate for the actual cost of retailing the bread. Since this was built into the bread price structure and bakers also acted as retailers, then we may reasonably assume that if the baker retailed the bread, he was entitled to that amount. The problem was that bakers could seldom sell all their bread without the grocers because the abundance of wheat made for stiff competition in bread retailing. The baker's need to sell his bread, even though the urban population was rising, gave the *pulpero* (grocer) considerably more clout than the baker in negotiating the purchase of bakery goods. Other consequences were that marginal bakers quit business or went bankrupt and that well- financed bakeries, usually in collusion with large grocers, tried to consolidate their control over the bread market.

A process of consolidation did in fact occur in the last quarter of the eighteenth century. More than seventy bakeries were listed in 1770 but only half that number by 1780.[78] By 1793 the number had risen to fifty-eight.[79] At the mill level, to process on average 100,000 cargas per year would require each operation to produce 38 pounds of flour per day. On the other hand, at the bakery level, if we assume a 16-ounce loaf and 262 loaves per carga, we can see that the bakeries could (or should) produce 26.2 million loaves. An average of fifty bakeries would have to produce more than 0.5 million loaves per year or nearly 1,500 loaves per day. For this effort, according to bakery regulations, the average baker could expect a daily profit of slightly more than 75 reales per 3,500 pesos (28,000 reales) per year. If he retailed his own bread, he might earn higher profits; if he sold his bread to a retailer, he most assuredly could expect lower profits.

Kicza's investigations of Mexico City bakeries reveal that except for a few owned but leased by convents (which we can confirm), owners were Spaniards of modest or moderate wealth with few or no other financial interests outside the bakeries themselves. Merchants did not show much inclination to buy or even to invest in bakeries in contrast to their growing financial interest in the mills. By the end of the century a bakery could cost 10,000–20,000 pesos, which, if borrowed, had to be paid back out of the annual profits.[80]

Adherence to the bakery regulations must have been as much of an exception as the rule. Over and above the issues of distortion, fraud, and manipulation, the wheat/flour/bread market did not encourage much innovation or diversification. It remained fundamentally a one-dimensional market of providing a much-needed product through a well-established process at a heavily regulated price. Super's observation that Central Mexico could supply Mexico City's daily bread was by and large accurate. It is true that by the end of the eighteenth century, in response to greater demand and lower supply, wheat and flour prices had reached a permanent level somewhat higher than normal and this may have furthered the impoverishment of the capital's urban dweller. If such impoverishment was growing, it was the result not so much of a overutilized agricultural sector as of an ill-conceived economic policy.

As we follow the path from where the goods were produced to where they were consumed, we find an increasingly complex picture. Eighteenth-century Mexicans may have had access, as some have contended, to varieties of foodstuffs, although access for the average inhabitant must have grown less certain over time. It appears that weather was the principal instrument that determined whether the agricultural sector yielded a surplus or a shortage. It is possible that by the end of the century some large urban centers faced shortages because of climatic conditions as well as structural deficiencies, although shortages did not affect all urban areas equally. It is not immediately evident that despite growth in cities the increase was of such a magnitude that it forced changes on the rural economies or the urban markets. Wheat farming may have replaced maize farming in certain agricultural regions, and although some wheat producers could have made money from time to time (specifically in the two decades before the agricultural crises), they eventually had to come to terms with the fact that the demand for wheat, like maize, was normally insensitive to price changes. Withholding or limiting supplies, practiced by some large producers, could be effective in times of scarcity and may account for higher price levels in the quarter century before the Hidalgo Revolt. But highly leveraged estates, in need of revenue, may have determined that renting acres rather than producing crops and paying workers in food rather than in cash was preferable to expanding their financial links with urban markets. If the agricultural sector carried as heavy a burden of debt as some research indicates, it may have reached that stage because expanding food production for subsistence-oriented markets without structural innovations proved to be less than profitable. The spreading impoverishment, most notably but not exclusively in the capital, derived less from overutilization than from misappropriation of resources. Policies governing urban markets, although conceived to protect the public, increasingly failed to achieve their goals. In addition to fraud and mismanagement, which may or may not have had an economic origin, these policies were not conceived or designed to operate very well in an economy that had surpluses as often as shortages. The paradox that many have observed and some have been misled by was that the impoverishment was occurring in a time of expanding silver production, the matter to which the next chapter is devoted.

4

Production Trends in Silver Mining

The economic forces at work in the mining sector were different from those in the agriculture sector. Silver was a valuable commodity in and of itself, and the search for new deposits or the repair of old mines had little to do with population changes or market opportunities. Silver producers, like other commodity producers, had to be sure that the cost of extracting and refining the ore did not exceed the value of the currency that was cut from the bullion. Since the price of silver was more or less fixed by the mint, the cost of producing silver was the owner's chief concern.

Unlike agriculture, where the creation of wealth was incremental, the creation of wealth from mining could be explosive and instantaneous. The discovery of a rich vein in a mining camp meant more employment and business, and the impact of that growth could be registered in farming and fabricating villages many miles from the camp itself. When mines closed down, the camp and the areas linked to it underwent an economic contraction. By the eighteenth century several major camps had evolved into large provincial cities with commercial and administrative functions that complemented their mining activities. Still, the focus of the economy of a silver city or a silver camp was the extracting and processing of the ore.

Very little of the wealth that silver mining generated was ever invested in new productive enterprises. What was not spent for wages and supplies was usually exported. Extractive industries like mining fulfilled the basic mercantilistic objective of providing a resource that could advance primarily the financial and economic well-being of the mother country. A mining boom almost always caused a business upturn, but it seldom served as an instrument of structural change and intensive economic growth.

That Mexico's silver industry operated continuously from the middle of

the sixteenth century to the end of the colonial period (1821) made it a crucial
force in the colonial economy. It is important to point out that during these
two and one-half centuries the industry suffered no major depressions,
although some individual camps did. Colonial mining was certainly not
always profitable, and yet despite that the long-term silver production trend
followed an upward path. The industry suffered setbacks and experienced
periods in which for financial, technological, or other reasons output stagnated or declined. For the most part, though, the setbacks proved to be
manageable in that after time for adjustment the growth resumed. Even as
mining consumed capital, it also generated income in both the private and
public sectors. To preserve and expand mining was in the interest not only of
the state but also of the economy.

Colonywide Silver Trends

Because mining data exist for both colonial Mexico and Peru we can undertake some comparative analysis that is not yet possible with respect to the
agricultural sector. During the two and one-half centuries that the colonial
silver industry was active, it produced about 100,000 tons of silver worth
about 2.9 billion pesos. About 60 percent of the silver was registered in
Mexico and 40 percent in the Andean region. Although Peru had the richest
mining camp in the legendary Potosí, Mexico had higher ore grades that
allowed several of its major camps to expand their output over the long term.
The production of silver in Peru and Mexico rose at an annual rate of 0.5
percent from 1559 to 1810. That represents relatively slow growth, for nearly
130 years passed before production doubled. When the data for Mexico and
Peru are separated, we see more clearly why the total colonial figure rose so
slowly. Mexico's output grew by 1.0 percent per year for two and one-half
centuries while Peru's was flat. Peru's curve climbed sharply in the first half
century (1559–1610) at nearly 3.0 percent per year; the curve then turned
downward for the next century (1611–1714) at a rate of 1.3 percent per year;
finally, after bottoming out the curve resumed its growth for the last century
of the colonial period at a rate of 1.7 percent per year. By contrast Mexico's
curve had no prolonged contraction, although it had periods of declining
production. During the initial boom (1559–1627) production in Mexico grew
by 2.5 percent per year; during the next phase (1628–1724) the growth in
output slowed to 1.2 percent per year but did not turn downward; in the final
period (1725–1810) production continued at 1.2 percent per year.[1]

For eighteenth-century Mexico we can calculate growth rates from two
different silver series: tax receipts and mint registrations.[2] From 1700 to 1806
(when the tax receipt series ends) tax receipts show that output rose by 1.0
percent per year, while for the same period mint registrations increased by
1.3 percent per year. When the mint registration series is extended to 1810

or 1821 the rates change very little. Thus with rates between 1.0 and 1.4 percent per year silver output doubled every fifty to seventy years, and that was comparable to the growth in Mexican agricultural tithes during the eighteenth century. As such the rise in output of silver in the eighteenth century represented the third century of almost continuous growth.

To treat the seventeenth century as a period of growth in mining, albeit modest growth, is to revise further the "century of depression" interpretation. In light of the fact that the second phase of the Mexican silver curve (1628–1725) culminated at the end of the first quarter of the eighteenth century, a brief discussion of the depression thesis is relevant. In the last decade J. I. Israel has revived interest in the depression thesis, first put forward by Woodrow Borah, by broadening the conceptual framework.[3] Employing the "general crisis" model of European historians to describe the seventeenth century, he argues that if Europe were in the midst of a crisis, then that crisis affected and was affected by the New World. Specifically, in the economic arena, Spain's mounting debt, only one sign of its impotence and drift, caused Spain to try to exploit its colonies' wealth even more. In other words, the more the colonies produced, the more the Crown wanted. In Mexico, according to Israel, this led to strained relations between the government and those economic and social groups which it counted among its ardent supporters. Without actually analyzing economic data Israel contends that Mexico's mid-seventeenth-century economy had entered a state of decline that was made worse as the Crown redoubled its efforts to raise tax receipts. The longer and deeper the depression, the greater the desire of the business community to criticize and resist royal policy.[4]

There is no doubt that the Crown was hard pressed for revenue to keep the monarchy solvent, although a bankrupt royal treasury cannot be automatically attributed to a stagnant colonial economy. Important linkages between the economies of Europe and the New World clearly operated during the seventeenth century. A consensus on the mechanism by which they worked has yet to emerge. It is difficult to demonstrate empirically that a European economic crisis provoked a similar crisis in Mexico and vice versa. If one discounted Europe's "general crisis" to focus on the potential for or the existence of a "home-bred" crisis within the Mexican colonial economy, one would find, on the basis of the mining statistics at least, that the economy was remarkably vibrant.[5] While Mexico's general economy and its silver economy in particular grew sluggish at times, neither had became mired in stagnation or depression.

By the middle of the seventeenth century the silver economy, having come to the end of the boom that had begun in the sixteenth century, was clearly in need of repair and revitalization. Zacatecas, for example, now nearly a century old, continued to lure miners and investors who could attain success only if they were willing to recapitalize and reorganize local mining operations. Although this made mining costlier and riskier in Zacatecas and other camps, the cost and risk was not so onerous as to stop the growth in output.[6]

Examining the colonial silver curve in terms of its major peaks is one way in which to unravel its internal dynamics. In the period 1580–1809 major peaks occurred in 1627 and 1724, and each is followed by a downturn of five to ten years in duration.[7] In the initial period the rate was high because in the sixteenth century the veins were easily accessible and of good quality. As those veins began to disappear, miners began to exploit deeper veins of medium- and low-grade ores. The invention of the amalgamation process for refining the ore in the late sixteenth century made it possible to build deeper shafts and longer tunnels to reach these ores and to process them economically. Many miners lacked the capital or the expertise necessary for these undertakings, and either they abandoned mining or declared bankruptcy. But their places were filled by new groups of miners and their backers, many of whom were wealthy merchants.

By the middle of the seventeenth century, difficult problems—poor ventilation, underground flooding, cave-ins, and mercury (for refining) and labor shortages—had to be overcome if old mines were to remain productive and if new mines were to be opened. These problems were solved to the extent that the growth in output continued, although with some interruptions and lapses, into the next century. The growth was volatile and irregular during the second half of the seventeenth century but strong enough for Mexico to surpass Peru as the major producer after 1690. From the late seventeenth century through the early eighteenth century silver output climbed steadily as new mines were being discovered and old mines rehabilitated.

The importance of the seventeenth century to an analysis of the eighteenth century is that the changes undertaken to solve the industry's problems could have actually strengthened the mining sector. The eighteenth-century boom no longer appears in such sharp contrast to the seventeenth century because the latter was not as depressed or stagnant as earlier studies suggested. Moreover, despite the peaks and dips that punctuate the colonial curve, the industry had the capacity not only to overcome its problems but also to attain new highs.

The output of silver grew from an average of several hundred thousand marks in the first decade of the eighteenth century to several million marks in the first decade of the nineteenth century, a six- to sevenfold increase.[8] Between 1700 and the end of the colonial period (1821) Mexico produced about 180 million marks (45,000 tons), for an average of 1.5 million per year. The rate of growth from 1700 to 1821 or to 1810 (to avoid the war) is about the same, 1.4 percent annually. Thus output doubled just under every half century. But the magnitude of the undertaking is better appreciated when it is known that a total of 25–40 million tons of ore had to be extracted and processed between 1700 and 1821 to attain that growth.[9] Around 1720 silver registrations broke through the 1-million-mark barrier for the first time, and they seldom dropped below that level in the next fifty years before they reached 2 million marks. The rate of growth was comparable before and after 1750. In the first half of the eighteenth century output rose fairly steadily but it rose sharply during the late third and early fourth quarters, after which it leveled off somewhat.

Despite a moderately strong upward curve in the eighteenth century, the silver industry was at times hobbled. Downturns could be traced to the shortages of food and labor that famines and epidemics caused as well as to the scarcity of mercury needed to refine the ore. In 1736–37, 1759–60, and 1784–85 natural disasters were bad enough to derail the growth temporarily, and in 1799–1801 mercury shortages had a similar impact. Many of the year-to-year fluctuations, if the documentation existed, could probably be traced to such disruptions. Even though the industry was healthy enough to recover fairly quickly from short-term maladies, it had underlying weakness: increasing costs required larger investments with greater risks. Ventures to recover mines proved to be costly failures, although there were a few spectacular successes. An enduring characteristic of the colonial mining industry was the resiliency of several important camps repeatedly to overcome their problems. By the late decades of the eighteenth century the industry too may have reached a plateau in that capital formation was too small to cover the investment needed to maintain expansion. Halfway through its third century of operation with little changed in technology, the industry may have exhausted the potential for further growth. The industry could not avoid the inevitable fact that without a better technology costs would eventually outstrip revenues.

Silver Production in Mining Districts

As the silver-mining industry expanded, the Crown set up branches (*reales cajas*) of the treasury to supervise such activities as tax collections and mercury sales. The areas served by these cajas became in effect informal mining districts, although mine owners could do business with cajas outside their own areas. Since silver tax data exist for each caja, they can be used to construct production curves and calculate growth rates for the mining districts.

By the end of the eighteenth century Guanajuato had emerged as the colony's premier camp. Humboldt ranked the districts served by the cajas according to data that he collected and published for 1785–89.[10] His list was as follows: Guanajuato, San Luis Potosí, Zacatecas, Mexico City, Durango, Rosario, Pachuca, Guadalajara, Bolaños, Sombrerete, and Zimapán. Several cajas—Zimapán, Bolaños, and Rosario—were established in the eighteenth century, but most of them had been in operation since the sixteenth or seventeenth century. Chihuahua, also founded in the eighteenth century, does not appear on Humboldt's list.

By using eighteenth-century silver tax receipts we have constructed a different ranking of cajas and the districts that they served. Table 4-1 shows the caja, the total value (in pesos) of the registered silver, the caja's percentage share of colony's total silver, and the annual growth rate.[11] The century-long rankings are as follows: Guanajuato, Mexico City, Zacatecas, Durango, San Luis Potosí, Guadalajara, Pachuca, Sombrerete, Bolaños, Rosario, Zimapán, and Chihuahua.[12]

Guanajuato had only attained its first-place ranking in the early part of the eighteenth century. For the previous two centuries Zacatecas had been the top-ranking camp. Around 1700 silver production averaged about 110,000 marks at Guanajuato, while it averaged about 150,000 marks at Zacatecas. By

Table 4-1. Total Value of Registered Silver By Reales Cajas in Mining Camps, 1701–1810 (totals in millions of pesos)

Real caja or Camp	Total value	Share percent	Rate per year	R^2	Student t
Guanajuato	322.5	22.5	1.8	0.93	8.54
Mexico City	245.2	17.1	0.8	0.65	0.32
Zacatecas	208.6	14.5	0.3	0.58	0.77
Durango	170.5	11.9	0.7	0.19	3.77
San Luis Potosí	127.4	8.9	2.8	0.92	9.25
Guadalajara	91.3	6.4	0.5	0.54	2.82
Pachuca	86.3	6.0	0.1	0.64	0.28
Sombrerete	58.9	4.1	2.4	0.84	6.65
Bolaños	44.9	3.1	di		
Rosario	43.2	3.1	di		
Zimapán	32.7	2.3	di		
Chihuahua	9.9	0.7	di		
Total for Mexico	1,436.0	100.6	1.0	0.87	6.65

Source: TePaske, "Economic Cycles in New Spain," Biblioteca Americana.
Note: All series were corrected for autocorrelation. Student t's for Mexico City, Zacatecas, and Pachuca become extremely weak when the series is corrected for autocorrelation. Abbreviation "di" means data insufficient for calculating any trends. Colonywide Mexico total is based on tax receipts rather than on mint registrations in order to be consistent with the camp data. Growth rate for mint registrations is 1.4 per year.

the end of the century Guanajuato's annual output had grown to 0.5 million marks, and Zacatecas's had only climbed to 300,000 marks. From 1700 to 1810 output at Guanajuato rose by 1.8 percent each year, the second highest growth rate among the major camps. The rate of increase in output at Guanajuato was higher during the first half of the century than in the second half. Guanajuato's contribution in terms of silver taxes alone grew from 100,000 pesos per year to 0.5 million pesos. Even during the third quarter of the eighteenth century, when growth paused temporarily, silver tax revenues were still two to three times higher than they had been around 1700.

Guanajuato represented the ultimate triumph of entrepeneurial skill and drive to revitalize a local silver economy.[13] Valenciana, the colony's largest mine, illustrated how large-scale, vertically organized firms could overcome the costs and the risks that so often made mining unprofitable. The expansion in Guanajuato's silver economy meant that the general economy also grew. The more fundamental question is whether that growth also produced the conditions for a broadly based economic development. The gargantuan size of a silver enterprise like Valenciana cannot be interpreted as fundamental change, for it may simply reflect a move toward a more rational approach to how mining and refining had been traditionally carried out. But measuring and analyzing the economic change that may accompany such growth is difficult even in modern times. The local economy may well have come to depend even more heavily on mining because the growth in output of silver was so strong in the second half of the eighteenth century.

One way to try to assess the change is to examine shifts in occupations. According to the 1792 census the population of Guanajuato was more or less 50,000. Of the 11,000 adult males, by Brading's count, more than 55 percent worked in the mining industry. The remaining 45 percent had jobs in commerce, transport, crafts, agriculture, and government. It is not an occupational profile that was diverse in character or, more importantly, that was diversifying under the rapid growth in the mining industry. Even among those not specifically identified with mining and refining, their jobs were often related to the silver business: transport of ores, fabrication of tools, and sale of supplies. Brading remarks that clothes-making was "largely composed of tailors, hatters and cobblers . . . [and only] a handful of weavers and spinners." In occupational categories outside of commerce, mining, and government, all of which existed in connection with mining camps, about 12 percent of the adult males fit those categories. On the basis of a single census Guanajuato's occupational statistics remain fairly narrow and concentrated.[14]

By examining the census of the Intendancy of Guanajuato, an area of approximately 7,500 square miles and a population of 400,000, we find that agriculture, mining, commerce, government, and church account for 60 percent of the total (111,000) employed. Of the remainder, 16 percent were classified as day workers, usually temporary unskilled or semiskilled employees, and 24 percent were classified as *fabricantes* (weavers, for example) and *artesanos* (tailors, for example). The economy of the intendancy appears somewhat more diversified than of the city, although for both the intendancy and the city the dominance of mining and its related fields tends to limit economic diversification.[15] It was observed in the previously discussed elasticity test that Guanajuato's silver boom could have been an important stimulus in the nonmining economic sectors. Under ideal conditions that might have begun a economic transformation in the form of new ventures and markets around Guanajuato, but in reality it did not occur nor was it necessarily destined to occur. Mineral extraction had a way of simply concentrating more resources and efforts into production of more minerals that were often then exported.

Although no other camp enjoyed as much of a boom as Guanajuato, several had their own smaller versions. Apparently, very few of the camps linked to the Mexico City caja, which ranked second, were among them. How much growth these camps experienced is hard to determine because of the aforementioned confusion over silver registration data. An inventory from the early 1770s showed that of the approximately 400 registered mines in ten different camps 120 of them were reported to be in operation, 17 partially worked, and the remainder abandoned. In addition, more than 1,000 openings were listed in Zacualpa(n), a camp about sixty miles southwest of Mexico City and not far from Taxco. For a five-year period, 1769–73, these ten camps registered silver worth about 1.2 million pesos per year.[16] During the survey 218 mines were counted in Taxco but 171 were classified as abandoned because there was too little high-quality ore and too few investors willing to underwrite the necessary repairs and excavations.[17] Many of the scores of mines in operation were barely breaking even or were actually losing money. Some mines flourished for a year or two only to fall victim to flooding, ore exhaustion, or other problems. The depth of the mines had already reached several hundred yards and the quality of the ores, an important factor in deciding how much to invest, often petered out unexpectedly. The absence of merchant investors was an unmistakable signal that for them the area's mines had little potential to return a profit.[18]

Zacatecas, the colony's oldest major camp, represents another angle from which to measure the ebb and flow of the eighteenth-century silver industry. Zacatecas's silver curve in the eighteenth century was strikingly different from the curves for most of the other principal districts. After impressive growth in the century's first quarter, Zacatecas's production began to slide, slowly at first and then precipitously well into the third quarter. After an inventory in the 1770s public officials reported 82 mines in operation and 628 mines in various stages of abandonment and desertion.[19] In contrast to

Guanajuato, which turned in a strong performance in the first half of the eighteenth century and only slightly less in the second half, Zacatecas saw production both rise and fall in the first half of the century after which it followed mainly an upward path. In the first quarter of the eighteenth century Zacatecas achieved an annual growth rate of 3.4 percent by which output doubled in two decades. Between 1725 and 1810 production fell for half the period at about 2.1 percent per year, and then in a reversal it began to rise at 2.4 percent per year. When the curve reached its nadir around 1760, it had fallen to its lowest level (under 100,000 marks annually) since the turn of the century. As often happened in the mining economy, the circumstances that had caused the depression gave way to a resurgence of output between 1769 and 1780, when Zacatecas posted a gain in each year. In the 1780s the average annual production was about twice as high as it had been in the 1760s. Even though mercury shortages and natural disasters temporarily derailed the boom of the late third and early fourth quarters, the growth resumed in the quarter century before the Hidalgo Revolt (1810) at an annual rate that was about three times higher (3 percent versus 1 percent) in Zacatecas than in Guanajuato.[20]

Zacatecas's twin cycles contrast sharply with the almost continuous upward trend for the colony as a whole and for Guanajuato. In eighteenth-century Zacatecas it is not sustained growth that we must try to explain but how contractions developed and were remedied. Two points become immediately apparent. The first is that the way in which Zacatecas's industry was organized had to change to accommodate financial and technological challenges; and the second (although related to the first) is that a new, dominant group of outsiders usually engineered a resurgence after a downturn.

In 1774 Juan Lucas Lassaga and Joaquín Velásquez de León, a miner and lawyer, respectively, highlighted what they said were the industry's problems—too little capital, too much avarice, no education. These problems, they speculated, could be traced to the failure of sons to follow fathers in the family mining businesses.[21] Such turnover and influx could be unsettling in a society that valued order and continuity, and yet the devotion to order and continuity could be an impediment to the need for progress and change. Heirs, faced with mounting costs and dwindling resources, often served as obstacles to protect their properties rather than as fonts of knowledge that could contribute to growth and change in the local industry. In Zacatecas the turnover was so complete that none of the largest producers at the end of the eighteenth century had any links with the largest producers at the start of the century. No comparisons can be made because Zacatecas is the only camp whose owner roster has been systematically studied for the eighteenth century. In Guanajuato, for example, the long tenure of the Sardenata family at Rayas and the Obregón and Otero families at Valenciana stand out as possible exceptions to the Zacatecas pattern, although little is known about the many other Guanajuato miners whose eighteenth-century careers remain obscure. Even in Zacatecas one can find examples of family continuity over two generations (father and son). What is more impressive, though, is that with each quarter century an almost completely new group of miners, refiners, and *aviadores* (merchants who advanced credit to miners) had emerged at the top of and throughout the roster. Guanajuato and Zacatecas did share a common characteristic: that is, the rise in the number of Basque and other Spaniards who entered each camp during the eighteenth century.[22]

In 1800 despite the resurgence in mining, or perhaps because of it, Zacatecas had a narrower economic base than Guanajuato. In addition to mining Zacatecas had active commercial, governmental, and pastoral sectors. But mining predominated. Because the 1792 census has not been found, an occupational profile has not yet been constructed. A *donativo de guerra* (war contributions) conducted in 1780 and 1781 provides a glimpse of how mining dominated the camp's occupational classifications. Of 6,000 males in a population estimated at between 20,000 and 25,000, more than one-half were identified as owners and employees of mines and refineries and more than one-third were identified as government and ranch workers. Another 5 percent could be classified as employed in commerce and exchange. A few traditional professionals (doctors, notaries) and artisans (cobblers, tailors) were listed, although a city as large as Zacatecas must have had more skilled craftsmen than these figures suggest. Since the donations were solicited by street in the city but by place of employment outside the city, the donors may not always have been listed by their occupations. Nonetheless, the population of working adult males in late colonial Zacatecas was unmistakably tied to the economy's mineral sector.[23]

Further evidence of the heavy dependence on mining appears in a viceregal survey in the 1790s when it was reported that except for the silver refineries Zacatecas had no mills, not even a grist mill.[24] The magnetism of mining—that a lucky strike equals an immediate bonanza, especially when compared to other economic endeavors— remained a dominant force even in a camp as old and troubled as Zacatecas until the end of the colonial period.[25]

Other districts and camps could be analyzed for their own special characteristics within the context of the eighteenth-century silver industry. It can be useful, however, to broaden the scope by grouping the camps and their cajas into three zones. Zone 1 includes camps in the vicinity of the capital. Zone 2, the heart of the eighteenth-century mining industry, is an area bounded by the camps of Zacatecas, Bolañas, Guadalajara, Guanajuato, San Luis Potosí, and Charcas. The distance from north to south and east to west is about 200 miles each way. This zone embraced some of the richest mines—

Rayas, Valenciana, Quebradilla, and Puríssima—ever opened and registered 55–60 percent of all the silver taxed from 1700 to 1810.[26] The northernmost camps belonged to zone 3.

Although zone 2 registered the most silver, it had the slowest-rising growth curve at 1.2 percent per year. This can be attributed to some of the oldest and most troublesome mines being located there. After climbing steadily for most of the century zone 2's curve began to slow down and flatten out in the middle 1780s. During the quarter century before the independence movement the curve dipped sharply in the middle 1780s, due to agricultural crises; in the early 1790s for reasons unknown; in the late 1790s and early 1800s because of mercury shortages; and in the period 1805–10, for which we have incomplete data. During this quarter century the curve also reached a new high in 1804 because the colony began that year with a large supply of mercury that permitted the refining of ore stockpiled during the blockade.

Although the lack of data for two of the reales cajas after 1806 could affect the shape of the curve in the half decade before Hidalgo's Revolt, the data from the other reales cajas point to a flattening curve and perhaps a slight downward movement. Having several major camps made a depression at one camp, as happened at mid-eighteenth-century Zacatecas, less serious for the whole industry. Although zone 2 enjoyed important new discoveries after 1700 that added to its growth, it counted heavily on the expansion and repair of old mines for most of that growth. Despite zone 2's large share, the other zones played an important role in the eighteenth-century silver revival. Zone 3 produced about one-fifth of the total silver, and zone 1 probably produced between one-quarter and one-third of the total. Zones 1 and 3 grew at comparable rates of 1.5 to 1.6 percent per year, about one-third faster than zone 2. Although the curves for zones 1 and 3 are more erratic over the course of the century (in part because of the impact of the addition of new reales cajas), they also show a stronger upward slant toward the end of the century than zone 2's curve.[27]

Mining Costs and Profits

The key to success in eighteenth-century mining was managing the cost of extracting and processing ore. Producers had to take into account many different factors, some of which were beyond their direct control, as they tried to estimate or determine their costs. Precise cost figures rarely show up in archival documents because producers did not keep accounts that showed all capital and operational costs. Still, we can make some estimates about those costs from the sources that do exist. The most expensive phase by the eighteenth century, most would agree, was the extraction of the ore. Producers usually did not distinguish between capital investments to build the deep shafts and long tunnels and operational costs to remove the ore. In general, the cost of paying the workers, maintaining the mine, buying the supplies, pumping the water, and hauling the ore to the surface consumed between 40 and 50 percent of the value of the silver.

Producers could determine refining costs with greater precision and over time they had learned how to enhance their profits by making their refineries or methods more efficient. Refining costs ranged from 18 to 24 percent of the worth of the silver, although those costs tended to fall in the eighteenth century because the government twice reduced the price of mercury. Silver taxes accounted for at least 12 percent and mintage fees for another 6 percent of silver's total value. Finally, transportation and miscellaneous expenses add up to another 3 to 4 percent of the value of the silver. With total costs at 80 percent of that value the producer might realize gross profits of 20 percent, but with costs at 96 percent he would only earn 4 percent. We have more information about the big-time miners who made or lost large fortunes than we have about the small operators who may have just barely eked out a living in their mines.[28]

Over the long term a significant factor in mining-cost calculations was the grade of the ore. The invention of the amalgamation process in the sixteenth century made it possible to refine ores of low or moderate grades, and by the late colonial period 80–90 percent of all Mexican ore was refined this way.[29] The quality of ore in a given mine was usually only known once the ore was extracted and refined, although it was discussed and estimated as if it could be fully documented. More often than not ore yield predictions were based on the camp rumors that circulated about the past history of a particular mine, only a few of which turned out to be accurate. In 1743, for example, an extensive survey was made of Zacatecas's mines, many of which were closed or operating on a limited scale because of the high cost to drain and repair their shafts and tunnels.[30] At almost every mine the owner or administrator was asked to state what the yield might be if the mine could be recovered. Some of the figures reported to the officials are shown in table 4-2. All these reported yields were at least twice as great as the assumed colonial average of two to three ounces per hundredweight, and in two instances they were many times greater than that average.[31] The fact remained that what often attracted miners and investors was the potential of the mines. In the second half of the eighteenth century costly rehabilitations were undertaken at all the mines for which the high yields were reported, and in the case of Quebradilla three different projects were launched, even though none of the mines ever attained yields as high as the estimates.[32] Yields that high were not necessary to make a profit, however, and for several of the mines lower yields did produce a profit.

Yields from Zacatecas's Quebradilla mine can be studied in some detail

Table 4-2. Ore Yields of Selected Mines, Zacatecas, 1743

Mine	Ounces of silver per cwt ore
Vizcaíno	32
Urista	12
Esperanza	7–8
Bentillas	7–8
Quebradilla	6–8
Carmen	4–7
Palmilla	4–5

Source: AGI, Guadalajara, leg. 190.
Note: Palmilla had some veins, according to those interviewed, that yielded as much as 80 ounces per cwt.

from 1777 to 1779. The mine's owner, José de la Borda, won special concessions that required him to refine Quebradilla ore and ores from his other mines in separate batches. After his death the government launched an inquiry; it charged that Borda had mixed ores in violation of the agreement. We cannot be sure, then, that the ores are strictly from Quebradilla, although the administrator's report claimed that they were. The problem arose because Borda built a highly efficient refinery by the name of Sacrafamilia to process Quebradilla ore, but until it was ready he sent the ore to be processed at other refineries that he owned. Variations in grades of ores from a mine were common: San Miguel, for example, processed ore that yielded twice as much silver as ore from Puríssima Concepción. It is also possible that higher yields resulted because San Miguel was more efficient than Puríssima Concepción. The yield of silver from Quebradilla per 2,000 pounds of ore (a montón) could range from a low of 2.8 marks to a high of 31.5 marks.

How a mound of ore was arranged and treated could influence the yield, and some refiners were far more skilled than others, although few of them ever recorded their procedures and refinements. Borda hired Basque miners, some of whom were nephews and cousins, in part because they were thought to possess more knowledge about mining than other Spaniards or creoles. At San Miguel ore yields improved from 6.6 marks per mound in 1777 to 7.2 marks in 1778 to 10.8 marks in 1779. On the other hand, at Puríssima Concepción yields fell from 1778 into 1779. No explanation is given for this; it may be related to the relative efficiency of the two refineries or it may be a matter of coincidence. The amount of mercury needed to refine the ore varied insignificantly from one-half of a pound to seven-eighths of a pound per mark.

While we are left with many unanswered questions about variations in yields at two different refineries with ores from the same mine, we should note that the average yield of 2.6 ounces per hundredweight of ore (just slightly above the colonial average of 2.5 per hundredweight) was by eighteenth-century estimates enough to ensure a reasonable return on investment.[33] In spite of increasing mining costs during the eighteenth century 2–3 ounces of silver per hundredweight not only meant profits but more importantly maintained a flow of capital into mining for expansion. By contrast in Peru late colonial yields (especially at Potosí) were on average about half the Mexican yields, and although production rose in the eighteenth century throughout the Andean region, the industry never attracted the long-term investor in part because profit margins remained low.[34]

Another measure of performance and accountability was the ratio of silver registered to mercury purchased at the treasury or the *correspondencia*. The Crown had long kept records on the amount of mercury the treasury sold and the amount that silver miners reported so that mercury would not wasted or resold at a much higher price. By the eighteenth century the ratio had settled at about 100 pounds or 1 *quintal* of mercury for each 100 marks of silver. For individual camps or mines, though, it could vary considerably.

Around 1750 San Luis Potosí, one of the colony's ranking camps, had a ratio of 1 quintal of mercury to 80 marks of silver (along with other camps), whereas Guanajuato, the premier camp, reported a ratio of 1 to 125.[35] During the late third quarter and in the early fourth quarter of the eighteenth century Zacatecas, in the midst of a major revival, achieved ratios above the colonial norm. In 1770 and 1775 miners consumed 91,200 pounds (912 quintales) and 151,100 pounds (1,511 quintales) respectively, and they registered 96,240 marks and 191,707 marks respectively for a ratio of 1 quintal to 105 marks and 1 to 126, respectively. Except during the most troubled years of the second and third quarters Zacatecas exceeded the 1 to 100 standard. Indeed, around 1800 the Crown may have revised the colonial standard upward to 1 to 125 because camps like Zacatecas were reporting higher than usual ratios.

The variation among individual miners within the same camp could also be quite large. For the two years previously mentioned we know how much mercury each producer purchased and how much silver each registered in Zacatecas. In 1770 the three largest purchasers of mercury were Antonio Escalera, José Zeballos, and Manuel Rétegui, and their ratios were 1 quintal of mercury to 107 marks of silver, 1 to 155, and 1 to 148, respectively. In 1775, after output at Zacatecas had risen substantially, the three largest purchasers were Manuel Duque with a ratio of 1 to 88, José de la Borda with 1 to 127, and Marcelo de Anza with 1 to 154. All of the above except Duque had entered the local industry through the purchase of both mines and refineries. Duque, however, had begun as an aviador, who for a premium supplied miners and refiners with cash or merchandise, in particular mercury, and in the process acquired several mining properties. Because aviadores serviced small, marginal refineries, they often had ratios similar to or less than the colonywide standard.

Technically under the correspondencia, based on the standard ratio, one could not purchase any more mercury than the equivalent of the silver that was presented for taxation. That meant that the purchaser could only buy more mercury (say, to process the ore from a newly opened vein) if he was able to improve the efficiency of his refinery to realize more silver from the mercury he had just purchased. The rule was difficult to enforce, and by the eighteenth century the ability of the purchaser to pay for the mercury or to line up credit was the chief criterion that the treasury used, although it continued to keep the correspondencia records.[36] Not only did the real caja keep such records but it also sent annual reports showing who bought mercury, how much silver they had registered, and what they owed the Crown. The health of the industry was often described in terms of the ratio of mercury to silver.

Mexico's mercury-to-silver ratios were higher than Peru's in the eighteenth century. In general, Mexico had a higher grade of mercury and ore than Peru, and in addition Mexico paid less for its mercury than Peru. The evidence for Peru is somewhat less complete than for Mexico, but that which exists indicates that the standard ratio may have been less than but no more than 1 mercury quintal to 100 silver marks. With lower yields and higher costs Peruvians spent about one-third of the total value of the silver on refining, whereas the Mexicans spent about a quarter of that value. According to John Fisher, Peruvian refiners performed better in the period of the late 1780s and early 1790s than they did a decade or two later.[37] It was harder to make money in Peru than in Mexico, and that may help to explain why Peruvian merchants, who controlled a part of the colony's capital pool, were less willing to invest in mining than Mexican merchants.

Both the potential for huge profits and the threat of escalating costs can be seen in the late colonial history of the famous mine Valenciana, in Guanajuato. No other mine in Mexico was as large or productive as Valenciana.[38] During most of the eighteenth century Guanajuato held the ranking as Mexico's premier district by registering one-quarter of the total silver output, and Valenciana alone accounted for over 5 percent of that total. In the two decades before Hidalgo's Revolt the colony averaged 2.5 marks a year, with Valenciana contributing 165,000 marks or 6.6 percent. Although the mine came into operation in the 1760s, data that can be used to show operating revenues, costs, and profits only exist from 1788 to 1809.

It appears that the mine was more profitable in the first half of its late colonial history than in the last half. In the first half cost as a proportion of the ore's total value may have been under 50 percent, but in the second half it may have risen to over 60 percent. Nevertheless, both figures are considerably lower than 80–90 percent that may have been the average for the industry. On the basis of available data (1788–1809) costs rose rather steadily at an annual rate of 3.8 percent. Production followed an erratic downward trend at about 1 percent per year as profits also fell erratically, by 8.1 percent.[39] At the beginning of the period costs accounted for under 30 percent of the value of the production, but by the end of the period they had risen to over 80 percent. What the rapidly mounting costs just prior to 1810 signaled was the end of an era for Valenciana where, according to Brading, the owners "had already cut most of the ore worth refining."

Valenciana was probably unique even among the "great enterprises" in terms of size and output. On another level, however, it was typical of what had happened to mining in eighteenth-century Mexico: the emergence of large enterprises requiring heavy capitalization and complex organization. That Valenciana's profits had eroded as its costs rose may also underscore that Mexico's eighteenth-century silver boom had exploited most of the ore worth mining. Valenciana's superior performance stemmed from the continuing availability of high-grade ores (*apolvillado* ores yielded as much as 75 ounces per hundredweight) and efficiency-minded owners and managers.[40]

Government Reforms and Concessions

The cost of mining sparked numerous inquiries and proposals during the eighteenth century as the Crown and the industry sought ways to spur production and to protect their own special interests. Each reform had to be discussed in terms of its impact not only on the industry and the economy but also on the treasury. For example, in 1727 a meeting called by the viceroy, Marqués de Casafuerte, urged him to cut the price of mercury from 82.5 pesos to 55 pesos per quintal to allow the amalgamation of low-grade ores, but to no avail. The issue was raised again in the 1740s when one group of miners and officials argued that mercury was such a small part of the total cost that lowering prices would have no beneficial financial effect while another group averred just the opposite.[41] The price of mercury, which the Crown sold through a monopoly, had long been a target of reform for miners and refiners. From a high of 310 pesos per quintal in the 1560s, when mercury was auctioned off, it had fallen to and settled at about 82.5 pesos by the second decade of the seventeenth century. Toward the end of the seventeenth century the cost of transportation was added to rather than included in the aforementioned price, so that at the more distant reales cajas another 10–15 percent was added to the basic price.[42]

The impact of mercury prices on refining costs can be seen in the case of a Zacatecas refinery in 1801.[43] In that year the refiner had to pay 62 pesos per quintal because higher-priced Austrian mercury was being sold in lieu of lower-priced Spanish mercury. By 1801 mercury from Almadén in Spain had fallen from 82 to 41 pesos per quintal. At 62 pesos the refiner paid 180 pesos and 1 real for mercury and 419 pesos and 5 reales in total costs. Assuming all other costs to be constant, we find that the refiner would have saved about 9 percent in total costs if he could have bought Almadén mercury at the established price, or he would have added about 8 percent to total costs if he had to buy the mercury at the old price of 82.5 pesos. Mercury was an important part of the total cost structure, but as some of the critics of mercury price reductions suggested, lower prices had to be accompanied by other changes.

In 1765 José de la Borda, one of Mexico's most colorful and shrewd miners, made a comprehensive proposal for reducing mining costs based on his experiences in the Taxco camp prior to his departure to Zacatecas. Borda took the position that the industry was less productive than it could be because costs had to be cut drastically to raise profits that could be invested in new mining ventures. By citing data on taxes and fees from the previous half decade when Mexican silver output had fallen by one-eighth, Borda tried to demonstrate that the treasury would be better off financially if it lowered silver taxes, mercury prices, mintage fees, and other levies. He linked growth in treasury income to growth in silver mining; if mining continued to stagnate so would the treasury, but if mining began to recover, the treasury would see its income expand. Lower levies would mean that revenue per mark of silver would be less, but they would also mean that total revenue would rise as output grew. Borda viewed the savings from reduced taxes and fees (and presumably any other efficiencies that miners could introduce) as capital formation for new ventures.[44]

Borda's proposal came to the attention of José de Gálvez, who visited Mexico at the request of the king to study the relationship between the economy and the treasury. It is not clear whether Gálvez seriously considered implementing Borda's proposals for the whole industry, but it is well known that he favored lowering mercury prices; and when Borda specifically petitioned for concessions along the lines suggested in his 1765 plan to restore Zacatecas's Quebradilla mine, Gálvez endorsed the plan.

Over the next quarter or half century many other miners won similar concessions. Rather than embrace a policy of reform for all miners and risk the loss of revenue, at least in the short term, the government pursued a course of action that allowed some of the most prominent but not always most successful miners to reduce their costs for specified periods. The terms of the concessions varied from miner to miner as did the results of the concessions. Normally, the concessions were not enough to underwrite the repair of a mine, and though they could significantly lower operating costs, they could only do so if and when a mine became productive. The fallacy in Borda's proposal, as he himself found out, was that a substantial amount of capital could be sunk into a mine's rehabilitation without any ore being recovered or any income being generated; under these conditions the concessions offered little assistance. In short, the Crown's concessions were an inducement, but they had to be combined with capital investment and technical expertise to offer much financial relief.

Borda's Quebradilla project illustrates how the concessions could work under the terms granted by the Crown. There were two parts of Borda's grant: first, he was to pay no taxes on ore refined during the rehabilitation and could purchase mercury at cost; second, he paid one-half the *diezmo* (10 percent) and still purchased mercury at cost once the mine was in full operation. The Crown approved the concessions in 1768 and in 1769 Borda began work on the mine with a 50,000-peso unsecured loan. Within months he abandoned the project and turned his attention to a group of mines in Vetagrande, a few miles from Zacatecas, where he successfully recovered Esperanza and other related mines. Well on his way to another fortune Borda returned to Quebradilla where, armed with a reaffirmation of his concessions, he started a new venture in 1777. Although Borda died in 1778, his heirs continued the repairs until the mine was declared rehabilitated in 1779. Years later when the heirs had to present an accounting of the project in the aforementioned dispute with the Crown over how Quebradilla ore was allocated to the refineries the audit revealed the following items:

Quebradilla repairs	459,428 pesos
Hacienda de Sacrafamilia: construction, operation	260,585 pesos
Haciendas de San Miguel and Puríssima Concepción: refining operations	49,467 pesos
Mercury and freight, 780 quintales (30 pesos per quintal)	27,175 pesos
Assay fees	3,791 pesos
Transportation to mint	17,222 pesos
Miscellaneous taxes	3,874 pesos
Total	821,542 pesos

The heirs declared that 95,258 marks were needed (calculated at approximately 8.6 pesos per mark) to cover the expenses and therefore were exempt from taxation. If the Crown had collected its customary diezmos on 95,258 and sold the 780 quintales at 41 pesos instead of 30 pesos per quintal, a difference in income of 8,864 pesos, it would have realized 98,053 pesos. In effect, the concessions allowed Borda and his heirs to lower their operating costs by 11.9 percent.

Did that 100,000 pesos in savings made a difference in a project that cost more than 800,000 pesos? Would Borda have undertaken the project without the concessions even though he could not calculate what the savings would be? These questions cannot be answered with any precision. Certainly the concessions were an incentive because they included the provision that once the mine was in operation the tax on silver was set at 5 percent and the price of mercury remained 30 at pesos per quintal. Between 1779 and 1784, when the mine ceased operating, the Borda heirs gained another 85,748 pesos (77,451 pesos from silver taxes and 8,297 pesos from mercury purchases), savings that were worth about 6.1 percent against a total value of 1.4 million pesos in silver credited to the mine. This does not prove the case that if the Crown had dropped or eliminated silver taxes or the mercury monopoly, the mining industry would have seen a dramatic spurt in silver registrations. But it does show that once the operations were underway, miners could enjoy substantial savings in operating costs, and if those savings were plowed back into the operations, then the concessions contributed to further capital formation.[45]

Even though a decade passed before Borda implemented the concessions, other miners began to petition the Crown for similar concessions almost immediately after Borda's were approved in 1768. In 1770 Antonio Mauricio de Aramburu filed a petition for concessions like those granted Borda to restore the Bomba mine in the depopulated Capula camp north of Pachuca. By that time, according to the petition, in addition to Borda, Joseph Cayetano Núñez de Ibarra near Temazcaltepec and Diego Sánchez de Piña Hermoso and Manuel de Moya near Pachuca had been granted such concessions. These petitions began to take on a standard format. They described the miserable state of the particular mine ("collapsed tunnels" and "blocked entrances" in the case of Bomba) or of the mining camp (Capula depopulated and in ruins). References were made to other entrepreneurs who had invested enormous sums only to accumulate enormous debts.

Usually new tunnels for draining the mine and shafts for entering it were proposed as well as *malacates*, a system of whims, ropes, and buckets, for hauling water from the many different levels. The malacate system could be viewed as a more primitive technique than cutting the often long and expensive horizontal adits. Malacates, built in the existing shafts, did not require new adits that were used primarily for draining water, not for removing ore. In addition, though, adits only became more suitable alternatives to the malacate system where the depth of the mine penetrated the water table, a phenomenon that was more likely to occur in the eighteenth century.[46]

Estimates of the mine's yield of 2–16 ounces per hundredweight for Bomba are cited from Capula's parish records. In the case of Bomba the work had already begun and the expenses posted and anticipated were:

Shaft for ventilation and light	238,100 pesos
Clearing entrances/repairing galleries	401,000 pesos
Building refineries/buying equipment	835,000 pesos
Total	1,474,100 pesos

It became common for petitioners to refer to other projects to stress that great costs had to be expected before success was within reach. Cited in the Bomba petition was Pedro Romero de Terreros, later named Count of Regla, from Real del Monte because he (with José Alejandro de Bustamante) had spent 2.6 million pesos to repair the famous Vizcaína mine between 1739 to 1762. No mention is made of how much silver was extracted from Vizcaína, which according to the petition "had been thoroughly worked" by 1762. Brading reports that Vizcaína registered 20 million pesos of silver between 1738 and 1781, an amount that must have generated profits for the owner and revenues for the government in the early 1760s.[47] There was a caveat with the Bomba petition as with other petitions. The Bomba petition acknowledges that a second horizontal tunnel would have to be built at a cost of 1.5 million pesos, but it declares that no such undertaking could be tried until metals rich enough to pay the cost had been found. In reviewing the petition royal officials found themselves in disagreement over whether to support the project at Bomba, and in the end no decision was reached after nearly a year of debate and review.[48]

How many such petitions the government received is not yet known. In addition to petitions for concessions from Zacatecan mines, Pachuca miners may have presented one-half dozen petitions for relief, and miners from other camps where the cost of restoring and operating mines had risen sharply during the century may have accounted for another half dozen.[49] Government concessions could help to reduce costs, and perhaps both the government and the industry would have benefited if they had become permanent reforms. But the state of the industry had not yet reached the point where they were required to guarantee profitable operations.

Technology and Labor

In agriculture, as demand rose during the eighteenth century, the growth in food production depended more on intensive uses of labor than on major changes in technology. What helped to establish this pattern was that the colony never faced long-term food or labor shortages. Indeed, commercial agricultural operations developed in such a way that producers could compensate for the additional labor by reducing wages, substituting rations for wages, or a combination of the two. Agriculture, saddled with large debts and inefficient operations, could still control the supply of labor, the industry's most costly item. In mining a similar situation prevailed. Increasing costs in the absence of major technological changes could have reduced profit margins or eliminated them entirely except that a growing worker pool made it possible for mine owners to hold the line on wages and, in some cases, to cut wages for some job classifications.

The technique of extracting and refining the ore had changed little since the sixteenth century. In any working camp by the eighteenth century nearly all the ore was extracted from a honeycomb of underground shafts and tunnels, many of which were flooded. Across the landscape were scattered many thousands of abandoned pits and diggings from the earliest years when access to ore was much easier. In the eighteenth century the need to consolidate and streamline mining operations had imposed some order in how the extraction of ore was done. But Humboldt, who visited several camps in the early nineteenth century, found much to criticize. Mine owners may have had a more pragmatic and effective approach to the technical needs than Humboldt's observations and inquiries could relate. Mine owners understood the advantages of linking underground tunnels and connecting them to adits that could be used for "ventilation, drainage and easy extraction of ore and waste." By the eighteenth century explosives were used at the largest mines to extend old tunnels and reach new veins. Pumps and whims were used to carry ore and water to the surface.[50] In the end, however, mining still depended heavily on labor.

In Real del Monte, which Doris Ladd has studied during the strike from 1766 to 1775, "thirty different specialized tasks" had to be completed to extract the ore and load it on backs of mules and, in some cases, of humans.[51] The work was arduous and dangerous, even though the government passed laws and issued regulations to protect the workers. Some pounded the rock until it cracked; some worked in water up to their waists; some carried sacks of ore weighing 150, 200, or 250 pounds along tree-trunk ladders with "hundreds or even thousands of shallow steps." They worked long hours (usually twelve-hour shifts day or night); they breathed air filled with dust, fumes, and smoke; they took few breaks and ate cold meals underground.[52]

Even reliance on humans rather than on machines did not prevent the great miners in eighteenth-century Mexico from devising ways to manage these unwieldy labor forces and to earn profits from them. A labor-intensive industry with a relatively fixed technological base was not necessarily unproductive, inefficient, or unprofitable. In theory the efficiency of an operation derives from how the factors of production are employed with a given production technology, while productivity involves the technology that is employed. The fact is that colonial silver-mining operations performed at a level that allowed the industry to sustain growth in output over the long term.[53]

Technology played a bigger role in the processing of the ore than in its extraction. Ore continued to be both smelted and refined. Although smelters were less expensive to build and operate than refineries, they were limited to a few types of ores. Large producers maintained smelters for high-grade ores, but marginal producers, who could not afford refineries, used them with all grades of ores.[54]

Amalgamation involved the combining of finely crushed ore with mercury and other ingredients to separate the silver from the ore itself. This required the construction of stamps for crushing the ore and *arrastres* for pulverizing it further. The incorporation of the ore, mercury, and other reagents took place in a large *patio* (sometimes roofed) where the *harina* (milled ore) was arranged in montones that needed about six to eight weeks to complete the chemical reaction. The mixture was then washed in a vat with the *pella* (heavy amalgam of silver and mercury) settling to the bottom. Finally, the mercury was cooked off by applying heat to the pella. Amalgamation had been known since ancient times, but the technique just described was largely the invention of Bartolomé de Medina in the 1550s. The basic technique changed very little between the middle of the sixteenth century and the end of the colonial period. Local conditions and the special skills of the individual refiners led to innovations and adaptations in the Medina technique, such as the introduction of *magistral* (copper pyrites) to speed up the chemical reaction. For the most part, however, the persistence of the sixteenth-century Medina system rather than its modification is the most evident feature of the patio process.[55]

Refining was less labor intensive than mining. Machines were used for crushing and stirring the ore, although humans and animals were also used in the latter task. Labor above ground was less arduous and dangerous than work underground except that mercury poisoning (some waded around in the harina) caused many deaths among refinery workers. Some statistics on the labor force in the mines and refineries of Zacatecas indicated how the industry was organized during the late eighteenth century. Around 1780 the ratio of mine workers to refinery workers was 2.5 to 1. There were nearly sixty working mines compared to thirty such refineries with an average of fifty workers per mine versus thirty-eight workers per refinery. These averages can be misleading, however. Only one-fifth of the mines had fifty or more workers, and the four largest employed two-thirds (1,753) of all the workers (2,664). In the case of the refineries about one-third had thirty-eight or more workers, and the three largest refineries (484) employed 44 percent of all the workers (1,103). Not only did it take more than twice as many to extract the ore, but also the mining operations themselves had more employees than the refinery operations.[56]

The cost of labor was an important factor in both mining and refining the ore, but it was proportionately larger in the former than the latter. Brading estimated that labor in the mines accounted for about 70 percent of the total costs, whereas refinery labor consumed about 20 percent of the total.[57] It was easier to achieve efficiencies in the refineries than in the mines because the former were somewhat less dependent on manual labor. For example, refiners could try to recapture some of the mercury used in one batch to be incorporated in the next batch.[58] That mine and refinery workers may have "constituted a free, well-paid, geographically mobile labour force which in many areas acted as the virtual partners of the owners" did not make them immune from attempts by cost-conscious owners to curb or lower their compensation.[59] When draft labor was approved at times during the eighteenth century, it too may not have been so much the result of shortages of workers, as the owners complained, as further efforts at controlling costs through wage reductions.[60] Daily wages ranged from a few reales for the least skilled to 5–6 reales for the most skilled mine and refinery workers. Many underground workers earned a wage and a share of the ore (called *partido* or *pepena*), but surface workers whether employed by the mines or refineries normally received only wages. But the worker's total compensation included wages, partidos, and what he could steal. A serious and constant problem, theft was probably harder for the owner to control than other parts of the worker's compensation package.[61]

Owners' efforts to reduce workers' remunerations were often met with resistance and were only occasionally fully implemented.[62] Their success depended on the size of the enterprise, the supply of labor, and the attitude of the government. Employers may have been more successful in adjusting partidos than in lowering wages or catching thieves. Since only some categories of underground workers could claim a share and considerable variation existed in terms of who qualified and the amount of the share from mine to mine and camp to camp, presumably employers had some discretion in arranging for compensation among newly hired workers. Large employers probably enjoyed greater discretion than small employers, who often worked side-by-side with their employees. In some camps the workers and owners agreed to split what had been mined over and above a "fixed daily quota," and in other camps workers simply expected a percentage of the total ore mined.[63] Even before the pressure to end or reduce partidos became tied to cost-cutting in the second half of the eighteenth century, owners and workers in large and small enterprises had feuded over the size of the share, the grade of ore, and the disposition of the share. The long, bitter strike at Real del Monte (1766–75) is an example of how a dispute over partidos and other conditions could disrupt mining. Although the strike virtually closed down the camp for a decade, the resolution of the strike was to reinforce the traditional wage system of wages and partidos (for some workers at least).[64]

Even though their efforts to cut labor costs were blocked or delayed, owners continued to tamper with the workers' compensation system throughout the late colonial period. In Zacatecas, where the late colonial labor supply exceeded demand, owners increasingly resisted the payment of shares. In Guanajuato some owners succeeded in "suppressing the payment of all partidos," although when the proprietors of Valenciana terminated the partidos, they had to double the pickman's daily wage.[65] From the employer's standpoint, however, a slightly higher but fixed wage was preferable to shares because, for cost-cutting purposes, wages were easier to deal with than partidos.

Over the long term, growth in output of silver did not translate into higher wages for mine and refinery workers. Some cost savings could be realized through production or management efficiencies: clustering mines, linking tunnels, building adits, consolidating operations, and other actions. Given the level of technology, the state of the mines, and the role of government, there were limits to how efficient the operations could be made. Over the long term, increasing production was tied to containing costs.

Labor constituted the largest component in the cost structure, and it was a candidate for control. Wage data for mine workers are too fragmentary from which to draw any conclusions about eighteenth-century trends. The data we have collected, primarily from Zacatecas, do not indicate that the wage part of the compensation package rose at all during the eighteenth century. Many workers received neither partidos or rations, and static wage levels meant that little changed about their standard of living. For those who received partidos or rations the assessment of the impact of static wages on living standards is more complicated. The available evidence certainly does not indicate that owners willingly considered upward adjustments in nonwage components. In an economy with little long-term price inflation what can static wage levels mean? In Real del Monte, estimates Ladd, one real (of the 2–5 reales a worker might earn per day) could buy "a beef tongue, a pound of wool, twenty-eight ounces of mutton, or five pounds of beef or veal." In fact, though, the worker could simply fritter away the one real on food or drink in the mine itself.[66]

Other considerations must be taken into account before we determine how well off any worker was at any given time or over a period of time: how many days did he work, how was he paid, and how large a household did he support? More to the point, however, discretionary income can become an engine for economic change and development. Ladd's example is instructive in this regard. Mine and refinery workers could earn wages that provided them with their daily subsistence but apparently not much more than that. Even though these workers were better paid than others, the level of consumption as represented in these figures and in light of a relatively fixed compensation scale did not lend itself to a changing economic structure.

Mercury Monopoly

As noted earlier, mercury was essential to colonial silver mining because without it most of the silver ore could not be profitably refined. Through a royal monopoly the Crown controlled the production, distribution, and price. In Mexico's case the monopoly operated on both sides of the Atlantic Ocean. Mercury was mined and processed under royal auspices in Spain, and then it was transported from Spain to Mexico and from Mexico City's warehouse to the mining camps. The supply of mercury, as expected, climbed in the eighteenth century but at a rate just barely lower than the rate for silver production (based on Humboldt's series).

Historians have debated whether silver production, dependent as it was on mercury, was retarded because of the uncertainties and inefficiencies that were often associated with royal monopolies. The implication is that in a free market mercury supplies would have expanded or shrunk in terms of how much refiners needed or were willing to pay for; not only would mercury prices have been lower but supplies would also have been more plentiful, especially in times of increasing silver production. This would have benefited both the silver and mercury miners. There were risks, however. In the Crown's view, private ownership of mercury mines did not constitute a dependable system for maintaining a supply of mercury. Moreover, expansion in silver production was so directly linked to mercury supplies that such ownership opened up the possibility of price manipulation for private gain. Finally, the operation of a mercury monopoly was in line with other royal businesses set up not only for control but also for enrichment. With its royal monopoly, however, the Crown ended up with as many problems as any private owner had. The Crown also had to overcome such problems as poor ores, scarcity of labor or capital, and inept management in order to preserve vital mercury supplies.

Over the entire colonial period the monopoly may have provided Mexican mines with about as much mercury as they could consume, given the industry's problems. It took more than a year from the time that mercury was extracted in Almadén (or Idria in Slovenia) to the time it was incorporated with the ore, and shortages were bound to occur. Minor shortages because of delays were frequent, but major shortages that led to widespread curtailments in registrations or closures of camps were actually uncommon, and when shortages ended, whether minor or major, both mercury shipments and mining operations resumed quickly.

Mercury remained essential to an expanding mining industry because other options for processing the ore in the absence of mercury were so very limited. In times of shortages, processors might try to introduce greater efficiencies into their own operations by preparing the ore more carefully and by recapturing as much of the mercury as possible when it was separated from the silver at the end of the process. Processing ore in smelters was an alternative to amalgamation with mercury, and although smelting was more important than amalgamation in camps like Sombrerete because of the quality of the ore, it was not economical in most camps or with most grades. In camps counting heavily on amalgamation, the quantity of ore smelted could exceed the quantity amalgamated from time to time. In 1746 Guanajuato registered more smelted silver (205,681 marks) than amalgamated silver (199,114 marks), but over the course of the century smelting ore was a viable option only when appropriate conditions prevailed.[67] In addition to high ore grades, smelting required a supply of charcoal, a commodity that was not readily available in most camps. Mexico probably had more smeltable ore than Peru, and each year, even as amalgamation was expanding, Mexico registered a quantity of smelted ore (only about 10 percent by 1810).[68]

A series based on mercury deliveries from Spain to Mexico can be analyzed for the eighteenth century.[69] Mercury was distributed and sold in units of quintales (about 100 pounds), and Mexico received an average 18,000 quintales or 1.8 million pounds per year during the eighteenth century. Mercury deliveries rose at a rate of 1.3 percent per year during the century, a rate that was just slightly below the rate for silver registrations. By the end of the century, after a long period of steady but moderate growth in output of silver, the Crown was delivering enough mercury to Mexico to provide the camps with as much as 25,000 quintales in a year and to maintain a reserve of 15,000–25,000 quintales.

In early 1795 the colonial government drew up a summary of the sale and distribution of mercury to the cajas during the first half of 1794 with these results. Eleven cajas in mining camps had a balance of 13,980 quintales in January 1794 and received an additional 3,750 quintales in the first half of 1794 and 7,353 quintales in the second half. Of the total 25,083 quintales available for sale at the cajas in 1794, 6,440 quintales were sold in the first half and probably twice that much in the second half.[70] Just under two-thirds of that total was Almadén mercury, and the rest was from Idria's mines. In the first six months of 1794 the cajas reported that 880,137 marks of silver had been registered, and if that figure were compared to the 6,440 quintales of mercury sold, the ratio of mercury in quintales to silver in marks would be 1 to 137, a ratio higher than the standard 1 to 100 (or perhaps 1 to 125). But such a comparison can be distorted because the quantity of marks may include silver refined with mercury bought in 1793 but not reported until 1794. Over a much longer period than six months, the ratio of mercury to silver would probably be close to what contemporaries considered the average. For all of 1794 the government report projected that 2.3 million silver marks would be registered from about 18,000 quintales sold, for a ratio of just under 1 quintal of mercury per 130 marks of silver. In fact, for 1794 2.5 million silver marks were registered, although that included both *plata de azogue* (amalgamated silver) and *plata de fuego* (smelted silver). If 10 percent of the total silver were plata de fuego, then the remainder in plata de azogue would equal 2.25 million marks, a figure that was relatively close to the government's own projection. At the end of 1794, despite the sale of 18,000 quintales in the cajas, the total colonial reserve (in the cajas and the central warehouse) had reached 20,000 quintales or more, because 5,501 quintales had arrived in Mexico from Spain. Hence the colony had at its disposal about 38,000 quintales of mercury in 1794, of which it consumed about 18,000 quintales of mercury.[71]

Having such large reserves on hand was not typical of the whole century or perhaps even of the late decades. Severe shortages as well as inadequate supplies that could cripple both mine and refinery operations did occur periodically in the eighteenth century. But the rise in output of silver, more and more of which was plata de azogue, was strong testimony to the monopoly's own achievement to manage the growth in the demand for and distribution of mercury. The fact remained that if the supply were interrupted, the stockpile of 20,000 quintales in demand during the late eighteenth century could be exhausted in a year. The refusal or failure to develop a more broadly based supply system for mercury made the colony vulnerable when the production or transportation of mercury was in some way interrupted.

One of the most serious threats occurred at the end of the 1790s when, caught up in the wars between France and England, Spain found that it had to halt mercury shipments because of the British blockade of the Iberian Peninsula from 1799 to 1801. This was not the first time that war had threatened or interrupted the shipment of mercury from Spain to Mexico. During the War for Independence in the English colonies some shortages occurred, although not on the scale of the 1799–1801 shortage. Perhaps out of concern for the vulnerability of the long supply lines, in the mid-1770s Charles III authorized Viceroy Antonio María Bucareli to spend 160,000 pesos to determine if any exploitable mercury deposits existed in Mexico.[72] In Zacatecas in 1780 Ventura de Arteaga, a former general manager of the Borda enterprise, received a license to operate a small mercury mine that never became very productive. The new mining code of 1783, in reversal of a long-standing ban, permitted mercury mining.[73] Under Bucareli's successor, Martín de Mayorga, the reorganized miners' guild was authorized to spend 50,000–60,000 pesos in search of a domestic quicksilver supply but (so far as can be determined) to no avail.[74]

Certainly, Mexico's dependence on Spanish or European mercury was even greater by late 1797, when the first sign of an impending scarcity can be detected, or by late 1798 and early 1799, when Mexico was in the midst of a full-fledged mercury crisis.[75] The shortage of mercury triggered a plan, drawn up under the intendancy codes, that provided for scarce quicksilver to be allocated among the camps in accord with the amount of crushed ore awaiting amalgamation. How quickly the surpluses from the mid-1790s had been depleted! So little mercury was on hand in 1799 that a major camp like Zacatecas was allotted only 750 quintales, enough to refine at the highest ratios about 100,000 marks at a time when the camp's output of refined silver had been in the range of 200,000–300,000 marks. The government's supply was exhausted by 1801, although a quantity of rescate (used or recaptured) mercury did circulate among the camps.[76]

One strategy, put forward by the miners' guild and approved by the viceroy in 1801 or 1802, was to cut the diezmo by half to make the smelting of ore more economical. The impact of this policy change, which earned the king's reluctant approval, was evident in silver registration figures. Colonial registrations had dropped by 1.3 percent in 1797, 4.3 percent in 1798, 8.3 percent in 1799, 15.2 percent in 1800, and 10.5 percent in 1801, but they then rose by 12.5 percent in 1802.

In Zacatecas, where silver data are available by plata de azogue and plata de fuego, the registration of plata de fuego rose noticeably after 1797 but then took a sharp jump between 1801 and 1802. In 1802 Zacatecas's plata de fuego registrations increased to 103,267 marks from 32,216 marks in 1801, an increase of nearly 2.5 times:[77]

Date	Total (%)	Azogue (%)	Fuego (%)
1797	−7.4	83.2	16.8
1798	−11.9	76.1	23.9
1799	−25.7	70.3	29.7
1800	5.8	72.1	27.9
1801	−45.3	73.9	26.1
1802	100	54.4	45.7

When mercury became more plentiful in 1803 and the reduction in the diezmo was ended, registrations of plata de azogue rose twofold but those of plata de fuego fell by one-third. These figures dramatize how important mercury was to both the industry and the treasury, for if the colony had had to rely on smelted silver, both silver registrations and tax revenues would have suffered.

Mexico had its own mercury deposits, but neither the government nor the silver-mining industry ever showed much interest in exploiting those deposits. Part of the reason may have been that mercury supplies were generally sufficient to meet the demand. Had the mercury supply system worked less well, both the Crown and the industry, especially with the eighteenth-century mining boom, probably would have been more inclined to develop a local mercury source along the lines of Huancavelica in Peru. Humboldt investigated the state of mercury mining in Mexico and declared it to be virtually nonexistent. The diggings were at best superficial because the investors did not see how they could realize enough profits in the first years to justify a shift from silver (or other activities) to mercury. One mine, Durasno, was abandoned in the 1790s, after 700 quintales had been drawn in the early months, because it could not pay its own way. Humboldt contended that in this mine the high costs resulted from a poorly constructed mine rather than from any inherent disadvantage from mercury mining itself. In any event, Humboldt, who visited Mexico after the blockade, believed that the colony could operate profitable quicksilver mines.[78]

Under existing procedures mercury was supposed to be distributed to the reales cajas each year on the basis of how much had been assigned during the year, how much of that was consumed, and how much was in reserve. If a camp had a major discovery or strike, it could receive an additional allotment from the central warehouse or from a nearby caja. It is not clear how closely or consistently these allocation procedures were followed, although the cajas submitted annual reports that contained information from which such decisions could have been made. With enough mercury on hand the government was probably under no strong pressure to enforce the procedures rigorously. The major camps were generally assured of adequate supplies irrespective of their immediate past performance, although no caja, not even a major one, was ever permitted to stockpile too much mercury beyond its current needs. When the mercury administration drew up its annual report in 1787, it reported that the eleven cajas could have had at the outset of 1788 as much as 16,803 quintales: 11,403 quintales from 1787 and 5,401 to be assigned in 1788. We estimate (because the document does not say) that 12,000–15,000 quintales must have been consumed in 1787 to account for the 1.5 million marks of plata de azogue that were registered. In 1787 only 4,000 quintales were shipped to the cajas: Mexico City received the largest amount, 1,099; followed by San Luis Potosí, 900; and Guanajuato, 501. Six received between 150 and 300 quintales, and two, Rosario and Zacatecas, received none. With these shipments all the cajas had a minimum of 200–300 quintales, and five of them (San Luis Potosí, Durango, Mexico City, Guanajuato, and Guadalajara) had 1,000–1,800 quintales. When the 1788 allocation list was drawn up, Guanajuato, Zacatecas, and Mexico City were each slated for 2,103, 1,200, and 1,048 quintales respectively, or more than 80 percent of the 5,401 quintales to be assigned. But Durango, Guadalajara, Pachuca and Rosario were not assigned any new allocations (not yet at least), for at the end of 1787 they still held 4,500 quintales. The remaining four cajas were to receive 150–300 quintales. Thus when 1788 began only Chihuahua and Pachuca would have had less than 1,000 quintales in current or anticipated inventory, and the rest would have had between 1,000 and 3,600 quintales. Of the 16,803 quintales (1787 reserves plus 1788 assignments), Guanajuato had 3,577 quintales, Mexico City had 2,638, Zacatecas had 2,153, and San Luis Potosí had 2,027 for 62 percent of the mercury, a ranking not unlike that of the camps by production of silver.[79] The reserves of 1787 combined with the allotments of 1788 meant that the industry could register 2.2–2.5 million marks in 1788, and that amount was close to the year's actual registrations.

The distribution of mercury undertaken in 1794 revealed that the allotments among the cajas could be frequently adjusted. At the start of the year the eleven reales cajas had inventories that totaled 13,980 quintales, to which another 3,750 quintales were added in the first six months for 17,770 quintales total. The cajas sold 6,440 quintales of the 17,770 quintales, leaving a balance of 11,290 quintales. Guanajuato and Bolaños began 1794 with the largest balances, 2,547 and 2,244 quintales respectively, and Sombrerete (which smelted most of its silver) and Chihuahua with the smallest, 461 and 233 quintales respectively. Only six cajas received allotments, with almost half of that assigned to Guanajuato. During the first half of 1794 the cajas sold slightly more than one-third (36 percent) of their inventories; Durango, Zacatecas, and Sombrerete sold 45–47 percent while San Luis Potosí sold only 28 percent. Guanajuato had the most sales (1,470 quintales), and all the other cajas had sales under 1,000 quintales each, with the smallest (74 quintales) in Chihuahua. Documents also included how much silver was marked, although not all this silver was necessarily processed with the mercury sold during that half year. The ratio of mercury consumed to silver marked for those six months was one quintal to 137 marks, an impressive performance. In individual cajas the variation could be highly significant. Five cajas reported ratios that exceeded the 1:100 ratio, with the highest (and perhaps the most suspect) being 1:336 at San Luis Potosí. The other four had the following ratios: Mexico City, 1:169; Guanajuato, 1:156; Rosario, 1:133; and Zacatecas, 1:108. These were, of course, among the most important camps, and their higher ratios help to explain why they received as much mercury as they did. At the bottom of the list was Chihuahua with a ratio of only 1:60. At the outset of the second half of 1794 inventories at the cajas were as high as 2,577 quintales (22.8 percent of the total) and as low as 159 quintales (1.4 percent). They received another 7,393 quintales during the second half of the year, for a total of 18,684 quintales available to sell from July to December. Thus for all of 1794 the cajas had 25,124 quintales to sell. After July every caja except San Luis Potosí had received new allotments from a low of 150 quintales at three cajas (Pachuca, Guadalajara, and Chihuahua) to a high of 1,500 at Guanajuato. With the new deliveries, Guanajuato had on hand 4,077 quintales, three cajas—Bolaños, Rosario, and Durango— had 2,200–2,600 quintales each, and the remaining seven had 300–1,800 quintales each.[80] It is not surprising that Guanajuato, given its continuing high output, had nearly twice as much as any other caja. The large reserves available at Bolaños, Rosario, and Durango may be somewhat more surprising because they were not among the major camps in the late eighteenth or early nineteenth century.

As a result of the distribution after July 1794, several minor camps had larger supplies than several top-ranking camps. These figures do not reveal how much mercury was available to be shipped from the central warehouse to the reales cajas. What the 1794 distribution plan may underline was that the colony had a supply of mercury that was more than adequate to cover the output of the mining industry. If the more than 25,000 quintales available in the reales cajas had yielded silver at the aforementioned ratio of 1 to 137, production of plata de azogue would have risen to 3.4 million marks, a level that the industry did approach but (so far as we know) did not reach in the colonial period. Despite some impressive recoveries in the late eighteenth century, the industry probably lacked both the financial and technical resources to achieve such a level of production. Mercury shortages could occur quickly, as the late 1790s proved, but they were not so common as to represent a threat to the rising trend in production.

The supply of mercury was a constant concern, but its price sparked as much controversy as the transportation and distribution of the mineral. As the operator of a monopoly, the government could fix the price at whatever level it deemed appropriate, not only to recover the cost of production and distribution, but to enrich the treasury. In 1617 the price for Almadén mercury in Mexico had been set at 82.5 pesos per quintal, and that price remained in effect until 1768. The cost of extracting the ore in Spain and transporting it to Mexico varied from time to time, but the aforementioned price allowed the Crown to realize a profit of 100–300 percent per quintal. Miners had long pleaded with the government to lower the price, and in 1727 the Viceroy Marqués de Casafuerte recommended a price of 55 pesos per quintal, but in spite of the support of miners, merchants, and other government officials, the Crown rejected the recommendation because of the potential loss in income for the treasury.[81]

The movement to reduce mercury prices gained momentum when José de Gálvez proposed during his visita that mercury should be sold at cost (about 30 pesos per quintal). After much discussion Gálvez finally convinced the Crown to cut the price but only by one-fourth, from the 82.5 pesos to 62 pesos per quintal, to take effect in 1768.[82] Silver registrations rose sharply, and Gálvez recommended a second cut of one-third from the new price to 41.25 pesos. If enacted, that would have represented a 50-percent reduction from the 82.5-peso level, but it aroused the more conservative forces in the government to oppose another reduction because of the impact on the revenue at the treasury. In particular, the new viceroy, Antonio María Bucareli, who was under mounting pressure to boost treasury income, disagreed not only because of his fear that lower prices would adversely affect royal revenues but also because he felt that the opening of new, rich mines like Valenciana in Guanajuato and Esperanza in Zacatecas, which had occurred independently of recent reductions in mercury prices, accounted for the rise in registration of silver.[83] The mining boom of the late third quarter was already underway when the initial price cut was announced. But savings from that cut reduced costs, added to the capital pool, and helped to sustain the expansion, despite Bucareli's opposition.

Bucareli's opposition was shaped by the advice that he sought from the creole jurist, Francisco Javier Gamboa, with close ties to Mexico City's Consulado. In a confidential report that he prepared for Bucareli, Gamboa laid out much of the argument that Bucareli used in his own report to the king. The main case made by Gamboa and repeated by Bucareli was that the cut was not needed, for mining was recovering from the mid-century capital crisis (earlier detailed in his 1761 *Comentarios*), and that a cut would not help that recovery along as much as it would hurt future income at the colonial treasury.

But Gamboa raised two other points: mercury sold at cost in Zacatecas and Pachuca had not directly contributed to the recovery of the mines for which concessions had been granted because he correctly understood that larger capital investments than represented by mercury price savings were necessary for such undertakings, and that, second, mercury sold at cost or at a price lower than the new price would not benefit the owners of smelters, who by Gamboa's estimate had contributed more than half of the increase in total output between 1768 and 1773. In the end, given his traditionalist outlook, Gamboa concluded that the best prescription for the industry, as stated in his *Comentarios*, was to ensure that the laws governing the industry should be properly and systematically enforced. In short, no radical change from past policy was necessary.[84]

With Gamboa's help Bucareli managed to delay the enactment of the second reduction until after Gálvez became Minister of Marine and Indies for Charles III. But Charles III finally approved a second reduction to 41.25 pesos per quintal in 1777. This remained the official mercury price until the end of the colonial period, except for the continuing selective approval of special reductions for individual miners and for Austrian mercury priced at 62 pesos per quintal.

Silver mining was by far the most important mining activity, but it was not the only such activity. As silver mining expanded in the eighteenth century so too did gold mining, at least in the northern provinces for which we have some records. The reason for this was that silver and gold ores were often found together. The fact that the Crown reduced gold taxes from 20 percent to 3 percent was certainly an inducement for miners to pay more attention to the discovery and exploitation of gold.[85] Not much else is known about gold mining, and the main interest of the mining industry remained silver.

Copper mining existed in many places, although Michoacán was the center of the industry. Much of the demand for copper was in connection with the manufacture of arms and coinage of money. Crown policy vacillated between strict and loose control of the copper industry, with the result that despite efforts to revive and stimulate copper mining in the late eighteenth century as the demand for copper exceeded the supply, the industry never realized its full potential.[86]

Although Mexico was rich in other mineral resources, its miners and investors had the most experience with and the most interest in silver. Success in one mineral did not automatically transfer to other minerals. Nor did the long-term growth in silver mining necessarily promote other economic opportunities. Higher production meant more jobs and greater demand for basic goods and services that supported the silver industry. Recapitalization and reorganization along with some timely reforms in public policy added strength to the industry's long-term growth curve. But silver mining (in some ways like commodity agriculture) succeeded in large part without altering the basic technology except for small modifications in refining procedures. Adding more workers, building more malacates, and consolidating more operations only marginally changed the way in which the ore was extracted from the mine and converted to silver at the refinery. Changes in the silver industry, especially the move toward consolidation because of the greater operational efficiencies that this represented, were crucial to maintaining the growth in output. As far-reaching as these were for the industry itself, they did not lead to many other fundamental economic changes. Mining and mining camps largely became more highly specialized in the business of extracting and processing metal and did not broaden in any significant way the colonial economy.

5

Manufacturing and
International Trade

Agriculture and mining entailed processing to convert raw materials into items that could be sold and consumed. Wheat, for example, had to be milled into flour and flour baked into bread. Ore had to be amalgamated or smelted and then coined. In such cases processing could be viewed as an extension of producing the raw material and often took place where the raw materials themselves were produced. Manufacturing of finished products for sale to producers or consumers as an activity separate from producing and processing was forbidden. It is not that the colony had no manufacturing operations but that what it could fabricate was limited and regulated. It was permitted to establish processing facilities for basic needs, but it was not permitted to invest in operations that competed with Spanish manufactured imports. These mercantilistic policies had a profound impact, but in the end, the manufacturing sector was larger than strict enforcement of the commercial code would have allowed simply out of need.

The manufacturing sector had developed only limited capacity by the eighteenth century. The closest activity to large-scale manufacturing was the *obraje*, which Richard Salvucci says "superficially, at least, . . . resembled factories in their division of labor and apparently large-scale production." Contrary to earlier views that the obraje represented an incipient factory system, it proved too limited in its capacity to expand or change as circumstances may have demanded. That explains why it ultimately disappeared.[1]

In the absence of a manufacturing base, Mexico was heavily dependent on overseas commerce throughout the eighteenth century as its own economy was growing. Until the eighteenth century such trade was exclusively assigned to the Consulado of Seville and its branch in Mexico City. In the early eighteenth century the monopoly was shifted from Seville to Cádiz, and over the course of the century other reforms to make foreign trade more competitive were introduced. By the end of the century the monopoly had been selectively but not completely dismantled. Despite these changes, direct trade between Mexico and foreign countries outside the Spanish Empire was limited and continued to be regulated. That meant that the range and variety of merchandise were restricted and that the price was inflated, although less restricted and inflated than before the reforms. The nature of the exchange changed very little: the colony imported manufactured goods, many of which were high-priced luxury items, paid for with silver. Over time the monopoly made the import-export merchants wealthy, and while the eighteenth-century economic reforms forced important changes on the ways that these merchants acquired and managed their wealth, the reforms did not seriously challenge their financial position.

Size of the Manufacturing Sector

What the colony processed or fabricated was high-volume, low-price merchandise; what it imported was the opposite. Although the wealthy class consumed a substantial volume of all manufactured imports, the general population needed common manufactures such as clothes, household items, and tools. Some important studies on eighteenth-century Europe point to the rise of rural industrialization, what is called protoindustrialization, prior to the Industrial Revolution. As the feudal system broke down, towns expanded their manufacturing base in response to demographic change and economic growth. Eventually merchant capital shifted "industrial production from the town to the countryside" where labor was cheap and available.[2]

Demand, transportation, and capital were needed if a rural area were to undergo protoindustrialization. For demand to be effective, it had to extend beyond local domestic demand. The dynamism of protoindustrial change lay not only in expansion but also in the "utilization of heretofore idle resources" for which the internal economy had little use.[3] In an overview of protoindustrial development, Peter Kriedte observes:[4]

Proto-industrialization stands between two worlds: the narrow world of the village and the world of trade that crosses all boundaries. . . . The agrarian sector contributed labour, commercial and entrepreneurial skill, capital, products, and markets. Merchant capitalism opened up foreign markets on whose capacity for expansion the rural handicrafts depended if they were to enter proto-industrialization. The dualistic structure of pre-industrial European societies thus became the soil on which capitalism could grow. Merchant capital, by drawing an essentially pre-capitalist social formation—namely peasant society—into its sphere, promoted the process of accumulation and became the pacemaker of the general acceptance of the market principle. If the process of accumulation was to continue, merchant capital needed the heretofore unused productive reservoir of the peasantry, once the urban production capacity had proved too inelastic. By changing peasant society into a supplier of either industrial or agricultural products, merchant capital opened it to specialization and created the precondition for sustained economic growth.

Although some agricultural regions linked to major Mexican cities in the eighteenth century exhibited an economic transformation that could have represented steps toward industrialization, the European model applied only selectively to eighteenth-century Mexico. After a detailed study of the Pueblan regional economy, Guy Thomson concluded that while "it would be tempting to use the term 'proto-industrialization' to describe the social processes, commercial practices and product specialization," it would also overstate the case.[5]

In both the agricultural and mineral sectors the processing of the raw materials was often an extension of the raising of crops or the extracting of ores.[6] Some food- or ore-processing mills, though attached to estates or mines, were large, complex operations that required special managerial staffs and substantial capital investments.[7] How then do we distinguish processing from manufacturing? Processing was an extension of production and extraction that made the raw material useful. Manufacturing, by contrast, may be defined as fabricating goods that exist independently of the original products. Manufacturers not only created and designed new products but found ways to market and distribute them—in short, to convince the public to buy or use products that may be new or unfamiliar. Manufacturing consumer goods for less-established markets entailed risks different from those experienced by commodity producers and small farmers.

It is not surprising that manufacturing was "less advanced" in eighteenth-century Mexico, not only because of the uncertainty of the market for such products, but also, according to Alexander von Humboldt, because Spain in pursuit of its mercantilistic policies had "thrown insurmountable obstacles" in the way of the development of the manufacturing sector.[8] Spain's aim to supply all finished products proved infeasible as the colonial population grew and spread out. It was too expensive to import ordinary, common merchandise, and it was too much of an economic temptation for the colonial businessman to ignore the low end of the consumer marketplace. Although the Crown might prohibit the manufacture of specific products, it did not (and could not) prohibit all manufacturing.[9] Still, little active encouragement of manufacturing at the highest governmental levels emerged due to the long-standing bias in favor of the Spanish mercantile community.

How much of a manufacturing sector did the colony actually possess in the late colonial period? That remains a difficult question to answer for two reason: how to define manufacturing as opposed to less-developed forms of processing or fabricating, and where to collect the data. John Kicza, who has carefully reconstructed the structure of Mexico City's economy in the eighteenth century, believes that manufacturing comprised more than the dozen or so obrajes, the hundreds of small weaving operations, bakeries, slaughterhouses, and printers, as well as the factories that made apparel and tobacco. Although he acknowledges a difference between processing and manufacturing, he groups all these ventures as manufacturing because the scale and form of these operations were different from the processing linked to estates and other agricultural ventures. Bakeries, for example, could require thousands of pesos in capital and employ dozens of workers; moreover, many had become big enough to gain from "a separation between ownership and management." Partnerships were common, and while the church invested in bakeries, merchants as a rule did not (at least in Mexico City). Merchants did provide "bridge loans" to bakeries that lacked capital to pay for grain or for equipment, to be repaid at 5 percent over five years.[10] Kicza makes a vital point that the growth of the city's population and its consumer market forced changes on how local businesses organized, managed, and financed their operations. Except for the obrajes, however, the manufacturing sector failed to penetrate much beyond a level that was small in scale and oriented toward standard household products that did not specifically have to be marketed.

According to Guy Thomson, Puebla may have been the "first region in the New World to acquire a broad base of industries, introduced by European artisans, using European technology and producing for the settler population." Although the manufacture and sale of products such as textiles, saddlery, glass, pottery, and ironwork became identified with Puebla, they did not become so deeply rooted that they transformed the basically agrarian economy. Thomson's discussion concerns primarily textile manufacturing. The size and diversity of manufacturing suggest that the colonial economy might have been changing and expanding. But if it were, then imports of manufactures should have suffered from a severe cost disadvantage because of high transportation costs. Mexico's silver covered the differential and made the transportation cost factor less urgent. The comparative advantage in buying manufactures from abroad rather than producing them at home is difficult to determine without more concrete data. We may assume that because mercantile capital continued to flow in ever-increasing amounts into late colonial mining, manufacturing and mining were not yet in competition for capital and other resources. Being expensive and risky was not so great an obstacle for mining, for unlike manufacturing, mining could yield higher returns faster.

Within the manufacturing sector the scale and type of venture varied significantly, and that difference surely affected investing decisions. Investments in flour mills or retail bakeries, for example, did not lack for risk, but from the standpoint of marketing and pricing, mills and bakeries may have appeared to be more predictable for investments than pottery shops, ironworks, or even textile mills. When Thomson studied loans made by individuals and institutions in the Pueblan area from 1800 to 1810, he organized them into the three broad categories of industrial, commercial, and agricultural. Loans under the industrial category constituted the largest percentage, slightly more than 50 percent. The average loan was about 10,000 pesos. Since the industrial category is not broken down more precisely, it cannot be analyzed in terms of how the loans were distributed within the category. Nor is it entirely clear how the loans were used. It would be helpful to know whether the loans were granted to cover previous debts, to purchase inventory, or to invest in plant and equipment to expand production. Still, Thomson's general point must be taken seriously: from time to time in the late colonial period domestic manufacturing was an attractive opportunity for investors. Although it never became the dominant sector, domestic manufacturing apparently competed with foreign imports and exploited domestic markets under conditions that allowed investors to expect some returns. Data from a single decade (1800–1810) may not accurately portray economic conditions or trends. It is worth noting, however, that the amount of money for loans under manufacturing declined in the second quinquennium from the first. The significance of this is not known. To underscore an earlier reference to Thomson, whatever the degree of proto-industrialization around Puebla and across Mexico, it was advancing slowly and unevenly.[11]

Without precise figures the size of the manufacturing sector is a matter of speculation. Humboldt estimated the manufacturing sector to be worth about 7–8 million pesos annually, a figure based on obraje output. In 1810 José María Quirós, secretary of the Consulado of Veracruz, presented a much higher figure of 72 million pesos. Neither of these estimates can be corroborated. Quirós's manufacturing data were calculated by multiplying an estimate of the quantity of product by an estimate of the product's average price with the result, according to Thomson, that Quirós "exaggerated the stake held by manufacturing by including raw material values which properly should belong to agriculture."[12] If all processing were included under manufacturing, the annual value of processing/manufacturing surely amounted to tens of millions of pesos. If a distinction were made, however, then genuine manufacturing may amount to no more than 10 or 15 million pesos.

A narrow definition of manufacturing, along the lines proposed by Salvucci, would probably consist primarily of woolen manufactures. According to figures which he has collected from various sources, the several dozen obrajes produced cloth worth 1–1.5 million pesos, and, he adds, even if the output of the *telares sueltos* (in-home operations) were included, the figure would only be several million pesos.[13] Woolens may have been the core of the manufacturing sector, but since they did not post much growth in output between 1700 and 1800, they cannot have represented a dynamic and expanding sector.

In Guadalajara where a detailed report was prepared, manufacturing was estimated to be worth 10 million pesos, or 40 percent of the economy's total output. According to the survey more than two dozen agricultural and pastoral products were produced in the intendancy, with a total value of about 1.5 million pesos, the largest of which was salt worth about 500,000 pesos, followed by tallow and soap, each worth about 275,000 pesos. These were surely more closely allied to the processing of raw materials on the farm or ranch where they were produced, than to manufacturing.[14]

Of more interest in this respect is the development of a Guadalajaran textile industry, which was valued at more than 1.6 million pesos. Guadalajara had long produced cotton textiles, mostly by Indians who raised much of the cotton in their communities and produced much of the fabric on backstrap looms for local consumption. During the eighteenth century mestizos in the towns and cities assumed control of the weaving business. By the end of the century in the intendancy of Guadalajara (with as many as 450 *fabricantes de algodón* [cotton fabric makers] in the city itself) the production of cotton *mantas* (pieces of cloth) reached nearly one-quarter million, worth an estimated 1.3 million pesos or 80 percent of the total textile industry. Since cotton cloth was seldom produced in obrajes and most of the textile business was in cotton rather than woolen cloth, obrajes may have been far more scarce in Guadalajara than telares sueltos. In his report to the Consulado of Veracruz in 1803, the intendant claimed that the region lacked an obraje, although both Eric Van Young and Salvucci refer to the establishment of obrajes sometime in the late eighteenth or the early nineteenth century.[15] Moreover, the intendant reported that the region lacked the knowledge and equipment to produce fine-quality fabrics, a deficiency that was more pertinent to the woolen industry than the cotton industry. The intendancy still imported textiles, perhaps worth several hundred thousand pesos; it also exported textiles of about equal value. Besides mantas the region produced and presumably exported at least a few shawls, sheets, blankets, and bedspreads.[16] Even though we do not know how many obrajes operated in Guadalajara, we do know that textile manufacturing remained small in scale, with firms having one or two looms. The intendancy had a ready and relatively cheap supply of cotton and wool that could have encouraged the establishment of more large-scale manufacturing operations than actually existed. But labor for these operations, especially for obrajes, was in short supply, and convict labor often had to be used where such operations were attempted. In woolens, at least, Guadalajara's obrajes could not compete with Querétaro's obrajes, in part because of labor constraints.[17]

We have not made any attempt to describe or analyze all the textile centers (either for woolens or cottons) that came into existence during the eighteenth century. Salvucci's research has fairly clearly established that in addition to several dozen obrajes, primarily devoted to woolens, there were hundreds of small operations that concentrated on cotton cloth during the eighteenth century.[18]

The long-term growth of the eighteenth-century textile industry remains unclear not only because of incomplete production data but also because of foreign cloth competition. In particular, the growth of Caribbean trade in British cloth (both wool and cotton) during the second half of the eighteenth century presented a challenge to Mexican producers, whether in the obrajes or in the telares sueltos. Great Britain could not trade directly with Mexico, but because of a flourishing contraband trade, many British fabrics found their way into the Mexican economy. In addition, Spanish cloth makers and exporters took advantage of fewer commercial restrictions to sell as much as they could in Mexico.

The rise in production of silver in Mexico helped to sustain this flood of fabrics and textiles from Europe (including Spain). Salvucci has determined that when compared (that is, the signs of the regressors) "[s]ilver output has a positive sign—the more that it was mined in Mexico, the more printed cottons were exported to the British West Indies. Obraje output has a negative sign—the less wool woven, the more British cottons exported, and vice versa." This is (to use Salvucci's phrase) a "hypothesized relation" between silver and cloth, but it is well worth considering. More silver was produced in the eighteenth century, and yet a concurrent rise in production (or consumption) of domestic cloth did not flow from that increase in silver. Domestic cloth was less competitive, especially with English textiles whose costs may have dropped by as much as 70 percent between 1780 and 1812. English manufacturers produced more cloth at a lower price through mechanization, whereas Mexican manufacturers could only do so by "driving labor harder." Although all Mexican producers may have suffered in competition with the British in particular and the Europeans in general, the obrajes may have suffered the most in that their cost effectiveness depended on forced labor, and because of that they were "rendered . . . increasingly obsolete."[19]

Triumph of Woolens

The textile industry represents the best example of nascent colonial manufacturing.[20] Textile manufacturing, first established in Puebla in the sixteenth century, had spread to the Valley of Mexico, the Bajío, and Nueva Galicia by the eighteenth century. The colony produced both cotton and woolen fabrics, but the system of manufacture differed for the two fabrics. Cotton was produced mainly in the home, in contrast to woolens, which had moved out of the home, first into small shops (*trapiches*) and then into factories (*obrajes*). It was not that obrajes were notably or especially efficient. Rather, in what Salvucci calls an "imperfect" market (i.e., little or no competition from cotton or other textiles), the obraje proved to be effective in the control of those uncertainties arising out of the supply of wool and labor. When cotton became more of a competitor in the late colonial period, the obraje became more of an anachronism. Although inefficient, it was not necessarily irrational because it served a particular purpose at a particular time. It could be viewed as a *protofactory*, because it was "an organizational precursor of the factory that lacked only machinery, yet realized economies of scale." In other respects the obraje defied the application of the term *protofactory*, and its demise demonstrated its disutility. At the end of the colonial period (based on Salvucci's distinction) the cotton industry had yet to develop a system of large-scale production, whereas woolens had created a form that proved to be a dead end.[21]

The Puebla-Tlaxcala region was the main producer of cotton goods. By the eighteenth century, however, Mexico City had a substantial and at times prosperous cotton industry. Mexico City's woolen obrajes (like Puebla's) had lost ground to the competition in Querétaro and other Bajío cities. The production of cotton cloth and fabric in Mexico City differed from that in Puebla and Tlaxcala in that the move toward multiple ownership of looms and the combining of several steps under single owners led to the creation of large-scale facilities instead of in-home operations. In 1797 the capital had more than 350 looms, of which more than half were owned by forty-five master weavers. On average, each master owned about four looms, although one had at least twelve. If the need to raise capital and to improve productivity among woolen manufacturers was a cause of the growth in the obraje, then some cotton producers surely faced the same pressures and opted for similar remedies toward the end of the eighteenth century.[22]

By the eighteenth century most of the manufacture of woolens had been transferred out of the home into shops or obrajes. Woolen facilities had been built in towns and cities from Puebla north to Querétaro and west to Guadalajara, although Querétaro emerged as the woolen manufacturing center in the eighteenth century. In the late seventeenth and early eighteenth centuries the number of obrajes in Querétaro doubled—from six to more than a dozen—and in the first half of the eighteenth century it more than doubled again. By the end of the century, however, the number had dropped to about twenty.

Even though the number of obrajes declined in the second half of the eighteenth century, the remaining obrajes concentrated their control over the operating looms as the number of looms in each obraje rose from 100–150 to nearly 300. The obrajes had some competition from the trapiches, which accounted for 1,000 or more looms, but even so the obrajes still had a capacity five or six times greater than the small shops.[23] The difficulty with these estimates is that the number of looms under the control of the obrajes appears to have increased as the number of obrajes declined. This points to an even greater concentration of looms in obrajes because fewer obrajes were possibly adding looms.

Over the years obrajeros from Querétaro serviced markets beyond the city either by setting up retail outlets or by negotiating with other merchants in the more densely populated Valley of Mexico and similar urban areas.[24] The data on the consumption of wool and the concentration of looms may be linked to the precarious state of the balance sheet in the textile industry. Despite their past dominance and success, Querétaro obrajeros increasingly functioned in a marketplace where prices of some raw materials were rising and, more importantly, where competition from many local trapiches was increasing. Textile manufacturing was not immune from the economic dislocations associated with the frequent, although not always severe, agricultural upheavals nor from inadequate supplies of credit and currency.[25] Many obrajeros constantly confronted cash flow problems. They bought wool on credit and they sold cloth on credit. Since they were not always paid in cash, they did not necessarily have cash to pay off their creditors.[26]

There were other obstacles of an even more fundamental nature to developing a more dynamic textile manufacturing in eighteenth-century Mexico. Few obrajeros (or few colonial entrepreneurs for that matter) were experienced in the task of assessing the risk and uncertainty in establishing new markets and formulating the strategies for exploiting those markets.[27] According to Salvucci, to succeed, Querétaro obrajeros had to become more adept at making decisions about where to buy their wool, how to organize their factories, what to price their product, and where to distribute their cloth. On average, obrajes had 200 workers and an output of 10,000 yards of cloth per year. Size alone forced owners to a level of decision making about how to use resources and workers that small-shop operations seldom faced.[28]

To be profitable a textile factory had to function as an "integrated unit" in which "various stages of manufacture were gathered together" for the purpose of achieving levels of productivity and efficiency that could give it an advantage in the marketplace over the telares sueltos and trapiches. During the eighteenth century Querétaro's obrajeros proved that they could manufacture a product at a price that smaller, local competitors could not match. Even in Puebla, Mexico City, and Tlaxcala, woolen obrajes could not compete with Querétaro because it was more expensive to ship wool from

Querétaro to those places and then manufacture the cloth than to buy finished cloth from Querétaro.[29] Different explanations, all revolving around controlling transaction costs, can be advanced to try to understand why woolen obrajes in Querétaro did better than similar obrajes in other places. Querétaro's success in dominating the woolen-manufacturing market was aided by its location, for "the obrajes of the Bajío were best positioned to capitalize on . . . demographic . . . change and the shift in regional demand that it implied."[30]

An additional factor that favored the Querétaro obrajero over the long term was that wool prices did not rise much during the eighteenth century and may in fact have declined or been flat until the last quarter. Humboldt estimated that each year the obrajes consumed more than 1.5 million pounds of "sheep-wool," or 60,000 arrobas worth about 600,000 pesos. Salvucci offers a modest annual series between 1765 and 1810 that shows consumption of wool between 36,000 and 74,000 arrobas. In this series wool consumption rose and fell in a cyclical pattern but established no discernable or verifiable trend.[31]

Cecilia Rabell Romero has published wool price data (based on tithes) from 1686 to 1804, although the series contains some gaps, especially in the last quarter of the eighteenth century. Wool prices were higher at the end of the colonial period than at the beginning of the eighteenth century, but it is difficult to track them long term with precision. Up to 1777 the curve was flat and perhaps even declining slightly. After that, a gap of twenty years exists in the series before data appear again. If Rabell's data reflect a trend in the Bajío with which Querétaro was economically linked, then a flat price curve for the principal raw material, which accounted for more than 50 percent of the production costs, served to strengthen the hand of the obrajero in the marketplace.[32]

For the last quarter of the eighteenth century wool prices may have started to climb a little. A price series exists for the sale of unfinished wool in Zacatecas. Since some of the wool sold in Zacatecas came from local ranches, it was less affected by transportation and other transactional costs. From 1760 to 1810, with one-third of the years missing, wool prices rose at an annual rate slightly under 1 percent.[33] Rabell's wool prices from San Luis de la Paz, as in Zacatecas, show a slight rise from the late 1790 into the early 1800s. A drought in these northern regions in the early 1790s decimated the herds and may well have caused a slight increase in local wool prices. Up to the late eighteenth century the obrajero in Querétaro could sell his cloth outside of the city at a price less than what local producers had to charge and still cover his costs for wool, labor, and transportation. What a small rise in wool prices might mean for obraje finances is difficult to determine. At a time when competition from cotton manufacturers and foreign importers must have contributed to depressed woolen sales, any change in the obraje's variable costs could have made its products less competitive.

As adaptive as some obrajeros were, the obraje system was coming under increasing stress from other factors even as woolen prices were relatively static. For one thing demographic changes could have further undermined the position of the obrajero during the eighteenth century.[34] Obrajeros functioned in an imperfect market. They could not always use the normal incentives of wages and amenities to hire enough permanent workers. Workers too operated in an imperfect market because they lacked mobility and information, even though they probably had more of both in the late eighteenth century than before. The overall advantage lay with the employer, and yet the labor system in the woolen industry may have evolved to a point where the worker could exercise some leverage. Obrajeros had to resort to slave, apprentice, and peon labor for 40 percent of the labor force in order to supplement free or wage labor because some potential workers simply rejected obraje employment. If workers were hard to recruit or keep, why did employers not raise wages or improve working conditions? In some locations that was probably unnecessary because enough workers were available despite the low wages and harsh working conditions. In Querétaro, which dominated the obraje-manufactured segment of the woolen industry, obrajeros faced labor resistance and yet refused to raise wage compensation. Obrajeros cited two reasons: first, higher wages meant higher costs and that meant a less competitive product; and second, higher wages did not necessarily attract more workers, especially those needed. Concerning the first reason, there is little debate. Obrajeros had long used low wages to compensate for manufacturing inefficiencies. When they could use coercion to avoid paying higher wages, they could retain their market share against their colonial competition. To avoid paying a full wage they could also assign part of the wage of the worker to the truck system (company store). Under the truck system as much as 25–50 percent of the wages were paid in merchandise purchased from the owner or in scrip redeemed by the owner. If part of the wage were based on what the owner determined the merchandise or the scrip was worth, then that wage could be adjusted as needed in order to control costs. But from the owner's view the "whole pay" consisted of the wage, however it was paid, and the value of what the worker pilfered. The effective daily wage was probably higher than 1.5–4 reales (in cash and merchandise or scrip) if the pilfering is accounted for. Too little is known to say whether the worker was able to steal enough to make up for any adjustment in his "whole pay" through the company store. The second reason, that obrajeros believed that workers did not need more because they could not really spend more, is less likely to have been accurate, given that bare subsistence was so widespread in the late colonial society and often limited economic choice. Was this reason a rationalization offered by employers who did not want to pay higher wages or perhaps could not afford to pay higher wages? Or was it an explanation based on accurate observations of how workers behaved within the late colonial economy? How much the worker needed to survive, and how the worker would have spent what he did not yet have, remain elusive questions. How much the employer truly understood about what the worker needed and anticipated is equally difficult to pinpoint.[35] In broad economic terms, however, to continue to coerce workers made it difficult to ascertain the true worth of the obraje product as well as to intensify the development of a more dynamic and diverse consumer market that might have led to other structural changes.

The matter of the worker and the obraje is further confounded by the fact that the population in most urban areas was increasing and this increase alone should have strengthened the hand of the obrajeros in determining wage levels and working conditions. On the other hand, changing demographic and economic patterns around Querétaro and other obraje towns may also have began to work to the disadvantage of the obrajero, whatever his views about the workplace and the wage system. One unexpected consequence of eighteenth-century population growth was that with more potential workers, small producers like trapiches could add to their in-home work force without significantly raising their costs or cutting their profits. A further advantage enjoyed by the trapiches was that they could more easily switch to lighter woolens or to cottons as the demand for the latter increased.[36] Until the latter half of the eighteenth century, obrajeros in Querétaro enjoyed certain economies of scale over other large- and small-scale producers, but after that the competition from within and from outside the colony made substantial inroads.[37]

The rise of Querétaro as a textile center in the eighteenth century came at some cost to other regions. And conversely the decline or at least the stagnation that Querétaro experienced in the century's late decades benefited its competitors. One region that had suffered at the hands of the Querétaro obrajes was Mexico City and the surrounding valley. In 1798 "a partial listing" revealed at least thirteen obrajeros but with relatively small and fairly heavily encumbered plants in the capital.[38] That number did not change much over the course of the century. In Querétaro, according to Salvucci, "liquidity rather than solvency was the principal problem," and obrajeros who could arrange for financial backing to see them through the time from purchasing the wool to selling the cloth had the best chance of success. As in mining (and perhaps other fields), an "extended kin group" was one way to find a degree of financial stability and protection. But even this was not always enough to prevent the sale or liquidation of obrajes whose owners failed as cloth manufacturers or simply sold out to pursue other opportunities.

Obrajes could make money. In Panzacola, a large Mexico City obraje under the Vértiz family for nearly a century, the return on equity was between 3.5 and 5 percent, with profits in the range of 5,000–7,000 pesos each year for three years between 1802 and 1805.[39] These figures compare favorably to those for some large agricultural enterprises, the only other sector for which we have precise data; although gross profits from mining could be enormous, the rate of return on capital invested often cannot be accurately calculated.[40] A rate of return in the range of 5 percent may well have become the standard for late colonial businesses in manufacturing, agriculture, and even mining, although the potential was much greater in mining than in the other two fields. What needs to be studied more thoroughly in light of so many marginal if not insolvent businesses is whether 5 percent was enough to carry the economy into the next phase of expansion and development.

Finding workers was as much a problem in Mexico City as in other textile centers, and owners used various strategies including petitions to the court to assign "delinquent and idle youths" to work in the obrajes, technically as apprentices. Hiring and holding workers may have grown increasingly serious during the eighteenth century as the size of the work force in the average obraje climbed from around fifty to perhaps twice that number. Some Valley of Mexico obrajes may have reached 200 or slightly more workers, but none, it would appear, ever reached the size of the largest obrajes in the Bajío or around Puebla. The problem in the capital as in other cities was that except for weavers, obraje wages were lower than a day laborer's wage and working conditions were probably worse.

Salvucci notes that even though wages in Querétaro and the capital were comparable, 1–4 reales per day, Querétaro had evolved a labor system based on debt and peonage, whereas Mexico City had a system that depended on debt but without peonage.[41] At least one owner of a Mexico City obraje testified that peonage did not work very well because workers with debts were relatively free to leave their jobs without paying their debts. His workers owed him 4,000 pesos, but a combination of government intervention and worker mobility made it unlikely that he would collect what he was owed.[42] What this meant was that the labor system in Mexico City obrajes was less coercive than in Querétaro. Being in debt in the capital did not mean being "a captive" of the employer.

Salvucci found that among Mexico City's obrajes the average debt of the individual worker did not become abnormally high. Indeed the owners themselves may have contributed to the creation of a less rigid linkage between indebtedness and peonage. When times were prosperous some owners were known to boost advances to workers and then not to deduct those advances later from their workers' wages. When the economy turned sour the owners were not only forced to release workers but also to "excuse" them from paying off their debts because workers lacked the wherewithal to do so. Letting workers go, of course, is different from having workers decide to leave. It may be that in bad times obrajeros everywhere had to let workers go, but in good times some obrajeros used cash incentives, such as advances, rather than coercion and enslavement.[43]

For part and perhaps even most of the eighteenth century, obrajeros in Querétaro were more successful that their counterparts in Mexico City, who may have seen less need or had less latitude to coerce workers. So long as Querétaro could contain the cost of labor more effectively than other regions, like Mexico City, it could compete effectively. But the growth in population eventually eroded the power of the obraje, even in Querétaro, to remain competitive even with coercion because it was possible for small producers to hire enough workers to raise their output but not necessarily their per unit cost. The opportunity arose for the small producer to operate at a scale that allowed him to compete with increasing success against the obrajes.

Competition from Cottons

The growth in competition from cottons also adversely affected the obrajes. During the second half of the eighteenth century Puebla, which had lost out to Querétaro in woolen production, saw its cloth manufacturing sector improve at the expense of its long-time Bajío competitor. Thomson has traced the development of cotton manufacturing around Puebla (including the cities of Cholula, Huejozingo, and Tlaxcala) during the eighteenth century.[44] Cotton textile manufacturing was not confined to the Puebla region, and by the end of the century it was well established in Oaxaca, Valladolid, Guadalajara, and Mexico City. Puebla gained some advantage because of its proximity to cotton growers along the Atlantic and Pacific coastal areas within the Puebla district. In addition, though, "[t]he cotton textile industry," writes Thomson, "proved particularly well suited to the peculiarities of the region, merchant capital and enterprise linking an independent and culturally distinct creole artisanate to a dependent Indian labour force, providing a solution to the problem of subsistence of this growing Spanish and mestizo population and of the demographically fertile yet disease-ravaged Indian population."[45]

The merchant community became involved as investors, middlemen, and retailers, but seldom did it enter the production side of cotton cloth manufacturing. Merchants preferred a "cash relationship over a putting-out system," but in spite of that preference their greater involvement meant their greater control over raw and spun cotton. As this network evolved, the merchants as the middlemen (*algodoneros* and *regatones de algodón*) assumed a powerful role in the Pueblan cotton industry, eroding the economic and social status of the weavers themselves. In a city where 20 percent of the population may have been employed in textile manufacturing, the merchants created the mechanism that joined the disparate parts of the industry from the production of cotton to the sale of the fabric.[46]

The extensive role of mercantile capital and management did not ultimately lead to mechanization. The cotton guild in Puebla strongly resisted such a change because they believed it would only reinforce the political and economic instability that already existed in the late colonial decades. The "unstable economic conditions and the general poverty which had nurtured the early growth of the industry during the first half of the eighteenth century also account for its survival in a traditional form over the first thirty years of the nineteenth century." The traditional approach survived even after independence because it required less "fixed capital investment" than a mechanized system and it could also function with a "flexible and subsistence" labor force. The producer, namely the weaver, never completely lost control over his operation to the merchant. But even though he continued to produce the cloth, he became more dependent on the merchant for the credit that he needed to purchase his raw materials and to market his finished goods. What merchants did for cotton cloth producers was what they had done for miners and refiners in the form of *avíos* (credits) for more than a century. Carlos Chávez, a Puebla cloth dealer and retailer, illustrates how extensive the role of a merchant could be. During the early nineteenth century he had advanced credit to "360 individuals in over fifty towns, villages, and haciendas stretching from Tabasco in the southeast to León, Lagos and Silao in the Bajío" in amounts from a few pesos to thousands of pesos. His business, like so many other cloth dealers, dealt in both domestic and foreign textiles, for to specialize in one or the other was unwise given the uncertainty of the economy.[47]

The presence of wholesalers and brokers from Veracruz, Mexico City, and Oaxaca, no matter how important they were to local commerce, did not win universal approval. The guild of weavers in Tlaxcala complained loudly that the outsiders had created a "lamentable" economic situation for the local membership. The feud between the *gremio* (guild) and the outsiders, so typical of what the economic reforms and changes could generate, endured from the middle to the end of the eighteenth century. In 1744 and again in 1747 Viceroy Conde de Fuenclara issued *cédulas* (decrees) that upheld the "ancient laws" that protected the gremio. It was lamentable, complained the gremio, that outsiders bought up so much of the local cotton output in the nearby towns and villages that little was left to be sold by Tlaxcala's gremio, or more specifically its officers, who had controlled the trade for many years. Consequently, both the city's weavers and its retailers, who sold what weavers brought to Tlaxcala, suffered great economic hardship. Not even the eighteen or twenty master weavers could afford any longer to pay the high prices that resulted from the competition for fiber, thread, and fabric. There was no evidence that the Tlaxcalan gremio was ever able to block or limit penetration of its traditional economic domain by outside interests, who were better equipped than the gremio to advance credit and to market cotton.[48]

A merchant's investment in cotton cloth production could only yield a profit if he could find a market for his product. Finding that market was crucial to the weavers (and other employees) as well because their livelihood was linked to how many orders the merchant placed with them, and how much credit he was willing to give. The market appeared to be growing in the late eighteenth century. Thomson provides some figures on the amount of cloth from Puebla that entered Mexico City's *aduana* (customs house). The growth was erratic; the volume nearly doubled between 1785 and 1801, after which it turned down until it was no greater than the 1785 volume.[49]

Most of the cotton cloth from Puebla passed through Mexico City, but its final destination was the areas where the manufacture of textiles was more limited, often northern silver cities. Other cities beside Puebla had developed a cotton textile industry, so that Puebla's cloth was only part of the total domestic output. The recurrent hostilities in the Atlantic world during the late eighteenth and early nineteenth centuries that made European supplies less dependable probably helped to boost domestic production. The basic change that favored the growth in cloth made of cotton was a preference by the consumer for lighter fabrics over heavier, costlier woolens. Even some cloth (Puebla *rebozos*) was being exported. The growth of cotton cloth production in Puebla, and perhaps elsewhere, did not involve the creation of obrajes, although toward the end of the eighteenth century the influence of cotton merchants and brokers helped to push the industry toward greater consolidation. But it was not ever strong enough to transform an industry of small production units into a modern manufacturing sector, at least during the colonial period.[50]

An occupational profile, based on a 1791 military census, shows the influence of the expanding textile industry in and around Puebla. With a total of more than 10,000 workers in Puebla and three adjacent rural districts, more than 2,500 were employed in businesses broadly defined as textile manufacturing, from cloth making to dress making. If metal-, wood-, and leather-working are included as a part of the manufacturing sector, then 30 percent (rather than 25 percent) of the total work force belonged to this sector. Agriculture, with slightly more than one-quarter, was the next largest sector. Both transportation and trade, as Thomson stresses, had large numbers. When compared to other cities Puebla apparently had a more diversified economy that affected the evolution of the social structure as well. Thomson writes that Puebla contained "a larger middle sector, with its economic core composed of manufacturers, artisans and shopkeepers, living decently and enjoying considerable political influence." He also contends that below the middle class was "a plebian artisan class—engaged in similar occupations to those of the middle class, aspiring to achieve its independence and respectability, but failing [over time] in the face of uncertainty and instability which threatened to submerge its members within the city's large 'underclass.' "[51] Thomson's analysis, it must be pointed out, is shaped by what happened to the economy and society (with greater emphasis on the latter than the former) in the half century after the colonial period. Before Puebla found itself caught up in the independence struggle, it may have reached a point of stagnation in its own economic development. The merchants and, to a more limited degree, the spinners and the weavers failed to anticipate or to initiate the next step of mechanizing both the spinning of cotton and weaving of cloth.[52]

The Atlantic Commercial System

In the absence of a large manufacturing sector Mexico had to depend on imports to satisfy its needs. Since it had few raw materials or finished products to sell, it balanced its foreign accounts with silver. Some have argued (most recently Thomson) that silver mining (in particular the eighteenth-century boom) skewed the economic outlook in favor of the extractive industries and away from product-based enterprises. Without silver, or with less of it, Mexico's economy would have had to pursue a different course. Silver mining allowed the Crown to impose a form of mercantilism that had the effect of limiting the development of manufacturing.

In statistical terms we can see the effect of the amount of silver produced and the amount of silver exported to Europe. Using Michel Morineau's figures for silver exports arriving in Europe and our figures for silver registrations, we have found that for every 10 percent change in output there was a 6.2 percent change in exports. Presumably most of the exported bullion paid for imported merchandise, although some of the bullion belonged to the Crown. Still, the relationship between bullion exports and bullion arrivals is highly elastic, a finding that confirms what we have known from other sources.[53]

What silver did was to make the cost of transacting business over long distances affordable, regardless of how efficient such activity was. Goods that had a narrow market but a high cost were conspicuously represented among the colonial imports. The economic issues that need to be investigated are whether the outflow of silver to cover imports not only denied the colony the use of its own wealth but also gained the colony little that could be used to broaden its own economic base.

Long series of eighteenth-century foreign trade statistics do not yet exist. Even without them, however, we can propose a general outline of how Mexico's import-export sector developed in the eighteenth century. In the sixteenth century Mexico relied on imports to supply basic commodities, manufactured goods, and luxury items. As the colony's agricultural economy grew, however, its import trade became identified with costly fabrics, liquor, spices, and furniture. How much the import business was worth during the colonial period can only be roughly estimated. Between 1580 and 1700 TePaske and Klein have calculated that Mexico exported bullion or coin in the king's account worth 100 million pesos, for an annual average of 800,000–900,000 pesos. In the eighteenth century currency exports to cover private transactions (private or individual accounts) were seven to eight times greater than the Crown's exports. If a similar ratio prevailed in the seventeenth century and even earlier in the sixteenth century, then bullion or currency exports to discharge private balances could have ranged from 5 to 10 million pesos annually.[54]

For the eighteenth century several series, based on currency exports to cover private transactions, can be studied for possible trends in trade between Spain and the colonies. One series, developed for the period 1717–1796, shows that shipments of gold and silver by private individuals to Spain grew by 2.2 percent per year.[55] These figures are not broken down by colony, and although we can assume that Mexico was the leading exporter of gold and silver coins, we can only speculate that Mexico's currency-export curve duplicated Spain's currency-import curve. It is worth noting, however, that the shipment of currency by private citizens grew almost twice as fast as the growth in silver output from colonial mines.[56] For the late eighteenth century when figures exist for the export of currency from Mexico specifically, we can also note that exports grew faster than silver registrations, which at the time were higher than they had ever been.[57] It is likely, therefore, that over the course of the century currency exports from Mexico to Spain, primarily to pay for imports, rose in the range of 2 percent annually. The currency-export curve from the colonial side (or the currency-import curve from the Spanish side) oscillated throughout the century, but the curve's upward movement probably peaked around 1780, after which it leveled off or perhaps declined slightly. The cause of this shift could have resulted from several factors: a saturation of colonial markets with imported goods that caused a drop in prices; an increase in contraband trade that did not show up in the official statistics; and a slowdown in silver production that reduced the demand for such goods. In addition, recurrent European wars had an impact on the movement of trade across the Atlantic, with dips in currency shipments resulting from interruptions in that trade and peaks resulting from resumptions in that trade. All the data collected thus far for the last quarter of the eighteenth century demonstrate that while the volume of exports of merchandise, both foreign and Spanish, from Spain to the colonies moved up and down, the trend was virtually flat. Moreover, when the volume for the last quarter is compared to the third quarter, little if any growth can be detected.[58]

Although eighteenth-century trends in commerce between Spain and Mexico remain unclear, trends during the second half of the century can be studied more precisely. Some figures for individual years—1761, 1763, 1766, and 1770—show that a total of 50.9 million pesos were exported from Mexico and that 42.8 million pesos (84 percent) were to cover private sales. Although private account exports for those four years averaged 10.7 million pesos, the amount actually doubled from 7.7 million to 15.8 million pesos between 1761 and 1770. Part of the increase may be attributable to the high prices charged for the imported goods, but most of the increase probably resulted from the restoration of the Atlantic commerce after the Treaty of Paris in 1763.[59]

What we can compare is the growth in foreign imports (as measured by currency exports) to the growth of silver registrations. For the period 1752–71 a total figure (225 million pesos) exists for both private and public accounts, and if private transfers amounted to 80–85 percent, then the annual average over the entire period was 9–10 million pesos, or comparable to the average for the decade of the 1760s.[60] During the same period the mint coined about 12 million pesos per year. The equivalent of three of every four newly minted silver pesos was required to cover all private account transfers.[61] Without an expanding silver industry Veracruz could hardly have become the "most important destination" for Spanish exports in the late eighteenth century.[62]

Even though the "Reglamento y aranceles reales para el comercio libre de España a Indias de 12 de October de 1778" ushered in an era of *freer* trade between Spain and the colonies, it was not extended to Mexico until 1789.[63] The Reglamento was a codification of earlier decrees concerning commercial privileges, and the *Aranceles* was a list of prices (where applicable) for all Spanish and foreign goods shipped to the colonies and the duties that they would pay. The Aranceles listed many different products, some of which were hardly ever imported and some of which were regularly imported. Under the letter C in the first schedule more than fifty Spanish or foreign products are listed, and of this single group more than half were quilts, belts, cloth, and fabric. One-fifth were foods, ranging from coffee to prunes, chestnuts to honey. The remainder were various items for the home or shop, such as crystal, bolts, nails, quills, and glue.[64]

When José Ortiz de la Tabla Ducasse examined what he called the "structure of imports from Spain" at Veracruz from 1802 to 1812, he calculated that textiles amounted to 48.7 percent; wine and liquor, 20.6 percent; paper, 15.1 percent; metal, 5.3 percent; with the remaining 10.2 percent miscellaneous.[65] More research and analysis of the import trade in eighteenth-century Mexico are needed, but these few indicators point to a structure heavily weighted toward costly consumer goods that had little impact in broadening or diversifying the colonial economy.

The commercial reforms, as important as they were, did not result in the sustained economic growth that their advocates had envisioned. Although designed to provide, in John Fisher's words, "a combination of freedom and protection which would promote the settlement of empty territory, eliminate contraband trade, generate increased customs revenues as an expanded volume of trade compensated for the reduction in the rates of duties and, above all, develop the empire as a market for Spanish products and a source of materials for Spanish industry," the reforms surely fell short of their intended goals.[66] The reasons arise from both economic and military considerations.

In the last quarter of the eighteenth century the export trade between Spain and the colony did not show any significant growth in the long term in spite of a higher than ever silver curve. Clearly, there was a limit to what the colony could spend on imports both foreign and Spanish. As Spain's biggest customer, Mexico bought one-third or more (on average worth 6–7 million pesos per year) of the merchandise exported from the peninsula, although that figure varied sharply from year to year. Cádiz handled most of the trade before 1789, and as much as 75–80 percent of it after 1789. Exports from Cádiz to Mexico declined by 3.2 percent annually (82 percent confidence level) between 1785 and 1796, while exports from Cádiz to all Spanish America dropped 3.4 percent (87 percent confidence level). The commercial link between Cádiz and Veracruz was more complicated than the negative growth rate suggests. Between 1785 and 1792 exports from Cádiz to Veracruz rose sharply (at an annual rate perhaps as high as 5 percent), after which they dropped precipitously until 1796.[67] The end of hostilities between Great Britain and the United States may account for part of the growth in exports during the 1780s, although that growth eventually created a glut of goods in Veracruz and a loss of profits in Cádiz. The Consulado of Cádiz called for embargoes, first of foreign goods and then of national goods, to correct the oversupply and to restore profits, but the Crown refused. Instead of embargoes the Crown extended "free-trade" status to Veracruz, after a delay of a decade, in an attempt to let the marketplace set the volume of imports and thereby the level of profits. In the early 1790s the deterioration in relations between Spain and France (that included the expulsion of French merchants from Cádiz) began to affect trade between Cádiz and Veracruz adversely. A harder question to answer is how the new competition among the Spanish ports affected trade between Cádiz and Veracruz in 1785–96. The impact may well have been minimal, although it cannot be measured yet with precise figures. Fisher's data show that exports from all the Spanish ports permitted to trade with the Spanish colonies rose until the middle 1780s, and then declined, albeit in an irregular fashion, until the middle 1790s.[68]

The commercial reforms did not unleash any long-term growth in exports from Spain to Spanish America in general or to Mexico in particular. Another consideration that might explain the downward movement of the export trade from the mid-1780s to the mid-1790s was the drain of currency from Mexico to pay for more contraband trade and public account transfers.

The other side of Mexico's international trade equation was the extent to which the promulgation of free-trade policies and other commercial reforms stimulated the export of merchandise from the colony within and beyond the empire. From 1778 through 1796 the value of all goods exported from the colonies to Spain, including gold and silver to cover foreign purchases and treasury transfers (especially tobacco income), increased sevenfold. The series is possibly distorted for two reasons: lack of data from 1778 and 1782; and relatively low export figures for the years 1778, 1782, and 1783 because of war-induced disruptions. From 1784 (when war was no longer a factor), to 1796, colonial exports to Spain rose by slightly more than twofold, although a trend as such cannot be verified. Although exports of merchandise were growing, perhaps by 9–12 percent per year, they were still overshadowed by exports of currency to cover overseas purchases and royal transfers that rose at an annual rate of at least 20 percent per year. In total value the merchandise export accounts each year were small, that is, in millions of pesos, relative to the private and public transfers of currency in tens of millions of pesos.

Within the merchandise category for all Spanish America, indigo and sugar exports experienced the strongest annual growth of 22.0 percent and 20.4 percent, respectively. *Cascarilla* (Peruvian bark) followed the clearest downward trend, perhaps by as much as 24 percent annually.[69] Merchandise export categories are not yet available by colony. Not surprisingly, as Mexico imported more from Spain than any other colony, it also exported more. Spain accounted for 35–40 percent of the total colonial export trade (currency and merchandise). According to Fisher, Veracruz's share of exports to Spain between 1782 and 1796 rose from about 5 to 25 million pesos per year, an annual rate of 13.7 percent.[70] Among its exports were cochineal and other dyestuffs, but far and away the largest item of export was silver. Without silver Mexico could hardly have maintained the level of import trade on the basis the volume of export trade.

For the period 1796–1810 we must turn to a different set of trade statistics.[71] It is unfortunate that Fisher's data cannot be linked up with Lerdo de Tejada's data to provide a long series for the last quarter of the eighteenth century and the first quarter of the nineteenth century. The differences in the series cannot be easily reconciled. In 1796, the only year that the two series overlap, Fisher's exports from Cádiz to Veracruz are 50 percent lower than Lerdo de Tejada's imports from Spain into Mexico. The data on Spanish exports to Veracruz from Cádiz concern shipments in official values, based on the Aranceles of 1778, while the data on Spanish imports at Veracruz cover shipments in current values from all Spanish ports. When the two data sets are compared, however, they reveal that the trend in the export trade between Spain and Mexico changed in a way that transcended the intrinsic differences in the datasets. Fisher's series indicates that export trade between Cádiz and Veracruz (and presumably Spain and Mexico) declined between 1785 and 1796, whereas Lerdo de Tejada's series suggests that trade climbed from 1796 to 1810. Lerdo de Tejada's detailed statistics on imports at Veracruz, whatever the trends, deserve scrutiny.

His figures are divided into three broad categories that include both exports from and imports into Veracruz: trade with Spain (on the import side, that means both Spanish and non-Spanish goods); trade with foreign countries (only a brief period in the early 1800s); and trade with America. The total value of Veracruz's imports and exports between 1796 and 1820 was 540 million pesos. Trade with Spain amounted to 71.4 percent, with foreigners 10.1 percent, and with America 18.5 percent.[72] Exports (including private and royal currency transfers) added up to 51.8 percent and imports to 48.2 percent. On average, Veracruz exported nearly 12 million pesos more to Spain than it imported from Spain and exported nearly 11 million pesos more to foreigners than it imported from them. In the category *Comercio de América*, however, Veracruz imported just under 2 million more pesos than it exported.

These accounts pose several problems. Although they concern mainly private transactions, they also include treasury transactions that cannot be sorted easily from the private ones. In addition, the notes that accompany the accounts reveal that large but imprecisely specified government monies were not included in the accounts themselves. For example, in 1802 the accounts show that Veracruz handled about 60.5 million pesos worth of private-sector business, but the notes also reveal that Veracruz handled another 21 million pesos worth of transfers for the government, some of which may have involved goods purchased from the private sector.[73] A further problem is that although the accounts show currency being exported, presumably to pay for imports, they do not contain currency exports that match up year to year with merchandise imports, and they do not contain currency imports to pay for Mexico's merchandise exports. Despite these and other problems, some useful trends can be detected. Until independence in 1821 the commerce (imports plus exports) through Veracruz could have risen by 2–3 percent per year.[74]

Not surprisingly, the upward movement peaked in 1809–10 when the insurgency began. Between 1796 and 1810, however, the trend for total commerce was generally but irregularly upward at a rate that could have been as high as 11 percent per annum.[75] After 1810 trade fell off sharply from 36.3 million pesos to 21.2 million pesos in 1811, and for the next decade it stayed in the range of 18–20 million pesos per year. The period from 1796 to 1810 was an extraordinary time in the Spanish Empire, from the British blockade of the Spanish peninsula to the brief suspension of commercial restrictions against foreign merchants, and this activity affected trade patterns and therefore growth rates.

The examination of the separate categories of commerce sheds further light on the changing character of the imperial economy. *Comercio de España* totaled 380–385 million pesos between 1796 and 1821, but 260 million pesos (or two-thirds) of those transactions were completed before 1810. In fact, there was little activity between 1804 and 1808 when foreign merchants (*Comercio de Extranjeros*) dominated the merchandise import trade in Veracruz. Although both national and foreign imports from Spain to Veracruz rose between 1796 and 1810, the growth in foreign imports was faster than the growth in national imports. In this period of blockades, wars, and other disruptions the capacity of Spain to supply its colonies was greatly diminished. Contraband took up part of the slack as a result of Spain's incapacity, and registered foreign imports took up another part.

Although the export of merchandise from Mexico to Spain was also rising, its value was not more than one-quarter of the value of imports from 1796 to 1810. In the absence of a large business in export of merchandise from Veracruz to Spain to counterbalance the imports, one would expect currency exports to climb sharply, and they did at a monumental rate of 25.4 percent (91 percent confidence level).[76] Currency exports grew faster than merchandise imports because they included payments for goods, government transfers, and shipments for citizens. On the export side, Mexico's two chief products were sugar and cochineal, and while cochineal exports grew in the decade before 1810, sugar exports probably did not.

In addition to trade in national and foreign goods between Mexico and Spain, Mexico traded with other Spanish colonies. Comercio de América accounted for about one-fifth of the total commerce at Veracruz. Since the ratio of imports to exports in the Comercio de América was about the same (4–5:1) as it was in the Comercios de España and Extranjeros, the difference there also had to be made up through bullion exports.

The pattern of trade at Veracruz between 1796 and 1810 presents a somewhat more complicated picture than previously assumed. When all three categories—Spanish, foreign, and American—are combined, the result shows that the total merchandise trade grew rapidly during the period 1796–1810 in spite of the hostilities between England and Spain. The hostilities may have had some impact, however. Even though overall growth in commerce at Veracruz was high, it was twice as fast from 1805 to 1810 as from 1796 to 1804.[77] To cover the imbalance in the merchandise accounts, currency exports by private citizens also grew rapidly from 1796 to 1810, with faster growth after 1805 than before.

Flotas, Fairs, and Consulados

During the eighteenth century the Atlantic economy underwent large structural changes as the volume of products grew and the competition among traders intensified.[78] Long-established, state-sponsored commercial monopolies, such as Spain's system of annual fleets and commercial guilds, began to crack apart under the pressure to accommodate these changes. With a rising silver curve Mexico became a dual battleground on which Spaniards who wanted to protect the old system were pitted against those who wanted to replace it, and Spaniards were pitted against foreigners. The sheer volume of merchandise for sale overcame the resistance or inertia that often accompanied such developments. In the early eighteenth century, even before many commercial reforms had been implemented, Mexico was being flooded with merchandise that left the *flotistas* (Spanish fleet shippers) and the Consulado struggling to find buyers and make profits.[79] Overstocking became a common feature of the import business during the century, with the result that the conduct of trade and the structure that supported it had to be modified.

The import trade was organized in several different ways before the advent of free-trade regulations in the last quarter of the eighteenth century. Under the fleet system, the merchandise (usually several thousand tons) from the Spanish convoy could be sold in Veracruz or shipped to and sold in Jalapa, where a fleet fair was authorized. Since fewer than twenty fleets sailed between 1700 and 1778, merchandise arrived on special-registry ships during the intervening years.

In a 1750 *informe* (report) the Consulado spelled out its objections to these uncertain and changing circumstances. The report underscored not only the causes of the present crisis but also the barriers to the future restoration of the Atlantic monopoly. It cited, for example, the importation of Oriental silk through Acapulco as the first step toward the gradual dismantling of the fabric trade between Mexico and Spain. Such action reduced the demand for Spanish fabrics, with a loss of thousands of jobs in Spain and millions of pesos in business at Valencia, Murcia, Jaen, and Seville. But the Consulado was also concerned that the cheaper Far Eastern imported fabrics would encourage colonial cloth and clothing producers to substitute Manila fabrics for Spanish fabrics. The informe speculated that any number of the 140–50 woolen producers in Querétaro, Cholula, and Mexico City could lose business to the silk manufacturers, although it failed to demonstrate that such a shift from wool to silk clothing had started or was imminent. In reality, the Consulado cared little for the domestic cloth manufacturers, who were in technical violation of prohibitions against any form of manufacturing. But they were preferable to the "idolators," or those who dealt in fabric and cloth from the Far East. The Consulado demanded that the Far Eastern silk trade be stopped to prevent any further temptation to Mexicans to expand their domestic fabric and cloth trade at great cost to Spanish businesses. The Consulado, dominated as it was by *peninsulares* (colonists born in Spain), identified its own economic interests with the Crown's economic needs, which the Consulado said were best met through the restoration of the commercial monopoly. Although the informe was a protest specifically against an earlier (1732) relaxation in the commercial monopoly, it was also an attempt to warn all those who benefited from the monopoly of the potentially adverse consequences.[80]

Even among import-export merchants there were disagreements. For example, the Mexico City Consulado objected to the activities of the flotistas, who were members of the Seville or Cádiz Consulado and were licensed to sell their merchandise at a fair in Jalapa (beyond Veracruz toward Mexico City), usually held after the arrival of the fleet. The flotistas did most of their business with merchants from the Consulado in Mexico City, but they could also sell any remaining inventory to merchants and shopkeepers outside the guild or directly to consumers. The law required that the flotistas maintain two price lists: one for consulado merchants, who would then resell the merchandise, and a second, which was higher, for non-consulado members. Adherence to the pricing policies was essential in order to preserve the consulado's authority over the colony's international commerce.[81]

Among other things, flotistas were forbidden to conduct business beyond the month designated for the fair or to travel to other fairs and cities to sell their merchandise. Mexico's Consulado complained, however, that the flotistas were not living up to the agreement. Not only did they charge all buyers the same prices (to the disadvantage of the Consulado) but they also carried on business throughout the year in Jalapa and other places. The Mexican Consulado made a veiled threat that damage to its financial interests could affect other colonial organizations like monasteries, *obras pías* (religious foundations), and charitable foundations, who depended on donations of time and money by its members. The violations of the rules and the threats to the foundations, notwithstanding, from at least the 1740s on the flotistas had more to sell than the colonial market could absorb.

The flotistas and the Consulado, who had been and should have continued to be allies, came into conflict because as competition in the Atlantic economy began to intensify their positions began to diverge. Despite the conflict and even as new consulados were being formed, Mexico's Consulado both proved tenacious in the defense of its prerogatives and adaptable in pursuing its goals.[82]

The fair at Jalapa combined the old and the new. With rules governing access, prices, credit, and deliveries the fair can be seen as perpetuating the old system of regulated markets. But at the same time the establishment of the fair itself, the admittance of flotistas to the colony, and the competition for sales among flotistas indicated that the system was opening up. Before the fair, flotistas sold their goods from ships anchored in the harbor at Veracruz. Once on land, even though they were not supposed to leave Jalapa, they certainly had easier access to the internal colonial market and posed a greater threat to Mexico's Consulado. Since the consulado merchants controlled most of the circulating specie that was the standard currency at Jalapa, they should have had a distinct advantage in dealing with the flotistas over other buyers. But the flotistas had far more to sell than the consulado merchants could or would buy, and, therefore, they were forced to accept whatever terms they could arrange with peddlers, petty merchants, and retailers to move their merchandise.[83]

In 1736 an alcalde from Jalapa reported that coins worth 3.6 million pesos were registered by merchants from Puebla, Mexico City, and other cities between 15 July and 1 September. Business was much slower than the flotistas had expected. With merchandise worth 8.2 million pesos to sell, the flotistas sold only 2.7 million pesos worth in 1737. Limited demand along with high fixed prices created large unsold inventories (5.5 million pesos worth) that flotistas had to clear out by negotiating with buyers not necessarily accredited to do business at Jalapa. Two years later (in May 1737) they finally sold off all the remaining merchandise.[84]

In 1758 and 1761 the Jalapa fairs were as controversial as earlier ones. Technically the 1758 fair was a continuation of the 1757 fair that opened after the arrival of the fleet in the spring of 1757.[85] In April twenty-five flotistas were licensed to sell what was left of the 1757 inventories, and by October twenty were still in business. Among the twenty on the list in October were three names that did not appear on the April list. Although no explanation was given, one possibility (that concerned the Consulado) was that traders, who did not qualify as flotistas, had gained licenses to sell in Jalapa. Mexican merchants complained that Spanish merchants violated regulations by selling merchandise directly to consumers in competition with the Consulado.

Flotistas had introduced a huge volume—54,612 bundles with a value of 16.0 million pesos, and by April 1758 they still had 2.6 million pesos worth to sell.[86] Between April and October 1758 the flotistas sold another million pesos worth of goods, so that the balance of the unsold inventory from the 1757 fair was 1.5 million pesos.

The individual inventories of the merchants registered at Jalapa in April and October illustrate why the Consulado complained. Spanish merchants could use unsold inventories as a cover at Jalapa to make other deals that brought them added business. At the top of the list in April were Francisco de Montes, whose inventory was 380,000 pesos, or 14.6 percent of the total, and Juan Batista Costa, whose inventory was 290,000 pesos, or 11.1 percent. By October they had reduced their inventories—Montes's fell to 58,396 pesos, or 3.9 percent of the October total, and Costa's to 109,600 pesos, or 7.3 percent. It appears, at least, that they were legitimately trying to reduce their unsold merchandise, although that cannot be verified. At the top of the list in October was José Belio, whose inventory had only dropped slightly from 240,000 pesos to 196,000 pesos as his share of the total had risen from 9.2 percent in April to 13.1 percent in October. In contrast to Montes, Costa, and Belio, however, Valentín de Otaola reported a fivefold increase in his inventory between April and October, from 37,935 pesos to 187,972 pesos (his share had jumped from 1.5 percent to 12.5 percent in the six months). Similarly, Juan Martín de Aguirre with 163,480 pesos in October had doubled his inventory of 80,000 pesos in April (from 3.1 percent to 10.9 percent). These figures raise questions rather than provide answers: Had the flotistas misstated or misrepresented their inventories in either April or October? Had they bought out other flotistas in the intervening half year? Or had they added to their original inventories domestic products that they attempted to sell in October? Whatever the explanation, in Jalapa, even a year after the fair, there was still merchandise to sell.[87]

A larger fair was organized around the arrival of the fleet in the fall of 1760. The colony was already well supplied with foreign goods. In addition, the French and Indian War (Seven Years' War) caused money to be diverted from commercial activities to military enterprises. In granting the flotistas permission to extend the fair through April 1762 the government was recognizing that a crisis had developed. A year after the fair the unsold inventories remained a staggering 14.1 million pesos. The total worth of the merchandise in the fair of 1760 was not stated in the survey, but it was surely greater than the 1757 fair inasmuch as the fleet delivered nearly 8,500 tons of merchandise in 1760 compared to 7,000 tons in 1757.

The economic plight faced by the commercial sector can be seen in the list of at least seventy-five flotistas (probably more if all the partners and associates had been enumerated) with unsold stocks. Nearly fifty of them had inventories in excess of 100,000 pesos. This was not a new experience for all of them, since perhaps a dozen and one-half of the names also appeared on the April and October lists of 1758. At the top of the list, Francisco de Herrasti y Ysturiz had unsold goods worth 819,771 pesos for 6.0 percent of the total, a figure that was nearly seven times higher than his 130,000 pesos in April 1758 and almost twelve times higher than his 68,452 pesos in October 1758. Juan Antonio de la Llano, also a veteran from 1758 with 30,000 pesos and 16,500 pesos from April and October, respectively, had seen his unsold inventory rise modestly to 46,000 pesos for 0.3 percent of the total in 1761. Miguel de Reinolina Cavo reported a smaller balance of 63,000 pesos in 1761 (0.5 percent of the total) than the 80,000 pesos in 1758. On the other hand, Francisco de Almanza had leftover stock of 4,000 pesos in 1758 compared to 120,000 pesos (0.9 percent) in 1761.

Although these comparisons reveal a degree of continuity among the wholesale merchants doing business at Jalapa in 1757 and 1761, the flotistas with the largest carryovers in 1762, except for Herrasti y Ysturiz, were newcomers. They included Miguel Rivero and his company, with an inventory worth 720,000 pesos, or 5.3 percent of the total, Juan Ignacio de Vertiz with 692,000 pesos, or 5.1 percent, and Gaspar Días Covian with 600,000 pesos, or 4.4 percent.[88]

The ultimate disposition of these inventories remains unclear, although José Joaquín Real Díaz has speculated that these surpluses combined with the uncertain international scene "occasioned a great commercial disorder." He attributed the disorder to the fact that the flotistas turned to the mining camps in direct competition with Mexico City's Consulado, the traditional supplier, because the flotistas' merchandise was exempt from sales taxes and therefore was cheaper.[89]

Despite the turmoil and animosity caused by the fairs, four or five were held from 1760–61 until 1778, when the fleet system was finally abandoned.[90] In tons of goods arriving at Veracruz on the fleet and presumably heading for Jalapa from 1757 to 1776, the range was between 5,000 and 8,000, a range that was two to three times higher than what it had been in the first half of the eighteenth century.[91] One clear pattern to emerge from the final fairs was that merchants from Mexico City's Consulado continued to lose ground to the combined forces of flotistas and non-Consulado merchants. More was imported than could be sold at Jalapa, and the unsold stock was disposed of through sales, technically illegal, between flotistas and provincial merchants. When the 1769 fair ended in February 1770, only about 40 percent of the merchandise sold at the fair was bought by merchants from Mexico City's Consulado; when the 1772 fair ended in August 1773, just over one-third was consigned to them; and when the 1776 fair ended in January 1777, only about one-quarter headed for the capital. Only with the fair of 1769 do we know how much unsold inventory remained (37 percent) after the fair and its extension ended. It cannot be shown that that was the case at each fair.

More than half of each fair's merchandise almost certainly was sold to non-Consulado members either in Jalapa or in the provinces, with the result that the Consulado's role in the Jalapa fair was probably shrinking. Although figures on market shares do not exist, the fact remains that if the flotistas' inventories averaged 15–20 million pesos, and if Consulado merchants purchased up to 5 million pesos worth of merchandise at Jalapa, then 10–15 million pesos worth still had to be sold.

Flotistas faced numerous obstacles, from boycotts by the Mexican Consulado—at least until it gained more favorable prices[92]—to many undercapitalized provincial and local merchants, who bought small lots usually on credit. In addition, provincial sales could mean higher costs and lower profits for flotistas, who had to cover travel expenses and accommodate discounted prices. Many flotistas understood that the longer the wait, the greater the risk for financial failure. Whether they made or lost money depended in part on how much the original markup was and how much of that could be preserved.

Because so much was being delivered under the fleet system the length of time needed was growing. During the Casa Tilly fair (1769–70) the flotistas still had more than one-third of their stock to sell a year after the fair started, and during the last fair (1777–78) they sold only one-third during the first six months or so. When Antonio de Ulloa left Veracruz to return to Spain in January 1778, a year after the fair opened, he registered 27.5 million pesos in currency and merchandise. Of that amount, only 9.8 million was in silver to cover foreign imports (mostly Jalapa sales), although 11.1 million pesos more than that had been credited to transactions at Jalapa.[93]

Eight months after the fleet's departure (and a year after the opening of the fair) the viceroy received a petition from the flotistas to reduce all internal taxes (such as the alcabalas) to speed the sale of remaining inventories. New merchandise, of course, continued to arrive at both Veracruz and Acapulco, so the colonial market was once again awash in imported goods.[94] It was likely that consumers of foreign merchandise benefited from the increasing supply and competition in the commercial sector, although by what amount remains obscure. In terms of overall policy, however, the fleet-fair combination did not function as smoothly and effectively as its creators had envisioned.

What did flotistas have to sell to Mexicans, especially as the volume of merchandise rose in the 1760s and 1770s? The fleet manifests show a variety of goods that presumably were not widely produced in the colony, although they may have been available from sources outside the imperial system. Total tonnage per fleet (excluding naval transport) averaged 7,300 tons, or more than 14 million pounds. Among the products on the manifests were iron and steel, paper, honey, spices, oils, cloth, liquors, wines, pots, medicines, and clothes. The volume in each product category could vary significantly from fleet to fleet. For some items—clothes; iron, steel, and other metals, beeswax, spices such as cinnamon and pepper; olive oil; paper and linen pieces; and brandy—some patterns emerge during the third quarter of the eighteenth century, although they cannot be precisely measured.[95] Shipments of several of these products rose during the third quarter, but shipments of several others either declined or remained unchanged.

The quantity of clothes (broadly defined) imported probably exceeded 50 percent of the total and was the highest of all product categories. In 1757 more than 0.5 million containers probably weighing several million pounds were registered, and although the volume dropped off in 1765 and 1768, it rebounded to nearly 900,000 containers and more than 10 million pounds in 1776. Metals, which were needed for tools and parts, were also a major item that actually declined from 4.6 million to 2.9 million pounds from 1757 to 1776. As a share of total imports, metals inexplicably dropped from one-third to one-sixth. Beeswax, a widely used item for candles, imported in hundreds of thousands of pounds, accounted for 6.1 percent of the total in 1757, for 8.5–9.5 percent in the 1760s, but for less than 1 percent in 1776. Imports of cinnamon and pepper rose slightly from 1.2 to 2.7 percent, whereas imports of olive oil, a staple in cooking, declined (about 400,000 pounds to under 200,000 pounds) from 3 percent to 1 percent of the total tonnage. Paper and linen followed somewhat similar paths in that quantities rose between 1757 and the early 1760s and then declined irregularly after that, with a greater drop in paper than in linen. Brandy was fairly stable over the years at 17,000 barrels, except for a sharp drop in 1772.

This represents only a selective analysis of the fleets' manifests, but the inference to be drawn from these data was that while total tonnage delivered to Mexico grew in the third quarter of the eighteenth century, the product categories varied from time to time. We do not know the extent to which these variations were reflections of changing economic conditions such as more foreign competition or more domestic production.

The more merchandise that Mexico imported under the fleet system, the more bullion it had to export. Had the flota system operated as it was designed, merchants should have sold their merchandise during the fair for bullion that they would have shipped out, shortly after the fair ended, when the fleet returned to Spain. We have already noted the irregular schedules of the flotas and the fairs during the eighteenth century until the 1778 decree. Despite this irregularity, however, other ships were commissioned by the Crown to deliver mercury, for example, and to return with bullion and a few commodities. Table 5-1 shows the number of arrivals with merchandise for documented fairs and the number of departures with bullion, primarily from those fairs.

Table 5-1. Fleet Arrivals/Departures and Currency Exports

Arrivals	Tonnage	Departures	Currency export
1732	4,458	1733	10.8
1736	3,141	1737	12.9
1757	7,070	1758	14.0
1760	8,493	1761	5.5
1762	-?-	1763	12.8
1765	8,013	1766	14.0
		1768	13.9
1769	5,588	1770	14.0
1772	7,675	1772	1.0
		1773	19.5
		1774	1.0
		1775	7.0
1776	8,176	1776	3.0
		1777	2.0
		1778	10.1
	52,613		141.5

Source: Real Díaz, "Las ferias de Jalapa," fig. 3; and Garner, "Exportaciones de circulante," app. 3.
Note: Currency exports in millions of pesos.

The eight fairs that took place between 1732 and 1776 averaged about 6,600 tons each, and based on currency export figures, each fair had merchandise worth about 17.7 million pesos. A figure of 17.7 million pesos is plausible in light of the fact that the earliest fairs were worth 10–15 million pesos and the last was worth about 27.5 million pesos. For the two fairs before 1750 the average tonnage was 3,750 worth about 3,000 pesos per ton. The six fairs between 1757 and 1776 averaged nearly 7,500 tons, with a value of approximately 15,700 pesos per ton. Not only did the volume double after 1750 but the value may also have risen five times. The figures on exports of currency are not related to specific fairs because the sources from which they were drawn did not always indicate whether these exports came solely from the sales at the fair. Given the rise in tonnage, however, exports of coins in these amounts were not unrealistic. Certainly a substantial part of the private currency exports were to settle the fair accounts.[96] What paid for most of this was silver output, which doubled about every half century. These currency exports did not include what left the colony to pay the contrabandists, who by Mexico's Consulado estimates pocketed 2–3 million pesos a year. Nor did it include the millions that left in the royal coffers.[97]

An increase in commodity exports from Mexico might have made it less dependent on silver to cover its international accounts, but that proved hard to accomplish. Dyes—cochineal and indigo—were Mexico's principal exports, but among its secondary exports were condiments, spices, sugar, leather, extracts, and purgatives. Prior to 1778 (the period of fleets and fairs) for years in which data exist, exports of commodities ranged between 1.5 to 3 million pesos. During those years total exports fluctuated between 7 and 16 million pesos. In most years exported commodities seldom exceeded one-quarter of the total, but in some years they reached one-third or one-half of the total. In 1758 commodity exports were uniformly high, with 32 million pounds of cochineal, or five times the average from 1733 to 1776.[98] If we exclude 1758 from the dataset we find no growth in commodity exports from 1733 to 1776. One reason for the lack of growth was that the chief exports—the dyes themselves—had a mixed performance: cochineal may not have increased at all, while indigo may have declined sharply. Other products either did not experience any substantial growth or, if they did, they represented only insignificant shares of total exports. It is not clear in view of the growing competition among the agricultural producers in the Atlantic world what commodity export industries Mexico could have exploited if that idea had been enthusiastically embraced. With only a limited manufacturing base Mexico had no finished products to sell in the international marketplace. The expanding mining industry paid for Mexico's expanding international commerce.

The Pacific Trade

Trade with the Far East through Acapulco posed a modest challenge to Veracruz and its various merchant communities. This trade has been less fully reconstructed and analyzed than the Veracruz trade. Pierre Chaunu, John TePaske, and Herbert Klein present data for the seventeenth century that show an increasing outflow of both public and private bullion from Acapulco to Manila.[99] The public money was needed primarily to pay for military expenditures in the Far East, but the private bullion was used to pay for costly spices and fabrics in demand by the colonial elite. Perhaps a substantial part of the Far Eastern luxury trade was then reexported from Mexico to Spain at substantial profits to Mexico City traders, most of whom belonged to the established commercial houses.

    In the eighteenth century an annual fair was approved along the lines of the fairs at Porto Bello and Jalapa. Faced with extremely hazardous voyages, the so-called Manila galleons kept irregular schedules (for example, there were sailings in 1722, 1728, 1729, 1733, 1737, and 1738), although they were no more irregular than the sailings of the flotas from Spain to Veracruz.[100] The size or the worth of this trade over the course of the eighteenth century is still undocumented. One way to try to measure it is to examine the outflow of bullion from Acapulco.

    From 1772 through 1804 (for the twenty-six years in which we have data) bullion worth 16.1 million pesos in private accounts was exported through

Acapulco, an annual average of 665,000 pesos. Although highly volatile, the growth may have been in the range of 3–3.5 percent per year. At these rates bullion transfers by private citizens doubled about every quarter century. Mexico also exported a few commodities to Manila through Acapulco. They included indigo, sugar, and medicine, but as in the Atlantic trade, they never covered more than a fraction of the cost of the merchandise imported from the Orient. Bullion made up the difference (not surprisingly) between imports and exports.[101]

Some of the merchandise imported from the Far East was sold through a fair that had been conducted at San Juan de los Lagos (in Jalisco) off and on since the seventeenth century. The Lagos fair was not as directly linked to the galleon trade as the Jalapa trade was to the flota trade. In 1792 Charles IV exempted the fair from the alcabalas against the advice of the Consulado and other established merchants, who properly interpreted this action as giving a price advantage to the fair sellers over the established merchants. Analysis of the fair and its economic impact remains to be done, although enough is known to indicate that the fair enjoyed some financial success. Each year thousands of persons attended the fair and traded goods worth hundreds of thousands of pesos. By 1807 the fair was open from the first of November to the middle of December, nearly twice as many days as was permitted in the original decree.[102]

In conclusion, the manufacturing sector and the commercial sector were interlocked. A domestic manufacturing sector beyond the processing of mainly agricultural commodities for urban markets had only limited growth in the eighteenth century. Mercantilistic policies placed major obstacles in the way of expansion in manufacturing. They could not absolutely prevent the rise of a domestic manufacturing sector because the cost of transport from Spain or Europe for many goods made their importation prohibitive. Except for textiles and a few other products, however, processing rather than manufacturing characterized the creation of products needed by consumers. Mexico depended on imports for what it did not produce itself, and it had the silver to pay for those imports. The rising silver curve in the eighteenth century attracted a flood of imported goods that may have eventually risen faster than the output of silver itself. The loss of silver to pay for these imports, which probably exceeded the actual demand, meant that the colony had less silver to undertake its own economic endeavors. Even the importation of goods worth millions of pesos each year did not offer the colony much opportunity to change its economic order. On the basis of what is known about the imports, they were consumed rather than used in the creation of other products or even reexported to other places, both of which could have stimulated change. But the international side was only part of the commercial system that evolved in eighteenth-century Mexico. Internal trade was also an important aspect of the late colonial economy.

6

Domestic Exchange and Commercial System

The commercial network that evolved during the eighteenth century existed on several planes. The colony had thousands of wholesalers and retailers, from the grand mercantile houses to peddlers who hawked their wares in the streets and plazas of the towns and villages. Such a description does not capture the widespread business of buying, selling, and bartering that operated outside the formal exchange network. Duties and taxes were imposed at various points: when goods entered the colony, when they were moved from one taxing district to another district within the colony, and when they were finally sold. Enforcement was arbitrary and uneven, and the collection of some duties and taxes had been removed from the royal treasury and handed over to town councils and merchant groups. For nearly two centuries all legal overseas trade passed through the hands of the merchants located in Seville and in Mexico City.

In Mexico the Consulado in the capital retained sole authority over import-export trade until the 1790s, when new consulados were authorized in the cities of Veracruz and Guadalajara in order to make the import-export business more competitive. The wealth acquired by import-export merchants (or wholesalers known as almaceneros) under the commercial monopoly was increasingly invested in other businesses, mainly but not exclusively mining. Even as the monopoly was being dismantled, the merchants who belonged to the Consulado or had links to the Consulado retained a strong influence over the colony's commercial life in large part because of their wealth. The creation of regional consulados only elevated to a higher status merchants who could not join the Mexico City Consulado but who were already powerful and wealthy in their own regions.[1]

The merchant was obviously at the center of the colony's commercial life, but he was also deeply involved in many other economic activities. Although his role as supplier of credit in mining and manufacturing and later as investor has been treated in earlier chapters, the relationship between the merchant community and the credit market was more extensive and profound than the mining or manufacturing links suggest. The credit market had two main sources, the church and the merchants. The church restricted its lending principally (but not exclusively) to rural and urban real estate. Merchants too invested in the real estate, but as a group they undertook far riskier economic ventures than either the church or private citizens. The transfer of money, either in the form of cash or paper—a basic need of every economic system—was largely in the hand of the merchants, not only for private transactions but also for public agencies.

If the economy had a linchpin, it was the merchant. His involvement was not a matter of altruism, but rather a matter of business. Commerce, and by extension merchants' profits, depended on the capacity of the economy to move goods from those who produced them to those who consumed them. It could almost be assumed that as the economy expanded in the eighteenth century, the merchant had little choice but to try to manage that expansion in such a way as both to protect and to advance his interests.

Measuring Domestic Trade

Trade at the local level had always been less regulated than at the international level, and although local public officials had the legal authority to regulate various economic activities, they seldom had the knowledge, resources, or expertise needed to make the exercise of that authority effective. By law each city was supposed to have a minimum number of grocery stores (*pulperías de ordenanza*) that could do business without buying a license. Other grocery stores (*pulperías de composición*) could only go into business if they purchased a license. Pulperías were more like the modern-day variety store, for they could sell an array of household, personal, and business items as well as foodstuffs.[2] But retail trade, especially in urban centers with growing populations, was more varied than the pulpería suggests. Some cities had wholesale grocers (who may also have sold to the public) and small food-retail shops in addition to their pulperías. A city's retail network could include specialized (and often licensed) stores that sold bakery goods, meat products, dry goods, and alcoholic beverages as well as shops like those run by tailors, hatters, or shoemakers. Finally, every city had its pool of peddlers, tavern owners, and open-market sellers (*puesteros*).

In an 1816 survey of Mexico City 679 commercial outlets of various sizes and functions were listed. They ranged from import houses to pottery stores, from grocery stores to pawn shops.[3] The scale and variety of the retail trade in smaller provincial cities was more limited than what existed in the capital or in larger cities. In the last quarter of the eighteenth century Zacatecas, with a population one-fifth that of the capital, had about 100 retail outlets, many classified as pulperías and puestos. There were a few other specialty outlets—bakers, butchers, tailors, cobblers, barbers—but in general there was much less variety than in other, larger cities.[4]

Counting the number of retail establishments in any eighteenth-century town or city can offer no more than a partial view of the commercial structure, for alongside the formal system functioned an ill-defined system of barter. How many such transactions occurred in the cities and across the countryside can never be recovered and studied, but they were probably numerous and certainly continuous.

The movement of merchandise within the colony became a matter of increasing concern because of the expense, time, and distance involved with the expansion of urban supply lines. Modifications in policy and law were designed to allow merchandise to move into and through the system with fewer delays and at lower costs than before, although uniform enforcement continued to be a serious deficiency. With the establishment of internal customs houses (*reales aduanas*) the government sought both to raise revenue and to expedite traffic by standardizing procedures. To this end the aduanas operated a *guía* (voucher) system that made it easier for merchandise that was properly registered to pass duty-free through several taxing districts until its final destination where the tax was collected. The real aduana could still impose barriers (from time-consuming inspections to bribe-demanding officials), but royal interference was less serious than the inadequacy of the transportation system.

So little was invested by the government in expanding or maintaining the highway system despite a rising treasury revenue curve that merchants often underwrote the cost of building and upgrading highways. Although a considerable amount of interregional or interurban trade existed by the end of the eighteenth century, the cost of transport certainly placed a limitation on how far products could be shipped or how much markets could be exploited.[5]

It is difficult to measure with precision the internal commercial activity of diverse groups such as wholesalers, shopkeepers, hawkers, craftsmen, ranchers, or monastics. John Kicza's analysis of the capital's commercial life only underscores how large and diverse it was.[6] The greatest deficiency is that reliable and standardized colonywide statistics do not exist, and without them measuring commercial activity is rendered far more difficult. Some statistics such as the alcabalas can be used to identify and measure trends and cycles within the colonywide commercial sector and on the smaller scale within or between regions.

The flaws in the alcabala record are well known. Not all transactions were subject to sales taxes; some transactions were taxed at the wholesale level and others at the retail; and transactions could be treated differently from region to region. There were other important drawbacks as well. The same item could be taxed several times between the initial and final transaction, with the result that the total revenues from many of the calculations made could be decidedly inflated. Since the tax was repeatedly farmed out before the 1777 order restricting but not ending such collections, a colonywide series can only be partially complete.[7]

Whether the tax was collected by the treasury or by an outside agency, the collections were eventually remitted to the colonial treasury. These data can be used to try to pinpoint and analyze in gross terms any long-term trends in domestic or internal commerce. Alcabalas receipts rose 2.0 percent per year between 1701 and 1810.[8] This meant, roughly speaking, that colonial commerce doubled about every forty years. This was slower than the rise in total treasury income but faster than the rise in tithe revenue and silver output. What cannot be ascertained precisely is the percentage of the alcabalas that came from domestic goods and from foreign goods, for the tax could be assessed against both.

The curve is of interest because it rose irregularly until the middle of the 1780s after which it declined until 1810. Indeed, the decline at 10 percent per annum was exceedingly pronounced. Although a sharp drop in alcabalas could definitely signal an economic slowdown, the downturn was probably also attributable to changes in collection procedures and tax rates as to economic circumstances. In any event, the long-term trend points to a century of growth in commerce at least until the agricultural crisis of the middle 1780s, after which the growth slowed and reversed itself. The long-term rate suggests a more robust economy than other indicators in the eighteenth century. The downturn after the 1780s was also sharper. Slowly rising prices (about 0.5 percent per year) accounted for part of the expansion in commerce, and price volatility during the late eighteenth century may have produced an erratic pattern of growth in the commercial sector (as the curve suggests).[9]

Alcabalas collections by regional offices present the opportunity to analyze commercial activity in a disaggregated form.[10] Numerous obstacles exist, however, not only because of gaps in the series but also because of problems in determining whether items were taxed or not taxed and how often they were taxed. When computing growth rates for each aduana during the second half of the eighteenth century Litle found considerable variation. In Bolaños, for example, alcalabas revenues fell by 2.4 percent from 1764 through 1806 (with three years missing), whereas in Acapulco and Michoacán they rose by 5.4 percent and 5.3 percent for 1768–1809 (four years missing) and 1760–1807 (sixteen years missing), respectively. Other aduanas reported growth rates between those two extremes. It is worth summarizing Litle's findings: although rates varied from aduana to aduana, most of the provincial aduanas witnessed a rise in alcabala income during the last quarter of the eighteenth century. In Veracruz and Mexico City, where much of the battle over tax reform and alcabala administration took place, no trends can be validated in that quarter century. If alcabalas do reflect internal commercial activity, then the interior of the colony appears to have been more dynamic economically than the port or the capital. Even if a part of the rise in revenue was attributable to more effective tax collection, another part—less than 1 percent in some places and more than that in others—stemmed from a growth in trade and commerce.[11]

After 1790 or 1800, we can observe several patterns. At some aduanas receipts grew at a slower pace; at others they flattened out or declined. For a third group the data ceased to exist or became too inconsistent to be of much use. In an effort to overcome the deficiencies related to single-aduana series we grouped aduanas by regions, with the result that the pattern just described seemed more apparent for the clusters than for single aduanas. Statistically, the computations do not inspire much confidence. One exception was the cluster made up of aduanas from Guanajuato, Michoacán, San Luis Potosí, and Saltillo. From 1760 to 1810 (with several years missing) the alcabalas averaged 345,000 pesos a year (one-fifth of the colony's average alcabalas) and rose at an annual rate of 4.3 percent.[12] Even with this cluster, however, the income curve climbed sharply up to 1795, after which it remained flat though volatile until 1810. Although the statistical evidence is not beyond qualification, it tends to match contemporary reports of an increasingly troubled economy and impoverished population in the quarter century before 1810. Based on alcabalas revenues, stagnation had replaced growth in the commercial sector.

For Mexico City and Zacatecas we can examine another feature of the alcabalas dataset. The ledgers usually were divided into several sections: *aforos*, which combined the subsections called Europa, China, Ultramarino, and Reino, which were the places where merchandise originated; *vientos*, which included grain, meat, cloth, and other household or personal items (called "perishables" by Litle); property, including slaves; and *iguales*, which were payments made by landowners in lieu of tax assessments.[13] To begin with, total alcabalas revenue in the two cities followed different paths; in Zacatecas it rose by more than 3 percent a year in the last quarter, whereas in Mexico City it was flat. The vientos receipts, however, in both cities were flat during the last quarter of the eighteenth century.[14] The difference in the alcabalas curves for the two cities may have derived not from the vientos, which were similar, but from the aforos, which rose in Zacatecas but followed no trend in Mexico City. Zacatecas's "imported goods" market was growing and must have contributed to Zacatecas's rising total alcabalas curve. In

Mexico City, where tax administration was always more complicated than anywhere else (except perhaps in Veracruz), the flatness of its alcabalas revenue curve may well mean that neither vientos nor aforos was growing in the quarter century before 1810. In both cities, however, if vientos revenues reflected ordinary day-to-day commerce, then given the rise in the urban population, they should also have risen. That they did not, for whatever reasons—high prices, low wages, unemployment, dislocation, or some combination of these—could be a sign that people were making do with less. Was this the statistical equivalent of the growing impoverishment of the colonial population to which contemporaries and historians have alluded?

For economic reformers the expansion of trade within the colony was an important component of the overall plan to develop and diversify the colonial economy. When new consulados were established in both Guadalajara and Veracruz in 1795, the aim was both to diminish further the authority of the Consulado of Mexico City and to encourage merchants to compete for business and investment in those regions and throughout the colony. Intendants were instructed to present a comprehensive plan of their district that described its economies, products grown or manufactured, and opportunities for growth and development.[15] No standard format was used for reporting or analyzing all the data from the intendancies, nor can the accuracy of the information be determined. The report from Guadalajara's intendant, for example, was among the most detailed, with figures on how much of each product was produced locally, imported into the province, and included in any locally fabricated merchandise for export. By contrast the report from Puebla (Manuel de Flon) was not much more than a description of each city and town with only a few statistics. Although important historical documents, these plans did not effect much change in the commercial or economic structure. A mechanism for implementing these plans did not exist, and the grip of Mexico City's Consulado, although weakened, remained firm because so much colonial trade, foreign or domestic, still passed through the capital.[16] Above all, economic growth required a more fully developed system of transportation and communication than the colony had in the eighteenth century.

Transportation System

By the eighteenth century Mexico had at best a modest overland highway system. The government, in spite of a substantial rise in revenue, invested little to expand or upgrade the system, and the consulados more often than the government assumed responsibility for construction and repair of interurban links. Even as the commercial structure was being opened up, it still greatly depended on a highway plan that radiated from the capital out to the provincial cities. How costly it was to move goods from the ports to the

Map 2. Section of Mexico and Guatemala corrected from original information communicated by Simon A. G. Bourne, Esq. By Sidney Hall. Published in London by Longman, Rees, Orme, Brown & Green, 1828. [This map was taken from an 1830 edition.] From Harvard College Library (4370.1828). Boundaries shown are for states established after independence in 1821. Mining districts are represented by crosses (+). Of special importance are the markings for roads, many of which correspond to late colonial roads.

capital and from the capital to the provinces remains largely unspecified because evidence is so scarce. In examining various obstacles to economic development in Mexico during the late eighteenth and early nineteenth centuries, Coatsworth has pinpointed a crucial missing link for more rapid economic development: the colony lacked cost-effective alternatives to overland transportation such as rivers and waterways.[17]

Some figures exist for estimating overland transportation costs. Transporting mercury from the central warehouse in Mexico City to the various mining camps offers one measure of shipping costs. Although the government charged the purchaser at the time he bought the mercury for the cost of transporting it from the warehouse to the camp, the government was not the carrier. Private haulers under contract to the mercury administration delivered the mineral to the mining camps. For eighteenth-century Zacatecas, about 300 miles from the warehouse, the cost may have fallen from 7 pesos per quintal to 4.5 pesos per quintal. Because the price of mercury declined in the eighteenth century, the proportion of the transportation charge to the purchase price actually increased slightly from 8.5 percent to 10.4 percent. When quintales are converted to cargas (we chose an average of 250 pounds), the cost to the buyer in Zacatecas over the whole century ranged from one-fourth to two-fifths of a real per carga mile, and it probably averaged from one-quarter to one-third of a real for each carga mile.[18]

In the late eighteenth century to haul grain thirty or thirty-five miles from the haciendas into Guanajuato cost on average one-fourth of a real per carga mile.[19] Juan Antonio de Yermo reported in 1785 that the cost of transporting a carga (converted from fanegas) of maize per mile to Mexico City was less than one-fifth of a real per carga mile, a figure slightly below the cost in Guanajuato.[20] Yermo claimed that the cost of delivering maize to Mexico City absorbed about half of the grain's sale value (compared to 10 percent for mercury shipments). That claim, though, was based on a price of 11 reales per fanega at a time when the price at the alhóndiga swung between the upper teens and the low thirties. More than likely the freight cost 10–20 percent of the price, although the cost of transporting maize may have been more stable than the price for selling maize.[21] In Guadalajara around 1800, the cost of shipping a carga of merchandise 211 leagues or 750 miles to Veracruz was said to cost 30–34 pesos, or about one-third of a real per carga mile. Taken together, these rates suggest an average of one-fourth to one-third of a real per carga mile (about 1.6 reales per ton kilometer or about 2.5 reales per ton mile).[23]

Although an average of 2.5 reales per ton mile may not appear high, it was probably high enough to preclude the transport and thereby the sale of low-priced agricultural and pastoral products much beyond 100 miles. The prices of many comestibles and some household items sold for such low prices that the cost of transportation would quickly exceed the value of the product itself. To test this hypothesis we have constructed a table that demonstrates how far it would be feasible to transport maize, at a given price, from the Upper Bajío to the Valley of Mexico and vice versa (a distance of about 200 miles). The key is the differential in maize prices between the two regions, for a producer would only ship out of his own market area if the price in another region was high enough above the local price to justify the cost and risk. We have computed three ton-mile figures (2.5 reales per ton mile ± 0.5 reales) in order to account for the range of possibilities with less than reliable data at hand (fig. 6-1 and appendix 2).

The maize price differential generally favored movement of maize from the Upper Bajío to the Valley of Mexico and not the reverse, but that differential was seldom ever great enough to justify a delivery of more than 100 miles, which was only half the distance from the Bajío to the valley. Indeed, for most years the cost-effective distance was fewer than fifty miles. At the end of the eighteenth century, when maize prices were higher than the century's average for both regions, trips above fifty miles could occur with greater frequency. Even then, however, it was expensive to transport maize from the Upper Bajío to or near Mexico City.

The purpose of these numbers is not to hypothesize how far producers sent maize in the absence of concrete documentary evidence, but rather to illustrate how costly transport could have been to move certain classes of goods out of a producing area into a consuming area.[24] Surely some comestibles were regularly shipped in the range of 50–100 miles because urban centers like Zacatecas, a mining camp that had very little local agricultural production, had no alternatives. Zacatecas's grain prices were generally slightly higher, and that was attributable in part to higher transportation costs.

A highway system connecting the main cities (Veracruz, Puebla, Mexico City, Guanajuato, Zacatecas, for example) had been in place since the sixteenth century, but it had never been significantly improved or expanded since then. Many secondary and tertiary roads, built to connect new towns and settlements with the main highways, were no more than footpaths and could not accommodate carts or wagons. Even along the royal highway between Zacatecas and Mexico City the mode of transport for two important items, bullion and mercury, was leather bags on pack animals. One to three months were needed to complete a trip of several hundred miles.[25]

Mail surely moved more quickly than freight. Around 1800 mail between the two cities required on average sixteen days for travel.[26] Puebla at less than 100 miles from Mexico City and Querétaro at slightly more than 100 miles required nearly a week for mail, while Veracruz and Acapulco, the principal ports each about 200 miles from Mexico City, required two weeks

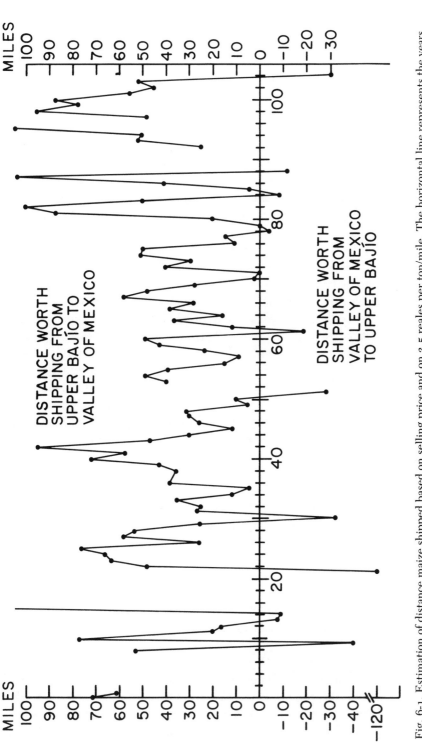

Fig. 6-1. Estimation of distance maize shipped based on selling price and on 2.5 reales per ton/mile. The horizontal line represents the years 1700 to 1806. *Source:* See chap. 1, note 59.

or more. The distance to Santa Fe, New Mexico, was twelve or thirteen times greater from the capital than the distance to Querétaro, but the number of days required to move the mail was more than thirty times greater. Mail between Mexico City and Parral (600 miles north) took more than a month, but freight took three to four times longer.[27]

The inadequacy of the system of transportation and communication did not escape the attention of the government or the business sector, and yet it did not receive the attention that it deserved if the system were to be changed. How much road work was undertaken by the public or private sector in the eighteenth century remains undocumented. From time to time and place to place merchants assumed the obligation for building and repairing roads because they were so crucial to the success of their businesses.

In 1797 for example, the Consulado of Guadalajara discussed a repair project on the highway that linked Guadalajara to Mexico City and Veracruz. The distance to be repaired was about one-fifth of a mile—380 yards long and 15 yards wide—from the point where the highway passed through the pueblo of Amalco outside of Guadalajara. In addition, several bridges along the road needed immediate repairs.[28] A decade later, when the Consulado reported on construction projects that it had undertaken, the above-mentioned project was said to have been completed at a cost of 13,030 pesos: road improvements at 2,055 pesos and bridges repairs at 10,975 pesos. The per-mile cost for just the road work was 10,500 pesos and for both road and bridge work (this assumes that the bridges were included in the stretch of road being repaired) 65,000 pesos. Seven other projects, including one at Fresnillo, 100 miles north of Guadalajara, and at San Juan de los Lagos, 100 miles west, were included on the list, with a total cost of 28,000 pesos, or 4,000 pesos per project. Finally, the list revealed that the Consulado had contributed 40,500 pesos to the rehabilitation of the part of the royal highway that served the Guadalajara region.[29] In total the Consulado of Guadalajara contributed about 80,000 pesos for ten projects over ten years, a modest amount for a region of many thousands of square miles, especially in the absence of any major governmental role.

Trade between Cities: Case of Zacatecas

Despite the handicaps related to cost, distance, and uncertainty, internal trade probably had to expand in the eighteenth century simply to accommodate the rise in demand. All major cities participated in commerce that ranged from basic commodities to luxury goods. In cities like Zacatecas, where mining was predominant, a large trade network was crucial to the city's survival. Except for some ranching in the vicinity of the city, silver mining was Zacatecas's only industry. During a viceregal survey in the middle 1790s, local officials reported that outside the silver refineries the city lacked even *molinos* (mills) for grinding wheat into flour.[30] A decade later the intendant, in a report to the Consulado of Veracruz, described the economic potential of the Zacatecan intendancy but then conceded that mining so preoccupied the business community that little of that potential was ever pursued.[31] Thus, as rich as it was in silver, the city depended on an ever-larger commercial network to sustain its economy.

From basic staples like maize and flour to luxury items like liquor and silk, merchandise flowed into Zacatecas week after week throughout the year. Maize and flour were essential, and by the end of the colonial period Zacatecas received deliveries from dozens of towns, villages, and haciendas in an area that extended fifty miles to the northwest and southeast and 100 miles to the southwest from the city. From the alhóndiga records in the 1750s more than two dozen places were identified; from the records of the 1790s more than three dozen; and from 1815–20 more than four dozen.[32] The heaviest concentration of places extended from Zacatecas southwest into the Upper Bajío, and although the quantity of grain from each place can only be computed with difficulty, the large number of places from which grain was shipped from the southwest to Zacatecas is probably an indicator of the increasing reliance on that region for the city's grain supply.

With the introduction of the guías system by the real aduana in the last quarter of the eighteenth century, however, it is possible to detail the aforo commerce with considerable precision.[33] Aforo trade in contrast to viento trade covered foreign imports and domestic products, although the former was more heavily represented. Although trade with Zacatecas originated in many colonial cities, the three with the most guías in our sample years— 1781, 1791, 1801, and 1810—were Mexico City, Veracruz, and Puebla (table 6-1). With nearly 980 guías from these four years Mexico City accounted for 38.7 percent of them, Veracruz for 15.3 percent, and Puebla for 12.2 percent. In each year Mexico City had the highest number of guías, but in 1791 Mexico City and Veracruz had almost an equal number of vouchers at 64 and 60, respectively.

Most large provincial cities as well as a few small towns participated in trade with Zacatecas. Other cities with substantial Zacatecan trade were Parras (wine), Querétaro (cloth), San Luis Potosí, and Guadalajara. The majority of the places were within a radius of 250 miles, with the Upper Bajío being heavily represented.[34] Guías were used to expedite traffic and not to designate a type of merchandise, and while imports dominated the merchandise from the capital or the ports, they could also show up in merchandise from the interior cities. In general, though, interior cities were sources for domestic products like cloth or wine and the capital and ports were sources for imported products.

Table 6-1. Originating Cities in Trade with Zacatecas, 1781, 1791, 1801, 1810

City	1781	1791	1801	1810	Total
Mexico City	120	64	91	104	379
Veracruz	7	60	32	51	150
Puebla	41	33	39	7	120
Parras	28	12	0	29	69
Querétaro	6	3	25	13	47
San Juan del Río	19	4	9	7	39
Aguascalientes	35	1	1	0	37
San Luis Potosí	0	4	1	18	23
Guadalajara	1	2	11	8	22
Celaya	7	0	10	0	17
Acámbaro	0	1	13	14	28
Lagos	0	0	1	12	13
León	3	0	0	7	10
Acapulco	5	0	3	0	8
San Miguel (El Grande)	3	0	2	2	7
Zamora	6	0	1	0	7
Fresnillo	4	0	0	0	4
Oaxaca	0	1	3	0	4
Sierra de Pinos	3	0	0	1	4
Guanajuato	0	0	0	3	3
Mazapil	3	0	0	0	3
Total					980

Source: MiU-C, Zacatecas Collection, *Alcabalas*, 1781, 1791, 1801, and 1810.
Note: Zero denotes that no guías were found from that city in that year.

In addition to determining the origination of trade, we can calculate how much it was worth in most years between 1766 and 1821 (table 6-2).[35] In the 1760s aforos trade averaged about 150,000 pesos a year; twenty years later it had doubled to 300,000 pesos; and twenty years after that it had increased by 50 percent to 450,000 pesos. From 1766 to 1810 the annual average was close to 400,000 pesos, nearly one-fifth of the output of silver (in pesos) per year. During that period silver production grew at an annual rate of 2.7 percent, while aforo trade climbed at an annual rate of 2.6 percent.[36] Since aforos data are concentrated in the period from 1780 to 1810, we made some short-term computations of growth in trade to compare with silver. Calculations indicate that from 1780 to 1810 or from 1788 to 1810 the trade and silver curves diverged.[37] Silver output rose at about twice the rate of aforos. These were among the most productive years in Zacatecan mining, and quite possibly

Table 6-2. Value of Aforos Trade to Zacatecas, 1766–1821 (in pesos)

Date	Aforos	Percent change	Percent of silver
1766	131,747		15.4
1767	169,920	22.5	17.3
1768	152,248	– 11.6	16.7
1780	429,550		24.4
1781	360,650	– 16.0	15.0
1786	210,450		11.4
1787	312,980	48.7	12.8
1788	323,547	3.4	15.7
1789	343,800	6.3	16.6
1790	295,038	– 14.2	14.6
1791	419,689	42.3	23.8
1792	505,018	20.3	20.3
1793	444,920	– 11.9	20.1
1794	284,903	– 36.0	14.1
1795	466,941	63.9	21.8
1796	594,163	27.3	19.8
1797	582,629	– 1.9	21.0
1799	374,215		20.6
1800	400,047	6.9	20.8
1801	326,425	– 18.4	31.1
1802	346,916	6.3	16.5
1804	557,683		nd
1805	397,550	– 28.7	8.6
1807	466,973	17.5	15.3
1808	692,083	48.2	12.9
1810	354,200		10.3
1814	428,757		16.9
1815	280,407	– 34.6	17.9
1820	378,057		nd
1821	197,529	– 47.8	9.2
Average	382,472		17.3

Source: MiU-C, Zacatecas Collection, Alcabalas, 1766–1815.
Note: Figures from 1810 and 1821 are incomplete. No data were found where "nd" appears.

more silver was being produced than the aforo trade could absorb, especially given the growing international conflict. Nonetheless, the two series are highly correlated, and the rise in trade was heavily dependent on the expansion in silver. The power of silver to drive the economy remained strong to the end of the colonial period.

Merchants and aviadores made up the principal participants of the aforos transactions (table 6-3).[38] Other persons participated, but usually they placed small and infrequent orders. For the two years of 1787 and 1788 we have

Table 6-3. Aforos Transactions Between Zacatecas and Selected Mexican Cities, 1787 and 1788

Zacatecas			
Businessman	Status	Aforos	Percent of total
Fernando Torices	Pulpero	57,279	9.0
Juan Bolado	Aviador	32,427	5.1
Vicente del Castillo	Aviador	31,220	4.9
Lorenzo Carerra	Aviador	30,246	4.8
Juan Cenos	Aviador	26,812	4.2
Total of five		177,984	28.0
Grand total		636,527	

Other Cities				
Merchant	City	Aforos	Percent of total	Percent by city
Miguel Lizardi	Veracruz	45,290	7.1	37.3
Juan Necochea	Puebla	44,815	7.0	35.9
Manuel Bolado	Mexico	22,158	3.5	15.9
José Olloquí	Mexico	19,542	3.1	14.0
Manuel Mantilla	Puebla	16,765	2.6	13.4
Casa de Múñoz	Veracruz	16,509	2.6	13.6
Joachín de Haro	Puebla	13,442	2.1	10.8
Pedro Berasueta	Mexico	12,988	2.0	9.3
Franco de la Torre	Veracruz	11,270	1.8	9.3
Juan Dosamontes	Mexico	10,454	1.6	7.5
Pedro Savala	Veracruz	10,026	1.6	8.3
Total		223,259	35.0	

Source: MiU-C, Zacatecas Collection, Alcabalas, 1787 and 1788.
Note: "Percent by city" refers to the share of trade that a shipper had among all those sending merchandise from a given city. Only those merchants from other cities are listed if their total shipments were 10,000 pesos or more. Aforos shown in pesos.

reliable data from which we can positively identify eighteen buyers in Zacatecas: ten were aviadores and eight were pulperos (grocers). Fernando Torices, who owned the largest licensed pulpería, handled more aforos trade than any other person: 9 percent of the trade worth 57,279 pesos in 1787–88. Torices also acted as an aviador for some local miners and refiners, but he remained primarily a wholesale/retail merchant. Torices was followed by four aviadores: Juan Bolado, Vicente del Castillo, Lorenzo Carrera, and Juan Cenos, each of whom accounted for 4–5 percent of the aforos trade. The five together purchased 28.0 percent of the total trade, which was 177,984 pesos worth of the total 636,527 pesos.

Eleven shippers each sent merchandise worth more than 10,000 pesos in those two years. Four of them were from Mexico City: Manuel Bolado (related to the Zacatecan aviador Joseph Bolado), José Olloquí (an investor in the city's mining company, Vetagrande), Pedro Berasueta (who also became a Mexico City baker), and Juan Dosamontes.[39] From Veracruz there were also four: Miguel Lizardi (with the largest aforos trade, 7.1 percent), Casa de Múñoz, Francisco de la Torre, and Pedro Savala. The third city, Puebla, had three shippers: Juan Necochea (who was second with 7.0 percent), Manuel Mantilla, and Joachín de Haro. More than half of Lizardi's trade was with Torices and nearly one-quarter of Necochea's trade was with Cenos. Among these major shippers, almost two-thirds of them had 70.1 percent of the total and were from outside Mexico City. The two largest shippers (Lizardi and Necochea) were from Veracruz and Puebla, respectively. This confirms what was noted in the analysis of the guías, that other cities could compete with the capital for business in an expanding commercial system. In 1787 and 1788 these three cities accounted for more than 60 percent of all the guías, which they shared equally (about 20 percent each).

Zacatecas's commercial activity reflects the special circumstances of its location and economy and may not, therefore, be typical of other cities, other regions, or even other camps. There can be no doubt, however, that this was a large, complex market structure that transcended local and regional boundaries. A mining camp during a relatively productive period could act as a strong stimulus on the commercial sector, not only for the import merchants but also for domestic producers and purveyors. This was true despite the costs and delays imposed by an inadequate transportation system. The total value of wholesale/retail trade, based on projections from alcabalas in Zacatecas, could have reached 1,000,000 pesos for some years in the late eighteenth or early nineteenth century. Total commercial activity may have equaled up to half of the value of the camp's silver output. The multiplier effect is clear even if it cannot be precisely calculated. But the commercial activity entailed a relatively narrow range of products—basic staples, household items, mining supplies, luxury goods—that merchants, agriculturalists, and manufacturers at home and abroad benefited from, and yet it provided little stimulus to expand Zacatecas's own economic base.

Consulado Reorganization and Internal Commerce

Until the late eighteenth century the Mexico City Consulado, made up of peninsulares with strong links to Cádiz through the flota, exercised a virtual monopoly over import-export trade in Mexico. The original Consulado was empowered to assess a 2 percent levy (avería) against the value of all imports and exports.[40] At times the Consulado members, who had acquired great wealth by the control that they had over international commerce, donated part of the avería to various public works. Eighteenth-century reforms led to the end of the capital's total monopoly with the creation of two new consulados in Veracruz and Guadalajara in 1795.[41] The authorization for these new consulados meant that merchants in these cities could organize into guilds and assess the avería on all imported merchandise that was sold in their respective jurisdictions. The boundaries of the consulados were never precisely defined, but they basically created a tripartite division: Veracruz in the east and southeast, Mexico City in the center, and Guadalajara in the west and northwest. Although each consulado had a jurisdiction (thereby an aspect of the old commercial monopoly survived), it was apparently free to pursue business (commercial or otherwise) outside that jurisdiction.

The two new consulados could collect the avería on goods that its members imported or exported. The rate was initially set at one half (0.5) of 1 percent, although it was soon revised upward at Veracruz until it reached 1.5 percent. The Consulado of Mexico City had traditionally paid 2 percent, and if that rate continued in effect until the end of the colonial period, the oldest consulado was at a competitive disadvantage with the two new consulados. At Guadalajara some goods could be taxed at more than the standard 0.5 percent.[42]

The Consulado of Veracruz was authorized to collect the avería on "generos, frutos, y efectos comerciales" from overseas except sugar. Coastal trade was also exempt from taxation at Veracruz.[43] Nor could the Consulado of Veracruz tax imports or exports under the auspices of other consulados. The instructions of the Consulado of Guadalajara stated that it could collect the avería on goods that entered or left by any port in the Guadalajaran district; were unloaded at Veracruz and sent by guía from there to Guadalajara; were sent by guía from Guadalajara and loaded at Veracruz; and were introduced at and purchased at the fair of San Juan de los Lagos. Thus, consistent with free-trade reforms, merchandise could move from a port to the interior or vice versa without approval of or interference from the consulados whose districts the merchandise might pass through.

Although the avería may seem to be a light tax in the range of 0.5–2.5 percent on the value of imported or exported merchandise, the total tax burden was still very large. When European or Spanish merchandise, already high-priced, was sent by way of Cádiz to Veracruz and then to the interior in the late eighteenth or early nineteenth century, it could end up being assessed as much as 35–40 percent in taxes, that is, in duties, alcabalas, and fees.[44] The demand for silver in the mercantile community arose out of the need not only to meet foreign obligations but also to settle tax claims.

How did the new consulados fare in this deregulated climate? It was assumed that more consulados could increase competition and lower prices, which would stimulate growth.[45] We know more about the expectations of a more open system than about the results. Whatever the economic impact, it has to be measured against the backdrop of a rapidly changing international scene that included the blockade of Spain, the introduction and then the recision of free trade between Mexico and neutrals, and the abdication of the monarch.

Despite the fact that Mexico City lost its absolute monopoly over the colony's import-export trade, merchants there still retained enormous influence and power over international trade because of their knowledge, experience, and wealth. Some scattered avería accounts from the mid-1790s to 1810 allow us to make a preliminary assessment of the impact of the change. In the period 1795–1801, based on avería income, Veracruz's Consulado may have accounted for one-quarter to one-third of the total of the traffic that passed through the port. What is more difficult to determine is whether its share of the total grew over time or remained relatively fixed at about the figures just cited.[46] There is no doubt that the Veracruz Consulado's business grew rapidly and substantially after its incorporation, in part by virtue of its location in the port itself. But credit must also be given to the merchants themselves who actively pursued and won business clients outside their own region.[47] In the end, despite its accomplishments in a relatively short time, the Consulado of Veracruz did not supplant the older, larger Consulado in the capital.

The Consulado of Guadalajara was the smallest of the three and quite possibly the least independent. Although designed to help to break the stranglehold of Mexico City over trade with interior cities, the Consulado of Guadalajara may have grown increasingly dependent on Mexico City for merchandise and credit to serve its widely scattered clientele.[48] When avería revenue collected by Veracruz and Guadalajara are compared, Guadalajara's business was from one-fifth to one-half as large as Veracruz's. In the earliest years (1795–98) Guadalajara's avería per year actually dropped from nearly 16,000 to about 6,000 pesos. This decrease could mean that the value of the commerce handled by the local consulado fell from about 3 million to 1 million pesos. Income declined so sharply in 1798 that the Consulado had to arrange a loan of 10,000 pesos to carry on with its business.[49]

In 1798, however, the format in which the avería was recorded was revised: goods were thereafter listed under three categories: *país*, *nacionales*, and *extranjeros*. Although the categories were not explained, they appear to refer to imported merchandise bought in the colony from large wholesalers in other consulados and, more typically, merchandise imported from abroad, principally Spain. This change could be a backward step in the effort to reform internal commerce; not only could the avería be collected more than once, but such financial arrangements could also give the almacen-eros who owned much of the unsold inventory a chance to assert their influence over that commerce. Whatever purpose or effect the change had, it was followed by a rise in avería income and commercial activity under the control of the Guadalajara Consulado. Moreover, the Consulado's income increased not only because of more commercial activity but also because avería rates were raised as high as 3 percent on some merchandise and other revenue sources were tapped. After an inauspicious start the Consulado of Guadalajara found a niche that seemed to derive more from the remnants of the old restrictive mentality than from the new competitive outlook.

As the Consulado's income rose so too did its expenditures. The cost of administering the guild could amount to several thousand pesos a year. But as noted earlier, consulados were expected to undertake road and bridge repairs in exchange for the privilege of collecting the avería. In the first decade of the nineteenth century the Consulado of Guadalajara invested about a quarter of its income in such projects. That amounted to a total of a some 10,000–20,000 pesos, and given the pressing need to improve and expand transportation that investment could only have had a marginal impact.[50]

In addition to reporting receipts and disbursements, the Guadalajara accounts summarized on an annual basis (although not for every year) the volume of trade between the Consulado and various cities, usually by the categories mentioned above. Table 6–4 presents the annual totals by cate-gory for all cities with transactions in given years. A breakdown of the cities that the Consulado served, the total value of trade between the Consulado and each city, and the number of years for which data exist for each city can be found in appendix 2. Taken together, the three dozen cities under the jurisdiction of Guadalajara's Consulado collected the avería on goods worth 25 million pesos, or 3.6 million pesos per annum over seven years (1799–1802 and 1807–9). Seventy percent of that trade belonged to the país category, 20 percent to nacional, and 10 percent to extranjero. Direct importation (or exportation) by Guadalajaran merchants was apparently a small part of the Consulado's overall business. Guadalajara accounted for the most traffic under the authority of the Consulado with 15 percent, but several other places—Charcas, Saltillo, and Chihuahua—were not far behind with 10 percent. This did not mean that the traffic physically passed through the city but rather that the Consulado earned the avería from any merchandise sent to or from these cities.

The figures also reveal that the Consulado benefited from the exchange that grew out of several major silver camps to the northeast of the city.[51] One such camp was Zacatecas, where the total value of the goods paying averías and the total value of goods paying alcabalas under the aforos can be

Table 6-4. Value of Trade under Consulado of Guadalajara (in thousands of pesos)

Year		Total	País	Nacional	Extranjero
1799		2,050	1,174	367	509
1800		3,059	2,130	639	291
1801		3,698	2,480	835	382
1802		4,695	3,940	540	215
1807		5,206	3,699	1,158	350
1808		3,880	2,599	952	330
1809		2,445	1,675	514	256
	Total	25,033	17,696	5,003	2,334

Source: AGI, Guadalajara, leg. 526–31.

compared for 1800, 1801, 1802, 1807, and 1808, although 1802 has been ignored because the figures are incomplete. First, the comparisons show that the two sets of figures rose or fell in step: lower in 1801 than 1800 but higher in 1808 than 1807. Second, the figures based on the averías were lower than the aforos in three of the four years by 77 percent and in the fourth year by 85 percent. The difference between averías and aforos arose from the fact that averías were to be collected on imports and exports, whereas alcabalas under aforos was assessed against all shipments of foreign or domestic merchandise. If the various public agencies maintained these distinctions as they levied the various taxes, then what the difference allows us to do is to estimate that certainly more than half and perhaps as much as 75 percent of the aforos consisted of imports or, if any, exports. This affirms again that consumption of expensive imports could command a substantial part of a locality's economic base, in this case silver.[52]

Who could join a consulado was determined by the guild's own members. How many merchants throughout the colony could or did join consulados is not yet known. The Mexico City guild had a membership that approached or exceeded 100, although the capital had many more persons who were engaged in various commercial activities.[53] Although Guadalajara's membership is also unknown, there were probably scores of members, including as many as a dozen agents from outlying cities and towns. Actually, Guadalajara's guild may have had more than 100 active merchants in the late eighteenth century.[54] Among the city's largest merchants (and guild members) may have been Venturo García Diego, Eugenio Moreno de Tejada, and Manuel González Vallejo.[55]

Although we cannot document actual transactions (as suggested by the país category) between Guadalajara and Mexico City, we can say that some merchants in the city and the region had extensive dealings with import-export houses in Veracruz. They included José Zumelzu, Mariano Pachero, and Juan Ángel Ortiz from Guadalajara and Estaquillo de la Cuesta in Tepic,

Antonio Martínez y Zavala in San Juan de Lagos, Juan Martín de Echevarría in Zacatecas, and Francisco Espinoza in Rosario.[56] Although not stated, some of these merchants must have been members of the Consulado in Guadalajara.

The Consulado of Guadalajara did not apparently attain the degree of independence that may have been envisioned at its founding. It earned the avería on the trade that involved its merchants, but it exercised little direct control over the trade itself because its merchants had to transact business through the more experienced international merchants in the other two guilds. Under these conditions the formation of new consulados led to the end of the dominance of Mexico City's guild but not to the end of the power of guild-based commerce.

Dye Production under Commercial Reform

In addition to silver, which was the main commodity for balancing its overseas accounts, Mexico had only a few other products to sell in foreign markets. Among those products were various dyes sold to European cloth and textile manufacturers. Since the founding of the dye trade in the sixteenth century merchants had participated not only as middlemen but also as investors and financiers. The other great lender was the church, but it maintained a portfolio that was dominated by real estate and commodity agriculture. Though merchant participation in the dye trade was intertwined with the much-criticized repartimiento system, it is the financial aspect that is relevant here.

Dye production was centered in southwestern Mexico around Oaxaca. Although the industry had languished during the first half of the eighteenth century, it became the focus of official attention during José de Gálvez's visit from 1767 to 1771. Typical of Gálvez's approach to other economic matters, he concluded that cochineal production suffered mainly because the government had failed to establish a coherent and efficient policy for the industry. Gálvez's reforms, which were also championed by some clerics, proposed the elimination of the corrupt system of repartimientos. Under this system merchants provided the capital and equipment for the dye producers, who in turn delivered their products to those merchants or their agents to be sent abroad. Financing was complex and inventive, but the merchants tended to dictate the terms, usually with the approval of the government. Alcaldes, appointed by the Crown to serve under the *corregidores* (local royal officers), often acted as middlemen between the Indian producers of cochineal and the Spanish merchants. By replacing the corregidores and alcaldes with intendants and subdelegates in 1787 and by permitting the Consulado of Veracruz to extend avíos and make contracts directly with the producers after 1795, the government (in line with Gálvez's earlier proposals) contended that producers (Indian producers in particular) would earn higher prices and therefore would increase their output to take advantage of those higher prices. Since the government wanted to add to its own revenues, an expanding cochineal industry would assist in that effort.

Not all in the government agreed with the proposals of Gálvez or his successors. Antonio Bucareli, who became the viceroy after Gálvez's visit, and one of his advisers, Francisco Leandro de Viana (Count of Tepa), opposed Gálvez on the grounds that reform of the existing system was preferable to replacing it. Once the reforms and changes were introduced, however, Spain and Mexico became caught up in the European wars of the 1790s and early 1800s, and since the shipment of cochineal from Mexico was irregular and unpredictable, its production, regardless of continuing high world demand, failed to attain the levels that had been anticipated.[57]

From the outset the problem with the cochineal industry was that the dyes ended up in European textile centers (England rather than Spain), and the colonists had to buy fabrics colored with their dyes for much higher prices than they received for those dyes. This led to an outflow of bullion from the empire, and in the neomercantilist view this could become a crippling factor, not only for the cochineal industry but also for the whole imperial economy. Even before the intendancy system ended the repartimiento system, the government had begun to tinker with the commercial network, of which the cochineal industry was a part, with an eye toward reversing its dominance by foreign traders and manufacturers.[58] In short, if the colonies bought more Spanish cloth made with Mexican dyes, the wealth created by these transactions would belong to Spaniards and not to foreigners.

Statistics on the production and price of cochineal registered in Oaxaca from 1758 to 1810 indicate first growth and then decline.[59] Over the half century the volume of cochineal from Oaxacan district actually declined at an annual rate of 2.2 percent, while the price remained volatile and without any trend. Prices rose until the mid-1770s, declined for the next twenty years, and then climbed again until 1810, after which they declined again during independence. Total revenues from cochineal sales (volume times price) declined by 1.9 percent per annum.[60] The highest price of 33 reales per pound was recorded in 1809 with output of only 350,000 pounds (compared to an average of nearly 700,000 pounds from 1758–1810) for revenue of 1.4 million pesos. By then, however, the cochineal industry in Mexico as well as the cloth industry in Spain, though still protected in spite of deregulation under *comercio libre*, had fallen on hard times due to warfare and to an increasingly competitive environment.

The most productive period for the late colonial cochineal industry was during the third quarter of the eighteenth century. From 1758 through 1774 all three variable—output, price, and income—exhibit somewhat more positive trends than for the total period 1758–1810: output rose 2.3 percent annually (only a 95 percent confidence level), prices rose 3.7 percent, and income rose 5.8 percent.[61] During the third quarter, price reached its highest point in 1771, when 1.1 million pounds sold for 32 reales per pound and earned 4.2 million pesos. Production attained its zenith in 1774, when 1.6 million pounds sold at 17.6 reales per pound for 3.4 million pesos. After 1775 (until 1810) production dropped at a rate of 3.1 percent per year as prices climbed (more slowly than before) by 2.3 percent per annum. Because of the sharp decline in production, revenues declined by 1.8 percent.[62] In the third quarter about two-thirds of Oaxaca's annual cochineal production (800,000–900,000 pounds) was exported, and that left about 300,000 pounds to be sold to domestic cloth manufacturers or to enter the contraband market. By the end of the century nearly all of Oaxaca's cochineal production (now averaging about 400,000 pounds each year) was exported.[63] Production had risen during the third quarter of the eighteenth century because two giant Spanish commercial houses (Cinco Gremios Mayores de Madrid and Casa de Uztáriz) had been given control over the export of cochineal from Mexico and the manufacture of cloth in Spain (at Guadalajara), with the result that as more Spanish cloth was sold demand for dye grew.[64]

In the fourth quarter economic conditions did not favor dye production in Mexico and cloth manufacture in Spain. At the end of the century the Crown was confronted with dye and cloth industries that had become less productive and competitive, and beginning in late 1798 it was also confronted with a British blockade of the Spanish peninsula. To counter the blockade, the government granted concessions to Spanish and neutral merchants to export the cochineal stored in Veracruz to take advantage of prices that were higher (by a few reales per pound). In return, the government granted to neutrals the right to bring into Mexico "a large quantity of British [no less!] manufactures, carried on United States ships." As high as cochineal prices were (they had been and would be higher), they would not cover the cost of the imported merchandise. Thus, as the drainage of bullion accelerated, the Crown reviewed the concessions and rescinded them in early 1799. How to deal with cochineal, which involved rival consulados in Veracruz and Mexico City, was not satisfactorily resolved during the first decade of the nineteenth century, with the result that production continued to fall as prices continued to climb.[65] In Hamnett's view, the failure of the Oaxacan cochineal industry to reverse the decline in production in the late colonial period stemmed from several wars, "the flight of investment," and the brief exemption to neutrals.[66]

The matter of investment directly involved the merchant community. Until the last half of the eighteenth century the Consulado of Mexico City, as the colony's only commercial guild, had provided the financing and the marketing that was necessary to support the production of cochineal. The merchants' local contacts were the alcaldes who arranged for the shipment of often useless but expensive merchandise from the merchants to the Indians in exchange for the cochineal, a system known as repartimiento.[67] The creation of intendancies and the liberalization of commerce and all of the ramifications of these reforms so disrupted the system of repartimiento and in turn the production of cochineal that the region was plunged into an economic crisis.

An attempt was made to gauge the extent of impact of the reforms on Oaxaca's economy in the first five years from December 1786 until October 1791.[68] Each pueblo (presumably under jurisdiction of a *subdelegado* now) was listed with the products that it had to trade and the volume of business from repartimiento that it supported (table 6-5). Almost all the pueblos and their districts produced cochineal, but they also produced cotton, slaughtered animals, raised wheat, and sold fabrics. The places with the most repartimiento business (more than 100,000 pesos in the first full year) were Nejapa, Villa Alto, Xicayan, and the four villages linked to the estate of the Marquesado (Cortéz) heirs. Four to five years later (years four and five were combined) they still had the most business, although the volume had fallen to 50,000–80,000 pesos. The total business in the first year was 1.3 million pesos and in the fourth/fifth year was 715,000 pesos, a decline of 43.5 percent.

When population figures (1793) are used to calculate per capita cost of the forced sales (total amount for each district), the range is from a few pesos per person to 27 pesos per person. Many of the pueblos had sales of 10–15 pesos per person, a relatively high figure given the fact that these included adults and children.[69] As averages of sales declined over four or five years, per capita costs rose. Costs were probably much higher in the late 1780s than in the early 1790s.

Repartimiento sales declined after the change to the intendancy. The production and price of cochineal held fairly steady. It is hard to compare individual years because the repartimiento figures were based on sales for each twelve-month period from late 1786, when the ordinances were promulgated, whereas cochineal sales were based on regular calendar years. In the first year of the ordinances the amount paid for dye was about equal to the amount sold under repartimiento, but in the fourth/fifth year it was twice as much. Did this mean that merchants were willing to buy cochineal even though they sold less merchandise in exchange; did it mean that producers were able to find other outlets (including contraband) that did not rely on forced sales; or did it mean that the two datasets are incompatible?

Forced sales, even as they declined, were still substantial, in the range of 750,000 pesos per year. The response by the merchants who directly suffered losses under the new policy was to reduce their investment in both cochineal cultivation and general agricultural production (maize or cattle). Certainly,

Table 6-5. Value of Merchandise Sold under Repartimiento by Pueblos, Intendancy of Oaxaca, December 1786–October 1791 (in thousands of pesos)

Pueblos/Products	1st yr.	2d yr.	3d yr.	4/5th yrs.	Total
Quatro Villas del Marquesado	100	60	60	60	270
[17,740 or 15 p/p; no products listed]					
Religious orders	80	50	50	40	220
[no population or products listed]					
Jalapa del Estado	30	?	?	?	30
[413 or ?; cattle]					
Acayucá(n)	50	35	25	25	135
[?; cotton, cattle, efectos comerciales]					
Huajolotitlan	25	20	20	15	80
[?; no products listed; misery of Indians stressed]					
Huamelula	30	20	15	15	80
[3,833 or 21 p/p; cochineal]					
Igualapa, Ometepec	40	30	20	20	110
[?; cochineal, cotton]					
Ixtepeji	30	25	20	20	95
[5,585 or 4 p/p; cochineal]					
Juxtlahuaca	30	30	20	20	100
[8,171 or 12 p/p; cochineal, efectos comerciales]					
Miahuatlan	80	60	50	40	230
[16,003 or 14 p/p; cochineal]					
Nejapa	120	120	80	80	380
[14,060 or 27 p/p; cochineal]					
Nochistlan, Peñoles	30	20	20	20	90
[5,955 or 15 p/p; cochineal, wheat, wood]					

merchants were more careful about the volume, size, and duration of their loans. But merchants were never excluded, and because the subdelegados were among the most lowly paid public officials, they eventually had to pursue business practices like those of their predecessors, the alcaldes, in order to meet their own personal and financial obligations. Moreover, the treasury soon discovered that it had less income because, since Indians had been liberated (partially at least) from the control of merchants and alcaldes, they were less inclined to pay their taxes or to invest their profits. By the middle of the 1790s the old system of repartimiento once again reappeared, although in an altered form.

The difference between the old system of repartimiento and the altered form concerned both the merchants and the subdelegados. Formerly, the merchants from the Consulado of Mexico in concert with the alcaldes had controlled the cochineal industry and other industries through the repartimiento system. The reforms ended the Consulado of Mexico's monopoly, and in time they caused

Table 6-5. Continued

Pueblos/Products	1st yr.	2d yr.	3d yr.	4/5th yrs.	Total
Tehuantepec	70	60	40	40	210
[21,746 or 10 p/p; cochineal, fish]					
Teotitlan del Valle	50	40	40	30	160
[12,432 or 13 p/p; cochineal]					
Teotitlan del Camino	60	60	40	40	200
[19,367 or 11 p/p; cochineal, slaughtering, *quepeles?*]					
Teozacualco, Teococuilco,	40	40	30	20	130
Teoxomulco					
[12,938 or 10 p/p; cochineal, wheat]					
Teposcolula	30	30	20	20	100
[43,591 or 2 p/p; cochineal, wheat, slaughtering]					
Teutila	40	30	25	20	115
[23,906 or 5 p/p; cotton, vanilla]					
Villa Alta	100	80	60	60	300
[58,280 or 5 p/p; cochineal, cotton, yarns, shawls]					
Xicayan	100	80	80	80	340
[28,749 or 12 p/p; cochineal, cotton]					
Yanhuitlan	80	60	40	40	220
[?; cochineal]					
Total	1,265	999	795	715	3,774

Source: British Library, Additions 13978, fols. 11–13 with population data from Hamnett, *Politics and Trade,* 188.

Note: Several places listed in the survey were in other intendancies. Abbreviation "p/p" means pesos per person for the five-year period.

a shift in the cochineal business from the Consulado of Mexico to the Consulado of Veracruz. In addition, though, the subdelegados, as the principal contact with the Indian pueblos, exercised greater control over trade than the alcaldes, who were financially dependent on the merchant community. The commercial arrangements that the subdelegados negotiated or dictated were not different from those under repartimiento except in one crucial respect: the subdelegado, not the merchant, set the terms of the contracts.

By the early 1790s the flaws in the reforms were evident to proponents and critics alike. Both the government and the church had criticized repartimiento and had supported reforms in order to free cochineal producers and to insulate royal officials from the merchants. They had not, however, anticipated the need to provide the services that the merchants had offered or to monitor the subdelegados. The merchants themselves, whether from the capital or the port, were ready to exploit the deficiencies that they encountered, but with or without their exploitation, the new system showed itself rather quickly to be inept and corrupt.

Cochineal production had been falling since 1782 (1.1 million pounds), and although prices had moved in a relatively narrow range of 15–18 reales per pound, revenues had obviously shrunk. The decline in output had already begun before the administrative and commercial reforms of the late 1780s, and the decline continued, slowly and irregularly, as the reforms were being implemented (but not as fast as the apparent decline in repartimiento sales). Ten years later, in 1792, production was only 433,115 pounds, a drop of 58.2 percent; and while the price had only fallen by 1.5 reales from 17 reales per pound to 15.5 reales per pound, the income from cochineal registered in Oaxaca had decreased from 2.3 million to just over 800,000 pesos.

A report probably written in the early 1790s, as Gálvez's reforms came under fire, described the business climate around Oaxaca as deteriorating. Cochineal output was said to have fallen from 1.5 million pesos to half that amount, with the result that Indians could not even afford to purchase seeds for maize and other staples. Not only were seeds scarce, but so too were workers to trim and maintain the *nopaleras* (the prickly-pear cactus supporting the cochineal), which without such care would become unproductive. The bleak conclusion was that in the absence of merchants to finance the cochineal farmers and alcaldes to discipline them, the dye economy was collapsing.

Finally, not only was the economy in ruin but public order had also disintegrated. The remedy, some urged, was to reestablish repartimiento and, in particular, to permit the merchants to deal directly with the Indian pueblos and their financial needs. It was also proposed that safeguards be enacted to protect the Indians against illegal activities by private merchants or public officials. In brief, whatever the abuses under the old repartimiento system, the merchant had to be returned to underwrite the cochineal producer and to protect the royal treasury.[70]

Events rather than goals and policies begin to shape the reform agenda in the 1790s. Increasingly, the government at all levels suffered from indecision. The subdelegados, whose official and entrepreneurial activities could hardly be distinguished from those of their predecessors, the alcaldes, rightly reasoned, as Hamnett points out, that the long delay in resolving the dispute was a sign that repartimiento would be restored. Although never officially restored, the prohibition against it was never rigorously enforced and was ultimately suspended.

In the meantime new players, mainly the merchants of Veracruz, entered the scene, and unlike their counterparts in Mexico City who had loudly complained about the reforms but generally refrained from accommodating the reforms, Veracruz merchants pursued the new economic environment in a more imaginative and aggressive fashion. They sought to create a similar commercial network in which, through their Oaxacan agents, they made contracts with producers of cochineal and other products for their output in exchange for advances in cash or shipments of merchandise. Faced with a more competitive situation they or their agents tried to bypass local administrators and to negotiate directly with the producers, and even to offer less exorbitant terms. How successful the Consulado of Veracruz was in competing with the Consulado of Mexico or in dealing with local administrators cannot be easily answered. Just as the Veracruz merchants became more active in the cochineal industry, the industry itself was changing. From the mid-1780s through the first decade of the nineteenth century production of cochineal was volatile but generally followed a downward path, while income from cochineal actually rose slightly because prices climbed from 15 reales to 25 reales per pound. The rise in price was presumably the result of the shortage of dyes in Oaxaca, and that could have meant higher profits for merchants from Veracruz (and for the producers from Oaxaca). By one measure the Veracruz merchants expanded their business in Oaxaca as Mexico City merchants retreated from the region when prices began to turn upward.

To avoid the danger of transporting cash overland, merchants used the facilities of the treasuries in Oaxaca, Mexico City, and Veracruz to square their accounts. During the 1790s such transfers, which probably do not account for the region's total commerce, totaled 3.1 million pesos or 277,000 pesos per year. By the end of the 1790s Veracruz merchants commanded a larger share (in pesos) of the transfers than Mexico City's merchants. Although the Veracruz merchants outpaced their Mexico City rivals over the decade, the annual value of the dealings between the merchants and the treasury is best described as flat. But the production of cochineal was also flat during the same period.[71] This suggests that the volume of dyes available for export was a major determinant of the level of transactions carried out at the treasury. Despite generally stagnant production, slowly rising prices could have meant higher profits for merchants and even for producers if the data actually reflect the condition of the market for cochineal.

Whether trade in cochineal and a few other products from Oaxaca was more or less profitable in the late eighteenth century because of the commercial reforms, it functioned under a different structure. The treasury transactions involved about one hundred different merchants; from Oaxaca, forty-one; Mexico City, twenty-six; and Veracruz, twenty-four.[72] The merchants identified from the treasury transfers included some who had long been active in Oaxacan commerce and some who had only recently entered that commerce. As a general rule, Oaxacan merchants dealt with both consulados, although the recent arrivals probably had closer and stronger ties to Veracruz than Mexico City. As was true of other cities and businesses,

Oaxaca's merchant community had a fairly oligopolistic character. Based on treasury transfer data from 1790 through 1800, eight Oaxacan merchants handled 1.8 million pesos (67 percent) of the total 2.7 million pesos worth of transfers drawn from the merchants lists. Each had total transfers worth 100,000 pesos or more. Two established merchants, Francisco Antonio Goytia and Alonso Magro, were at the top of the list. Goytia's total transfers amounted to 482,000 pesos (18 percent of the total transfers) and Magro's to 372,000 pesos (14 percent). In both cases their transactions with Mexico City merchants fell during the course of the decade. It was also evident that a few merchants in the capital or in the port handled a major portion of Oaxaca's trade, although that trade probably was more widely dispersed in Veracruz's Consulado than in Mexico City's.

For the whole decade Mexico City merchants may have had a slight edge in the total value of the Oaxacan transfers over the Veracruz merchants (1.3 million against 1.2 million pesos). Only two Veracruz merchants—Casa de Unanué and Pedro Miguel de Echeverría—had transfers that exceeded 100,000 pesos, although their combined totals equaled more than 40 percent of the total transfer business between Oaxaca and Veracruz. With respect to Mexico City four merchants—Pedro Alonso de Alles, Matías Gutíerrez de Lanzas, Francisco Ignacio de Iraeta, and José Rafael de Molina—each had transfers worth at least 100,000 pesos, or almost 56 percent of the total transfers between Oaxaca and Mexico City.[73] Echeverría from Veracruz conducted transfer business worth 345,000 pesos, followed by Mexico City merchants Gutíerrez de Lanzas and Iraeta, each of whom had about 250,000 pesos worth of business. Several merchants from these two consulados have also turned up on lists of merchants conducting trade between the port or the capital and northern urban centers, such as Zacatecas and Guadalajara, both before and after Mexico City's monopoly was ended.[74] For some mercantile houses Oaxaca's trade was only part of a much larger and perhaps expanding colonial enterprise.

Whether from Oaxaca, Mexico City, or Veracruz, an established or a recently arrived merchant had to possess capital or have access to it in order to finance his dealings. Producers and administrators often required working capital beyond what merchants themselves could provide. One source of capital for all parties was through loans with various religious foundations. These loans may have become more crucial after the reforms because the guaranteed sales under the repartimiento contracts made business riskier.

Some of the old-line mercantile houses (principally in Mexico City), perhaps ill-prepared to participate in a more competitive climate, abandoned the Oaxacan market because the risk appeared to be too great. Exports rose after the end of the blockade in 1801, in part because a surplus had accumulated, but then the promulgation of Consolidación de Vales Reales in 1804 caused enough economic stress to forestall any further growth in cochineal market.[75] Between 1804 and 1808 tens of thousands of pesos were paid into the treasury to redeem loans or shares of loans that religious foundations had made to businessmen, some of whom were engaged in cochineal trade. The tightening of credit surely made it harder to raise the capital necessary to expand the industry, but the exact relationship between the impact of consolidación and the production of cochineal remains vague. In the previous twenty years, since the middle of the 1780s, production had not shown any sustained recovery or growth. To be sure, the disruptions (in addition to consolidación) had been serious and numerous, and they must be considered in any attempt to describe the long-term developments. On the other hand, the sign of improvement between the blockade and the consolidación could have been equally misleading.[76]

By 1810 the cochineal industry in Oaxaca had reached such a deplorable state that this sparked another vigorous debate about reinstitution of repartimiento. Those who favored repartimiento recognized the problem of the current scarcity of capital, but they also viewed it as a long-term consequence of ill-conceived reforms. Those reforms trimmed the powers of the alcaldes or replaced them, but they did not directly provide for the services that the alcaldes had performed.[77] In the long term, however, the cochineal industry did not undergo the transformation that was anticipated for a variety of reasons covering both internal as well as external circumstances. Fashioning a policy to deal with new conditions or to achieve new goals proved to be more difficult and disruptive than reformers had realized.

Some of the pueblos just discussed figure in Marcello Carmagnani's recent work on how Oaxacan Indians reconstituted their ethnic identity in the seventeenth and eighteenth centuries. His purposes are different from ours, and yet economic affairs—namely, the organization and management of the natives' economies—occupy a crucial place in the argument for reconstitution of identity. Briefly Carmagnani postulates that Indian communities were far more flexible and inventive in adapting to economic pressures and governmental intrusions than is generally accepted in the conventional view of their constant struggle to defend and expand territorial rights. Land was still central to the communities' economic lives, but it was not their only economic resource. They learned to develop new strategies to exploit economic resources that allowed them to maintain their populations and to fulfill external obligations such as tribute and repartimiento. The adaptability of native communities to economic changes is convincingly related by Carmagnani. Certainly the productive capacity of the native had to rise, but did the rise in capacity simply allow native economies to keep pace with the demands of the populations as well as the merchants and bureaucrats, or did it add to the communities' economic well-being?

Carmagnani provides some data to show that funds accumulated by the communities and their religious endowments grew during the last quarter of the eighteenth century. More needs to be known about the components of these funds—for example, if the communities or endowments were simply assessing their members more—and about what happened to these funds after the 1790s, when both the series ends and the economy falters. Moreover, the accumulated funds were not large. In five communities with perhaps thousands of inhabitants, the balance of accumulated funds was under 10,000 pesos. Finally, since much of the trade within communities and between them was based on barter but outside the communities it was based on money, the terms of trade—how the products were valued within the whole network—can be a crucial factor. If goods being introduced from the outside carried high prices and goods being shipped to the outside carried low prices, then the communities could suffer a drain of wealth. From an economic viewpoint the new strategies had an uncertain impact.[78]

Credit and Debt

In silver mining, cloth making, and cochineal the merchant's role can be clearly observed and analyzed. But the credit market upon which much of the colony's economic activity was based was both more complex and mysterious than these earlier discussions have perhaps indicated. The merchant's role grew because of his wealth or, more accurately, his access to wealth.[79] Although some merchants were certainly wealthy enough to underwrite their own activities, many others had to borrow to conduct their businesses. Merchants borrowed from each other, and to a more limited extent they borrowed from the church. Although the church tended to favor loans to agriculturalists—in Brading's words "the colony's land bank"—it ended up lending money to merchants for purchase of property as well as for other business ventures.[80]

The church normally acquired its wealth from several sources.[81] The main sources were tithes paid by landholders, rents from urban and rural properties owned by the church's various branches, and interest payments on loans and mortgages made to citizens and businesses from religious endowments. The church's total assets cannot be easily accounted for because they were spread through so many agencies from the regular to secular branches and from ecclesiastical to lay organizations. There is agreement that the church controlled (passively or actively) a substantial part of the colony's tangible wealth, but there is less agreement on exactly how it exercised that control.

Recently, Arnold Bauer has tried to advance the discussion of the church's financial role by distinguishing among the various instruments used by the church to acquire or lend its assets. It is important, argues Bauer, to distinguish between liens and loans, or *censos-grávamen* and *censos-prés-*

tamo. A lien was an encumbrance on a property that resulted from an agreement to finance a church activity but not to transfer any money except for the annual interest of 5 percent on the amount subscribed for the activity. A loan, on the other hand, was an act of advancing credit to someone who agreed to terms concerning payment of interest and repayment of principal. In either, the interest could be used for church needs, loans, or both. "The problem," writes Bauer, "is to determine to what extent the church acted as a financial institution lending capital at interest and to what extent it merely soaked up 5 percent annuities off the top of the economy."[82]

Trying to untangle the confusion over terms is especially acute when any effort is made to use contemporary sources that estimated the amount of wealth held or invested by the church. One example is a protest, probably from the Ayuntamiento in Mexico City, after the proclamation of Consolidación de Vales Reales in 1804. In that protest the writer declared that religious endowments, called simply obras pías, were worth about 50 million pesos with the following breakdown: "los bienes especificos de obras pías" were worth 25 million pesos and "las acciones al numerario disperso en los vasallos" 18–19 million pesos. Another 7 million pesos, less clearly defined, was also included to reach the total of 50 million (plus) pesos. The document further stated that 20 million pesos of the obras pías were held in two archbishoprics and seven bishoprics.[83] The document distinguishes between what appears to be property (called *sus fincas* in another place) and capital held by the obras pías. The fact that the protest also claimed that the 50 million pesos earned 2.5 million pesos suggests that the total principal outstanding covered both liens and loans. Because these figures cannot be corroborated, even the 2.5 million pesos may be no more than the application of the standard rate of 5 percent to the 50-million-peso total.[84]

Since most of the ecclesiastical liens and loans were secured by land, scholars have concluded that land, a readily available asset, was heavily encumbered. Bauer, for one, has observed, "On one thing everyone agrees: by the end of the eighteenth century, rural and urban property was heavily laden with financial charges."[85] Even merchants and traders became landowners by borrowing from the church.[86] While the church was not a harsh lender because it did not often foreclose, it may not always have been an intelligent lender.[87] The extent to which the church was lenient about the payment of interest or repayment of principal affected the amount of lendable funds that could be recycled through the economy. The amount was not insignificant. Based on the above figures, the per capita debt was 10 pesos for every man, woman, and child. If nonecclesiastical liens and loans were included, the per capita debt might then double. At 20 pesos, it would not be far below what we have estimated for per capita income. This may well have become a substantial burden for an economy that was still basically at a subsistence level. The consolidación was a factor in the emerging financial crisis, but the level of indebtedness, especially under the control of the church, may have been a bigger factor.[88]

The extent to which family assets and church obligations became so entangled as to limit any further formation of capital can be seen in the mayorazgo belonging to José Gregorio Guerrero Dávila Moctezuma, one of Mexico's oldest and noblest families. Several plans for resolving a dispute over a part of the mayorazgo were drawn up in 1786. Each property held by the mayorazgo was listed with a description of the property, the name of the renter, and actual and potential rents for the year.[89] The rents were derived from several dozen properties in Mexico City, its suburbs, and the countryside. The documents do not reveal how the properties were acquired or whether any encumbrance against the estate resulted from the purchases of the properties.

A typical procedure was for the founder of an endowment to use a piece of property as collateral in perpetuity and to agree to an annual interest payment (usually 5 percent) for the amount of the endowment that was, in effect, charged against the property itself. The rentals were listed as houses, stores, properties, and combinations of the three, and the annual rents ranged from a few dozen pesos to 1,000 pesos per annum. The highest rentals were concentrated in the Calle de San Bernardo (in the capital), where seven properties (two houses with stores, four houses with properties, and one house) averaged 900 pesos per year. Total rents from all properties was approximately 25,000 pesos per year, and the average rental was about 500 pesos per year. Only a dozen properties rented for under 100 pesos per year, and since the rest exceeded that level, the properties as a group could be classified on the high side of the rental market. The total value of all the properties was not given, although it probably was between 0.25 million pesos and 1 million pesos.

More pertinent to the present discussion than the rentals are the loans which the mayorazgo recognized, the lenders, and the interest due or past due for each one. Most of the censos listed appear to be liens (grávamenes) on properties used for founding religious endowments. They amounted to about 165,000 pesos with another 30,000 pesos in censos that could have been religious liens or private loans. The total outstanding debt could have reached 195,000 pesos with an annual interest charge of 9,700 pesos. The largest lien was for 50,000 pesos held by the Convento de San Bernardo, but the average lien was about 6,000 pesos. A survey of the liens indicates that the endowments included parish churches, monastic orders, and ecclesiastical and lay organizations. A major portion of the annual interest charge was current, with arrears being more evident among the contested censos. Little can be learned from the survey about the individuals who were listed as lenders, although several had names of prominent Mexico City mercantile families. Hence all the liens and loans could cost the mayorazgo about 9,500 pesos per year, and no part of any principal was repaid during the year.

But there were other costs. In addition to interest payments on the liens and loans, the estate had to pay *alimentos* (allowances) to various members of the family or household in the neighborhood of 10,000–13,000 pesos, and when that was combined with the interest on the liens and loans, the mayorazgo was left a balance of 5,000 pesos or less.[90] Because ecclesiastical censos and family alimentos entailed annual obligations, the estate had no power to alter how it spent more than half of its rental income. Although this money could have been used by church agencies or family members to promote social good or economic development, we know nothing about how these funds were in fact spent.[91] From the estate side, however, what is of interest in terms of capital and credit is how little money was invested in productive enterprises. In the late eighteenth century private citizens as well as church agencies had increasingly turned to the security of rental income as opposed to the risk of business investment. If this mayorazgo is representative of how merchant families, who along with the church owned a major part of the colonial wealth, organized their financial affairs, then the capacity of mercantile wealth to expand the pool of available capital was hobbled.

Additional information about the credit market and the merchant's role can be gleaned from the Guadalajara region. By analyzing data from *Libros de Hipotecas*, ledgers in which loans in Guadalajara were registered, Greenow constructed a profile of lending and borrowing operations that presented a more complex network than emerged from focusing on church affairs. During the eighteenth century 19 million pesos were lent, with only one-third ever being completely repaid. After 1770, even though loans were repaid more promptly, the time often amounted to twenty years. Faster repayments probably helped to sustain the "surplus of credit" toward the end of the eighteenth century when capital was both more scarce and more expensive, but given the credit-worthiness of many borrowers, faster repayments may not have been possible or larger loans may not have been prudent.[92]

Merchants accounted for 5.3 percent of all loans between 1720 and 1820. Merchants borrowed about 2.6 million pesos but lent only 1 million pesos. Of those borrowing from merchants 27.1 percent were religious groups, 10.4 percent were other merchants, 9.3 percent were clergymen, and 52.8 percent were in a large, miscellaneous category. It is worth noting that the church was known to be a lender, yet its clergy could borrow. From the borrower side, the percentage of loans between merchants was relatively small; but from the lender side, the percentage of loans by merchants to merchants was higher, at 28.9 percent. Also from the lender side, the percentage of "other" or "occupation not indicated" dropped from more than half (on the borrower side) to less than one-third.

In analyzing the amount rather than the number of loans, Greenow uncovered that shopkeepers preferred ecclesiastical credit for loans up to about 8,000 pesos and that merchants called upon each other to finance loans above 20,000 pesos. Merchants could arrange large loans among themselves because, as owners of haciendas or as members of families that owned them, they used them as collateral, an option that many less wealthy traders and retailers lacked.[93]

In the last quarter of the eighteenth century merchants changed their pattern of borrowing. Before 1780 the church was tapped for 40–60 percent of the loans, but after that it was used for only 15–20 percent. The Consulado did not fill the void left by the church, for it provided only a fraction of what merchants borrowed. Increasingly, individuals served as lenders: from 35.7 percent in the 1720s and 1730s, to 84.1 percent in the 1780s and 1790s, and down to 79.6 percent in the first decade of the nineteenth century. Although the individuals cannot always be identified, many of them were merchants and operated within an informal network of business associates and family members.[94] The point can be made that the continuing or expanding reliance on family for capital would not create what Mexico mainly needed, a stable, functioning, institutionalized credit market.

There can be no doubt that the colony depended on credit—advances, loans, and other such arrangements. Even the libranza was a form of credit, although it ultimately had to be paid in specie or the drawee was declared to be in default.[95] It can be argued that by the late colonial period land, as one possible source for financial credit and thereby economic expansion, was already so heavily encumbered that it could hardly bear much more. Indeed, church policy may have enhanced the burden on land not only by encumbering the land, but also by extending the repayment time and more or less maintaining the 5 percent rate of interest. Although the staff of Mexico City's *Juzgado de Capellanía* was, according to Michael Costeloe, diligent in protecting the agency's interests and funds, the agency's procedures for making loans indicate that few of the loans were repaid within the specified time and most became perpetual mortgages on which heirs to the properties continued to pay interest. Actual figures on how much the church had lent or had to lend in the eighteenth century are not yet available. Various estimates point to a growing demand for loans and a shrinking supply of funds.[96] That could only retard business activity.

In regard to the church as lender Margaret Chowning writes that the "church was an endlessly patient creditor." In analyzing the impact of consolidación in Michoacán she found that leniency was still evident in the policies and decisions of the juntas that were charged with enforcing consolidación. For example, those who "composed" (that is, renegotiated the terms of their debts) rather than redeeming their loans made a lower "initial payment" and took longer to repay the renegotiated loan than the law specified. Further, perhaps as many as 40 percent (more than 2,000 persons), with loans worth about 2.5 million pesos or more, simply "did not comply with the decree." Up to 1808 consolidación may have yielded about 1 million pesos for the government out of a total of more than 6 million pesos in loans and liens.[97] Whatever the impact on the public, and by extension on the economy, the amount of money actually collected under consolidación was probably permanently lost to the credit market once it passed to the government.

Nonpayment, although perhaps helpful for the individual borrower, had the effect of restricting the velocity of money. If money did not recirculate, especially in a situation where the pool of currency may have ceased growing, then economic expansion was less likely. What nonpayment did, quite simply, was to increase the burden of debt.

Although businessmen—merchants and retailers in particular—had long acted as lenders and brokers, their role may have grown in the late eighteenth century as the demand for credit rose and the liquidity of the church shrank. In Michoacán beginning in the 1780s the volume of private lending rose until it may have exceeded the volume of church lending around 1805.[98] Businessmen were probably more rigorous in setting terms and demanding repayments, since unlike the church, they could not survive very long on annual interest payments. Private lending, as noted, had obvious limits.

In his study of the business community in Mexico City, Kicza found credit to be widely used: an economy "based on credit," he wrote, "meant an economy based on trust, or at least on enforceable agreements, and this proved both a boon and a threat to merchants." Loans could be secured by properties or by fiadores, and since so many properties were already encumbered, fiadores became the only option available for many in search of capital. As uncertainty caused by reform, warfare, and indebtedness grew in the late eighteenth century, merchants had to learn how to balance opportunity and risk. Moreover, after the commercial reforms had begun to take root, few merchants could afford to specialize in a single product line or trading area. The internal market, argues Kicza, "lacked the size, the amount of circulating coin or currency, and the rapid transportation system necessary to support mercantile specialization." Credit was necessary to make the quickest possible sales. Sales had to be made as quickly as possible to avoid the cost of holding inventory or paying interest on loans to buy that inventory. Advancing credit to consumers was a way to help move merchandise. Although credit was a business that merchants could expand into more readily than other businessmen because they had wider contacts and possessed greater assets than most, they were also limited by the availability of capital, the existing level of colonial indebtedness, and the degree of credit-worthiness.[99]

As many other scholars have demonstrated through the study of marriage contracts, wills, and other legal documents, marriage was a common way of consolidating wealth and influence. Several well-known families—Iraetas, Iturbes, and Icazas—represented just such consolidation. Francisco Ignacio de Iraeta (Yraeta), was a Basque party member and then *consul* (presiding officer) (1789–90) of Mexico City's Consulado. He pursued various business projects that took him far afield at times from traditional commerce to protect his assets and optimize his opportunities. He, like others mainly from the merchant sector, was not necessarily bound to any established system for investing or acquiring wealth.[100] He had a son, Gabriel de Iturbe e Iraeta, and two daughters, María Rosa and Anna María.[101] Gabriel, whose wife was Margarita, was the executor of his father's estate. Gabriel, like his father, Francisco, was elected as a consul (1805–6) on the Consulado for the Basque party, was a city official, and was tapped as a *caballero* (knight) in the Order of Charles III. María Rosa was married to Isidro Antonio de Icaza, who was consul in the Consulado of Panama before moving to Mexico City, and who, like his father-in-law and his brother-in-law, was elected by the Basque party as a consul (1805–6) in the Consulado of Mexico City. He served as a municipal officer and was also elected as a caballero in the same order.

Sorting out the various inheritances (especially since María Rosa had also died) is difficult. Francisco's estate was estimated to be worth 1.2 million pesos. Francisco owned a commercial house in which Gabriel was a minor partner. Probate documents contained the following figures:

Value of inventory	367,689 pesos
Money on hand	376,281 pesos
Good loans	242,403 pesos
Doubtful loans	74,832 pesos
Bad loans	88,406 pesos
Total	1,149,611 pesos

It should be pointed out that this mercantile family, which was not known to be deeply involved in mining, carried only about one-third of its assets in inventory and the remainder in cash and various loans, a situation not unlike what Brading discovered in Guanajuato. Liquidity was obviously important, but as the figures are examined further, they reveal other problems with respect to how this well-to-do mercantile family used or could have used its assets.

Moreover, the fact that these documents were drawn up to provide for the distribution of the estate raises an additional question of whether such distributions diluted or enhanced the potential for investment of such a large family estate. Charges against the assets, perhaps largely in connection with the inventory itself, amounted to 345,650 pesos, so that the assets to be shared by the heirs were 803,959 pesos. More than one-third of the total assets or one-half of the unencumbered assets were in loans, 40.4 percent of which had been more or less written off. That would amount to more than 300,000 pesos!

The bulk of the 1.2-million-peso estate—perhaps 770,000 pesos—remained in the company, founded by Francisco but now under Gabriel's control. Anna María, Francisco's youngest daughter (twenty-five years old), and the children of María Rosa (Francisco's other daughter) and Isidro split a share worth about 420,000 pesos. María Rosa's three children—Isidro, who became the rector at the university, and Mariano and Antonio, who joined their father Isidro's firm—actually inherited 153,310 pesos, whereas Anna María received 148,673 plus another 30,035 pesos from her deceased mother's estate. (María Rosa may have already received her share of her mother's estate, perhaps as a dowry.)

Their inheritances included a roster of bad debts: 15,811 pesos in *dependencias dudosas* and 27,332 pesos in *dependencias perdidas* for a total of 43,143 pesos each. Their part of the uncollectable debt appears to have included a part of 50,000-peso loan made by Francisco to the miners' guild. Francisco's daughter and grandchildren received "dinero efecto," which consisted of cash, bills of exchange, and redeemable loans: 129,923 pesos for Anna María and 133,560 for the grandchildren. Among the items in Anna María's inheritance were notes drawn on the Consulado, tercios of cacao, property at the Hacienda de Sotepingo, and household goods. Each received 100 shares, worth 18,750 pesos, in a Philippine company.[102] Icaza was himself the son of a well-established mercantile family, and by this marriage the links between two well-to-do families were further cemented.[103]

Francisco Ignacio de Iraeta was probably one of Mexico's most successful and important merchants, and yet when he died, he left an estate that was by eighteenth-century standards very large but also lacking in liquidity. That meant that just under half of the value of the estate was effectively lost. Moreover, one-third of the estate (including both assets and liabilities) was split among four persons—a daughter and three grandchildren—in an action that spread out the liabilities but also the assets. A major mercantile fortune was probably less capable of extending credit or lending money after the death of the founder than before.

The Consulado of Mexico, like some of its members, carried a heavy debt load in the late eighteenth century. By the end of the colonial period, in two separate accountings, the Consulado had acquired at least two sets of loan obligations for a total of just under 3 million pesos. One set carried interest of 4–4.5 percent and the other 5 percent. The interest rate schedule could not be characterized as treating one type of borrower, such as the church, differently from another type, such as a widow. The audits took place in 1782 and again in 1804, and the names of the lenders and the amounts of their loans did not change for the most part. The loans at 4–4.5 percent totaled 1.6 million pesos in 1782 and again in 1804, but the 5 percent loans may have fallen from 1.2 million pesos in 1782 to 1.1 million in 1804. Interest payments, which amounted to 130,000 pesos per year in 1782, had also fallen to 120,000 pesos in 1804. It is not clear, however, that all interest payments were current. Interest was to be paid from the avería with each loan being assigned to one of the four avería categories, and it was to be paid every four months.

What were the loans used for? That question is harder to answer. It is possible that these loans were raised in connected with the Consulado's role to repair and maintain the Desagüe of Huehuetoca, a canal that passed from the city to a place called Nochistango in the pueblo of Huehuetoca. From 1607 when the canal was first built until 1777, money was assigned to the cost of building, maintaining, and repairing the canal from the wine and meat monopolies, granted by the municipal government. From 1607 and 1777 one account showed 5.7 million pesos in revenue, 5.4 million pesos in cost, with a balance of 0.3 million pesos. When the figures are actually added up, however, the total income was 5.7 million pesos and the total expense was 5.8 million pesos, for a loss of about 100,000 pesos. From 1667 to 1777 revenues (2.0 million pesos) exceeded costs (1.6 million pesos), based on the corrected totals, by just under 0.4 million pesos. In those 100 years it appears that income was sufficient to cover costs. In the ten years from 1767 to 1777, though, considerable work may have been required on the canal because expenses (567,000 pesos) outpaced revenues (383,000 pesos) by 1.5 times.

The Consulado made at least one loan of 275,000 pesos to the city for work on the canal prior to 1777, perhaps to help finance the renovations of the early 1770s. Since 1777 (up to 1789) the Consulado spent 800,000 pesos to rebuild the canal. It is unclear how this was financed except that it combined cash and loans, some or all of which show up in the aforementioned categories. From the Consulado's viewpoint it was not only a worthy project but also a necessary one: without an operating canal, commerce through and around the city was greatly slowed and often curtailed. Unfortunately, despite such large expenditures to build a new tunnel, the work was not satisfactory. There were numerous complaints about its design and operation.[104]

Whatever the loans were for, whether for needed public works or for other concerns, they entailed a substantial amount of late colonial capital held by the church and private citizens. A vast majority (perhaps two-thirds) of the loans to the Consulado came from religious organizations. The largest— 485,000 pesos—was provided by the Patronato of the Marquis of Castañiza, a recently deceased Basque merchant and Consulado member.[105] The next three largest were also ecclesiastical loans, but the fifth largest of 206,000 pesos was from a citizen, José Zeballos. Zeballos was not identified, although a José Zeballos was then an active miner and aviador in Zacatecas. Others can be identified as merchants, hacendados, and miners, whose loans ranged from thousands to tens of thousands of pesos.

By 1804 a few lenders had been repaid a part of the principal. Among the top five lenders (each in excess of 200,000 pesos), a loan from Patronato de Castañiza was 100,000 pesos lower. In addition, another Castañiza endowment (*Colegio de Indias*) had received a payment against the principal of 60,000 pesos. The similarity in the 1782 and 1804 lists reinforces what Brading and others have concluded: lenders came to prefer public projects to more speculative investments in productive industries even at the low annual interest of 4–5 percent.[106] Whether the Consulado could have repaid the loans may be moot if lenders did not insist that they be repaid.[107] As it happens, the avería was barely adequate to cover the costs of the Consulado's operations including the interest payments. The longer the money from religious foundations and private citizens was tied up in the Consulado's debt, the less quickly it could be recycled through the economy for other projects and needs.

Even in an economy driven by an expanding silver industry, lending and borrowing were necessary and potentially beneficial activities. In the absence of formal banking institutions those with wealth or with control over wealth became the lenders. Merchant wealth derived from a long-standing monopoly over Atlantic commerce (and to a more limited degree Pacific commerce). The church too had an equally long-standing monopoly over the colonist's spiritual life. The Bourbon reformers, who found such traditional economic practices incompatible with their more rationalistic fiscal policies, forced a series of changes on the way in which capital was formed and invested. But the changes may not have gone far enough or may not have moved in the right direction to produce the economic transformation that the reformers hoped for. Both mercantile and ecclesiastical capital contributed to the growth of the economy, but since so much borrowed capital was never repaid, the borrowings themselves and the indebtedness that they represented simply became obstacles to growth. The church, which may have been more interested in providing for its own support than making its capital more productive, could well have exhausted most of its lendable funds by the late eighteenth century. The mercantile community, which unlike the church was both lender and borrower within a much riskier economic world, may have reached its limit as well. Nearly every merchant whose estate can be examined had large credits for loans made or large debts for loans owed, or both. How much capital was generated, needed, and invested may never be known. By the end of the eighteenth century millions of pesos were tied up in liens or loans for a variety of activities, some of dubious or no economic value, that may have diverted ever-increasing amounts of money to pay for the burden of the debt rather than to refund the debt in order to recycle the capital. There is an additional player in this drama, however. The government itself controlled a large stake of the colonial economy with particular reference to the size and nature of the debt.

7

Royal Treasury and Economic Policy

Economic growth and change cannot be divorced from the goals and policies of the Crown and, in particular, the royal treasury. Although the state owned and operated some businesses (such as mercury, salt, and tobacco), the principal sectors—mining, agriculture, and manufacturing—were held and managed privately. The state's power and influence extended far beyond what businesses it owned and operated. Products, sales, and transfers were subjected to heavy taxation and regulation that derived not only from the government's ordinary fiscal needs but also from numerous special undertakings at the imperial and international level. Mercantilism remained at the heart of the Bourbon commercial policy, as it been for the Hapsburgs.

A distinction, however, can be drawn between the mercantilism of the Bourbons and their predecessors. Faced with a bankrupt treasury and a stagnant economy, the Bourbons sought to introduce a more rational and logical imperial system that had a direct bearing on the economy itself. There was no single, overarching plan that was conceived and implemented at once by the eighteenth-century Bourbon rulers. From Philip V through Charles III to Ferdinand VII, reformers tried a variety of experiments to streamline the administrative structure and to reinvigorate the colonial economy. The pace and intensity of these reforms varied markedly from reign to reign, but the reforms themselves had a common aim of both extending and consolidating control over the empire. These reforms, either in their theoretical formulation or in their direct application, were not intended to diminish or limit the power of the state, although they may have changed the manner in which the state performed its role or exerted its influence.

What the Crown gave up with one hand, it often took with the other. In the end the Bourbons may have proved to be more efficient than the

Hapsburgs but also more exploitative. Richard Morse's description of the eighteenth century (at least after 1750) as a time when Mexico, technically a "kingdom" within the empire, truly became a colony relates directly to the reforms and the changes that they induced.[1] In economic terms, the colonies, Mexico in particular, had less and less opportunity to guide or finance their own development at a time when their own productive capacity was expanding. What the colonies would have done if the imperial noose had not been drawn so tightly remains a matter of speculation. In important ways these economies were still driven by extractive industries and bound by legal restraints that made change slow in coming and full of controversy. But the option to choose a different course or to modify the existing course was severely limited because of Bourbon policy.

Revenue Trends

If one has any doubt about the implications and ramifications of the reforms, one can turn to the operations of Spain's treasury during the third and fourth quarters of the eighteenth century, when the reform movement had entered high gear. From 1760 to 1788 the treasury spent more than 15 billion *reales de vellon*, or approximately three-quarters of a billion pesos. Of that amount 6.4 billion reales de vellon, or 43 percent, were spent over the first half of the period, 1760–73, while 9.4 billion, or 57 percent, were spent during the second half, 1774–88. Expenses were high at the beginning of the 1760s during the later years of the Seven Years' War and then declined in the late 1760s and early 1770s. Expenses began rising during the second half of the 1770s until they peaked in 1780. Although they declined after that, they were still higher than they had been in the previous two decades. Even though the expense curve contains two distinct phases, a long-term rate of 1.8 percent per year has been calculated.[2] In the first phase, because it begins in the middle of the war, expenses follow a downward course, and in the second phase, expenses first rose and then retreated.

Without data for the period after 1788, as European warfare intensified, we can assume that the outflow from the treasury also intensified. In short, to meet ever-increasing growth in outlays the Spanish Crown was faced with the task of tapping new sources of revenue and further squeezing existing sources. Part of the burden was obviously borne by Spain's inhabitants, but part of it, perhaps a major part of it, was borne by the colonies, in particular by Mexico.[3]

Describing the treasury and how it worked in the eighteenth century is a subject large enough for its own book. Here our aim is to examine the treasury in terms of those functions that had a major impact on the colonial economy.[4] Even without a full-fledged history of Mexico's treasury, the scope of the treasury can best be examined through the recently published royal accounts. The debate over how to use these accounts and exactly what they contain will continue well into the future. In time, no doubt, a highly reliable version of the accounts will appear. Still, the accounts are much too valuable a statistical source to be ignored until that version appears. An approach that includes precautions and qualifications is to be preferred to no approach at all.[5]

The series have flaws, but they all yield growth rates that are relatively close in the long term. For short-term analysis, however, one series may be superior to another. For ease of reference we have dubbed them series A, B, and C.[6] We will begin with series C, for if the annual totals are accepted as they appear in the ledgers, then the treasury's total income between 1701 and 1810 was 1,374.3 million pesos, for an annual average of 12.6 million pesos. The growth rate is 3.2 percent each year.[7] Beginning in the late 1780s and the early 1790s the yearly totals show a dramatic jump from 10–15 million pesos to 20–30 million pesos. Then in the first decade of the nineteenth century the totals reach 40–50 million pesos. One can quickly see that about one-half of the total revenue for the whole period came from the last quarter (1780–1810).

The annual totals for series C point to a rapid acceleration in the collection of revenue in the fourth quarter of the eighteenth century. When the accounts themselves are examined for clues that might explain this rapid increase, they are not very helpful. Instead of reflecting changes in the economy's productive capacity, they are primarily concerned with transfers, loans, and other such transactions. For example, if we aggregate all the receipts for borrowings from citizens and organizations from the middle of the 1780s (when the first item appeared) to 1809, the total exceeds 150 million pesos, or equal to 6 million pesos per year. It is possible that the government was able to extract that amount of money from an economy that was producing only 15 million pesos worth of silver each year, but it is highly improbable. The exact level of the public debt is not yet known, although it could have been as high as 80 million in 1817.[8] In any event, what is clear is that the treasury's debt grew from a few million pesos to several tens of millions of pesos in a quarter of a century. Although this series has some obvious defects, it more than any other series alerts us to some significant changes in late colonial fiscal policies and trends.

Series A is certainly less controversial because it has been trimmed to a more conservative estimate of late colonial treasury receipts. If one regards series C as overstating income, one could argue that series A understates it. Total receipts in series A amounted to 790.6 million pesos, about half of series C's total, from 1700 to 1810. The annual average income was 7.3 million pesos, and the growth in income for the period was 2.3 percent yearly, not quite a full percent less than series C. Although one-third slower than series C, series A still grew at a rate that meant that treasury income was doubling every thirty years. Even at the slower rate royal revenue was growing considerably faster annually than either agricultural or mineral (1.0–1.4 percent yearly) output.

Series A grew faster in the second half than in the first half of the eighteenth century, and the surge in receipts that characterizes series C in the 1780s only showed up more moderately in series A after 1800. Still, in the first decade of the nineteenth century series A may have grown five times faster than the annual growth rate from 1700 to 1810. At some point between the agricultural crises and the Napoleonic wars, both series confirm that royal revenue was climbing at a decidedly higher rate. We need to underscore the point, however, that the difference between the two series concerns the high annual receipts in the last fifteen to twenty years and not the long-term structural change evident in all three revenue series and occasioned by the Crown's long-term need for money.

Series B is closer to series A over the long term but different from both series C and A in the short term. In series B the total revenue was 844.3 million pesos, for an annual average of 7.8 million pesos. The annual growth rate was 2.6 percent. The rise in revenue was faster in the second half of the eighteenth century than in the first half more or less along the lines established in series A. One difference, however, is that series B does not exhibit any surge of growth until 1804 or 1805, after which for the next five years it may have risen more rapidly than any time in the eighteenth century. In general, though, this series does not differ substantially from the other two: slower growth until the 1780s, after which it climbed rapidly. If we discount series C because it may contain some double-counting, then we are left with two series that tend to agree that revenues rose 5–6 percent a year from the middle 1780s until 1800, after which the growth may have reached twice that rate until Hidalgo's Revolt in 1810. Over the long run the more serious consideration is not so much the burst of collection of revenue at the end of the colonial period but the steady rise comparable to or in excess of growth rates for other economic sectors.

Caja Structure

The treasury was only as successful as its branches were in carrying out their duties and responsibilities. By the end of the eighteenth century nearly two dozen branches had been opened around the colony. Each of these reales cajas received instructions from and remitted funds to the central treasury in Mexico City. But the central treasury also served as a real caja, primarily for the area around the capital, and because of this dual role the possibility existed that the remissions of the funds from the branches to the capital could become intermingled with the funds collected directly at the real caja of Mexico City.

The problem shows up in a recent essay by Herbert Klein, who has used treasury accounts to analyze economic trends and structures.[9] His totals, which are decennial rather than annual, for each branch and for the whole treasury system are derived from an estimating procedure rather than from actual entries in order to overcome the gaps created by the missing ledgers from the reales cajas. The total revenue from 1700 to 1810 based on this technique is 2.1 billion pesos, compared to 1.3 billion pesos cited earlier in connection with series C. It is unfair to highlight the difference between the two totals (although the difference is significant) because Klein's aim is not to try to estimate a new grand total but to try to chart the role of the reales cajas in the overall treasury operations. The estimates of both the decennial totals and the grand total for the reales cajas appear reasonable in most cases. For example, we have studied the remissions from Zacatecas's branch to Mexico City between 1700 and 1810, and while Klein's estimate of those remissions is higher than what the certificates add up to, they are still close enough to make estimating procedures with some refinements a viable approach for overcoming some of the defects in the ledgers.

It is the estimates for Mexico City's caja that raise red flags, especially between 1780 and 1810. Up to 1780 its estimated receipts—in the range of 3 million pesos per year by decade—were consistent with what we expect from the caja in the city and region with the densest population and in comparison with other cajas. From 1780 to 1810, however, the estimates for the capital's caja rise so sharply that they total 759 million pesos, for an annual average of 25.3 million pesos. Except for Veracruz, which averaged about 12 million pesos per year (and which may also be suspect although it benefited from being the principal port), no other caja experienced a tripling of its estimated annual receipts. In short, the central treasury, as a branch rather than as a depository, collected nearly twice as much revenue as all the other cajas together from 1780 to 1810.[10]

These figures offer strong evidence for a two-pronged economic policy: to liberalize where possible in order to stimulate economic growth and to upgrade the administration of the treasury as much as possible in order to benefit from that growth through rigorous collection of taxes and fees. Behind these figures, however, lurks an important question: to what extent could local economies sustain the economic growth necessary for the state to collect the revenue calculated for all the various treasury series.

It proves easier to analyze the performance of the treasury system than to assess the economic impact for the colony as a whole or for specific localities with reales cajas. But the fact remains that the administrative reorganization would have yielded little new revenue without economic growth either on a local and regional basis or on a colonywide basis. Based on his interpretation of treasury revenue trends, Klein posits an eighteenth-century cycle of depression, boom, and stagnation.[11] With a long period of growth, speculates Klein, the economy may have acquired wealth that was increasingly spent on consumer purchases, some of which the government taxed in order to raise much-needed revenue. Thus if the colony's productive capacity began to falter in the late eighteenth century due to a lack of capital, part of the explanation for the continuing rise in receipts at the royal treasury was that the savings from the period of growth were being spent on consumer goods rather than on capital goods. The savings issue hinges on the long-term growth cycle. Without real growth, any savings would seem hard to achieve. We do not think that treasury data allow us to estimate accurately real economic growth.

Klein's work represents another approach that underscores that the economy had reached a troubling stage in the late eighteenth century. He is less ambivalent about the fact that the colony carried a greater tax load than the metropolis—in the 1790s, 8 pesos per person compared to 4.8 pesos per person respectively—and he implies that the colony was able for the most part to bear the burden.[12] That Mexico had a large tax bill is evident enough, but whether it could afford that bill is less apparent.

The real caja at Zacatecas has been studied more extensively than other treasury offices.[13] What can be reconstructed for the Zacatecan fiscal archives are not only the receipts and expenditures for the real caja, but also the remissions from the real caja to the Central Treasury in Mexico City for most years from 1750 to 1810 and for many years between 1700 and 1750. The remissions are important because they represent what was available to the colonial government from the total receipts minus expenses to operate the real caja.

The remitted funds can also be broken down by *ramo* (treasury division) within the caja. Over the whole colonial history of the Zacatecan real caja, the most important ramo was the collection of silver taxes: the *quinto* (fifth) in the sixteenth century and the diezmo (the 10 percent tax on silver) during the seventeenth and eighteenth centuries. In the case of the diezmo there were few if any expenses because the miner paid an additional 1 percent tax to cover the ramo's expenses. With the alcabalas, which was not permanently incorporated into the caja until 1777, the administrative costs were much higher, one-fifth to one-quarter of the total receipts, so that the government only received a portion (substantial though it was) of the actual receipts. All of the ramos had their own special considerations, but none was exempt from the drive to make them both efficient and productive in behalf of the Crown, especially during the second half of the eighteenth century.

When growth rates are computed for receipts at or remissions from Zacateca's real caja for the whole eighteenth century, they are among the lowest of all the reales cajas and much below the growth in central treasury revenue regardless of which series is used. The reason for this is well known: Zacatecas was the only major mining center to undergo a period of contraction and stagnation from 1725 to 1765. Between 1750 and 1809 data for total remissions between Zacatecas and Mexico City exist for almost every year. Data for several important ramos also exist for most years in which the ramos were functioning. Total remissions from 1750 to 1810 came to 23.8 million pesos, for an annual average of 425,000 pesos. Its remissions grew by 2.3 percent per year. The rise in remissions after 1750 reflected the recovery of mining and the expansion of the treasury. Productive mines were an essential condition to the economic health of Zacatecas as well as Spain's economic solvency.[14]

As with the central treasury, the rise in remissions from Zacatecas was related to economic recovery, population growth, and administrative reorganization, the last being especially important because it added such money-making ramos as *tabacos* to its revenue sources. The major ramos in terms of receipts at Zacatecas were diezmos (silver taxes), azogues (mercury sales), alcabalas (sales taxes), *salinas* (salt sales), and tabacos (tobacco sales). The first two ramos were a part of the real caja in 1750, the third became a part in 1777, the fourth in 1779, and the fifth in 1791.

Silver taxes and mercury sales, long-standing treasury functions, provided 10.4 million pesos (43.5 percent) and 4.4 million pesos (18.5 percent), respectively. But the benefit to the treasury of adding or expanding functions can be observed in the other ramos. Opening an outlet for the sale and distribution of tobacco in Zacatecas yielded 2.6 million pesos (10.9 percent) in remissions from 1790 to 1810. Sales taxes and salt purchases (salt used primarily in processing ore) added 2.1 million pesos (8.9 percent) and 1.3 million pesos (5.5 percent), respectively, to the remitted funds. If we rank these five sources according to their annual average for the years in which they functioned between 1750 and 1810, we find the following results (in pesos per year):

Silver	173,333	averaged over 60 yrs.
Tobacco	130,000	averaged over 20 yrs.
Mercury	73,333	averaged over 60 yrs.
Sales tax	63,636	averaged over 33 yrs.
Salt	41,936	averaged over 31 yrs.

The importance of the addition of alcabalas and tabacos can be seen in the fact that tabacos ranked second, ahead of mercury, and alcabalas ranked fourth, behind mercury. While diezmos and azogues receipts had been the mainstay of the Zacatecan caja for many years, they grew more slowly than receipts from ramos added to or incorporated into the treasury during the last quarter of the eighteenth century. The revenues from alcabalas or tabacos were more broadly based than diezmos and azogues, and they represented income sources that Klein generally described as taxes on commerce or as products for consumption.

Revenue from diezmos and azogues probably grew somewhat more slowly because some large mining enterprises were exempted from the diezmos, and the price of mercury was slashed by half in the second half of the eighteenth century. The impact of the exemptions from the diezmos can be seen when silver registrations are compared with silver remissions: the former rose twice as fast as the latter from 1750 to 1810. Still, there can be no doubt that by expanding treasury functions, the Crown tapped both new and heretofore underutilized revenue sources that could mean higher annual remissions, even in a local economy so inextricably bound to a single industry, such as silver mining.

With respect to alcabalas and salinas, the government placed under direct royal administration functions that had long been viewed as royal prerogatives but had been farmed out to the highest bidders. The royalization of the alcabalas probably entailed the most far-reaching administrative reorganization in that a separate office of the real aduana was set up in Zacatecas. Alcabalas receipts could be volatile because they depended on the general health of the local economy, and yet despite some volatility, remissions appeared to have more than doubled from 1778 to 1810. Salinas remissions, by contrast, after an auspicious start fell sharply from 1778 to 1810. When royal management began, they were at a very high level—generating nearly 90,000 pesos per annum in the first decade—because all payments for salt had to be made in Zacatecas (usually distant silver refiners used local merchants). The reason for the decline in salinas remissions was that the government eventually permitted refiners to pay for salt at their own local cajas without that payment being credited or remitted to Zacatecas. After that the annual remissions fell to about 30,000 pesos. (Under the prior arrangement the contractor paid his annual installment either in Mexico City or Zacatecas, but the installment was much smaller than the net income under royal control.) Finally, the establishment of a tobacco outlet in the early 1790s to serve the Zacatecan region resulted in some annual remissions that were in some years as large as silver tax remissions.

The variability in the remitted funds from the major ramos cannot hide the fact that half of the money remitted from 1750 to 1810 was raised in the last two decades, or that 40 percent was raised in the three new ramos (alcabalas, salinas, and tabacos). Nor can we ignore the fact that remissions from

Zacatecas to Mexico City rose at a rate equal to or even slightly higher than the increase in output of silver in Zacatecas. If Zacatecas's remissions averaged 400,000–500,000 pesos per annum between 1750 and 1810, that represented nearly one-quarter of the annual average value (2 million pesos) of the registered silver. It is evident that in the late eighteenth century a substantial portion of locally produced wealth was transferred to colonial and imperial needs.[15]

A longer but less specific dataset can be examined for Guadalajara's real caja. Although Guadalajara had several large mining camps within its borders, its economy was more dependent on farming and ranching than Zacatecas's was. From 1701 through 1804 Guadalajara collected revenues of 41.3 million pesos, for an annual average of just under 400,000 pesos (about the same as Klein estimated). About three-quarters of Guadalajara's income (approximately 30 million pesos) was received in the second half of the eighteenth century.[16] In eighteenth-century Guadalajara, total receipts probably grew twice as fast as Zacatecas's receipts, and this may point to an economy that was both more diverse and more robust for most of the century.[17] From 1701 to 1804 caja receipts in Guadalajara grew by nearly 2 percent annually, with growth in the second half 1.5 times greater than in the first half.[18] The rise in treasury receipts was slower in Guadalajara than for the colony as a whole. One possible reason is that the flow of receipts may have moderated in Guadalajara after the agricultural crises of the middle 1780s, although as yet this cannot be fully documented statistically.

The combined contribution of these two cajas to the central treasury was probably no more than 5–7 percent of the total royal income in the eighteenth century. But the impact of the real caja on the local economy could vary because it depended on the economy's main function, not its size. Cajas like Guadalajara, which had fewer units of silver to tax or mercury to sell, actually reached more deeply into the economy in per capita terms than cajas like Zacatecas did.

The treasury could only accomplish its goal of raising its revenue if the various cajas performed their duties with a degree of efficiency and dispatch. Although the system continued to be plagued by sloppy bookkeepers, fraud, and inconsistent policies, the operation of the system was improved over the course of the century and in particular after a heavy dose of administrative and financial reforms during the late third and early fourth quarters.

A survey (table 7-1) made of the performances of the cajas in 1770, just as the reforms were being discussed and implemented, showed that the 14 cajas reported spending 29.4 percent of their receipts, or 2.4 million pesos, on administrative costs.[19] Three of the cajas—Acapulco, Mérida, and Campeche—had costs that were 1.8–3.1 times greater than their receipts, and when they are removed from the list, the percentage of receipts to cover

Table 7-1. Receipts and Expenses for Reales Cajas and Other Treasury
Departments, 1770 (in thousands of pesos)

Real Caja/Ramo	Receipts	Expenses	Percent
Guanajuato	558	21	3.8
Durango	364	34	9.3
Guadalajara	341	39	11.4
Zacatecas	247	17	6.9
San Luis Potosí	226	22	9.7
Pachuca	169	6	3.6
Bolaños	127	10	7.9
Acapulco	125	390	[3.1]
Zimapán	84	4	4.8
Los Álamos	75	29	38.7
Campeche	44	78	[1.8]
Sombrerete	25	3	12.0
Mérida	19	55	[2.9]
Tabasco	10	1	10.0
Total	2,414	709	29.4
Veracruz	716	3,657	[5.1]
Mexico City	2,222	2,559	[1.2]
Total	5,326	6,925	[1.3]
Mint	947	234	24.7
Aduana	677	69	10.0
Pulque	228	7	3.1
Naipes	83	25	29.4
Puebla Account	168	160	95.4
Grand Total	7,455	7,420	99.5

Source: TxU, G 206–7.
Note: Puebla's special account concerns the privilege to provision departing ships.
See AGI, *México*, leg. 821 and 2,485 for more details on Puebla. Our totals differ
slightly from those given because of rounding off the figures. Numbers in brackets
show how many times greater expenses were than receipts.

costs falls to 8.4 percent. Why these three cajas had such high costs in 1770 or
whether 1770 was typical of other years was not discussed in the survey. But
two other cajas—Mexico City and Veracruz—need to be added to the list.
Veracruz's expenses were 5.1 times greater than its receipts, and the capital's
were 1.2 times greater, and when the totals are calculated, costs outrun
receipts for all the cajas by 1.3 times.

Zacatecas illustrates how cost effective a caja could be, even if it was not
typical. From 1760 to 1796 the costs to administer the caja and to collect the
revenue seldom exceeded 10 percent of the total receipts and were more
often than not in the range of 4–5 percent.[20] Over and above the cajas' costs

were many other fiscal obligations, such as justice, defense, interest or debt payments, and shipments of coin to Spain, on which the cajas' receipts were expended. Normally, these obligations were handled through Mexico City's treasury.[21]

The majority of the reales cajas, then, were expected to manage their operations primarily to generate income that could be funneled to the central government (and beyond) to meet its many obligations. In a system where most decisions of a local nature, such as repairing a road or building a jail, required central government approval, the massive outflow of money from the branches to the capital was not surprising. What appeared as costs in the ledgers of the caja in Veracruz, Mexico City, or Acapulco included more than the simple day-to-day administrative expenses of a treasury branch. How these costs were allocated or determined among the cajas remains to be investigated. If the calculations were made simply on the basis of the costs to keep an office open, to collect and remit taxes, and to manage the affairs of the treasury, then the evidence suggests that the ratio of costs to revenues was relatively low or within acceptable limits.

Treasury Operations

One obvious goal of the Bourbon reformers was to end or at least to limit severely the practice of farming out taxes to the highest private bidder. Although the reforms did not completely eliminate this practice, important functions such as the administration of alcabalas and salinas were restored to the treasury largely under plans prepared during the visita of José de Gálvez from 1765 to 1771. Whether farmed out or administered directly, the ever-expanding duties of the treasury meant that the government commanded a larger and larger share of the economic pie. Although the shape of the royal revenue curve has sparked considerable controversy, the expansion of treasury's functions, and therefore its receipts, cannot be denied.

Some functions had never been farmed out because they were too important to the Crown. That was especially true of the collection of silver taxes and tribute taxes. Tribute was a head tax that households of Indians and castas, except for mestizos, had paid since the middle of the sixteenth century, when the Crown began to exercise more control over the financial side of the encomienda system. The amount of revenue collected in tribute depended mainly on the size of the indigenous population at any given time.

The procedure for assessing the annual tribute had become standardized over time, although it was hardly simple and routine. Lists of tributaries (usually but not exclusively heads of households) were maintained for all settlements where tributaries might be found. Corregidores and alcaldes, local royal bureaucrats, were responsible for transmitting tribute payments from their localities to the reales cajas. The standard assessment per tributary was 1 peso and one-half of a fanega of maize (which could be computed at 9 reales per fanega, or 4.5 reales). In the Indian communities (blacks and mulattoes also paid tribute) the actual collection, based on what the local royal officials calculated the number of tributaries to be, was left in the hands of the Indian authorities themselves.[22]

During the depopulation of the late sixteenth and early seventeenth centuries, the total tribute declined. For example, in 1600 the treasury reported about 100,000 pesos from the various tribute categories, while twenty-five years later it reported only about half that amount. From the middle of the seventeenth century, as depopulation was followed by repopulation, the income from tribute grew. By 1700 it may have exceeded 300,000 pesos, and it may have doubled by 1750 and doubled again by 1800.[23]

Although tribute never ranked among the highest revenue sources once the eighteenth-century administrative reforms were underway, it remained an important source in those areas with large tributary populations, in part because it was not costly to administer. In 1770, for example, the government spent for administration about 10 percent of the 852,000 pesos that it collected in tribute. That was still the case in the 1780s, when the government collected 9.6 million pesos at a cost of 1.2 million pesos. Inasmuch as collectors were often reimbursed a percentage of what they collected (thus public officials were equivalent to tax farmers), the ratio of costs to receipts changed very little.[24] More than 90 percent of the tribute was collected for or deposited in Mexico City's caja, 5 percent was recorded in the cajas of Guadalajara, San Luis Potosí, and Guanajuato, and the remaining 5 percent in all other cajas.[25] At times tribute was designated for use by or in behalf of the Indians and other tributaries, but increasingly it simply became another source of state income.

On the level of the village or community where the tribute was raised, there was a definite and obvious link between economic activity and tribute policy. Except in periods of famines, when tribute might be excused, leaders had to collect whatever the community was assessed without regard for the prevailing economic, demographic, or political circumstances for that community. As tribute payments became identified with money payments, usually in hard currency, Indian communities had to organize their business affairs with reference to the Spanish colonial economy to ensure that money would be available to make the payment.[26] Tribute came to represent a transfer of wealth from Indians and castas to the government, and although growth rates cannot yet be verified from the existing tribute series, they probably corresponded minimally to the growth in numbers of tribute payers. Based on a 1 percent rate or less, the tribute-paying groups could see their total contributions doubling every seventy years or more.[27] The extent to which this was a burden depended on factors such as the ratio of those earning income to those assessed for tribute, the state of the economy in the area of the tributaries, and the availability of currency with which to pay the tribute. In addition, a shift of wealth from the tributaries to the state yielded few if any direct benefits to the tributaries themselves.

Alcabalas and tribute involved mainly effective periodic collection, but other treasury functions involved direct day-to-day management. Such was the case with at least three ramos in the mining sector: powder, salt, and mercury. All three items were sold through the cajas at prices and in allotments set by the Crown to ensure not only an adequate supply for the miner, but also a tidy profit for the government (as discussed in chapter 4 with reference to the mercury monopoly). The deeper the mines, the more vital powder was for the extraction of the ore in the eighteenth century. Although powder monopolies were common in Europe, as reported by Alexander von Humboldt, they were no more efficient there than in Mexico. The disadvantage for the state was that the ingredients for explosives were so readily available that they could be made almost anywhere. Humboldt calculated that the government sold a few hundred thousand pounds of explosives each year, but several times that amount was consumed in late colonial Mexico. The Crown sold its powder for under two pesos per pound, whereas contrabandists sold theirs for half that price.[28]

In the case of salt from Peñol Blanco near Zacatecas, the Crown had alternated between management by the royal treasury and by private contractors. A type of salt mined there was crucial to refiners because when it was mixed with ore, mercury, and other ingredients it improved the refining process. For most of the eighteenth century (until Gálvez's visita) merchants, usually from Zacatecas, held the contracts to administer and operate the Penal Blanco salt mines under which they could charge 4 reales per fanega for salt sold to refiners. The stipend paid to the Crown each year fluctuated between 10,000 and 30,000 pesos, but the profits earned by the contractors could be twice that much.

Gálvez reasoned that under royal management the Crown would earn more than the contractors now paid. In the first decade after incorporation in 1778, Gálvez's projection was largely realized, as the profits from salinas averaged 80,000 pesos per year. After that, salinas income dropped to levels comparable to what the Crown had earned under the contract system. Part of the decline occurred, as explained earlier, because buyers were accorded the convenience of paying for purchases at their own cajas. It is also known that the government at times had trouble maintaining output at Peñol Blanco because of too much rain or too few workers. This may have caused salinas income at Zacatecas to decline as buyers had to seek other outlets. Finally, it is possible that Peñol Blanco's declining remissions were a sign that it had become a less productive operation and served primarily the Zacatecan mining district.[29] For the colony as a whole, salinas revenues probably moved in step with silver production, although this does not indicate how productive or profitable the various salt mines were either under the royal treasury or private contractors.

The mercury monopoly presented the treasury with a special problem. Mercury was expensive even for the richest miners and refiners. For most of the eighteenth century it sold for 82 pesos per hundredweight before it dropped to 41 pesos. The correspondencia was devised not only to keep track of a valuable commodity but to keep all accounts current by requiring purchasers to pay for their next batch of mercury with newly registered silver. But this plan was not always effective because often miners or refiners lacked the silver to pay for the next purchase of mercury, without which their operations would come to a halt, with a great potential loss for the royal treasury and the local economy. Although the treasury expected immediate payment for mercury purchases, as prescribed by the correspondencia, it in fact allowed purchasers to pay for mercury after the ore for which it was needed was processed.

Regardless of various precautions, the treasury could find itself with unpaid mercury debts, some of which could rise sharply in periods of declining output. The real caja, which was directly responsible for collecting the debt, could threaten the purchaser with legal action such as confiscation of property, and in some cases the threats had the desired effect. But the ultimate weapon, foreclosure, was not always in the best interest of the real caja because the mine or refinery for which the mercury was purchased had to be kept in operation or restored to operation to recover the debt. The treasury did not often try to manage these operations directly. If it could not find a leasor, then both the property and the debt could be classified as "nonperforming."

Information on Zacatecas's management of mercury debt accounts reveals how intractable the indebtedness became from time to time, and how the Crown tried to prevent or reduce such indebtedness. As early as the late sixteenth century, according to Peter Bakewell, the real caja distributed mercury on credit, and by 1620 the Zacatecas treasury was confronted with "very considerable debts" in the amount of 356,000 pesos when yearly silver registrations were not much more than 250,000 marks, worth about 2 million pesos. (At Potosí, mercury debts reached 3 million pesos when silver registrations were worth 6–7 million pesos.) As a result of these and other debts the Council of the Indies ordered viceroys to accept only cash, which was often not available.[30] At the same time all old debts had to be collected and the money remitted to Spain. The "instant collection of the debt was impossible," writes Bakewell, "for miners did not have the wherewithal to pay." Since miners had to pay in cash, the treasury was more discreet about distributing mercury than before the council's order. One result was that merchants known as aviadores became much more visible in mining as backers of miners and refiners who lacked the cash to buy their mercury. "Few long-term debts," declares Bakewell, "were incurred after 1650."[31]

In the first half of the eighteenth century, in spite of these safeguards to forestall long-term indebtedness, Zacatecas's treasury found itself with a rising level of past-due accounts from mercury sales. The ledgers show that producers who had been active during the 1720s and into the 1730s, some of whom had only enjoyed modest success, had quit business by the late 1730s or early 1740s without paying off their mercury debts. As was true in the past, the downturn in mining was the chief culprit. The downturn may also have led officials to a less strict enforcement of mercury policy, which only compounded the problem.

In the 1750s, with the mining economy still sagging and the mercury debts still rising, the treasury was again ordered to take action to reduce and eliminate such indebtedness. Mercury debts had reached 112,000 pesos at a time when the output of silver was about 100,000 marks, with a value of 800,000 pesos. One-third of the accounts were more than twenty years old and probably uncollectible. The treasury's actions, however, were limited because unless the miners could arrange to pay off the debt, either completely or in installments, the choice was to take over the properties or to write off the debts. Confiscations were not enthusiastically pursued because the low state of the silver industry prompted little interest in the leasing of these embargoed properties. By the middle of the 1750s, although most of the current and recent debts had been settled, none of the long-term chronic debts had been resolved.

In 1757 the Crown notified all branches of a revised policy: credit would be approved only when the buyer had no accounts past due, when he presented a cosigner, and when he agreed to pay the debt in six months.[32] From that point onward long-term mercury indebtedness faded from the treasury's agenda. In 1787, for example, the real caja reported debts of over 35,000 pesos, none of which was past due; in 1792 its mercury debts had risen to more than 54,000 pesos, only a few of which exceeded the six-month limit. Finally, in 1795 it reported debts of under 34,000 pesos, again none of which was past due.[33] In these years the local industry was producing on average 250,000 marks of silver worth about 2 million pesos, a much more favorable ratio than what existed in the middle of the century.

The fiador became a crucial component in the advancing of credit for mercury purchases. Few miners or refiners had the financial resources to pay for mercury at the time of the purchase. It helped producers financially that silver output was on the rise and that the price of mercury was on the decline during the eighteenth century. But even the largest producers depended on credit to make their purchases and on fiadores to be approved for credit. Included among fiadores were miners, refiners, family members, and local businessmen but mainly merchants, such as aviadores, who had links already to the mining industry or to individual purchasers. Although not flawless, the fiador system effectively served the needs of the treasury and the industry.

The arrangements between the fiador and his client are partially revealed in the treasury documentation from which we have drawn examples. In 1724 Juan Alonso de Solis, a miner, used Lucas de Solis Argüelles, a merchant-aviador but also a relative, as a fiador in the purchase of 9 quintales (900 pounds worth about 750 pesos) of mercury. That was enough mercury to refine 900 marks of silver, and at the time the debt was due, Solis actually registered 3,422 marks, worth over 27,000 pesos, more than enough to pay the debt and release the fiador. In another case, Juan Antonio de Llano Villanueva, a miner, bought 6 quintales of mercury (to yield about 600 marks of silver) on credit with Miguel de Oses Villanueva, a merchant and relative, as fiador. The debt was never paid, and although it was small, it was typical of many debts, which in total amounted to thousands of pesos and eventually had to be written off as uncollectible. A third case involved a triad of two merchants and a miner. Domingo Sánchez de Quirano was the aviador to Gerónimo Pérez Namorado, a small miner, and Diego López de Aragón, a merchant, served as Sánchez de Quirano's fiador when he purchased 17 quintales of mercury to be sold to his clients including Pérez Namorado. This particular debt was never satisfied, even though Sánchez de Quirano and López de Aragón continued to do business with the caja in behalf of Namorado, a marginal producer, and other clients.[34] The standard arrangement granted the purchaser six months to pay his debt to the caja, and in some cases the arrangement was only approved if the purchaser presented a fiador and left a deposit in coin or silver when the mercury was purchased.

During the 1770s, when mining conditions were more favorable, the fiador system not only served its basic purpose effectively but it also proved to be highly adaptable—even if some of the variations may have increased the risk for the caja. In a 1772 example, Phelipe Garcés, a miner and refiner, bought mercury on credit with the aviador Francisco Ayala as his fiador, while at the same time Garcés was serving as a fiador for another refiner, Francisco Javier Eguía. A few years later, in a similar arrangement Miguel Meléndez, a miner and refinery owner and an aviador, purchased a sizable lot of mercury with cash and on credit with José Zeballos, another miner-refiner-aviador, as his fiador, while Zeballos was acting as the fiador to Francisco Camara, a miner. And finally in 1779 Marcelo de Anza, a prominent miner-refiner and sometime aviador in Zacatecas, presented José Arrieta as his fiador and then presented himself as fiador to Sebastián Unsain, who served as manager and adviser to a prominent Zacatecan miner-refiner,

Manuel Rétegui. In all these cases where the fiador system revealed potential risk, the debts were duly retired within the allotted six months.[35] That merchants or aviadores participated as fiadores was logical in light of their overall financial commitment to mining.

Whatever the risks to the treasury, small producers and some large ones could not have survived long without the fiador system. Whether other reales cajas had similar experiences in the administration of mercury accounts cannot yet be answered. It was another function within the treasury system, however, that had to be managed with attention and care if the Crown were to realize the goal of increasing the revenue, especially after implementing a large cut in mercury prices.

Among the most ambitious of Spain's reforms were to bring the various internal commercial taxes and duties often grouped under alcalabas under direct control and to expand them.[36] Few other treasury functions had as broad an impact because most commercial transactions (including sales of commodities, properties, and slaves) were subject to taxation. After introducing the alcabalas in the sixteenth century, the Crown moved away from direct administration toward contracts auctioned off to the highest bidders, such as city councils, merchant guilds, or even individual citizens. By the eighteenth century the bidding was seldom competitive, and at times the government had trouble finding bidders who offered prices that it considered reasonable. The Bourbons began to subject these contracts to much closer scrutiny and to reject some as financially insufficient. Never totally abandoned even after the real aduana and its branches were in place, the contracts eventually came to be viewed as producing insufficient income in an expanding economy. As the treasury vacillated between farming out and reincorporating in the middle of the eighteenth century, it found itself with even less revenue than before. Reincorporating was often ineffective; the treasury lacked staff and experience and could not even match in revenue collection the former contract. It might try to reduce its losses by calling for new bids, but usually it discovered that new bids reflected its own recent performance rather than the previous contract price. At the same time, if the treasury's reincorporation proved itself effective in the collection of the alcabalas, the merchant guild might try to regain control by offering a higher contract price.[37] In 1777 the vacillation mainly came to an end. The process of the royalization of the collection of sales taxes and other imposts began in earnest.

Adding this function to the reales cajas and establishing policies and procedures for governing its activities presented major challenges to colonial reformers. The rules for determining what was taxed, what was exempt, and how the local aduana should exercise its duties and resolve any conflicts were lengthy and complex documents, which many bureaucrats did not understand or chose to ignore. In many cajas the aduanas were probably the largest departments, with rosters of a dozen or more employees. The aduana was also the one department that touched a wide segment of the business community and the general public. In 1789 the treasury reported nearly 600 authorized positions in more than two dozen locations, with total annual salaries of almost 237,000 pesos.[38] In Zacatecas, the aduana's accounts show that to collect 50,000 pesos on average each year required an outlay of one-quarter of that for administrative costs, a ratio that may have applied throughout the system.[39]

Although not officially authorized in 1777, the real aduana system began to take shape under Gálvez, who was interested in streamlining the movement of trade as well as in improving the collection of revenue. His approach varied from place to place. In Veracruz he opted for a plan in which city government administered the alcabalas, and in Guanajuato he chose the merchants again. Regardless of who controlled the administration and collection of the alcabalas, Gálvez issued detailed rules and regulations to cover the contracts. Issued in February 1767, the contract held by Veracruz's municipal government contained nearly one hundred provisions. They ranged from the powers of the *escribanos* (notaries) and alcaldes to monitor commercial traffic and inspect the purveyors' books, to rules on the guía system, by which merchandise could move unimpeded to its final destination, where the tax was collected and where a portion of the guía would be returned to the originating aduana (in this case Veracruz).[40]

In general Gálvez's approach to standardize the assessment and collection of the tax in order to limit delays and minimize fraud, combined with consistent and strict enforcement, was not altered significantly down to 1810. The volume of complaints and investigations concerning these and other matters suggests that the rules were far from perfect, but the rising income from the real aduana also indicated that the rules were working well enough to justify their continued enforcement. Of course merchants, hacendados, shopkeepers, and others tried to derail Gálvez's plans during the ten years between his first reform proposals and the final decision to create a colony wide aduana.

One point that raised a strong protest was Gálvez's efforts to tax grain dealers more rigorously. Grain sales by ecclesiastical bodies and native communities normally enjoyed exemptions from alcabalas, although there were frequent disputes about whether the sales qualified for the exemptions. Maize purchased at an alhóndiga was also normally exempt. Flour, on the other hand, even if purchased at a public granary could be taxed. Increasingly as the government stepped up the enforcement of the alcabalas, even before royal incorporation in 1777, grain producers and dealers tried to devise ways to escape taxation. A 1770 report from the Chalco district, a main supplier of grain to Mexico City, revealed that when laboradores repaid nearby hacendados for advances or loans in wheat instead of selling the wheat for cash to repay their debts, they were able to avoid paying the alcabalas.[41]

The guía system, devised by Gálvez, remained a crucial element in the overall strategy of the real aduana. Attached to shipments of goods was a bill of lading that listed the items, quantities, and prices along with the city where the shipment originated and the city of destination. Once at its destination, the seller (or the buyer) was required to pay the tax, based on the "current" or the market price, and to present a record of the payment of the tax within ninety days (according to a decree of 12 October 1779). One example of how the system worked involved Juan José Quintana. On 23 December 1796 he received a guía to ship merchandise said to be worth 321 pesos and 3 reales from Querétaro to Petatlan, about one hundred miles north of Acapulco. In Petatlan on 25 April 1797 he apparently presented his voucher that showed that he had sold his goods for just under 400 pesos, or an increase in value of about one-quarter over the original declaration. Only three items traded for the prices that appeared on the Querétaro guía, while the remaining thirteen fetched higher prices, some of which were twice as high. Paper and vanilla each declared at 4 reales per unit sold for 8 reales or 1 peso. Some cloth listed at 20 pesos for the lot sold for 30 pesos, and some metals listed at 49 pesos for the lot sold for 76 pesos.[42] Because he paid a tax based on the market value instead of the declared value, the treasury was the obvious beneficiary.

The guía system was open to fraud, evasion, or bribery, especially with the rise in the volume of trade. Bribery in particular was a constant temptation. A common form of bribery was for the guards at the garitas (inspection stations) along the highways to demand a share of the merchandise in exchange for falsifying the records or reducing the taxes, although the taxes were seldom paid at the garitas. Also aduana officials were not above accepting bribes in exchange for allowing dealers and merchants to ship their goods into the cities under the cover of darkness.[43] But despite these and similar problems (in particular, the amount of paperwork required), after many decades of uncertain procedures the guía system introduced a fairly uniform set of rules to enforce internal customs that survived until the end of the colonial period. The Crown may have undermined its own commercial reforms by trying to impose an elaborate system of internal duties and taxes, because in the end colonists quite correctly perceived that while the system was more rational, it also was more intrusive than before. For the Crown the alienation caused by such enforcement was more than compensated for (in the short run) by the real aduana's rising receipts. Moreover, a completely free internal commerce was simply not a part of the neomercantilistic outlook of the financially driven Crown reformers.

Not only did the real aduana system help to boost the receipts from the alcabalas (a standard commercial levy of 6 percent), but so did the growth of the economy. By the end of the eighteenth century it was contributing several million pesos annually to the government coffers. In the 1790s the viceroy (Conde de Revillagigedo) reported that the receipts from the alcabalas at the aduanas from 1765 through 1777 amounted to 19.8 million pesos, for an annual average of 1.5 million pesos, compared to 42.6 million pesos, or 3.2 million pesos from 1778 through 1790.[44] Part of the increase in receipts during the second period (1778–1790) was attributable to a higher rate, 8 percent, imposed in 1781 to help to defray military costs and maintained for the rest of the decade. As much as 8.5 million pesos of the income reported by the viceroy may have resulted from the higher rate.

The colonial government received numerous petitions for reductions in or exemptions from the alcalabas. Shortly after royal incorporation in 1777 the Crown exempted from taxation the produce of ecclesiastical properties donated to or inherited by the religious orders, but did not exempt the produce from properties that the orders bought or rented.[45] Indians were also granted exemptions on goods that they bought or sold, although many disputes arose because mixed bloods also requested exemptions from alcabalas. Administrators had to be warned occasionally not to be so rigorous in refusing exemptions because that could violate Indians' rights. Even miners and hacendados were granted exemptions on products like flour, horses, metal, and tools bought as a part of their business operations.[46] During the agricultural crises of the middle 1780s the government issued a temporary blanket suspension in the collection of the alcabalas on products and transactions in certain regions to spare the population any further hardship.[47]

While the government had to deal with complaints over rates and exemptions, it also received requests to impose additional commercial taxes. As restoration of the 6 percent rate was being considered in 1791, the Consulado in Mexico City proposed that the reduction in the basic rate be accompanied by a new levy of 3 percent on all merchandise that entered Veracruz and was then shipped directly to the interior, bypassing Mexico City's Consulado. The Consulado had more than the treasury's fiscal plight in mind with this proposal. It paid a higher tax than the other consulados to move goods from the port to the interior, and that made its goods more expensive. The fiscal was not sympathetic because, he declared, such a tax would have an adverse impact on free-trade policies. Citing the example of a merchant in Durango who bought merchandise in Veracruz, the fiscal tried to demonstrate that if this tax were added, it could result in boosting the cost for taxes, storage and transport, and other expenses to 40 percent of the price of the product. Experience had shown, wrote the fiscal, that trade commerce had grown by moderating colonial and municipal taxes, not by raising them.[48]

Another project on the scale of the real aduana but more aligned with neomercantile strategies than free-trade policies was the creation of the tobacco monopoly. This is a further example of the Bourbons' pursuit of a dual track: adding new monopolies and taxes while discarding or modifying old ones. Again Gálvez was deeply involved, although the monopoly had been authorized in January 1765 several months before his arrival.[49] What gave some urgency to the establishment of the monopoly during the visit was the need to finance the debt from the recently concluded Seven Years' War.

The government began by buying up all tobacco on hand and by closing down all tobacco-producing farms outside the designated crop area just west of Veracruz. As a result of these initial actions, Humboldt reported, the population in certain Guadalajaran districts, where high-quality leaf tobacco was grown, began to decline (and presumably so too did economic activity).[50] To assure success, the plan developed by Gálvez extended control over all phases, from raising the crop to selling its products. His most difficult task was to raise the initial working capital to pay the planters, to build and supply the factories, and to develop a network of branches and outlets at a time when the treasury could least afford to invest in such a complex network. Private loans arranged by Gálvez may have yielded as much as 600,000 pesos to supplement the revenue from the tobacco sales. By the late 1760s annual profits reached several hundred thousand pesos, but by the 1770s they exceeded more than 1 million pesos, and twenty years later they topped more than 4 million pesos. As of 1771 the monopoly employed 6,000 persons and generated an operating surplus in the range of one-half of the total annual sales. Between 1765 and 1809 the monopoly's annual, average profits were 2.6 million pesos, and at that level the monopoly became one of the most lucrative, if not the most lucrative, ramo in the treasury.[51] Humboldt, by no means a defender of monopoly, recognized that it was effective enough to raise millions of pesos annually. By decree tobacco profits were reserved strictly for the use of the king.[52]

The impact of the tobacco monopoly for a real caja and the local economy can be seen in Zacatecas, itself a large city but located in a sparsely populated area. Since a retail tobacco shop (*estanquillo*) was not opened until 1790, tobacco products before that were distributed through private contractors whose operations did not come under the scrutiny or control of the local caja. With the implementation of the intendancies in 1788, six outlets were opened in the intendancy of Zacatecas, with the largest shop in the city itself. Within a few years these shops became the second largest revenue source, with one-quarter to one-third of total treasury receipts, and for several years they produced more income than the silver taxes.[53]

Although municipal governments (with Crown approval) had imposed their own commercial taxes since the sixteenth century, some reformers viewed these local assessments as much an obstacle to the flow of trade as royal taxes were. These taxes varied from municipality to municipality. Humboldt listed them as *derecho del consulado* (from 0.5–1 percent), *derecho del fiel executor,* and *derecho del cabildo* (the last two of varying rates).[54] The derecho del consulado was the avería collected by the several consulados. The fiel executor inspected weights and measures and regulated prices in a city, for which he could charge a one-real tax on each wholesale transaction for his salary and expenses.[55] The derecho del cabildo was any tax imposed by the municipality to support local institutions such as the alhóndiga or pósito. But the miscellaneous derechos of the municipal governments showed little uniformity from city to city, so that the goal of the reformers to eliminate or standardize local levies was far from complete.

A partial list of local taxes still in effect in the early 1800s can be constructed for one-half dozen cities. In Puebla the cabildo collected 3 granos, or one-quarter of a real, for each carga of flour delivered to the city, in part to help retire a long-standing debt for grain purchases. Oaxaca's cabildo, on the other hand, collected 4 granos on each carga of sugar and 4 granos on each carga of cacao to be applied to the maintenance of a *piquete de 12 soldadas* (local garrison) and the local courts. In four northern cities the tax assessments and the products taxed showed even further variation. Guanajuato charged 1 real per fanega of maize and 2 reales per fanega of flour to support a local garrison, to open a new road, to clear the river, and to construct other public works. At nearby Sayula, Salvatierra, Salamanca, and Acámbaro a tax of 1 real per carga of flour was levied to pay for the maintenance of the *Regimiento de Querétaro.* In Guadalajara the schedule of local taxes and fees was even more extensive. It paid for local militia costs from its municipal revenues that were raised from a 2-real tax per carga of wool, a 1-real tax per carga of flour, and a 4-real tax per barrel of wine and brandy, although the last was overruled because it violated current rules on royal assessments. Finally, San Luis Potosí was an exception to the aforementioned in it had fewer diverse taxes because it did not specifically impose any levies for military purposes.

By the early 1800s the need to raise local militias to defend the colony may have reversed a tendency in the last quarter of the eighteenth century to limit local taxation in order to spur commercial growth. By 1800 the Crown was encouraging, if not mandating, local governments to upgrade their militias and to levy the taxes necessary to accomplish that.[56]

Municipal taxes were as much a nuisance or an inconvenience as they were a burden for local wholesalers and retailers. Compared to the array of new and old royal taxes, the municipal taxes paled in significance. Nonetheless, based on a 1771 report of municipal fiscal operations, 75–95 percent of the total municipal income derived from levies (such as taxes and fees) and from monopolies. In 1771 these municipalities filed reports: Mexico City, Puebla, Oaxaca, Veracruz, Pátzcuaro, Sayula, Zacatecas, Valladolid, Chihuahua, San Luis Potosí, Guanajuato, León, and Córdova. The report acknowledged that only some of the largest municipalities were included, but it did not explain why that was so.

Total revenues over three years exceeded 625,000 pesos, and if several other major cities, such as Querétaro or Guadalajara, had reported revenues, the amount could have reached 750,000 pesos. On an annual basis the cities could have collected as much as 250,000 pesos through their various taxes. Revenue sources were diverse, although taxes on grains, liquors, and similar products were the most common. In Mexico City more than 90 percent of its 1768 income could be classed as assessments against merchants and traders (including those who held city contracts) and taxes on certain commercial transactions. In Puebla, however, these sources may have contributed only 70–75 percent of the total 1768 income. For other towns and cities the data were not sufficiently detailed to provide even percentage estimates, but so far as can be determined, none fell below the Puebla figure and few exceeded Mexico City's figure.[57]

Although the total municipal tax revenue equaled a few reales per person per year for the colony as a whole—not large in and of itself when compared to royal tax income—it must be treated in the wider context as an additional cost to doing business in Mexico. Direct commercial or commercially related taxes no doubt underwent periodic review and reform during and after Gálvez's visita. In the last quarter of the eighteenth century these taxes did not shrink in any substantial form, especially after 1780 with the demand for revenue to underwrite the rise of new, large military expenditures. The extent of control by the royal treasury and its adjuncts was perhaps wider than ever after the so-called fiscal reforms.

Treasury Borrowing and Currency Exports

As long as the arm of the treasury had grown by the late eighteenth century, it was apparently not long enough. In addition to new or revised taxes and monopolies, the Crown resorted to "voluntary" donations, forced loans, and outright confiscations to augment a revenue base that was already several times larger in 1800 than in 1700. By 1800 the search for money, primarily to pay for military expenditures, both in the mother country and in the colonies, had reached a near frantic pace.[58] Private debt was alarmingly high by the late eighteenth century, and to this must be added an increasing public debt. The impact of this combined and intertwined debt is not easy to measure, except that in general terms, the more wealth soaked up by government (without returning it to the economy), the less capital flowed into private investment channels.

The Consolidación de Vales Reales, perhaps the most controversial action in the decade 1800–1810, may have netted 10 million pesos for the Crown, but various loans from individuals, corporations, and businesses may have brought in two or three times that amount. Because the Crown insisted on cash, the loans had a double impact; they reduced not only the capital pool but also the currency pool. Since so much of what the government borrowed was exported to the Caribbean or Spain, little of that wealth was ever recycled through the colonial economy.[59]

A major part of Mexico's annual bullion output had always been exported to pay for European and Asian purchases and to cover royal expenses. The total exported currency (private and public) grew in the eighteenth century (reflecting overall economic growth), but after 1750 this changed; the ratio between private and public exports began to reverse and royal accounts contained more bullion than private accounts. The rise in currency exports, whether private or public, left the domestic economy with less hard currency. The acceleration in the rise of both private and public exports resulted in an outflow of bullion that equaled or exceeded the output of the silver mines in some years.[60]

The history of the colonial public debt remains to be written. There is no doubt, however, that the government, the ecclesiastical orders, and the corporate bodies (merchants' and miners' guilds) had created over time a complex web of lending and borrowing money to meet certain critical needs. It was not uncommon, for example, for a consulado to borrow money from a variety of private citizens and religious foundations in order to finance public works like road and bridge construction in return for special tax favors from the Crown. Nor was it uncommon for the government to borrow money and to grant citizens, foundations, or corporations a share of the receipts from certain taxes or monopolies to cover the interest or to reduce the principal. We do not know how many such agreements were ever negotiated, approved, or canceled, but we do know that by the end of the eighteenth century many wealthy citizens and foundations had lent millions of pesos to the government or to other quasi-public corporate bodies to finance important public projects.

In 1817 in the midst of the independence movement, the treasury prepared a report on the public debt in a deliberate effort to try to improve its standing by determining not how to pay the debt off, but rather how to avoid paying it off completely. The actual size of the public debt could have been as low as 40 million and as high as 80 million pesos.[61] The debt was divided into three categories: preferential debts (to be paid off), nonpreferential debts (not to be paid off immediately, if ever), and internal debts (loans from bureaus within the treasury).

The largest of three, and unfortunately the least documented in this report, was the internal debt. It amounted to 41.0 million pesos, or 50.8 percent of the total. Only about one-quarter of the 41.0 million pesos was assigned to specific offices: 4.8 million to tabacos, 1.6 million to the mint, and just under 1 million total to *temporalidades* (which administered Jesuit properties), the post office, and the artillery fund. The remainder was simply listed under a subheading of various internal treasury offices, with the largest item, 24.3 million pesos, not specified any further. These were funds that belonged to the Crown or treasury and were used for purposes other than what the ramos that claimed them was expected to do. Hence revenues from the tobacco monopoly were transferred, say, to the navy instead of being spent on the monopoly or being assigned to the king (although the navy also belonged to the king). These internal loans were similar to moving unencumbered funds from one department to another.

The other two categories were more fully described. The preferential category, the next largest at 32.1 million pesos (39.7 percent), was divided among three subheadings: loans of 22.8 million pesos with interest obligations, loans of 5.4 million without interest obligations, and finally, 3.9 million in unpaid interest. Under the first two subheadings the following loans are listed with data on the loan, the lender(s), the account from which interest ought to be paid, and the amount of the loan. The interest-bearing loans were: (1) 12 October 1794, Merchants' and Miners' Guilds, tabacos, 6.8 million pesos (hereafter m/p); (2) 26 December 1804, Ecclesiastical Endowments (with Consolidación de Vales Reales), no data (hereafter n.d.), 10.5 m/p; (3) 26 December 1804, Mission and Jesuit Funds, n.d., 0.8 m/p; (4) 1814, 1815, Merchants' Guild, n.d., 1.1 m/p; (5) undated, General and Special Treasury Funds, n.d., 2.3 m/p; (6) undated, various bills of exchange (libranzas), n.d., 1.2 m/p; (7) undated, Will of Josefa Bergara, n.d., 0.1 m/p. Although the church, principally through consolidación, was the largest lender at 11.3 million pesos, the combined miners and merchants (more merchants than miners) were not far behind with 7.9 million pesos, or about 35 percent.

Loans not bearing interest could more appropriately be considered as "voluntary" donations—not contributions by the public but loans by the wealthy. They included: (1) 1798, 1809, Patriotic Loan (*préstamo patriótico*), 4.0 m/p; (2) 10 January 1810, Patriotic Loan (*empréstito patriótico*) 1.4 m/p; (3) 1812–13, Miscellaneous Donations, from church silver to customs taxes, 3.6 m/p. For reasons unexplained, item 3 was not included in the total. If it had been, the total preferential debt would have been higher by several million pesos.

The failure of the royal treasury to make interest payments on a regular basis represented additional loans for which interest should have been charged but probably was not. By 1817 the treasury was deeply in arrears for interest in the amount of one-sixth of the total value in interest-bearing loans. When the treasury fell behind cannot be determined, although because of the heavy borrowing after 1800 it may never have had the income to meet all interest payments. It is worth noting that interest-bearing loans carried different rates. Although 4–5 percent was the common rate both in private and public borrowing, a 3 percent rate was assigned to the funds acquired through the consolidación. At rates of 3–5 percent on 22.8 million pesos, the cost of interest after 1810 could have reached 750,000 pesos per annum. The Crown had obviously paid some interest or the 1817 figure would have been higher. The Crown could actually have repaid some loans before 1805 or 1810. It is possible that a substantial part of the unpaid interest after 1805 or 1810 could be traced to the consolidación whereby the Crown had agreed to pay interest on money that the church had surrendered, to compensate for any loss of earnings from loans by the church.[62]

The nonpreferential category of loans was 7.7 million pesos (9.5 percent). It contained loans of "quality" and loans lacking "documentation." This phrase implies that some were normal loans with proper collateral, and some were less well defined or documented and may have been gifts rather than loans. Given the dates on some of them, there was apparently no great urgency to pay interest or to reduce the principal. Three of the six items listed under this category were described as supplements to other requests made by the Crown because of continuing international crises. Both the merchants' and miners' guilds agreed to supplements in 1782, 1793, and 1794 in amounts of 2.4 million pesos for the former and 0.6 million pesos for the latter. Several audiencias (judicial bodies), unspecified religious endowments, and Indian communities advanced 1.5 million pesos, with another 234,596 pesos from juzgados intestados (probate courts) in Mexico City and Guadalajara and 419,635 more pesos from Indian communities of Mexico City, Valladolid, and Oaxaca. In addition, there were debts of 2.2 million pesos in libranzas drawn on the Renta de Tabacos (tobacco monopoly), that is, bills used by the Crown but not yet presented to or redeemed by the treasurer of the monopoly (perhaps because the money did not exist). Finally, two other items were listed: an unpaid bill of 100,000 pesos for paper bought by the tobacco monopoly and more than 800,000 pesos for old juros, or liens against taxes to cover earlier loans by the treasury. Again, in this category as in an earlier one, merchants and miners guilds had provided substantial loans, nearly 40 percent of the 7.7 million pesos, and if more were known about the libranzas and juros, the figure might be even higher.[63]

If the internal transfers within the various ramos of the royal treasury are put aside for now, then the total indebtedness from outside the treasury was 35–40 million pesos. Although government borrowing extended back into the early 1780s (and perhaps earlier), it tended to accelerate after the early

1790s. The size and the persistence of borrowing over time raise questions about how much this practice depleted the private capital reserve. The Crown's failure to pay interest or to repay the principal with any regularity must have made it difficult to maintain a level of lendable funds for private ventures. Toward the end of the century the guilds borrowed from their members in order to lend to the government, and if they were not paid the interest on what they had loaned to the government, they could not use that money to pay the interest owed to their members. The original lender as well as the intermediate lender lost a source of income from which to make new loans or conduct other transactions. Although lenders, individuals or corporations, may have willingly served their government in times of crises, they could not have understood or foreseen the stiff economic penalties that the government's policy imposed.

Linked to the treasury debts was the larger issue of currency exports. The export of bullion from Mexico to Spain and other colonies had long shaped the commercial relations between the mother country and the colony. Most years since the sixteenth century Veracruz had shipped millions of pesos in silver for the government and for private citizens, mainly merchants. But in the late eighteenth century exports of government-held bullion had increased much faster than of privately owned bullion.

One criticism aimed at the consolidación policy was that it would only aggravate the existing shortage of bullion in Mexico caused by more than a decade of heavy silver exports.[64] How much currency was actually in circulation in the early 1800s or at any earlier time can only be estimated. According to one report coins worth 31 and 36 million pesos had circulated between 1771 and 1791.[65] During the consolidación debate (1805), the miners' guild claimed that only 14–16 million pesos in currency were then circulating. Another consolidación critic contended that half of the coins had been minted in the current year (1804 or 1805), the other half had been minted in the last decade, and almost no coins from earlier years remained in circulation because the government had exported so much bullion.[66] At a time of unprecedented silver production in the colony, its currency level may actually have been shrinking rather than expanding. If the heavy debt load retarded expansion, the shrinking currency pool slowed business activity, and that in turn further eroded the potential for expansion. In an economy that lacked formal banking institutions that might have broadened the currency base (even libranzas, which became more popular, had to be settled in specie), the loss of too many coins could be serious.

Those writing in opposition to consolidación took an even longer view of the relationship between silver production and currency exports and the government's role in this matter. They pointed out, for example, that between 1739 and 1804 the mint coined 1.1 billion pesos, for an average of

15.6 million pesos per year. During the same period total currency exports (private and public) could be estimated as follows: 10–12 million pesos were exported each year to Spain (and Europe), 2 million to Asia, and 2–3 million were lost to contraband. If the lower figures prevailed, the colony would enjoy a slight gain, in that some of the coinage from any given year remained in Mexico to circulate; however, if the higher figure prevailed, the colony would witness a gradual diminution in its circulating currency. By any measure there was a fine line between exploiting the colony's wealth and eroding the basis for that wealth. By the end of the eighteenth or the early nineteenth century the line had probably been permanently crossed.[67]

From 1802 to 1805 alone, the colony exported 96.7 million pesos in both private and public accounts, and while that amount included currency (at least that heading for Europe) that had accumulated during the blockade from 1799 to 1801, it still consumed the equivalent of all the silver minted in those same six years. Part of the justification for alienating the funds of the obras pías was to reduce the need to solicit private funds and to stem the outflow of privately controlled currency. But the drain had been so heavy in the previous decade that the export of obras pías funds simply compounded the scarcity of coin by shrinking further the currency base. And one clear distinction between the impact of the policy of consolidación in Mexico and in Spain was that money claimed in Mexico and exported to Spain was irretrievably lost to the colonial economy.[68]

Recently, Pedro Pérez Herrero has offered a possible corrective to earlier research on the ratio of silver registrations to currency exports. He has divided the period from 1766 to 1810, for which there is more data than any other period, into three blocks: 1766–1788, when exports did not exceed coinage and when the circulation of money was not significantly reduced; 1779–1791, when exports began to catch up to coinage in part because the circulation of illegal silver (from stolen ores) was greatly reduced; and 1792–1810, when exports came to exceed coinage with a serious shortage of currency.[69] While there is disagreement about the total amount of currency exported from 1750 to 1810 or 1780 to 1810, there is general agreement that the export of currency began to accelerate in the late 1780s or early 1790s and soon surpassed the volume of silver produced or coined and may even have reduced the level of currency in circulation. The libranza was certainly used more widely in the eighteenth century as the demand for currency rose but the level fell, although at some point in the transaction even the libranza had to be redeemed in specie or written off as a loss.[70] Without knowing more about the actual circulation of libranzas, we cannot yet say to what extent they eased the shortage of currency.

The quality and quantity of the colonial currency were problems that the government had grappled with throughout the late eighteenth century. The quantity of the currency is a fairly technical subject that need only be reviewed briefly here. Gold coins occupied the highest level in the currency hierarchy but few gold coins circulated, and other metals, especially silver, were far more widely available than gold. In the early years 485 Spanish maravedís were equal to a gold *castellano* and 272 maravedís to a silver peso of 8 reales. But the fineness of the gold varied so widely that some gold coins were worth as little as 300 maravedís. In time the gold *tepuzque* came to equal the silver real with each the equivalent of 34 maravedís.

At a later date the Mexican government proposed a higher valuation of its silver reales (40 maravedís per real) in order to keep its reales home (since it took more maravedís to buy a real), but it never received approval for such a revision. The fineness of a peso (also called an eight piece) was originally set at 268 grains, with 67 reales being cut from each peso (or, more accurately, one silver mark being equal to one silver peso) in denominations of one-quarter, one-half, one, two, and three reales.[71]

Mexico's currency was more highly valued in commercial circles than the coins of Spain were because until the second half of the eighteenth century its coins generally contained the amount of silver (and gold for those few coins so minted) that they were supposed to. In 1735 the alcalde mayor at Jalapa, where the great commercial fairs were held, reported the local citizens' complaints that Spanish reales (probably fabricated in Seville) being circulated were worth about 10.5 fewer grains than Mexican reales, and as a result of the complaints, the alcalde mayor was permitted to post a notice that the Spanish coins were worth less.[72]

Several times during the eighteenth century (1728, 1772, 1786) the Crown ordered that the coinage be devalued by reducing the grains (finally to 258) contained in the coins and by increasing the reales (to 69 or more) cut from the marks.[73] This was necessary, it was explained, to bring Mexican coinage into line with European currency, reducing the outflow of the more highly valued Mexican peso and alleviating the shortage of coins in Mexico. The new coinage that was to replace the old coinage in 1772 never fully came about, as the government was forced to extend the period for turning in old coins for new ones until the effort was mostly abandoned by 1800. It was reported in the early 1790s that while the one-quarter real still retained most of its fineness, the one-half real had lost most of its fineness.

The viceroy prohibited the export of two, one, and one-half real pieces in 1773 because the colony was desperately in need of small coins for retail transactions. But as late as 1800, according to various reports, cacao beans were still widely used at a rate of 144–192 beans per real. Other products were also used as token coins. These tokens were usually called *tlacos,* and they often bore the symbol of the person who issued them and carried the value of one-eighth real. At both the retail and wholesale levels of business activity, the use of several types of paper money—which might even pay interest—was growing to counteract the shortage of specie.[74]

Hard currency had become scarce throughout the Atlantic world in response to the eighteenth-century commercial boom, and paper money had not yet achieved wide acceptability, at least in Spanish America. Even with libranzas and other such media of exchange, an accepted standard for assessing and redeeming obligations was required. Without a more elaborate system of money and credit in place, the risks in accepting various paper substitutes were significant, although the choices were limited. Mexico might well have suffered shortages under the normal strain of commerce expanding more rapidly than the coinage to support it. However, Mexico suffered for another reason: the increasing demand to ship bullion abroad restricted its capacity to erect a paper system based on a reasonable standard of specie convertibility.

Throughout Mexico's colonial history, some of its silver output had been exported. In the first half of the eighteenth century the ratio between exports in private accounts (to pay for goods) and exports in the name of the king may have been about 75 percent to 25 percent, respectively. This ratio began to shift during the second half of the eighteenth century, most notably in the 1780s, until public exports had an edge over private exports of about 60 percent to 40 percent. At the same time, however, the total amount of currency in public and private accounts was increasing, with public exports increasing faster than private exports. It was not solely a change in ratio but also a change in volume that had an impact on Mexico's economy.

Three series of currency exports from Veracruz between 1786 and 1804 range from 225.2 million pesos (11.9 million per year) to 271.7 million (14.3 million per year). During the same period 245.3 million pesos (12.9 million per year was registered at various Spanish ports. With about 385 million pesos worth of silver registered in that period (20.3 million per year), currency exports consumed the equivalent of 58.6–70.4 percent of the taxable silver each year. None of these datasets takes into account what was exported through other ports or contraband trade. Nor can we say that the mint figures capture all the silver that was actually produced. The growth in currency exports was highly erratic and the impact could be quite different from year to year. In some years exports rose quite sharply, only to reverse themselves several years later. Although the public share of total currency exports had been increasing since the 1770s, the great leap forward in the late eighteenth and early nineteenth centuries illustrates how great the demand for money was and how extensive the impact was.[75] One thing for certain is that between the 1730s, when about 6.3 million pesos in both accounts was exported each year, and the 1800s, when 20–30 million pesos was being shipped out each year, the change even against the backdrop of rising agricultural and mineral output was a major consequence of the newly reorganized state.[76]

The royal treasury had not only grown in size, but, to paraphrase Coatsworth, had also honed its skills in extracting more and more of the colony's wealth. Much remains to be learned about the treasury, its policies and its operations as well as its linkage to the general economy. More data need to be gathered and analyzed and above all refined to lessen the possibility that the series thus far constructed reflect the biases and distortions from a less-than-perfect accounting system. But based on what is available now, the role and the impact of the treasury in the development of the economy could have reached a substantial if not a destructive scale by the end of the colonial period.

8

Growth and Change

The presence of silver mining on the scale that existed in late colonial Mexico could easily impart a gloss of affluence or opulence to a society that was far less rich than it seemed. The new wealth of the eighteenth century led to a resurgence in construction of *palacios,* cathedrals, and public buildings as well as contributions to charitable and governmental projects. By the last decades of the eighteenth century or the first decade of the nineteenth century construction fell off sharply, and philanthropy turned from a voluntary to a coercive act.[1] But physical appearances aside, how did this new wealth spread through the economy and across the society? Furthermore, did this new wealth leave the social order so distorted that it was ripe for the potential upheaval that showed its face in the Hidalgo Revolt?

According to the Consulado's 1805 survey and to other reports and memorials written in the first decade of the nineteenth century, the social order was on the verge of disintegration. The question became moot, of course, because the invasion of Spain in 1808 set off a chain of events that ultimately produced the independence movement. It was possible, but by no means certain, that the turmoil in the cities or in the countryside was not yet deep enough to spawn insurrection.

Many examples of unrest can be gathered from the eighteenth century, but they are local or particular in origin and character. When the independence movement did take hold, it appears to have followed a more violent course in rural areas than urban centers. For a variety of reasons, which Van Young has considered, the hardship experienced by some urban populations did not suggest "a social situation in which the urban groups so often associated with mass direct action in the European context—the *menu* people, the *popolo minuto,* and so forth—were likely to have risen, nor in which other popular groups were likely to have picked up the banner of collective protest and rebellion."[2]

Cities certainly had full agendas in trying to provide municipal service for and to maintain public order among increasing populations, and they may have lacked the financial and structural base to perform these duties well in the late eighteenth or early nineteenth century. But whether conditions had reached the stage where uprisings against the government, local or colonial, were warranted cannot be yet demonstrated. Discontent was often evident, but the transposition of discontent into uprisings that seriously threatened civil authority remained unrealized.

On the other hand, the potential for rebellion at the village level in the rural countryside was understood to be serious and real. In discussing the background to the Hidalgo Revolt in 1810 within the Guadalajaran context, Van Young points out that while living standards for rural workers may have fallen and conflicts over land may have risen because of commercialization of agriculture, these conditions did not necessarily produce revolutionaries, or if they did, the linkages remain to be proven.[3] In focusing on evidence of unrest in Jalisco, a rural area that served Guadalajara, Taylor has observed that the city's expanding market left some Indian villages with a narrowed economic base that could disrupt and even destroy traditional communal patterns. But like Van Young, Taylor urges caution in postulating a link between the loss of economic autonomy and insurrection.[4]

Eighteenth-century village uprisings in central and southern Mexico, also analyzed earlier by Taylor, illustrate that rural villages and communities had a fairly well developed sense of their political and legal standing: they could "translate disaffection [boundary disputes, tax and service burdens, etc.] into political unrest" to try to correct the abuses, but they were less able to "comprehend the larger forces that threatened their independence" and to do something about them. "This local political unity and militant myopia made villagers good rebels but poor revolutionaries."[5]

Behind these contemporary and historical accounts and interpretations of what was happening to society are certain assumptions about the economy. Most agree that the wealth of Mexico was exploited and expropriated in so many ways that regional and local barriers to such economic intrusion and penetration were increasingly breached. One could add that such intrusion and penetration were expected, perhaps even accepted, within the colonial system that had evolved over 250 years. But questions arise over whether something had changed about the system and the relations that grew up around it because the economy and the policy that governed that economy had changed during the eighteenth century. Contemporary critics as well as modern historians have portrayed a system (in spite of reform) that left individuals, groups, localities, or regions worse off economically than before. Part of the problem, of course, is to determine what is meant by "before." Still, without knowing precisely what "before" means, we can examine some of the economic implications that such a view contains.

There is the obvious danger of putting too much emphasis on events and reactions to events in the quarter century between the agricultural crises and the Hidalgo Revolt. The colony was buffeted by a series of internal and external upheavals that left both the economy and government in disarray. To assume that the colony could accommodate these upheavals without adverse effects on public policy or economic development would be unrealistic. In recent years scholars have increasingly linked the late colonial period with the early national period for the reason that independence simply substituted one form of dependence for another. Whatever the similarities between the late colonial and the early national economic structures, independence removed Mexico from the Spanish imperial system even though it may have placed Mexico in a new imperial scheme. To understand how severe or profound the dislocations were in the late colonial decades, or at least to try to determine how much better off or worse off the economy was at the turn of the nineteenth century, the reconstruction of the eighteenth-century economic performance may offer a useful and necessary perspective.

Even before the well-known economic crises of the late eighteenth or early nineteenth century, progress toward reforming the economy was slow and uncertain. The key to progress for reformers inside or outside the government was economic growth. To stimulate the economy to produce more would not only have enhanced the welfare of the society but also would have restored solvency to the monarchy. Over time, of course, restoring solvency became so paramount that stimulating economic production lost whatever force it had. In the last half century of rule by Spain, Mexico exported 500–600 million pesos by public and private accounts, amounting to a substantial part of the colony's silver output. The impact of such massive and constant currency outflows on Mexico's economy can never be fully appreciated because the struggle for and the achievement of independence altered public policy as well as economic performance.

Despite the existence of several long datasets that clearly show that the eighteenth-century economy grew, the growth was largely extensive rather than intensive. How did increasing the output of maize, wool, or even such a valuable commodity as silver have any effect in modifying the demand curve, creating new markets, reshaping the entrepreneurial spirit, or improving the welfare of the populace? There can be little doubt that the colony produced more during the eighteenth century because the population needed more. That in itself had important effects because it required decisions about how to allocate resources and to react to opportunities in a changing economic climate.

The changing economic climate itself began to draw local and regional markets into larger entities and to challenge whatever autonomy they had known, although a more integrated economic system was just beginning to emerge. As urban populations grew, the links between cities and the regions that supplied them became more complex. Interregional and intracolonial markets became more visible and active over the course of the century, and yet the process was far from complete at the end of the century. How much or how fast that process occurred influenced the shape of the late colonial economic growth.

On this issue, the size of the economy is of interest and relevance. We do not yet have data for a precise measurement of the size of the economy and the degree to which it changed in the eighteenth century. We do have a range of estimates of Gross Domestic Product (such calculations can include items like farming, ranching, processing, manufacturing, mining, domestic investment, trade balances, and government purchases) from 100 to 250 million pesos.[6]

Despite some important agricultural advances—e.g., from capital improvement to crop diversification—the agricultural sector proved highly resistant to change. In the absence of a deliberate plan from the industry or the government to overhaul colonial agriculture (even if one put aside the matter of implementation), were "natural" forces (population growth, market demand, profit optimization, and the like) sufficient to bring about change?[7] For one thing, major agricultural innovations cannot be documented for the eighteenth century, although some agricultural practices had to change to permit any increase at all. In addition, except for Mexico City and two or three other cities, the urban populations did not reach such concentration or diversity as to generate in the long term a shift in demand that would have encouraged or required producers to make more than simple modifications to maintain existing practices.

The eighteenth century bore witness to some serious famines—on average one every quarter century—and many minor shortages that killed thousands of persons and disrupted economic activity. Although prices shot up in years of famines, the overall trend showed at most a modest rise of about one-half percent per year. Price movements were less predictable than long-term trends suggests. The rates for the interfamine periods (from the low immediately after the famine to the high of the next famine) moved appreciably faster than the secular rate. Although the higher-than-normal prices after the 1780 agricultural crises may indicate a narrowing between supply and demand, even they do not yet demonstrate the potential for a Malthusian demographic catastrophe.

One final factor to be considered is that household production, although it declined in volume with the growth of cities, remained an important item in the overall agricultural picture. Presumably, market forces played a much smaller role in 1700 than in 1800, and therefore nontraded or nonmarketed agricultural production (which escaped tithe and tax collectors and seldom showed up in any formal statistical rendering) bulked large in the total production. The supply network for the capital and other provincial cities was more compact and cohesive than the rise in population would permit a century later. Even though household production remained a factor in 1800, fewer people could depend on that production. Large agricultural producers, who served primarily the large cities, understood that change to the extent that they tried to limit grain supplies and conversely to boost grain prices. Over the long run the loss of household production was compensated for in the more formal market production sphere because of other economic developments.

The larger question was whether developments in the agricultural sector contributed to advances in the general economy. It is evident that since starvation was not a common or constant condition, the agricultural sector was capable of raising output. In the process of adding or converting land to cultivation; of building barns, irrigation ponds and ditches; and of generally upgrading facilities, landowners incurred heavy debts. Some landowners made money (but seldom equivalent to more than a 5–10 percent return on capital), but many others could barely cover operating expenses. As the principal lender in the agricultural sector, the church may have contributed as much to the limitation of credit as to the expansion in production. Not only did the church have many landowners among its borrowers, it also had many borrowers who were in arrears. Suspending or delaying principal payments (and in some cases interest payments) resulted over time in a shrinking pool of loanable funds and a growing network of marginal producers. Although landed estates were sold, consolidated, and even abandoned in response to heavy indebtedness, many others, including those owned and operated by the various ecclesiastical branches, never had to face a true financial accounting. By the end of the eighteenth century, land was so heavily encumbered that a major component of the colony's capital stock could no longer be used to maintain or expand economic growth.

Agriculture provided the livelihood for more people than any other economic sector. Yet not only did wages remain relatively low during the eighteenth century, they were increasingly paid with merchandise rather than with cash. The colony's largest wage-earning group could have influenced the shape of the marketplace but did not because it lacked a medium of exchange through which to exert that influence. Except for the insatiable demand of the well-to-do for imported merchandise, local markets were oriented primarily toward food for subsistence and basic household commodities. Few specialty markets came into existence either to accommodate the producers with new produce to sell or the consumers with new income to spend. In addition, transactional costs were so high (both in terms of weight and time) that they discouraged the growth of specialized and diversified markets. Even the growth in urban populations and a somewhat higher wage level did not significantly modify the subsistence-based markets. Urban inhabitants often lacked currency as well as permanent employment. The response of the market was not to exploit the potential of a group that basically lacked earning or consuming power but simply to exploit the group by selling contaminated, shoddy, and misrepresented products.

Mexico's slow-to-change agricultural sector was not its only major economic activity. Silver mining, although smaller in terms of numbers of workers (tens of thousands versus hundreds of thousands) and of total peso worth (to the extent that it can be measured), occupied center stage in debates over public and economic policy. Ore was more easily and immediately converted into tangible wealth (such as bullion or coin) than maize, cloth, or even land. When a mining camp experienced a large strike, its local economy became a powerful economic magnet by attracting investors, merchants, peddlers, workers, and transients who wanted to partake of the camp's good fortune. After the boom died, the camp could just as quickly be deserted and abandoned. In fact, the major camps survived the boom-bust cycles in part because they had also become commercial and administrative centers. But mining remained their economic core, and it could nearly subsume all other economic activities.

Despite the wealth that mining generated through the extraction of the ore itself and the business to support the industry, it did not often lead to a diversified local economy with a differentiated market structure. Public officials and contemporary critics saw "get rich quickly" as an impediment to the growth of a more rational and less cyclical economic system.[8] Whether or not the local mining economy induced any permanent changes, the silver industry itself was of profound importance to the colonial and the imperial economy.

By the end of the colonial era the silver-mining industry had undergone an evolution in structure that might qualify it to be described as a "mature" preindustrial enterprise. The structure evolved over time in such a way as to create large firms, which more often than not combined mining and refining in a vertical format, recognized the need for recapitalization, developed somewhat specialized job categories with differentials in pay and responsibility, and created more elaborate managerial and technical staffs. That by the late eighteenth century these organizations reached the size and complexity that they did and enjoyed the success that some had was testimony to a certain entrepreneurial resourcefulness, embedded in the industry and abetted by the state. Even the ore, which was so costly to extract, came in grades that could be refined profitably.

How much farther, though, could this model evolve before it reached a diminishing utility? Not only was it still heavily labor-intensive, but it had failed to spawn any related industries that could have served to change the mining industry on the one hand and to intensify economic development on the other. The structure of the silver industry had surely not reached the anachronistic point that has been claimed for the obraje and its forced-labor system, but neither did it contribute to modernizing the economy.

The mine and refinery workers were among the highest paid laborers and among the most troublesome when their compensation was tampered with. Even so, they did not enjoy any substantial gains because of economic growth and may well have suffered serious losses because of it. The full compensation of silver-industry workers is hard to calculate because it involved ore shares, merchandise, and cash wages. But no matter the size or shape of the package, over the course of the century compensation rose slightly, but not in step with rising silver output or with the inflation rate. Some owners also succeeded in altering the components of the compensation package so that the package was worth less to the worker, although how widespread this was remains undocumented. Earning perhaps two to three times more than rural workers, the mine or refinery workers existed above whatever constituted a subsistence level. How much remains a matter of debate.

Population growth created additional problems at the level of the lowest paid and least skilled worker whose replacement introduced opportunities for savings (albeit small per worker) in an industry that produced more ore mainly by employing more people. The militancy of the workers in Real del Monte, where strikes over wages closed the camp for nearly a decade, may be underscored as a sample of the power of the worker. In the end, however, the wages of workers were simply restored in a slightly different form. Maintaining worker's compensation was the issue, and that was accomplished for some but not all workers. After a decade of losses of income to owners and workers as well as to the state, the status quo was not only restored but preserved until 1821. The silver cities with better paid and more specialized work forces did not undergo or stimulate enough economic modernization to distinguish them or their economies fundamentally from an earlier time of less production and more stability.

The processing of agricultural or mineral products (wheat to flour or ore to bullion) continued to be narrowly viewed as an extension of production rather than as an opportunity for expansion independent of production. To be sure, the long-standing restrictions against the establishment of or the investment in a colonial manufacturing industry could shape such views. It is perfectly obvious that Mexico had to fabricate many items that would have been simply too expensive to import. The fabricated items ranged from foods to textiles, from vehicles to tools, but if these were not custom-made, they were made in small-scale firms of several employees and few machines. Except for silver refineries, woolen obrajes, tobacco factories, and perhaps sugar plantations, few businesses were organized to produce in volume, and not even these dealt with such market concerns as product differentiation or price elasticity. With many fabricated goods law or custom determined size, quantity, price, or design. Law and custom were barriers to an expanded manufacturing sector, but so too were the scarcity of currency and the cost of transportation. Above all, a consumer market could hardly evolve in an economy where potential consumers were increasingly paid in merchandise or forced to barter.

Even if the state had gradually lifted the ban on manufacturing, that action would not have automatically created a marketplace in which the manufacturer could assess or anticipate the risk. No doubt in the nooks and crannies of the colonial economy individuals dreamed of designing fancy cloth or creating new food. But while the economy possessed some of the resources needed for such development, it lacked more than anything else the structure by which to initiate and sustain those changes. What must have been most daunting was the absence of a mechanism for moving from production to consumption, from fabrication to sale. Dropping a mine shaft 500–1,000 feet was both costly and risky, but it was also a venture that was well understood and potentially successful. Creating a product and marketing it where no precedents existed, even if legal, proved to be more than the most inventive could accomplish.

At the center of the colony's economic activity stood the merchant. The term *merchant* embraced multifarious identities and roles. Merchants could be importers, retailers, and itinerants, and they traded in merchandise, silver, money, and credit. Although hardly a monolithic economic institution given the disputes and squabbles that they had among themselves, particularly after the commercial reforms were implemented, they shared a common function of directing or managing the movement of wealth through an economic system that had a highly localized and scattered character.

Economic autonomy characterized more regions at the opening of the eighteenth century than in 1800, although many regions undoubtedly retained a degree of autonomy even in 1800. Differences between regions like Oaxaca and Guadalajara or within large geographical areas like Michoacán can be observed in land tenure, Spanish-Indian relations, or product specialization. But differences become less distinctive features against an eighteenth century backdrop of demographic and economic growth that forced the more densely populated regions to expand their supply network. Regional economic autonomy had always been subject to penetration and influence from the outside because of the long commercial pipeline from the center or the periphery through Mexico City's Consulado to Asia, Europe, and even the rest of the New World. That pipeline also had an internal flow because the transfer of silver or cochineal to the capital or a port involved not only the distribution of European fabrics, Venezuelan chocolate, or Asian spices but also sugar loaves from southern Mexico or alcoholic beverages from northern Mexico.

The merchant's place in the far-flung commercial network was enhanced by monopolies and restrictions that limited competition in or access to the marketplace. This was most prominent in overseas trade, where control over prices and quantities had long existed, but it was also evident in domestic trade, where retail outlets were licensed and price schedules could be (although often were not) imposed. The commercial reforms were designed to open up the system, and yet the monopolies and restrictions that the reforms were supposed to curtail or eliminate remained in a diluted form. The flota was eventually abandoned, but even before that occurred Mexico was awash in imports that, in the absence of merchandise to export from the colony, had to be paid for with silver. By making imports cheaper, the deregulation of trade after 1778 contributed to continuing high levels of merchandise imports and silver exports.

In a further step toward a commercial restructuring, the state permitted the formation of three consulados to handle primarily but not exclusively Mexico's import-export trade. The desired result of a more competitive climate can be documented as the Consulados of Veracruz and Guadalajara did battle with the capital. Considerably more needs to be learned about the strategies and operations of these new commercial entities because while the new competition forced important changes on Mexico City's guild, it did not render the guild impotent. It continued to serve the region with the most dense population and to maintain trading relations throughout the colony. In the final analysis, though, consulados, whether one, three, or five in number, were at least quasi-monopolies that endorsed a system of importing manufactures and exporting a few primary commodities and a lot of silver bullion and coin. This may well be "reformed" mercantilism but a mercantilism nonetheless driven by an "engine of growth" that was located in the Atlantic economy rather than in the Mexican economy.

The terms of trade, as they evolved under reform, could not favor Mexico, for as Mexico City's Consulado clearly perceived, the colony had few raw materials and no finished products (except silver) to trade with other colonies or nations. In a long self-serving and enlightening report from Mexico City's Consulado to the King Charles III, Juan Antonio Yermo, a Consulado official, underscored a common feature of the late colonial economy: Mexico had 5 million sheep that produced annually about 5 million pounds of wool, almost none of which was of high enough quality to be exported.[9] Despite Yermo's alleged concern, the guild that he represented was hardly in the forefront of advocating or instituting the kind of change that would have improved the quality of the wool and its acceptance in the marketplace at home or abroad.

The economy of eighteenth-century Mexico began to grow basically as a function of the rise in population. But indisputably, growth was in the interest of the state that sought to replenish its treasury and refurbish its empire. What shape the colony should take after the reforms was only dimly perceived, if perceived at all. When the royal economic policy is followed through its various meanderings and stages, its intent, although at times ambivalent, is increasingly tied to the financial health (or malaise) of the Crown. A larger and larger percentage of what Mexico possessed and produced was earmarked for the government through taxes, fees, monopolies, and loans. If the state's total take was the equivalent of 1–2 pesos per inhabitant in 1700, it was surely several times higher in 1800.

By all accounts, whether the most conservative or the most expansive treasury series is chosen, government revenue collection ran ahead of general economic growth over the long term (but also over short spans) by as much as 1–2 percent. The economy could not appease the appetite of the treasury out of growth alone, so the government extracted an ever-larger share of Mexico's wealth. The capacity of the government to create an "extraction machine" (to broaden Coatsworth's metaphor) should no longer be in doubt. Of equal importance, this should not be confused with how wisely and efficiently the government spent what it collected. Since a part of what it collected was spent in the colony, government disbursements could contribute to the colony's domestic product. Some large ramos like silver, mercury, and (later) tobacco were reserved for the use of the monarch, and their receipts were generally exported to Spain.

But the most troubling aspect of a spreading revenue net concerned the category of donations and loans. In a matter of two decades the government may well have "borrowed" from its citizens and itself tens of millions of pesos to defend the empire and preserve the monarchy. These borrowings were in addition to what the Crown got from taxes and monopolies. More to the point, public debt, like private debt, was seldom repaid but simply rolled over. Even interest was in arrears.

Despite evidence of both nominal and real economic growth in the eighteenth century, that growth did not translate into development. In 1800 or 1810 Mexico's economy looked larger but not structurally different. One could argue that the structure had narrowed, not broadened, over time. Production of comestibles was more concentrated in rural haciendas, silver in mining companies, and textiles in woolen obrajes. To be sure, some important changes must be acknowledged: cottons, produced in trapiches, became competitive with woolens, and the commercial and administrative reforms facilitated the flow of trade and activated a spirit of enterprise. But these changes and others that might be identified were not enough to push the Mexican economy toward a broader base.

Although Mexico's eighteenth-century growth precluded a Malthusian catastrophe, it may still have been too narrow or too uneven or too incomplete to escape totally the Malthusian element. Cycles of growth and contraction and of change and stagnation reflected the capacity of the economy to expand and shrink without succumbing to the Malthusian calculus but the margin of safety was small. The colony was expected to ship staples to the mother country and to purchase from it manufactures. By and large Mexico paid for its imports with silver. This arrangement did little to expand the margin of safety.

Inquiries into both historical and contemporary colonial systems indicate that colonial economies, led by exports of staples, can combine both growth and development. The key is whether or not exports of staples lead to greater internal diversification. In a mercantilistic system the mother country will almost always have the advantage in manufacturing, but even so it cannot always control the various economic niches that exist between the production of staples and the production of manufactures. Why should an entrepreneur not take up the challenge of developing a "unique resource . . . of the colony, using the edge provided by cheap primary products to overcome constraints imposed by small local markets and short supplies of labor and capital . . . [or] tailoring semimanufactured imports to the tastes of the colonial populace."[10]

Even the growth in density of population will mean that the colony can manufacture some items more economically than they can be imported. Is it possible, though, that some staples are more effective at the "spread effect" than other staples? To answer this question one must consider two points. In what proportion does the production of the export staple utilize the factors of production—land, labor, capital, and management—and to what extent does it induce investment in other economic undertakings? There is an additional point: where does the "spread effect" take place, in the colony, in the mother country, or in a third country or colony? Although the staple-export theory has its critics—too deterministic, lack of evidence, exclusion of native Americans in economic systems, and regional variations—it does provide a vehicle for addressing the matter of growth and development.[11]

Does this model have any applicability to eighteenth-century Mexico? Over the course of the colonial period and especially in the eighteenth century silver was Mexico's chief export. It also exported grains, dyes, and a few other products, although compared to silver they were far less significant. Mexico imported some foods and beverages, but by and large it had attained agricultural self-sufficiency. This is not to comment on the quality or quantity of its agricultural product but rather to state that basic commodities were not generally included among imports. Under the terms of the model, however, silver was the staple that paid for the importation of manufactures, slaves, luxuries, and other items. It is easy to blame the preoccupation with silver for the failure of Mexico to develop a more broadly based staples economy, and yet it must be underscored that to concentrate on mining to the exclusion of farming or ranching was no doubt an economic decision—the return on silver not only in the early decades when it was readily accessible but even in the eighteenth century was greater than on any other business undertaking. No colony was expected to compete with the mother country in the production of manufactures except with those areas that the mother country had willingly relinquished—ordinary fabrics and textiles could be counted exceptions.

In Mexico's case internal economic diversification had to be related to the production of silver, for that was the main commodity that it had to export. In short, did the growth in output of silver make much difference in the domestic economy in general or in the export sector in particular? There could be a backward linkage (to use Albert Hirschman's terms) in that more food, candles, leather or mules would be needed to maintain the growth in output, and there could also be a forward linkage in that more goods and services relative to the export sector itself would be required.[12] Producing more of what was needed at either end, and in particular at the forward end, for minting and transporting coins was understandable. The question becomes one of what kind of growth could yield development. On the European side, of course, the impact could be profound because the silver provided the capital for manufacturing goods and underwriting services. In eighteenth-century Mexico, as more and more silver was exported, less remained to circulate in the domestic economy or to be invested in new or expanded businesses.

While the export of silver drained the wealth of Mexico, the production of silver, which remained largely labor intensive, offered little incentive or opportunity to change the way in which ore was mined and processed or in which silver was transported and handled. Even though mine and refinery workers were better paid than most other laborers and even though some among them possessed important skills, their presence in mining camps and silver cities did not give rise to much variety in local economies. If a "spread effect" cannot be identified outside the mining industry itself, neither can much innovation that significantly changed the level of productivity be documented within the industry. Drainage systems were enlarged but not necessarily enhanced, and refining processes were improved although not in any basic sense. Mine owners and silver merchants (in conjunction with the Crown) controlled most of the wealth derived from silver, and like the colonial planters, they spent this wealth in ways that benefited the international economy, not the domestic economy. In the absence of other export staples or some other factor, such as a change in the density of the population, Mexico as a colony was tied to silver.[13]

Although other commodities might have been more fully developed for export—cochineal, sugar, grain, wool—in the eighteenth century, only cochineal among the potentially exportable raw materials played any role. As the production of these and other commodities evolved during the colonial period, however, it elaborated a system based on plantations or haciendas that employed many low-skilled workers who spent their incomes on basic necessities. Indeed, in cochineal production repartos de efectos rather than money were the common medium of commercial exchange. Any economic impact in terms of broadening or diversifying local markets was virtually nonexistent.

Silver linked the economy to many points in the imperial and international markets, but whatever the linkages, they served a relatively narrow economic purpose or created a relatively narrow economic activity. At another level, almost incidental to the production and export of silver, was an economy responding to population growth and economic change associated with that growth. At the domestic level, economic growth created by demographic expansion was generally organized around basic products and the industries needed to transform raw materials into processed goods and to move them from where they were produced and processed to where they were consumed. Little evidence has yet emerged that these basic economic functions underwent much evolution. Under the conditions that existed—a narrow income base, an unskilled labor force, and a high debt level—new or different functions were hard to organize. The economy's cycles indicate that the growth began over time to press against supplies to the extent that famines and attendant epidemics resulted, but the pressure was never so great that either profound demographic or economic upheavals occurred. To some extent the rising silver output may have cushioned the economy against any severe shocks or disruptions. In the end, though, growth did not lead to a new abundance or fundamental changes.

As Mexico ended its colonial era and began its independent period, it was a nation with serious economic handicaps. Total output had risen steadily throughout the eighteenth century but did not lead to substantially improved living standards. For most citizens impoverishment was more of a prospect than was improvement. The economic growth of the eighteenth century required change but was accomplished largely without any fundamental reordering of the colony's economic system. What independent Mexico had to confront after a century of so-called splendor was a heavily burdened economy.

Appendix 1

Description and Explanation of Equations

Linear Regressions

Many works can be consulted for descriptions and procedures concerning linear regressions. On regression estimations and econometric models, see Peter Kennedy, *A Guide to Econometrics*, for a nontechnical discussion; see Ronald Wonnacott and Thomas Wonnacott, *Econometrics*, for an intermediate approach with numerous examples; and see J. Johnston, *Econometric Methods*, for an advanced discussion with special treatment of spline functions.

A linear regression refers to estimating the coefficients of an equation that is linear in the coefficients and not necessarily linear in the independent variables. The standard equation for estimating a linear regression is: $Y = a + bX + e$, where Y is the dependent or respondent variable, b is the coefficient from which the slope of the line is calculated, X is the independent variable (often time herein), a is the constant, and e is the error term. The error term acknowledges the presence of data that do not fall along the line. In perfect datasets, which obviously do not exist, the actual value for Y and the predicted value (from which the line is plotted) would be the same.

Since data are far from perfect, a straight line can only be drawn if a predicted value is used for Y (typically denoted as $\hat{y}$). Since several different lines might be calculated, the best-fitting line is obviously desirable. This is calculated through the principle of least squares. Under this procedure the vertical distance between each data point and the regression line is determined, the distance is squared, and all the squared distances are added together. The best-fitting line corresponds to smallest sum of the squared distances.

Growth Rates

Growth rates along regression lines were calculated by introducing logarithmic functions. In most cases log base$_{10}$ were used but in a few cases natural logs were computed. The equation reads as follows: $\log y = \log a + \log bX + e$. The actual rate is calculated by converting the estimated regression coefficient into an annual percentage figure based on P being compounded at a rate of growth, r, per year:

$$P_t = P_0 (1 + r)^t \tag{1}$$

where P_0 is the value of P at the base year. On taking the logarithm of equation 1 we have:

$$\log P_t = \log P_0 + t\log(1 + r) \tag{2}$$

Equation 2 is of the form

$$\log P_t = \alpha + \beta t \tag{3}$$

which is linear in the parameters. Since $\beta = \log(1 + r)$, the antilog β gives $(1 + r)$ which, upon subtracting 1, gives the annual average compound rate of growth in P.

Compound rates may be interpreted in the following manner: 1 percent per year for 100 years = growth of 2.7 times; 2 percent per year for 50 years = growth of 2.7 times; 4 percent per year for 25 years = growth of 2.7 times; 5 percent per year for 25 years = growth of 3.4 times.

Autocorrelated Errors

Autocorrelated errors arise most frequently when time-series data are used. In the basic regression model $Y_t = a + bX_t + e_t$, e_t is the random error (or disturbance) term reflecting that the proposed relationship is not entirely exact but may be subject to some error. The specification of an error term is typically justified on the following grounds: the omission of the influence of numerous chance events; error in the measurement of variables because of data collection difficulties or because some variables can never be measured exactly; and inconsistency in human behavior.

The occasion may emerge, however, when in the use of time-series data the error in one time period is related to the error in an earlier time period. Random disturbances have effects that persist over more than one time period. Dramatic examples are earthquakes, wars, and famines, which can affect the economy's operation in years subsequent to the event. Such an error process generates autocorrelated errors (that is, the errors are correlated with themselves). The most common specification of autocorreleated errors is the first-order autocorrelation which assumes $e_t = \rho e_{t-1} + u_t$, where ρ is a parameter less than or equal to 1 in absolute value and is known as the autocorrelation coefficient. u_t is another random error with zero mean and constant variance and is assumed not to be correlated with itself. Estimation by ordinary least squares will not provide the most efficient (minimum variance) estimates. This leads us to use generalized least squares techniques.

The Durbin-Watson statistic is used to identify the presence of first-order correlation. This statistic is calculated from the residuals of the ordinary least squares estimation. The test of the null hypothesis of no autocorrelation by the Durbin-Watson statistic can lead one to accept or reject or to an inconclusive result. If this statistic does suggest the presence of autocorrelation, a generalized least squares approach is taken to estimating the regression coefficients.

Spline Regression

Spline functions are useful in looking at data series where discrete shifts in behavior occur at specific points in time. For example, consumption behavior may be different for war years compared to peace years. A linear time trend offers simple examples of such a model where t represents time:

$$
\begin{aligned}
\text{period 1:} \quad & Y_t = a_1 + b_1 t + e_t & t \leq t_\alpha \\
\text{period 2:} \quad & Y_t = a_2 + b_2 t + e_t & t_\alpha < t \leq t_\beta \\
\text{period 3:} \quad & Y_t = a_3 + b_3 t + e_t & t_\beta < t
\end{aligned} \tag{4}
$$

where e_t is a random error term with zero mean and constant variance. Figure A-1a illustrates how the two periods may appear when period 1, period 2, and period 3 regressions are estimated separately. The key to the spline function is that it requires the two periods to meet at the switching point $t + t_\alpha$ and $t + t_\beta$. Figure A-1b illustrates a linear spline function that avoids the discrete jumps in the function at the switching point.

To incorporate the matching-up restrictions, consider the end of period 1. At this point in time the period 1 equation is $Y_{t\alpha} = a_1 + b_1 t_\alpha + e_{t\alpha}$. To match up with the beginning of period 2, which is $Y_{ta} = a_2$, requires that $Y_{ta} = a_1 + b_1 t_\alpha + e_{t\alpha} = a_2$. Similarly the end of period 2 must match up with the beginning of period 3, and requires that $Y_{t\beta} = a_2 + b_2 t_\beta + e_{t\beta} = a_3$.

Parameter restrictions must be developed to guarantee that the end point of period 1 matches up with the starting point of period 2, and the end point of period 2 matches up with the starting point of period 3. One way to do this is to define the following variables:

$$
\begin{aligned}
W_{1t} &= t \\
W_{2t} &= 0 & \text{if } t \leq t_\alpha \\
&= t - t_\alpha & \text{if } t_\alpha < t \\
\\
W_{3t} &= 0 & \text{if } t \leq t_\beta \\
&= t - t_\beta & \text{if } t_\beta < t
\end{aligned}
$$

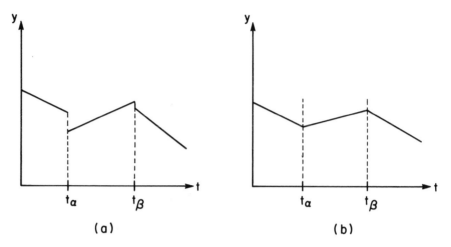

Fig. A-1. Illustration of trends by linear spline method.

Using W_{1t}, W_{2t}, and W_{3t} allows us to rewrite the three different periods as one equation:

$$Y_t = a_1 + \delta_1 W_{1t} + \delta_2 W_{2t} + \delta_3 W_{3t} + e_t \tag{5}$$

Equation 5 is equivalent to equation 4 as follows:

$$b_1 = \delta_1, \, b_2 = \delta_1 + \delta_2, \, b_3 = \delta_1 + \delta_2 + \delta_3$$

$$a_2 = a_1 - \delta_2 t_\alpha, \, a_3 = a_2 - \delta_3 t_\beta. \tag{6}$$

Equation 5 can be directly estimated by using ordinary least squares and guarantees that the estimated functions in periods 1 through 3 meet at the switching point. In addition, estimations of the a's and b's can be determined from the δ's by using the relationship in 6.

Response to Risk

The empirical measurement of risk focuses on the representation of the explanatory variable(s) that is (are) inherently random. In the case of Michoacán the price of maize is a random variable, and agricultural supply is a function of that variable. The specific price level cannot be known with certainty, and therefore the random variable can only be known to the extent that it can be determined through the characteristics of the underlying probability distribution (described by the mean and variance) for the price variable. By specifying agricultural supply as the function of the mean or the "expected" price and of the variation in price, we can make the model operational.

The mean price in year t is the price that the producer expects in that year. This can be estimated from the current price, but since few eighteenth-century producers had much reliable information about such prices, they could hardly make accurate predictions about actual prices. The second measure, a moving average of the average prices of the previous three years, may be a more realistic approach to what the producers might have known. The moving average price in year t is defined as $P(t) = [P(t-1) + P(t-2) + P(t-3)]/3$, where $P(t)$ is the "expected" price in year t. $P(t-1)$, $P(t-2)$, and $P(t-3)$ are the actual prices in years $t-1$, $t-2$, and $t-3$, respectively. By this definition the producer must rely on the past information on prices in order to predict what the current price is.

The variation in price represents a risk variable and is defined as a weighted three-year standard deviation of price deflated by the average price over the preceding three years. The specific definition is $V(t) = \{(1/2[P(t-1) - P(t-1)]^2 + (1/3)[P(t-2) - P(t-2)]^2 + (1/6) [P(t-3)-P(t-3)]^2\}$ $5/P(t)$, where $V(t)$ is the risk variable in year t. The weights $(1/2, 1/3, 1/6)$ reflect the relative greater importance of recent information over past information. Deflating the standard deviation by the average price, P, provides a risk variable that can be treated as the coefficient of variation of price.

Agricultural supply in Michoacán is assumed to be influenced by maize prices in Michoacán and in the colony as a whole. The colonywide price is included to capture whatever influence interregional marketing may exert on agricultural prices. The model for agricultural supply in year t is

$$Y(t) = b_0 + b_1 P_m(t) + b_2 P_c(t) + b_3 V_m(t) + b_4 V_c(t) + b_5 t + e(t) \qquad (7)$$

where Y = Michoacán tithe, P_m = expected price of maize in Michoacán, P_c = expected price of maize in colony, V_m = coefficient of variation of Michoacán maize price, V_c = coefficient of variation of colonywide maize price, t = time trend, 1746–98, and e = normally distributed random error with zero mean and constant variance. The definitions of $V_m(t)$ and $V_c(t)$ involve using Michoacán and colonywide prices respectively in 7. The b_i's $(i = 0, 1, 2, \ldots, 5)$ are regression coefficients to be estimated. Estimated coefficients reveal the direction and magnitude of how changes in prices affect changes in supplies. Estimate b_1 indicates how supply responds to a change in the expected Michoacán price, while the estimate of b_2 pertains to colonywide prices. The impact of the direction of prices and the magnitude of the changes in direction is reflected in the estimated coefficients: the sign of coefficients show the direction and the size of the estimate reflects the magnitude of the response. Since supply and price are directly related (that is, an upward sloping supply curve) b_1 and b_2 should be positive. The coefficients b_3 and b_4 measure the impact of any increased price risk (defined here as an increase in the coefficient of variation of the two prices) on agricultural supply. The risk-adverse producers respond to an increase by risk by increasing prices. Hence, b_3 and b_4 should be negative if the producers try to maximize the expected utility of profit. The coefficient b_5 measures the growth in supply for a positive value and decline in value for a negative value. The time trend reflects changes of exogenous such as technology, improvements in marketing and distributing of agricultural goods, and greater trade.

Appendix 2

Statistical Values for Regression Calculations

Datasets

To save on space, only the datasets that we have constructed appear herein. Datasets from printed sources generally available have not been reproduced. The latter datasets are fully cited in a note the first time that the dataset is discussed in the text. We have presented published data generally as we have found them. Even where we encountered gaps in series, we normally did not "manufacture" numbers in order to make the series analytically more manageable. In a few published datasets we have filled in estimated numbers and analyzed the series both without the estimated numbers and with them.

Below are the series that we have constructed and that do not appear in any published sources.

Treasury Revenue—Series B (thousands of pesos)

To construct this series we have subtracted from series C receipts (cargo) year-end balances, unspecified transfers and remissions from subtreasuries, and loans and donations. These figures should not be viewed as the actual annual income but rather as the computed annual income. An asterisk means a figure is estimated because the series C total is missing. From the middle 1790s on, even series B contains computations that may be considerably higher than what the treasury could have realistically had as income. (See chap. 1.)

1701	1,933	1708	1,924	1715	1,894
1702	2,649	1709	1,532	1716	2,157
1703	1,858	1710	2,756	1717	2,644
1704	1,886	1711	2,113	1718	2,410
1705	1,622	1712	2,470	1719	2,325
1706	1,756	1713	1,946	1720	2,999
1707	2,462	1714	2,767	1721	2,305

1722	1,778	1754	6,171	1786	8,097
1723	2,572	1755	5,633	1787	13,563
1724*	2,470	1756	6,276	1788	11,665
1725	1,477	1757	5,677	1789	14,008
1726	3,914	1758	5,807	1790	15,078
1727	2,542	1759	6,366	1791	14,187
1728	3,129	1760	5,722	1792	12,868
1729	2,516	1761	7,400	1793	14,128
1730	3,692	1762	4,960	1794	15,474
1731	3,747	1763	5,760	1795	23,269
1732	2,909	1764	5,978	1796	23,424
1733	4,185	1765	4,491	1797	37,620
1734	3,222	1766	5,288	1798	43,832
1735	3,919	1767	5,932	1799	32,136
1736	3,566	1768	6,229	1800	26,048
1737	3,568	1769	6,457	1801	31,169
1738	3,100	1770	7,992	1802	37,349
1739	2,888	1771	7,592	1803	26,631
1740	3,551	1772	7,123	1804	38,527
1741	4,317	1773	8,672	1805	34,759
1742	4,075	1774	6,777	1806	33,847
1743	5,489	1775	6,743	1807	35,902
1744	6,055	1776	7,406	1808	36,724
1745	3,980	1777	7,723	1809	49,535
1746	4,595	1778	8,420	1810	35,638
1747	3,870	1779	8,670	1811	30,892
1748	4,893	1780	9,207	1812	27,060
1749	4,850	1781	12,799	1813	40,000
1750	5,086	1782	16,291	1814	27,536
1751	5,033	1783	14,908	1815	30,644
1752	5,353	1784	9,556	1816	29,721
1753	5,798	1785	13,421		

Colonywide Average Annual Maize Prices

Below we show the colonywide average price (reales per fanega) and the number of different prices from which the average was computed. Sources are cited in chapter 1.

1700	9.90	4	1710	17.30	4	1720	4.75	2
1701	9.78	5	1711	10.25	4	1721	16.50	2
1702	7.47	3	1712	14.67	3	1722	8.00	3
1703	8.05	4	1713	24.43	3	1723	6.67	3
1704	7.25	4	1714	12.90	4	1724	6.75	4
1705	5.20	3	1715	2.77	3	1725	6.78	5
1706	5.23	3	1716	2.75	4	1726	10.26	5
1707	5.63	3	1717	3.43	4	1727	10.33	6
1708	9.07	4	1718	10.07	3	1728	6.98	5
1709	16.67	3	1719	11.00	3	1729	8.37	6

Year	Value	N	Year	Value	N	Year	Value	N
1730	13.13	6	1757	5.70	5	1784	11.32	5
1731	9.60	5	1758	7.24	7	1785	22.77	4
1732	8.25	6	1759	8.81	7	1786	36.92	5
1733	8.50	5	1760	10.42	5	1787	17.92	4
1734	9.55	4	1761	10.98	6	1788	14.70	6
1735	10.27	4	1762	8.93	7	1789	23.90	4
1736	6.00	4	1763	5.54	7	1790	13.20	3
1737	13.35	4	1764	6.53	6	1791	15.50	3
1738	12.40	4	1765	6.91	7	1792	10.20	4
1739	11.52	4	1766	7.50	6	1793	12.50	3
1740	10.55	4	1767	6.19	7	1794	19.90	3
1741	14.18	5	1768	6.38	4	1795	12.40	3
1742	11.40	5	1769	7.60	5	1796	12.80	3
1743	6.48	5	1770	11.68	6	1797	15.75	6
1744	6.78	6	1771	12.33	6	1798	16.42	4
1745	8.70	6	1772	15.05	6	1799	14.04	5
1746	11.73	6	1773	12.02	6	1800	15.67	3
1747	11.63	6	1774	10.16	5	1801	13.58	4
1748	11.66	5	1775	7.98	5	1802	18.40	4
1749	20.64	5	1776	12.20	4	1803	18.30	4
1750	23.85	6	1777	8.30	6	1804	15.57	3
1751	10.92	6	1778	9.00	4	1805	15.40	3
1752	4.63	4	1779	10.50	4	1806	16.30	2
1753	5.66	8	1780	12.64	5	1807	17.50	2
1754	5.86	5	1781	11.90	4	1808	12.00	1
1755	8.79	8	1782	9.96	5	1809	22.60	3
1756	8.71	8	1783	7.77	4	1810	38.30	2

Upper Bajío Average Annual Wheat Prices

Wheat prices (reales per carga) for this series have been collected from tithe records for three communities: San Miguel el Grande, Dolores Hidago, and San Luis de la Paz. We list below the average and the number of data. Sources are cited in chapter 1.

Year	Value	N	Year	Value	N	Year	Value	N
1700	64.00	1	1714	40.00	1	1728	80.00	1
1701	64.00	1	1715	24.00	1	1729	48.00	2
1702	39.00	1	1716	32.00	1	1730	44.00	2
1703	32.00	2	1717	96.00	1	1731	0.00	0
1704	32.00	1	1718	53.00	1	1732	38.00	2
1705	100.00	1	1719	80.00	1	1733	36.00	2
1706	56.00	1	1720	64.00	1	1734	72.00	1
1707	104.00	1	1721	56.00	1	1735	32.00	1
1708	56.00	1	1722	48.00	1	1736	32.00	1
1709	52.00	1	1723	48.00	1	1737	36.00	1
1710	48.00	1	1724	32.00	1	1738	64.00	2
1711	43.00	1	1725	32.00	1	1739	36.00	2
1712	48.00	1	1726	44.00	2	1740	48.00	2
1713	61.00	1	1727	40.00	1	1741	48.00	1

1742	50.00	2	1763	39.67	3	1784	62.00	2
1743	36.00	2	1764	40.00	2	1785	108.00	2
1744	68.00	2	1765	40.00	2	1786	104.50	2
1745	66.67	3	1766	36.00	2	1787	79.50	2
1746	53.33	3	1767	27.00	2	1788	73.00	2
1747	43.67	3	1768	41.50	2	1789	48.00	2
1748	52.00	2	1769	60.00	2	1790	40.00	1
1749	77.33	3	1770	56.50	2	1791	0.00	0
1750	37.67	3	1771	44.00	2	1792	0.00	0
1751	38.33	3	1772	30.50	2	1793	0.00	0
1752	54.00	3	1773	32.67	3	1794	0.00	0
1753	30.33	3	1774	25.50	2	1795	0.00	0
1754	30.00	3	1775	0.00	0	1796	48.00	1
1755	36.67	3	1776	58.00	1	1797	52.00	1
1756	42.00	2	1777	52.00	1	1798	58.50	2
1757	40.67	3	1778	45.00	1	1799	48.00	1
1758	42.67	3	1779	45.00	1	1800	41.00	1
1759	48.00	2	1780	71.00	2	1801	48.00	1
1760	46.00	2	1781	55.50	2	1802	36.50	2
1761	37.33	3	1782	46.50	2	1803	46.50	2
1762	36.00	2	1783	40.50	2	1804	22.00	1

Wage Data by Various Categories

Wage data are highly selective and should be treated only as rough indicators of wages paid in rural or urban areas and across the colony. Some wage data cannot be assigned to urban or rural categories. Data are payments in cash as pesos per month. Many years are missing. Column 2 contains urban average wages, column 3 rural average wages, column 4 average of data in columns 2 and 3, and column 5 is an average of wage data without regard to area. It should be recalled with respect to column 5 that for some years the average is based on a single entry and for others on many entries.

1704		4.50	4.50	4.50	1751		4.00	4.00	4.00
1709	6.00		6.00	6.00	1752		4.00	4.00	4.00
1710	3.00	6.00	4.50	4.50	1757	3.00		3.00	3.00
1718		4.00	4.00	4.00	1758	4.50		4.50	4.50
1723		6.00	6.00	6.00	1759	4.50		4.50	4.50
1725	8.25		8.25	8.25	1763	23.25		23.25	23.25
1730		5.07	5.07	5.07	1764		4.00	4.00	4.00
1732		4.25	4.25	4.25	1765	12.00	4.10	8.05	6.50
1735		4.00	4.00	4.00	1766		5.70	5.70	5.70
1736	11.88		11.88	11.88	1767	5.38		5.38	5.38
1740	5.25		5.25	5.25	1768	3.00	4.50	3.75	3.75
1745	11.67	5.00	8.33	5.03	1770	6.50	5.25	5.88	5.88
1746		2.38	2.38	2.38	1772		4.38	4.38	4.38
1748		5.25	5.25	5.25	1774	7.50		7.50	7.50
1749	10.50		10.50	10.50	1775	5.25	12.50	8.88	6.00
1750	10.50	2.50	6.50	6.50	1776	7.50		7.50	7.50

1777		4.00	4.00	4.00
1778	9.00	4.00	6.50	6.50
1780	12.50	4.50	8.50	10.50
1781		8.25	8.25	8.25
1783		3.75	3.75	3.75
1785		3.75	3.75	3.75
1786		5.25	5.25	5.25
1788			6.38	6.38
1790	9.00	7.50	8.25	7.90
1791		6.00	6.00	6.00
1793	5.41	4.50	4.95	5.70
1794	9.00	5.00	7.00	6.33
1795	6.00	3.00	4.50	4.50
1797	7.50	5.00	6.25	6.25

1798		3.00	3.00	3.00
1800	4.50	4.08	4.29	5.45
1801		8.25	8.25	8.25
1802	5.25		5.25	5.25
1803	13.19		13.19	13.19
1804	8.25		8.25	8.25
1806	9.00	6.00	7.50	8.00
1807	9.75		9.75	9.75
1810	11.00		11.00	11.00
1811		4.50	4.50	4.50
1812	7.50		7.50	7.50
1814	7.50		7.50	7.50
1815	9.00		9.00	9.00

Transportation Costs

Estimates on how much transportation costs added to the cost of maize shipped from the Upper Bajío to Mexico City or vice versa are based on comparing the price of maize in one location with that in another location and tacking on the cost of transportation. Positive numbers represent shipments from the Bajío to the capital, and negative numbers the opposite direction.

When transportation costs, based on maize prices year-by-year from 1700 to 1804, are estimated at 2, 2.5, and 3 reales per ton mile, the miles worth traveling are given below. A minus ($-$) sign means it is worth shipping maize from Mexico City to the Upper Bajío, a transaction that was probably not very common.

Year	2 Reales/ ton mile	2.5 Reales/ ton mile	3 Reales/ ton mile	Year	2 2 Reales/ ton mile	2.5 Reales/ ton mile	3 Reales/ ton mile
1700	69.0	71.2	59.9	1728	67.0	53.6	44.7
1701	77.0	61.6	51.3	1729	32.0	25.6	21.3
1708	66.0	52.8	44.0	1730	−40.0	−32.0	−26.7
1709	−50.0	−40.0	−33.3	1731	33.0	26.4	22.0
1710	97.0	77.6	64.7	1732	32.0	25.6	21.3
1712	20.0	16.0	13.3	1733	44.0	35.2	29.3
1713	−10.0	−08.0	−06.7	1734	15.0	12.0	10.0
1714	−12.0	−09.6	−08.0	1735	05.0	04.0	03.3
1719	15.0	12.0	10.0	1736	55.0	44.0	36.7
1721	−150.0	−120.0	−100.0	1737	01.0	00.8	00.7
1722	60.0	48.0	40.0	1738	45.0	36.0	30.0
1723	80.0	64.0	53.3	1739	54.0	43.2	36.0
1724	83.0	66.4	55.3	1740	91.0	72.8	60.7
1725	95.0	76.0	63.3	1741	72.0	57.6	48.0
1726	32.0	25.6	21.3	1742	119.0	95.2	79.3
1727	73.0	58.4	48.7	1743	59.0	47.2	39.3

Year	2 2 Reales/ ton mile	2.5 Reales/ ton mile	3 Reales/ ton mile	Year	2 2 Reales/ ton mile	2.5 Reales/ ton mile	3 Reales/ ton mile
1744	38.0	30.4	25.3	1774	65.0	52.0	43.3
1745	15.0	12.0	10.0	1775	62.0	49.6	41.3
1746	32.0	25.6	21.3	1776	14.0	11.2	09.3
1747	39.0	31.2	26.0	1777	18.0	14.4	12.0
1748	41.0	32.8	27.3	1778	− 05.0	− 04.0	− 03.3
1749	07.0	05.6	04.7	1779	01.0	00.8	00.7
1750	13.0	10.4	08.7	1780	26.0	20.8	17.3
1751	− 35.0	− 28.0	− 23.3	1781	109.0	87.2	72.7
1753	51.0	40.8	34.0	1782	125.0	100.0	83.3
1754	62.0	49.6	41.3	1783	63.0	50.4	42.0
1755	49.0	39.2	32.7	1784	− 09.0	− 07.2	− 06.0
1756	19.0	15.2	12.7	1785	06.0	04.8	04.0
1757	10.0	08.0	06.7	1786	52.0	41.6	34.7
1758	30.0	24.0	20.0	1787	130.0	104.0	86.7
1759	54.0	43.2	36.0	1788	− 14.0	− 11.2	− 09.3
1760	60.0	48.0	40.0	1790	156.0	124.8	104.0
1761	− 24.0	19.2	16.0	1792	32.0	25.6	21.3
1762	16.0	12.8	10.7	1793	65.0	52.0	43.3
1763	46.0	36.8	30.7	1794	63.0	50.4	42.0
1764	20.0	16.0	13.3	1795	131.0	104.8	87.3
1765	48.0	38.4	32.0	1797	59.0	47.2	39.3
1766	36.0	28.8	24.0	1798	120.0	96.0	80.0
1767	72.0	57.6	48.0	1799	98.0	78.4	65.3
1768	60.0	48.0	40.0	1800	109.0	87.2	72.7
1769	34.0	27.2	22.7	1801	70.0	56.0	46.7
1770	02.0	01.6	01.3	1802	58.0	46.4	38.7
1771	00.0	00.0	00.0	1803	67.0	53.6	44.7
1772	51.0	40.8	34.0	1804	− 38.0	− 30.4	− 25.3
1773	37.0	29.6	24.7				

Value of Commerce under Consulado of Guadalajara by City and by Number of Years with Transaction

Given below are data collected on trade conducted under the auspices of the Consulado of Guadalajara during the late 1790s and early 1800s. The list shows the city within the Consulado's jurisdiction, the total value of the commerce from which the Consulado collected the avería, and the number of years for which there were transactions.

Aguascalientes	377	5	Bolaños	83	5
Álamos	620	4	Charcas	2,095	7
Aquacatlan	19	6	Chihuahua	2,267	5
Arispe	565	6	Cienquilla	351	4

Coahuila	52	2	Saltillo	2,414	7
Colima	1,100	5	San Antonio Huerta	516	6
Cosalá	279	5	San Miguel de	330	3
Cucliacan	469	6	Horcasitas		
Durango	1,214	5	Sayula	1,094	7
Fresnillo	622	7	Sierra de Pinos	289	5
Guadalajara	3,708	7	Sinaloa	99	5
Jalapa	81	3	Sombrerete	1,359	7
Jéres	79	4	Tepic	612	6
Monclova	36	1	Veracruz	96	5
Rosario	238	3	Zacatecas	1,581	5

Notes

1. General Economic Trends in Eighteenth-Century Mexico

1. British Library, Additions 13978, fols. 116–19.

2. Sterling Library, Yale University (CtY), Latin American Collection, 12-E. The survey is summarized and discussed in the next few paragraphs. For other examples of such reports, see Enrique Florescano, *Precios del maíz y crisis agrícolas en México (1708–1810): Ensayos sobre el movimiento de los precios y sus consequencias económicas y sociales;* Stanley Stein, "Prelude to Upheaval in Spain and New Spain, 1800–1808: Trust Funds, Spanish Finance and Colonial Silver"; British Library, Additions 13978, fols. 204–214 (which Stein also cites in his essay); Asunción Lavrin, "The Execution of the Laws of Consolidación in New Spain: Economic Aims and Results"; and Manuel Abad y Quiepo, "Representación a nombre de los labradores y comerciantes de Valladolid de Michoacán."

3. See Gabriel Haslip-Viera's description of the underclass in late colonial Mexico City in "The Underclass."

4. British Library, Additions 13978, fols. 204–214.

5. See Pedro Pérez Herrero, *Plata y libranzas. La articulación comercial del México borbónico,* for an analysis of eighteenth-century libranzas.

6. For a discussion of recent economic studies see John Coatsworth, "The Economic Historiography of Mexico," also published with a few changes as "La historiografía económica de México."

7. Richard Morse proposed a new chronology in which the colonial period had the dates of 1760 to 1920 because this was "the period when the creole, Catholic culture and institutions of Spanish America lay open to influences and pressures" that had little impact in the previous two centuries

("The Heritage of Latin America," 165). Coatsworth in "The Economic Historiography of Mexico" (p. 11) admonished historians to stop writing colonial history as if it ended in 1810 or 1821, because political independence did not change the essential colonial character of Mexico during the nineteenth century. For a different view, see William Taylor, "Between Global Process and Local Knowledge: An Inquiry into Early Latin American Social History, 1500–1900," 170–71.

8.   Various scholars have tackled the matter of geography and economy in colonial Mexico. For an overview, see Wil Pansters and Arij Ouweneel, eds., *Region, State and Capitalism in Mexico: Nineteenth and Twentieth Centuries*, 6–8. Two European scholars describe colonial Mexico in schematic terms of circles and zones. In *Histoire, science sociale: La durée, l'espace, et l'homme à l'époque modern*, Pierre Chaunu organizes Mexico's economy into four concentric circles—rural, local, regional, and international (pp. 188–93). Bernard Slicher van Bath weighs economic activity in terms of centers, intermediate zones, and peripheries in "Economic Diversification in Spanish America Around 1600: Centres, Intermediate Zones, and Peripheries," in *Bevolking en Economie in Nieuw Spanje (ca. 1570–1800)*, 114–64, and in "De modelos referidos a la relación entre población y economía en Nueva España y Perú durante la época colonial." As intriguing as these approaches are, they cannot really be tested until the data base is large enough to allow for comparison of the economic activity at each level.

9.   This tends to downplay, for the sake of identifying and analyzing the long-term economic trends and the changes that they produced, the degree to which the area was more Spanish than Indian, more mobile than sedentary. See Ida Altman and James Lockhart, eds., *Provinces of Early Mexico: Variants of Spanish American Regional Evolution*, 3–28.

10.   Charles Gibson, *The Aztecs under Spanish Rule: A History of the Indians of the Valley of Mexico, 1519–1810*, 1.

11.   Claude Morin, *Michoacán en la Nueva España del siglo xviii: crecimiento y desigualdad en una economía colonial*, 16–23.

12.   Guy P. C. Thomson, *Puebla de los Angeles: Industry and Society in a Mexican City, 1700–1850*; Eric Van Young, *Hacienda and Market in Eighteenth-Century Mexico: The Rural Economy of the Guadalajara Region, 1675–1820*; and Michael Swann, *Tierra Adentro: Settlement and Society in Colonial Durango*.

13.   Eric Van Young, "A modo de conclusión: el siglo paradójico," 214–21. Pedro Pérez Herrero is also critical of economic analysis based on the assumption that a national market existed; see "El crecimiento económico novohispano durante el siglo xviii: una revisión," 81, 88. In the most economically advanced area of central Mexico, Horst Pietschmann finds diverse and dynamic native economies engaged in agriculture and industry. The latter in this instance is primarily processing and fabricating. How deeply integrated the native economy was with the Spanish economy remains to be analyzed. Moreover, many more details about the structure of

the native economy and how it functioned need to be collected and studied before any firm conclusions can be reached. Pietschmann is clear that Indian communities did not live with abundance but neither did they live in "absolute misery" ("Agricultura e industria rural indígena en el México de la segunda mitad del siglo xviii," 76–79, 83).

14. See J. D. Gould's discussion of Schumpeter in *Economic Growth in History: Survey and Analysis*, 438–43.

15. See Charles Tilly, *Big Structures, Large Processes, Huge Comparisons*, esp. 14–16 and his discussions of Fernand Braudel (pp. 65–74) and Theda Skocpol (pp. 105–15).

16. Transportation costs are discussed in chapter 7. The price and tithe series analyzed herein are discussed later in this chapter where sources will be cited. Mexico City/Upper Bajío Maize Prices: 1700–1804: ninety observations, $R^2 = 0.39$, Student t $= 7.59$; 1700–50: forty observations, $R^2 = 0.26$, Student t $= 3.79$; 1751–1804: fifty observations, $R^2 = 0.50$, Student t $= 7.02$. Oaxaca/Michoacán Tithes: 1701–1800: ninety-nine observations, $R^2 = 0.74$, Student t $= 16.9$; 1701–50: fifty observations, $R^2 = 0.18$, Student t $= 3.46$; 1751–1800: fifty observations, $R^2 = 0.64$, Student t $= 9.39$. Correlation coefficient $=$ square root of R^2.

17. John Coatsworth, "The Limits of Colonial Absolutism: The State in Eighteenth Century Mexico," 36–38; also for a European perspective see Gould, *Economic Growth in History*, 218–25.

18. Coatsworth, "The Economic Historiography of Mexico," 6–7. Since we have almost no year-by-year data before the second half of the nineteenth century and are relying on estimates, we have used a geometric ratio procedure to measure growth over time. The formula is

$$\left[\frac{X_n}{X_1} \right]^{\frac{1}{t-1}}$$

where X_n is the final year and X_1 is the first year and t is the number of years. The result is a figure, like a compound interest rate, that is cumulative because the increase (or decrease) in the value for a given year is a percentage of the value for the previous year. Since we have only estimates of GDP in the eighteenth and early nineteenth centuries, we have used this technique to suggest what growth rates would be realistic in light of what we know about the late colonial or early national economic systems.

19. More will be said about population growth later in this chapter. For a brief but good recapitulation of various eighteenth-century population rates, see Arij Ouweneel, "Growth, Stagnation, and Migration: An Explorative Analysis of the Tributario Series of Anáhuac (1720–1800)," 536.

20. Coatsworth, "The Decline of the Mexican Economy, 1800–1906," 41.

21. See N. F. R. Crafts, *British Economic Growth During the Industrial Revolution*, 45–47. Craft's calculations have been criticized, but even with revised British figures a gap exists.

22. John Coatsworth, "Características generales de la economía mexicana en el siglo xix," 173–74.

23. Linda Salvucci and Richard Salvucci, "Crecimiento económico y cambio de la productividad en México, 1750–1895," 69, 88. They also use an assumed annual rate of 0.41 percent. If the 0.41 percent rate were applied to the same 1895 figure of 2,441 in 1970 pesos, then the figure would be 1,350 for 1750 and 1,657 for 1800. This would result in figures for per capita income that would be twice as high as those estimated by Coatsworth in nominal terms. Obviously if the long-term growth were slower, then the eighteenth-century figures would have to be higher.

24. Paul David, "The Growth of Real Product in the United States Before 1840: New Evidence, Controlled Conjectures," 154–57. For a description of how a modern Gross National Product is calculated, see U.S. Dept. of Commerce, *GNP: An Overview of Source Data and Estimating Methods*.

25. There is a dispute about when the Mexican population reached its colonial nadir. Sherburne Cook and Woodrow Borah have written that "Most scholars . . . have found the turning point somewhere between 1610 and 1650. In the first decade of the seventeenth century, population was still declining. Shortly after the midcentury, the Spanish authorities began to recount Indian towns and found population increase. Obviously, the low point and the beginning of increase of population must have taken place at different times and perhaps under somewhat different circumstances in various regions" (*Essays in Population History*, 3:101). In the second volume of the *Essays in Population History*, published in 1974, they calculate the total population to be 1,498,068 in 1646 (p. 197). For an overview of Latin American colonial demography, see Nicolás Sánchez-Albornoz's two essays: *La población de América latina. Desde los tiempos precolombinos al año 2000*, chaps. 1–4, and "The Population of Colonial Spanish America."

26. For a critical discussion of this census as it was published in José Antonio Villaseñor y Sánchez's *Theatro americano. Descripción general de los reynos, y provincias de la Nueva España, y sus jurisdicciones*, see Cook and Borah, *Essays in Population History*, 2:182–85. Peter Gerhard's *Mexico in 1742* based on *Theatro americano*, offers a population total of 2.6 million in 1742.

27. Alexander von Humboldt, *Political Essay on the Kingdom of New Spain*, 1:97–99 and 1:280–81.

28. For example see, Richard Morse, ed., *The Urban Development of Latin America 1750–1920*, 95.

29. Delfina López Sarrelangue estimates that the Indian population alone rose by 44 percent in the last half of the eighteenth century. This is based largely on figures from Villaseñor y Sánchez in the early 1740s and from Revillagigedo in the early 1790s. Neither census is without defect but the figures that they contain are not farfetched and may be low. Such an

increase would only mean about 1 percent growth each year ("Población indígena de Nueva España en el siglo xviii," 529–30).

30. Cook and Borah, *Essays in Population History*, 1:310–12, 320–21, 355 with quote from 355.

31. Humboldt, *Political Essay on the Kingdom of New Spain*, 1:105–10.

32. For the relationship between rural and urban population growth rates, see Van Young, *Hacienda and Market in Eighteenth-Century Mexico*, chap. 2, and Swann, *Tierra Adentro*, chap. 3. D. A. Brading has noted that growth was estimated to be 1.82 percent per year (tributaries) around 1807 (Brading et al., "Comments on the 'The Economic Cycle in Bourbon Central Mexico: A Critique of the Recaudación del diezmo líquido en pesos,'" 532n.1).

33. Arij Ouweneel and Catrien C. J. H. Bijleveld, "The Economic Cycle in Bourbon Central Mexico: A Critique of the Recaudación del diezmo líquido en pesos," 492–94 and passim; and Ouweneel, "Growth, Stagnation, and Migration."

34. When corrected for autocorrelation the growth rate is 0.7 percent per year: 100 observations, $R^2 = 0.94$, Student t = 3.97. Ouweneel computes a 0.6 percent growth from 1720 to 1800 ("Growth, Stagnation, and Migration," 545).

35. David Grigg, *Population Growth and Agrarian Change: An Historical Perspective*, 1, 57–63 with quote from 60. For a more detailed account of the European urban growth, see Jan DeVries, *European Urbanization 1500–1800*.

36. More about tithes will be discussed in chapter 2. See Emmanuel Le Roy Ladurie and Joseph Goy, *Tithe and Agrarian History from the Fourteenth to the Nineteenth Centuries: An Essay in Comparative History*, 3–70; and Ouweneel and Bijleveld, "Economic Cycle in Bourbon Central Mexico," 479–557. Also see Morin, *Michoacán en la Nueva España del siglo xviii*, 102–7; and D. A. Brading, *Haciendas and Ranchos in the Mexican Bajío: León, 1700–1860*, 68–69 for more on tithe sources. The volume on the Michoacán tithe by Enrique Florescano and Lydia Espinosa regrettably came to our attention too late to be included in our study.

37. For this section we have used figures published in Walter Howe, *The Mining Guild of New Spain and its Tribunal General, 1770–1821*, 453–58, and Humboldt, *Political Essay on the Kingdom of New Spain*, 3:291–92; and both sets appear in Pérez Herrero, *Plata y libranzas*, 317–22, although Pérez Herrero collected the figures from the treasury archives. Because gold production was averaged or estimated, the figures did not change much from year to year up to the 1730s, and therefore we, like Pedro Perez Herrero, did not include them.

38. Morin in *Michoacán en la Nueva España del siglo xviii*, 103, and Elías Trabulse et al., *Fluctuaciones económicas en Oaxaca durante el siglo xviii*, various tables beginning on p. 66. On regression analysis, see Peter

Kennedy, *An Guide to Econometrics;* and appendix 1. Scholars have criticized regional studies that conform to ecclesiastical jurisdictions as in the case of *Michoacán en la Nueva España.* See, for example, Taylor's criticism of Morin's approach in "Between Global Process and Local Knowledge," 178 n.39. This is a valid criticism to the extent that regional economic studies have not been as carefully framed as they should have been. Van Young's *Hacienda and Market in Eighteenth-Century Mexico* is an example of a more carefully conceived study of a region whose boundaries are developed in terms of the social and economic links that grew up between the city of Guadalajara and the countryside. But the criticism should not be overplayed. The collection and analysis of economic data can be slow and tedious work and may represent the first stage of a long process. As Taylor points out, the ecclesiastical boundaries are used because economic data, especially the agricultural tithes, come from church archives that are organized by administrative units such as dioceses. The next stage may be to define more clearly and precisely how economies at the local and regional level are organized and then how they are linked. Ecclesiastical tithes do permit us to examine the patterns and trends in output of agricultural for a given district or jurisdiction, although the area may, from an economic standpoint, have a degree of artificiality. Criticisms may also be leveled against the Oaxaca study because data and jurisdictional boundaries are not as clearly defined as they could be.

39.   For different estimates see Henry Aubrey, "The National Income of Mexico"; Fernando Rosenzweig Hernández, "La economía novohispana al comenzar el siglo xix"; and Clark Reynolds, *The Mexican Economy: Twentieth-Century Structure and Growth.* Reynolds provides a summary of the work of Aubrey and Rosenzweig on pp. 311–14. As noted earlier, John Coatsworth offers a revision of the agricultural sector in 1800 in "The Decline of the Mexican Economy," 41.

40.   The R^2 values for the individual series, Oaxaca (100 observations) and Michoacán (131 observations), and for the combined series (100 observations) are very high—in the range of 0.80 to 0.95 when the series were corrected for autocorrelation. The series have not been adjusted for inflation. Thus the real growth of the combined Michoacán-Oaxaca series was lower than the 1.3 percent rate. Although we consider the inflation factor later in this chapter, we note here that over the long term it may have been less than one-half of one percent. The inflation rate like other rates was surely higher over the short run and could vary from region to region.

41.   See Linda Greenow's discussion of Robert Spillman's mapping of death rates from those crises in *Credit and Socioeconomic Change in Colonial Mexico: Loans and Mortgages in Guadalajara, 1720–1820,* 173–75. Also John Tutino, *From Insurrection to Revolution in Mexico: Social Bases of Agrarian Violence, 1750–1940,* 41–99.

42.   See Morin, *Michoacán en la Nueva España del siglo xviii,* 47–49, esp. cuadro II.2 on p. 49; and Sánchez-Albornoz, "Population of Colonial Spanish America," 2:26–27. One may argue, in line with Van Young's

analysis, that output rather than population was the independent variable and that as population rose so too did output primarily through the addition of land rather than the more intensive use of available land. In effect, this turns the Malthusian model upside down. Instead of population rising to and eventually overwhelming the level of production, production rises to the level of population with the duly noted disruptions that worked in such a way as to provide a brief respite (Van Young, *Hacienda and Market in Eighteenth-Century Mexico*, 103, 220–24, 348–49).

43. Brading, *Haciendas and Ranchos in the Mexican Bajío*, 13, 18.

44. William Taylor, *Landlord and Peasant in Colonial Oaxaca*, 153–54; and John Chance, *Race and Class in Colonial Oaxaca*, 144–51.

45. R^2 values are approximately the same for both series—0.94 versus 0.92 when corrected for autocorrelation. The discrepancies in the two series are most pronounced from 1733 to 1778. The year 1742 is most puzzling because one series reports a total of 8.9 million pesos worth of gold and silver and the other reported 16.7 million worth, nearly twice as much. If we exclude 1742 from both series, we have the same rates with slightly higher R^2 values. Either way the correlation between the two series is extremely high.

46. Data from John TePaske and Herbert Klein, "The Seventeenth-Century Crisis in New Spain: Myth or Reality?" 124–27; and TePaske, "Economic Cycles in New Spain: The View from the Public Sector," *Biblioteca Americana* (BA), 198–203.

47. See Garner, "Long-Term Silver Mining Trends in Spanish America: A Comparative Analysis of Peru and Mexico," for a discussion of patterns of growth in each viceroyalty from the sixteenth through the eighteenth centuries.

48. Data from TePaske, "Economic Cycles in New Spain: The View from the Public Sector," *BA*, 198–203. The trend in Guanajuato (100 observations) is well established: $R^2 = 0.93$ after being corrected for autocorrelation and Student t = 8.54. For Zacatecas (100 observations), because of the mid-century depression, the eighteenth-century trend is less verifiable. When corrected for autocorrelation, the $R^2 = 0.58$ but Student t = 0.77, far below an acceptable confidence level. In any event a growth rate of 0.3 percent yields basically a flat trend.

49. Salvucci and Salvucci, "Crecimiento económico," 73–74, 88.

50. We emphasize that these are strictly tentative findings. The calculations show a high degree of autocorrelation that cannot be easily corrected for. We offer these findings to encourage research along these lines rather than to present a definitive case for favorable elasticities.

51. The literature on growth and change in Europe's economies during the eighteenth and early nineteenth centuries is extensive. Three articles on the British industrial revolution present opposing views on how much growth can be documented from 1750 to 1850, whether it was agriculturally or industrially driven, and how it compared to other European economies: N. F. R. Crafts, "British Economic Growth, 1700–1850"; Jeffrey Williamson,

"Debating the British Industrial Revolution"; and Joel Mokyr, "Has the Industrial Revolution Been Crowded Out? Some Reflections on Crafts and Williamson."

52. For another approach see John Coatsworth, "Obstacles to Economic Growth in Nineteenth-Century Mexico."

53. The chief sources are John TePaske with José and María Luz Hernández Palomo, *La Real Hacienda de Nueva España: La Real Caja de México (1576–1816)*; and TePaske and Herbert Klein, with Kendall Brown, *The Royal Treasuries of the Spanish Empire in America*.

54. TePaske and Klein have undertaken sectoral analysis: TePaske and Klein, "The Seventeenth-Century Crisis in New Spain"; TePaske, "Economic Cycles in New Spain," *BA* and in Garner and Taylor (G-T); and Klein, "La economía de la Nueva España, 1680–1809: un análisis a partir de las cajas reales." Mention should also be made of John Coatsworth's essay, "The Limits of Colonial Absolutism." The most heated discussions have occurred in the pages of *Past and Present*. TePaske and Klein's article "The Seventeenth-Century Crisis in New Spain" was a response to an earlier essay, "Mexico and the 'General Crisis' of the Seventeenth Century," by J. I. Israel. In "Debate," Israel and Henry Kamen responded to TePaske and Klein, who issued rejoinders to their critics' responses. Many different issues are raised in these essays and in the rejoinders, but the underlying concerns for all parties, particularly for TePaske and Klein, are the reliability and trustworthiness of the treasury's figures. We should also note that Coatsworth's essay, "The Limits of Colonial Absolutism," sparked a rebuttal entitled "Facts and Figments in Bourbon Mexico," by D. A. Brading, and a rejoinder by Richard Garner, "Further Consideration of 'Facts and Figments in Bourbon Mexico.'" Finally, Samuel Amaral in "Public Expenditure Financing in the Colonial Treasury: An Analysis of the Real Caja de Buenos Aires Accounts, 1789–91," offers a critique of an earlier Klein essay, "Structure and Profitability of Royal Finance in the Viceroyalty of the Río de la Plata in 1790," that focused on a single year. For further discussion of Amaral's critique, see "Commentaries on 'Public Expenditures Financing in the Colonial Treasury'" by Javier Cuenca Esteban, John TePaske, Herbert Klein, and John Fisher (in the same issue of the *Hispanic American Historical Review*), 297–319.

55. Series C contains the annual receipts as listed in TePaske et al., *La Real Hacienda de Nueva España*. Series A is explained in TePaske, "Economic Cycles in New Spain in the Eighteenth Century," G-T, 130, 133–35. In constructing Series A TePaske eliminated year-end balances, temporary loans and deposits, and other cash infusions that were not by definition revenue. These revisions that seem so reasonable actually entail subtracting a very large category known as real hacienda en común on the debit side from the total receipts because in TePaske's view this came to represent year-end balances. On the revenue side real hacienda en común figures never reached the magnitude that they do on the debit side. Series B is somewhat artificial.

We have focused solely on the revenue side and in so doing we have removed accounts that might contain year-end balances and transfers, temporary loans and deposits, and other unusual items. More study of these accounts is needed but in these three series we have a range of possibilities.

56. In all three series (109 observations) the R^2 values are above 0.9 and the Student t's above 10.0. Series C had to be corrected for autocorrelation.

57. Richard Garner, "Exportaciones de circulante en el siglo xviii"; and Pérez Herrero, *Plata y libranzas*, chap. 8.

58. Coatsworth, "The Limits of Colonial Absolutism," 27. See also in the same publication TePaske's "The Fiscal Structure of Upper Peru and the Financing of Empire" for an assessment of the performance of Peru's treasury over the whole colonial period but with special attention to the eighteenth century.

59. See Garner for a discussion of sources and methods in the creation of a colonywide maize series in "Price Trends in Eighteenth-Century Mexico." Since the publication of that article the series has been expanded to include tithe data compiled by Silvia Galicia, *Precios y producción en San Miguel el Grande, 1661–1803,* 72, and also tithe data by Cecilia Rabell Romero, *Los Diezmos de San Luis de la Paz, Economía en una región del Bajío en el siglo xviii,* 191–201. The average prices that appear in table 4 differ from those that were published earlier, but growth rates for both series were almost identical. We stress that the colonywide series contains prices from various regional sources—public granaries, tithe sales, official estimates, and the like. It is created not to establish a single maize price—such a price did not exist—but to study the trends and movements of the price of a commodity that was grown nearly everywhere and was affected by similar conditions such as weather, yields, pests, inputs, transportation, and other factors. On Europe, see Le Roy Ladurie and Goy, *Tithe and Agrarian History,* 43–53. Also see critiques by Herbert Klein and Stanley Engerman ("Methods and Meanings in Price History") and John Coatsworth ("Economic History and History of Prices in Colonial Latin America") on work done thus far on colonial Latin American price history. Finally, the most comprehensive treatment of price history remains Fernand Braudel's and Frank Spooner's "Prices in Europe from 1450 to 1750," esp. 378–90 and 442–56.

60. Bronfenbrenner, "Inflation and Deflation"; and James Tobin, "Inflation: Monetary and Structural Causes and Cures," 3–8.

61. Y. S. Brenner, "The Inflation of Prices in Early Sixteenth Century England," 231–36.

62. Richard Garner, "Problèmes d'une ville miniére mexicaine à la fin de l'époque coloniale: prix et salaries à Zacatecas (1760–1821)."

63. After correction for autocorrelation (169 observations), $R^2 = 0.5$; Student t = 3.25.

64. After correction for autocorrelation (111 observations), $R^2 = 0.43$, Student t = 3.44.

65. The rates (r) and the statistical tests (corrected for autocorrelation)

for the interfamine periods are: 1700–1714: fourteen observations, r = 11.8 percent, R^2 = 0.59, Student t = 2.42; 1715–50: thirty-four observations, r = 2.7 percent, R^2 = 0.43, Student t = 1.95; 1751–86: thirty-four observations, r = 3.5 percent, R^2 = 0.47, Student t = 4.16; 1787–1810: twenty-three observations, r = 2.6, R^2 = 0.27, Student t = 2.26. These were not the only years of serious famines and epidemics, but they were the years with the highest recorded prices. For the period after 1786, the year 1810 is used as the terminal year even though it was not a year of famine or epidemic. See also Garner, "Price Trends in Eighteenth-Century Mexico."

66.   For quarter-century periodization we used a linear-spline technique, which, unlike the dummy-variable approach, recognizes that some linkage exists between periods with the result that the trends and rates for each period tend to be smoother and more in character with the overall growth of the eighteenth century. Corrected for autocorrelation (100 observations), R^2 = 0.38, Student t = 2.0.

67.   Somewhat different averages and rates occur if 1772, a year of some scarcity, is removed from the series. The data are drawn from Florescano, *Precios del maíz*, 233–34. With eighteen observations for each month, January–October, R^2 values seldom exceed 0.15, and Student t's cluster around 2.0.

68.   Garner, "Problèmes d'une ville miniére mexicaine à la fin de l'époque coloniale," 82; and Van Young, *Hacienda and Market in Eighteenth-Century Mexico*, 59–63.

69.   Arij Ouweneel, "The Agrarian Cycle as a Catalyst of Economic Development in Eighteenth-Century Central Mexico: The Arable Estate, Indian Villages and Proto-Industrialization in the Central Highland Valleys," 408.

70.   Galicia, *Precios y producción en San Miguel el Grande*, 74; Flor de María Hurtado López, *Dolores Hidalgo, estudio económico, 1740–1790*, 49–51; and Rabell Romero, *Los Diezmos de San Luis de La Paz*, 191–201. The coefficient with ninety-seven observations yields a negative annual rate of 0.1 percent with only a 43.3 percent confidence level. The R^2 is a −0.006.

71.   Virginia García Acosta: *Las panaderías, sus dueños y trabajadores. Ciudad de México. Siglo xviii*, and *Los precios del trigo en la historia colonial de México*. From 1741 to 1788, based on sales (forty-eight observations) of good and inferior wheat by harvest year, no trend can be verified. From 1754 to 1788, however, wheat prices (thirty-five observations) may have risen about 1 percent per year with an R^2 = 0.28 and Student t = 3.81.

72.   Garner, "Problèmes d'une ville minière mexicaine à la fin de l'époque coloniale." The R^2 values are unimpressive, in the range of 0.1 to 0.4. Thus the trend does not explain much.

73.   Ouweneel and Bijleveld also believe that inflation was more serious in the late decades of the eighteenth century or the early decades of the nineteenth century. They do not, however, offer any figures on how much inflation the fifty-one central Mexican provinces in their study suffered or

how much greater the inflationary trend was in the late colonial decades compared to earlier times ("Economic Cycles in Bourbon Central Mexico," 509, 515–19).

74. Reynolds, *Mexican Economy*, 11–14.

75. Haslip-Viera, "The Underclass," 294, 296. The source of these data is not, so far as we can determine, given.

76. Timothy Anna, *The Fall of Royal Government in Mexico City*, 231n.27, and in general chap. 1.

77. The data have been collected from many different sources, both primary and secondary. Eric Van Young's paper "The Rich Get Richer and the Poor Get Skewed: Real Wages and Popular Living Standards in Late Colonial Mexico" contains tables of urban and rural wages (pp. 65–73), which with the author's permission have been incorporated into our own data base. The statistical tests show up better for the series that includes all salary and wage data per year than the series based upon annual averages. For the former (186 observations) $R^2 = 0.1$ and for the latter (fifty-nine observations) zero, and the Student t's $= 4.68$ and 1.86, respectively.

2. Trends in Agriculture

1. By the early 1980s more than 200 studies bearing on haciendas and rural life had been published. See Eric Van Young, "Mexican Rural History since Chevalier: The Historiography of the Colonial Hacienda"; and Van Young, "Recent Anglophone Scholarship on Mexico and Central America in the Age of Revolution (1750–1850)," which updates an earlier piece by James Lockhart, "The Social History of Colonial Spanish America: Evolution and Potential."

2. Based on Van Young, "The Age of Paradox: Mexican Agriculture at the End of the Colonial Period, 1750–1810," 64–65, 80–81. For other views of the agricultural sector, see Brading, *Haciendas and Ranchos*, chap. 1; and Enrique Florescano, "The Formation and Economic Structure of the Hacienda in New Spain." John Coatsworth offers some challenging ideas on the eighteenth-century agricultural economy. "Estates agriculture enjoyed advantages not available to Indian villages, small landowners, or tenant farmers: economies of scale, access to outside credit, information about new technologies and distant markets, a measure of protection from predatory officials, and greater security of tenure." But these advantages did not eliminate the need for or the development of small-scale agriculture. What the large estates did better than the small holdings was to raise livestock, grain, sugar, and *pulque*. With other products "that required very close supervision (or highly motivated workers) either to produce or to transport without great losses," products such as fruits, vegetables, pork, fowl, or silk, small-scale operations did better. "Product specialization among units of varying size, location, and organization made Mexican agriculture more efficient than it would otherwise have been." Producers had to worry about

and act upon "what a modern economists would describe as an 'optimal mix.' " Coatsworth concludes that large haciendas, which represented concentration of landholding, "functioned to allow more efficient production of crops suitable for large units . . . without sacrificing the advantages of small-unit output for other produce" ("Obstacles to Economic Growth in Nineteenth-Century Mexico," 87–88).

3. Brading, *Haciendas and Ranchos*, 68–69; and Morin, *Michoacán en la Nueva España del siglo xviii*, 104–5. For criticism in using tithe data to analyze rural production, see Ouweneel and Bijleveld, "The Economic Cycle in Bourbon Central Mexico," and "Comments on 'The Economic Cycle in Bourbon Central Mexico,' " by Brading, Coatsworth, and Lindo-Fuentes with a reply by the authors, 531–57. Also see Héctor Lindo-Fuentes, "La utilidad de los diezmos como fuentes para la historia econónica."

4. Van Young explains the roles of the various sellers in Guadalajara's maize market, in *Hacienda and Market in Eighteenth-Century Mexico*, 79–88.

5. Brading's discussion of the tithe in *Haciendas and Ranchos*, 68–69, is reaffirmed in "Comments on 'The Economic Cycle in Bourbon Central Mexico,' " 533.

6. For maize output in León and Silao, respectively, R^2 = 0.33 and 0.64, Student t's = 6.97 and 13.85 for 107 and 128 observations. For the shorter period (1660–1768) Silao's R^2 = 0.62 and Student t = 11.99 with 107 observations. From 1700 to 1768 in León and from 1700 to 1789 in Silao the annual rates were 0.7 percent and 1.23 percent, respectively, R^2 = values 0.32 and 0.25, and Student t's = 2.35 and 4.92.

7. For León from 1660 to 1768, R^2 = 0.02 and Student t = 1.98; from 1700 to 1768, R^2 = 0.03 and Student t = 0.69. For Silao from 1660 to 1789, R^2 = 0.10 and Student t = 2.98; 1660–1768, R^2 = 0.02 and Student t = 1.42; 1700–1789, R^2 = 0.10 and Student t = 2.98; 1768–89, R^2 = 0.02 and Student t = 1.16. If the dataset is reconfigured to begin in the 1750s instead of the 1760s, the difference in the rates of the two variables is less pronounced, and the statistics for validating the trends are stronger. In the third quarter, therefore, prices appear to be climbing faster than production, but by how much more depends on how the dataset is arranged.

8. We have used two methods to calculate elasticities. For a general figure we regressed the log of maize output against the log of lagged maize price. For León (ninety-seven observations) 1660–1768, R^2 = 0.22 and Student t = 1.62 when corrected for autocorrelation, and for Silao (108 observations), R^2 = 0.53 and Student t = 1.96 when corrected for autocorrelation. The annual figures were derived from the regression coefficient of output regressed against lagged price multiplied times lagged price divided by output. For León 1660–1768 R^2 = 0.37 and Student t = 4.02 when corrected for autocorrelation, and for Silao 1660–1789, R^2 = 0.52 and Student t = 3.81 when corrected for autocorrelation.

9.   Tutino, *From Insurrection to Revolution in Mexico*, chap. 2, esp. 73–77.

10.   *World Almanac, Book of Facts*, s.v. "Mexico."

11.   Conflicts between Spanish haciendas and Indian villages over land was common. Each tried to avoid being forced to use marginal land, to surrender arable land, or to share water and timber rights. See Martin, *Rural Society in Colonial Morelos*, which details many such cases.

12.   Aguirre Beltrán, *La población negra de México*, 197–241.

13.   Van Young calculated that each Indian adult consumed about 7 fanegas or 700 pounds per year in "The Rich Get Richer and Poor Get Skewed," 33. In a later communication he proposed a revised calculation of 3.5 fanegas or 350 pounds per adult person. We have estimated that about 50 percent of the Indian population consumed at adult rates. The average maize consumption and the total Indian population figures are at best very rough estimates. Van Young uses a formula of 1 fanega equals 100 pounds so that the tonnages above would amount to 3.5 million fanegas and 5.3 million fanegas, respectively.

14.   Florescano, "Formation and Economic Structure," 2:171–82; and Brading, *Haciendas and Ranchos*, 9–12.

15.   See Ouweneel and Bijleveld, "Economic Cycle in Bourbon Central Mexico," passim, but the point is most resolutely presented in their rejoinder, p. 556.

16.   Data for Puebla from Medina Rubio, *La iglesia y la producción agrícola en Puebla*, 176, 180, 184, 187, 190, 194, 196; for Michoacán from Morin, *Michoacán en la Nueva España del siglo xviii*, 103; and for Oaxaca, Trabulse et al., *Fluctuaciones económicas en Oaxaca*, 66–67. There are problems with Oaxaca's series. Several datasets are published, but their arrangement is not always clearly explained. The authors claim to be more interested in fluctuations than trends, in local economic conditions than larger-scale units. On pp. 66–67 there is a table with the annual tithes under three columns: the first column has no title, the second has the title "Mixteca," and the third has the title "Obispado." Between 1770 and 1790 there are no data under the first column except for the years 1780 and 1781. It appears, however, that by turning to another table we can ascertain that column one is the total tithe product for the livestock ranchers and the wheat farmers. The other table, on pp. 88–91, shows the conversion of all tithe data to logarithms but in a somewhat confusing manner, with many more columns designating sources of tithes by regions and agencies: Costa de Alvar (Alvarado), Ganado Valles, Centrales, Costa Mixteca, Costa Sur, Diezmo Suelto, Trigo Valles, Costeras, Valles, Mixteca, and Obispado. When the logarithms for Ganado Valles and Trigo Valles are inverted, the sum of the numbers equal the totals under column 1. Logarithms for Centrales and Mixteca are exactly the same and this is a strong indication that they are the same data, one with a geographic reference and one with an ethnographic reference. Costa de

Alvarado, Costa Mixteca, and Costa Sur are all regions shown on the map entitled *Obispado de Oaxaca en el siglo xviii*, p. 24. The relationship of Costeras and Valles to the other coast or valley regions cannot be determined. Finally, while the authors state that the "most complete" series is Obispado (p. 25), they do not explain exactly what figures are included in the series. The total of all the columns on pp. 88–91 (but counting the figures for Centrales and Mixteca only once) is greater for any year than the number under the Obispado column. This may be an indication of double-counting in order to develop the geographic scheme. In any event, we have taken the authors at their word and we have used only Obispado in calculating trend lines and growth rates for Oaxaca. See critique by Lindo-Fuentes, "La utilidad de los diezmos."

17.   The Puebla series differs from the other two in that to fit the data from the sixteenth and seventeenth centuries with the eighteenth century, we have used not total receipts but receipts minus costs. The shape of the curve and the rate of the increase could be affected, although the shape of the curve was more likely to be affected than the rate. When corrected for autocorrelation, Student t's are above the 99 percentile but R^2's do not rise above 0.42 for 102 observations.

18.   For all four calculations—Oaxaca, Puebla, Michoacán, and total—without second-quarter data (sixty-nine observations) and corrected for autocorrelation, R^2's range from 0.6 to 0.9 and Students t's exceed 3.0. The absence of second-quarter data makes a difference in the shape of the curve and the rate of the growth along the curve. Ouweneel and Bijleveld estimated population for years that were missing, but using estimated data for so many years can make the statistical calculations less reliable. They have used five-year moving averages to smooth out the peaks and dips, although these moving averages are affected by the estimated values. When their series (100 observations) is analyzed, it yields a growth rate of 1.3 percent per year: Student t = 13.29, and R^2 = 0.98 when corrected for autocorrelation. Our eighteenth-century rate without estimating or averaging (seventy-five observations) was 1.0: Student t = 9.23 and R^2 = 0.83. The shape of the curve based on the estimates and averages was strikingly more upward for the whole century than ours.

19.   This figure is only an estimate. It is derived by dividing the total for these three dioceses by the total tithe collected during the period 1770–90.

20.   The 1800 figure is considerably below other estimates, although it is close to Humboldt's figure. See Reynolds, *The Mexican Economy*, 311–14 for estimates that range from 29.0 million to 106.0 million pesos in 1800, and Coatsworth, "The Decline of the Mexican Economy," 41–42.

21.   The linear-spline technique yielded the following rates: Michoacán (sixty-nine observations) grew by 1.6 percent per year for 1701–94, 1.8 percent before 1750, and 1.3 percent after 1750; Puebla (twenty-four observations), 0.8, 0.5, 1.3, respectively; and Oaxaca (forty-four observations) 0.7, 0.5, 1.3, respectively. After correction for autocorrelation the R^2 were

moderately high and the Student t's within the 99 percent confidence level, except for Puebla and Oaxaca in the second half of the eighteenth century the Student t's fall below the 95 percent confidence level.

22.   For a presentation of this technique, see J. Johnston, *Econometric Methods*, 392–96. R²'s and Student t's fall within acceptable ranges after correction for autocorrelation.

23.   In Mixteca, a region in the jurisdiction of Oaxaca, population growth rates fluctuate between a low of 0.2 percent and a high of 1.2 percent per year in the eighteenth century, although no long-term rate has been computed. Growth did not seem as strong decade by decade in the second half of the eighteenth century, when the tithe jumped, as in the first half (Cook and Borah, "An Essay on Method," in *Essays in Population History,* 1:107). Lindo-Fuentes also offers some population-growth percentages (0.7 to 0.8 annual rates) for Oaxaca in "La utilidad de los diezmos," 283.

24.   Morin, *Michoacán en la Nueva España del siglo xviii*, 38–83.

25.   Rabell Romero, *San Luis de la Paz*, 57–58.

26.   Brading, *Haciendas and Ranchos*, 58–59. In the adjacent diocese of New Galicia (not included in the Michoacán tithe collection but not far from León) Cook and Borah have calculated decennial growth rates between 2.0 and 2.8 during the eighteenth century. These calculations do not reveal that the rate of increase changed significantly from decade to decade during the eighteenth century (*Essays in Population History*, 1:312–21).

27.   Lindo-Fuentes, "La utilidad de los diezmos," 283.

28.   Calculations are drawn from Garner's "Price Trends in Eighteenth-Century Mexico," 282–83, 306–11, and some refinements that have been introduced since that essay was published.

29.   This description is at variance with the one presented by the compilers of the Oaxacan tithe series. They argue for substantial growth in tithe receipts and therefore in agricultural output during the seventeenth century. This is based on calculating growth rate from two points: 1624 and 1694. Using just two points entails many risks but it can and has been done by others. However, the figure of 3.5 percent for the two dates is twice the actual rate (1.7 percent) per year. The Trabulse team figure is also used to call into question Woodrow Borah's seventeenth-century depression thesis. Borah contends that tithes lagged in the second quarter of the seventeenth century because of Indian depopulation and then began to rise as a result of better collection and the expansion of the Spanish and mestizo economies in the wake of the declining Indian economy. The more moderate annual growth rate suggests a less dynamic economy and lends credence to Borah's contention that a more efficient tithe collection system combined with an economic recovery in the second half of the seventeenth century explain the rise in income from tithing. Furthermore, the conclusions of Trabulse for the eighteenth century seem at variance with the statistical evidence. They contend that the period from 1735 to 1770 is one of depression. In fact, when regression analysis is applied either to the yearly data or to the moving

averages—the most extreme being a ten-year moving average—for the *obispado* it yields growth not depression. The growth could be as low as 0.3 percent per year and as high as 0.9 percent per year from 1735 to 1770, the lower figure being derived from the yearly receipts and the higher figure from a ten-year moving average of those figures. As indicated above in the text, growth rates of the two middle quarter centuries are not much different from the century-long average (Trabulse, *Fluctuaciones económicas en Oaxaca*, 14, 33, 37–40, 95–96). See also Murdo MacLeod's "Review of Trabulse et al., Fluctuaciones economicas," in which some of these conclusions are highlighted. Borah, "Tithe Collection in the Bishopric of Oaxaca, 1601–1867," 386–409.

30.   Enrique Florescano, *Orígen y desarrollo de los problemas agrarios de México, 1500–1821*, 69. We have used a document found in the British Library, Egerton Collection, 520, fols. 199–205. Ouweneel and Bijleveld analyze the 1770–90 data briefly but primarily to highlight the differences among the various series in "The Economic Cycle in Bourbon Central Mexico," 484–85; and Brading, "Comments on 'The Economic Cycle in Bourbon Central Mexico,' " 533, in responding to Oweneel-Bijleveld's article raises the possibility of defects in accounting.

31.   Garner, "Price Trends in Eighteenth-Century Mexico," and "Problèmes d'une ville miniére mexicaine à la fin de l'époque coloniale." $R^2 = .23$ and student $t = 2.33$ for maize from 1770 to 1790.

32.   In an earlier section we argued that maize producers could use maize prices of the previous year to help to determine how much maize to plant in the current year. In general, the supply of maize proved to be inelastic. Changes in maize prices induced only marginal changes in maize supplies. We can run a similar test for the total output (based on tithes) of the agricultural sector. In short, how was supply (as measured by ecclesiastical tithes) affected by changes in prices (as represented by maize prices) in the fifteen years before the famines of the 1780s? The elasticity ratios based on agricultural tithes and maize prices do not differ very much from those based more narrowly on maize output and price (from Brading). What this may indicate is that the relative inelasticity in supply of agricultural sector products reduced the incentive to invest heavily in the expansion of the sector. It must be remembered, however, that these calculations are extremely tentative and have been introduced primarily to suggest ways in which scholars might use tithe and price data to test certain hypotheses about the performance of the eighteenth-century agricultural economy. For these calculations (twenty-one observations) (maize prices regressed against tithes) Student $t = 1.89$ and $R^2 = 0.12$.

33.   The towns of the sellers of maize and flour were identified in the alhóndiga records. See Garner, "Problèmes d'une ville miniére mexicaine à la fin de l'époque coloniale," for discussion of sources.

34.   See map 2, in Van Young, *Hacienda and Market in Eighteenth-Century Mexico*, 20–21.

35.   See Arij Ouweneel's study of a diary kept by the proprietor of a large Tlaxcalan estate in the 1760s, "Eighteenth-Century Tlaxcalan Agriculture: Diary 9 of the Hacienda San Antonio Palula, 1765–1766." His accounts show a concern for the prices received for the products and whether they were sufficient to cover the costs (p. 41), the best time to bring grains to market (pp. 56–57), and the yields of crops (p. 65).

36.   For the mathematics consult appendix 1. The modern literature on response to risk is extensive. For a review of the early literature, see H. Askari and J. T. Cummings, *Agricultural Supply Response: A Survey of the Econometric Evidence;* and J. R. Anderson, J. L. Dillon, and J. B. Hardaker, *Agricultural Decision Analysis.* More recent attempts are: A Sandmo, "On the Theory of the Competitive Firm under Price Uncertainty"; R. E. Just, "An Investigation of the Importance of Risk in Farmer's Decisions"; B. Traill, "Risk Variables in Econometric Supply Response Models"; J. M. Antle, "Econometric Estimation of Producers' Risk Attitudes"; and Y.-H. Luh and S. E. Stefanou, "Dairy Supply and Factor Demand Response to Output Price Risk: An Econometric Assessment."

37.   David Grigg addresses the issue of risk and leisure with respect to peasant communities in *Dynamics of Agricultural Change: The Historical Experience,* 98–99. Generally, he argues, because of the "high risk of harvest failure" peasants were disinclined toward risk taking. In all probability, those who took the risk in eighteenth-century Mexico were the large commercial producers. But they too had to devise a strategy that allowed them to try to calculate from the standpoint of inputs and returns, especially since their operations were more capital intensive, the degree of risk in expanding production or distribution.

38.   Grigg, *Population Growth and Agrarian Change,* 11–19, 44–47 with quotes from p. 44 and with special attention to figures 6 and 7, pp. 45–46.

39.   Ester Boserup, *The Conditions of Agricultural Growth: The Economics of Agrarian Change under Population Pressure,* 11–14 and passim. Also see Grigg's summary of Boserup's model in *Dynamics of Agricultural Change,* 37–43, esp. table 1, pp. 38–39.

40.   E. L. Jones and S. J. Woolf, *Agrarian Change and Agricultural Development: The Historical Problems,* 1–21.

41.   These ideas are taken from Grigg, *Dynamics of Agricultural Change,* 23–25, in his discussion of optimum theory. Eric Van Young believes that Boserup's approach as a "theory of agricultural growth explains, in a general way, the changes in the economic structure of the Guadalajaran region in the late-colonial period" (*Hacienda and Market in Eighteenth-Century Mexico,* 348–49). The growth of urban populations provided the critical mass necessary in certain regions to launch the commercialization of agriculture, although the capital needed to sustain the expansion in output may have been drying up. In León, Brading observes that while population growth initiated changes in the agricultural system, it could also serve as a "Malthusian brake" because of the region's limited resources and skills to

support agrarian development (*Haciendas and Ranchos*, 60, 200). Because of the cycle of famines and epidemics that mollified the pressure of population growth against agricultural capacity, the level at which Mexico's rising population posed a threat is hard to establish.

42. Charlton, "Land Tenure and Agricultural Production," 258–61. In the Oaxacan region, Marcello Carmagnani's investigations reveal that the use and acquisition of land by pueblos was more complex than the simple question of whether the Indians had enough land to support their communities might indicate. In some native communities land was insufficient, in others adequate, and in still others just one of the resources that Indians employed to meet their external financial obligations and to maintain their populations. The land question, as Carmagnani treats it, is part of an elaborate argument concerning the capacity of these native communities to manage their own economic affairs. We will consider that argument later. At this point we want to emphasize that it cannot be automatically assumed that Mexico's land base was being expanded and simultaneously marginalized during the late colonial period (Carmagnani, *El regreso de los dioses*, 110–16).

43. Hurtado López, *Dolores Hidalgo*, 15, 20–21.

44. Hurtado López did not report or compute an annual tithe for the parish as a whole so that we do not know for certain if his figures are complete. If they are incomplete, then the ratios could change.

45. Hurtado López, *Dolores Hidalgo*, 81, 83–85.

46. Two documents for 1802 and 1803 from AGN-AHH, Consulado, legajo (leg.) 917, exp. 1. The 1803 *relación* by José Fernando de Abascal y Sousa has been published in Enrique Florescano and Isabel Gil Sánchez, *Descripciones económicas regionales de Nueva España. Provincias del Centro, Sureste y Sur, 1766–1827*, 110–17. A version found in Seville was published by Ramón María Serrera de Contreras "Estado económico de la Intendencia de Guadalajara a principio del siglo xix: la 'Relación de José Fernando de Abascal y Sousa de 1803.' "

47. Van Young, *Hacienda and Market in Eighteenth-Century Mexico*, 26; and "The Rich Get Richer and the Poor Get Skewed," 49n.27.

48. Van Young, "The Rich Get Richer and the Poor Get Skewed," 11.

49. Van Young, *Hacienda and Market in Eighteenth-Century Mexico*, 206–7.

50. AGN-AHH, Consulado, leg, 917, exp. 2. See Garner, "Problèmes d'une ville miniére mexicaine à la fin de l'époque coloniale," 98–102, tables of prices. Only in the early 1790s when a severe drought in the northern provinces destroyed many flocks and herds did wool prices show any upward movement.

51. He cites three reasons for such changes: a limited supply of arable land, insufficient population base to justify major technological innovations, and too few specialized rural workers. The second of the three reasons is the most persuasive. The lack of arable land under mounting pressure to grow more should lead either to innovation or starvation. Neither of those oc-

curred on a major scale. Too few specialized workers could also be the result of an agricultural system that had not yet permanently confronted the need to change (Van Young, "The Age of Paradox," 69–71).

52. See Gibson on Aztec agricultural productivity in *Aztecs Under Spanish Rule*, 320–22.

53. Humboldt, *Political Essay on the Kingdom of New Spain*, 2:399–531; 3:1–103, esp. 2:478–79.

54. Ibid., 2:457–64.

55. Van Young, *Hacienda and Market in Eighteenth-Century Mexico*, 222–23.

56. Gene Wilken, *Good Farmers: Traditional Agricultural Resource Management in Mexico and Central America*, 7–9, 266–70.

57. Gibson, *Aztecs Under Spanish Rule*, 308–10. Using different calculations for maize yields in the Teotihuacán Valley, where Axapusco was located, Charlton also finds a wide range of ratios of seed planted to corn harvested. Based on kilograms of maize planted to maize harvested per hectare, his ratios are as low as 1:40 and 1:50 and as high as 1:80 and 1:100. It is of interest that his ratios cover yields on "floodwater-irrigated" lands, some of the best lands in the region. Charlton, "Land Tenure and Agricultural Production," 245, 256–57.

58. Brading, *Haciendas and Ranchos*, 65. See also pp. 66–67 for an enlightening discussion of how eighteenth- and twentieth-century yields compare.

59. Van Young, *Hacienda and Market in Eighteenth-Century Mexico*, 220–24.

60. Ibid. On the other hand, bean yields were possibly higher in Guadalajara than in León, with a ratio of 5 to 7 cargas for each sown compared to 3 to 1 cargas (Brading, *Haciendas and Ranchos*, 67).

61. Van Young, *Hacienda and Market in Eighteenth-Century Mexico*, 220–24.

62. Coatsworth, "Obstacles to Economic Growth in Nineteenth-Century Mexico," 92. Coatsworth offers a more sanguine view of the eighteenth-century agricultural economy than has been presented herein.

63. Both Richard Lindley and Eric Van Young believe that this became the case around Guadalajara toward the end of the century. Lindley describes unused properties as "small, arid, or poorly located" (Van Young, *Hacienda and Market in Eighteenth-Century Mexico*, 317–18; and Lindley, *Haciendas and Economic Development. Guadalajara, Mexico at Independence*, 44–45, 108).

64. The northern frontier, which had far more arable land than it was using, was too far away from the central core, where the pressure on arable land was the greatest, to be of much help. See Charles Harris III, *A Mexican Family Empire: The Latifundio of the Sánchez Navarros, 1765–1867*, 30, 32, 44–49; Enrique Florescano and Isabel Gil Sánchez, comps., *Descripciones económicas regionales de Nueva España. Provincias del Norte, 1790–1814*,

37–40, 95, 97–135; and Francisco Rendón, "La Provincia de Zacatecas en 1803."

65. Brading, *Haciendas and Ranchos*, 84–85.

66. Ibid., 79–80.

67. William Taylor, "Town and Country in the Valley of Oaxaca," 86–88.

68. Brading, *Haciendas and Ranchos*, 84–85.

69. Ibid., 83–85.

70. Ibid., 82.

71. Herman Konrad, *A Jesuit Hacienda in Colonial Mexico; Santa Lucía 1576–1767*, 22, 68–69, 176–77, 199.

72. Hermes Tovar Pinsón, "Elementos constitutivos de la empresa agraria jesuíta en la segunda mitad del siglo xviii en México," 184–86. This was certainly a plausible ratio for some former Jesuit properties in the late 1760s.

73. Taylor, "Town and Country," 81; Gibson, *Aztecs Under Spanish Rule*, 272–99; Brading, *Haciendas and Ranchos*, 61–65; and Van Young, *Hacienda and Market in Eighteenth-Century Mexico*, 110–13.

74. Brading, *Haciendas and Ranchos*, 84–85, 171–72. Wilken's *Good Farmers* makes the case against automatically dismissing small-scale operations simply because of their size or technology. In fact, the battle between the small and large producer was not driven by who was more efficient but by who was more powerful.

75. Martin, *Rural Society in Colonial Morelos*, 115.

76. Gibson, *Aztecs Under Spanish Rule*, 324–331.

77. Ibid., 331, 407–8; and Van Young, *Hacienda and Market in Eighteenth-Century Mexico*, 139–41.

3. Estate Operations and Urban Markets

1. For 1582–1773 (fifty-nine observations) $R^2 = 0.30$ and Student $t = 2.66$ when corrected for autocorrelation; for 1724–73 (thirty observations) $R^2 = 0.10$ and Student $t = 1.99$. Konrad, *A Jesuit Hacienda in Colonial Mexico*, 212–14, 391n.104.

2. Tovar Pinzón, "Elementos constitutivos de la empresa agraria jesuíta," 184–96.

3. Lindley, *Haciendas and Economic Development*, 44–45; and Eric Van Young, *Hacienda and Market in Eighteenth-Century Mexico*, 186.

4. Van Young, *Hacienda and Market in Eighteenth-Century Mexico*, 186; and Lindley, *Haciendas and Economic Development*, 45.

5. Eighty-two observations, $R^2 = 0.30$ and Student $t = 7.44$.

6. Van Young, *Hacienda and Market in Eighteenth-Century Mexico*, 179–81, for a list of the haciendas, and 178–82 for a discussion of them. The rate of growth was faster (1.7 versus 2.2 percent per year) in the second half of the eighteenth century compared to the first half, although the data cannot really be submitted to such precise trend analysis.

7. Greenow, *Credit and Socioeconomic Change in Colonial Mexico*, 137.

8. Águeda Jiménez-Pelayo, "El impacto del crédito en la economía rural del norte de la Nueva Galicia," 516–24.

9. Van Young, *Hacienda and Market in Eighteenth-Century Mexico*, 182–91 and 114–27, in which he discusses property transfers.

10. Ibid., 224–35; and Brading, *Haciendas and Ranchos*, 29–32.

11. Bancroft Library, University of California, Berkeley (CU-BANC), Mexican Manuscripts, 1872. See also Taylor's discussion of a Carmelite estate, San Juan Bautista, near Oaxaca, in "Town and Country," 88–89.

12. In Oaxaca, according to Taylor, small estates may have been worth more because their owners had to be more efficient in using their land and equipment than large estates, ("Town and Country," 82). Brading's observation bears repeating: the emergence of large landed estates in the Upper Bajío drove out of business more or equally productive small farms (see *Haciendas and Ranchos*, 88–91, 95–114). But the financial data remain to be collected and analyzed.

13. Richard Grassby, "The Rate of Profit in Seventeenth-Century England," 738–44.

14. See Wilken, *Good Farmers;* and Nola Reinhardt, *Our Daily Bread: The Peasant Question and Family Farming in the Columbian Andes*, esp. chap. 1. The assumption is that owners use their resources more effectively than renters.

15. CU-BANC, Mexican Manuscripts, 1872.

16. Grigg, *Dynamics of Agricultural Change*, 158–59.

17. Tovar Pinzón, "Elementos constitutivos de la empresa agraria jesuíta," 186.

18. Konrad, *A Jesuit Hacienda*, 98–100, 169–71, 294–95, 315–16.

19. Brading, *Haciendas and Ranchos*, 32, 98–99, 106, and 111.

20. Ibid., 103, 104, 107.

21. Ibid., 157, 202; and Tutino, *From Insurrection to Revolution in Mexico*, 237–38.

22. Van Young, *Hacienda and Market in Eighteenth-Century Mexico*, 224–35.

23. The ratio of urban to rural population has not been determined. If the populations of Mexico City and the capitals of the intendancies, as listed in Humboldt (*Political Essay on the Kingdom of New Spain*, 1:97), are summed the total is only about 400,000, or less than 10 percent of the total.

24. James Riley, "Landlords, Laborers and Royal Government: The Administration of Labor in Tlaxcala," 221–29; Taylor, *Landlord and Peasant in Colonial Oaxaca*, 147; and Van Young, *Hacienda and Market in Eighteenth-Century Mexico*, 238–41.

25. Van Young, *Hacienda and Market in Eighteenth-Century Mexico*, 246–47. Under certain economic conditions, which do not appear to apply in eighteenth-century Mexico, the intensification of agricultural labor and the

reallocation of labor from manufacturing to farming could have positive short-term results for terms of trade and investment in the agricultural sector; see George Grantham, "Agricultural Supply During the Industrial Revolution; French Evidence and European Implications," 69–70.

26.   Compare accounts in the previously discussed sources: Konrad, Tovar Pinzón, Taylor, Brading, and Van Young.

27.   As we reported in chapter 1, when rural wages are separated from urban wages, they grew very slowly or not at all. Precise figures are not possible yet because of inadequate data.

28.   Taylor, *Landlord and Peasant*, 147–50; and Harris, *A Mexican Family Empire*, 70–71; also cited in Van Young, *Hacienda and Market in Eighteenth-Century Mexico*, 256n.55.

29.   See discussions that encompass more than their regions (Guadalajara and Bajío) in Van Young, *Hacienda and Market in Eighteenth-Century Mexico*, 248–61; and Tutino, *From Insurrection to Revolution in Mexico*, 70–74.

30.   Van Young, *Hacienda and Market in Eighteenth-Century Mexico*, 268–69.

31.   Morse, ed., *The Urban Development of Latin America*, 95.

32.   Thomson, *Puebla de los Angeles*, 101–2.

33.   Ibid., 114.

34.   MiU-C, Zacatecas Collection, *Cargo y Data*, 1810–21.

35.   Van Young, *Hacienda and Market in Eighteenth-Century Mexico*, 43–58, with quote from p. 45.

36.   Thomson, *Puebla de los Angeles*, 130–35, with quote from p. 134.

37.   Ward Barrett, "The Meat Supply of Colonial Cuernavaca." This is a visual comparison of Barrett's graph (p. 535) and Van Young's graph in *Hacienda and Market in Eighteenth-Century Mexico*, 47.

38.   One could observe a similar development in Guadalajara, although yearly figures are not available to be analyzed. Van Young, *Hacienda and Market in Eighteenth-Century Mexico*, 47.

39.   Richard Garner, "Zacatecas, 1750–1821: A Study of a Late Colonial Mexican City," 359.

40.   Humboldt, *Political Essay on the Kingdom of New Spain*, 2:90–93.

41.   John Kicza, *Colonial Entrepreneurs, Families and Business in Bourbon Mexico City*, 196.

42.   Ibid., 197–198.

43.   Thomson, *Puebla de los Angeles*, 115.

44.   AMZ, leg. 17, exps. 4 and 17.

45.   Enrique Florescano, *Precios del maíz*, 55–67; Richard Garner, "Problèmes d'une ville miniére mexicaine à la fin de l'époque coloniale," 78–90; and Van Young, *Hacienda and Market in Eighteenth-Century Mexico*, 75. In both Zacatecas and Guadalajara all maize was supposed to be sold by granary, although that may have been hard to enforce in any municipality. Van Young states that Guadalajara tried to influence the price of maize

through operating a pósito (p. 77). Thomson also notes that Puebla charged a fee (*Puebla de los Angeles*, 115).

46. Van Young, *Hacienda and Market in Eighteenth-Century Mexico*, 75. The series combines private and public deliveries: R^2 = 0.30 and Student t = 4.96.

47. Garner, "Problèmes d'une ville miniére mexicaine à la fin de l'époque coloniale," 81.

48. Comments based on observations of Thomson's graphs, in *Puebla de los Angeles*, 117–19.

49. Ibid., 120–22, with quote from p. 122.

50. AMZ, leg. 24, exp. 10 and leg. 31, exp. 21; also in Garner, "Problèmes d'une ville miniére mexicaine à la fin de l'époque coloniale," 86–87.

51. Van Young, *Hacienda and Market in Eighteenth-Century Mexico*, 75–94; also see Thomson's comments about Puebla's pósito in *Puebla de los Angeles*, 114–30.

52. Thomson, *Puebla de los Angeles*, 18. For a discussion of the export of flour grown in the region of Puebla, see 18–32.

53. Van Young, *Hacienda and Market in Eighteenth-Century Mexico*, 60–61.

54. Ibid., 67–71. In Puebla, according to Thomson, besides bakery regulations the government experimented with fixed wheat prices to help the financially beleaguered wheat farmer (*Puebla de los Angeles*, 135–37).

55. Enrique Florescano quoting the documents concerning their organization in *Precios del maíz*, 46.

56. Ibid., 55–61; and British Library, Additions 17561, fols. 63–83.

57. Florescano, *Precios de maíz*, 201–35.

58. British Library, Additions 17561.

59. The R^2 is 0.36 and the Student t 2.97 with no apparent autocorrelation.

60. No clear trend can be identified. Without correction for autocorrelation the rate is a −0.8 percent per year, but R^2 = 0.02 and Student t = 1.50; with a correction the rate jumps to a −1.4, R^2 = 0.48 and Student t = 4.30. A 1 percent rate is no more than an estimate.

61. British Library, Additions 17561, fols. 63–83. We have converted cargas to fanegas on the basis of 1 carga to 2 fanegas.

62. Humboldt, *Political Essay on the Kingdom of New Spain*, 2:94; Clara Elena Suárez Argüello, *La política cerealera en la economía novohispana. El caso del trigo*, 112, 146; John Super, "Bread and the Provisioning of Mexico City in the Late Eighteenth Century," 163; and García Acosta, *Las panaderías* and *Los precios del trigo*.

63. Super, "Bread and the Provisioning of Mexico City," 182; and Suárez Argüello, *La política cerealera en la economía novohispana*, 58–76, 80–83. On bakeries the best is García Acosta, *Las panaderías*.

64. Suárez Argüello, *La política cerealera en la economía novohispana*, 132–33, 143–45; García Acosta, *Las panaderías*, 116.

65. With a wheat price series and a flour supply series we have attempted to analyze what might be called "elasticity of demand." Unfortunately, as stated above, the two series do not match up well. In one model we hypothesized the flour deliveries in year t depended on wheat prices in year t, and although the demand was inelastic, the slope coefficient was statistically insignificant. In another model we hypothesized that flour deliveries in year t depended on wheat prices in year t-1 (one-year lag). This assumes that those demanding flour arrange for prices in advance, with much of the flour being delivered late. Again, the result was that demand was inelastic. The t values were significant but more than 80 percent of the variation could not be explained. There are some observable economic forces at work in terms of the data, but because of inadequate figures and exogenous factors such as public regulations we cannot yet describe the dimensions of these forces.

66. Super, "Bread and the Provisioning of Mexico City," 167–70. We both examined the same documents with respect to the Gálvez plan at the AGI, *México*, leg. 2779. Further documentation appears in AGI, *México*, leg. 2780.

67. See Herbert Priestley, *José de Gálvez, Visitor-General of New Spain, 1765–1771*, 296–98, for a brief discussion of Gálvez's plan.

68. AGI, *México*, leg. 2779; García Acosta, *Las panaderías*, 118–37; and Super, "Bread and the Provisioning of Mexico City," 170–71.

69. AGI, *México*, leg. 2779.

70. Ibid. The other bakers were Bandember, Calvete, and Huerta. Basilio Bandember and Juan Huerta show up on García Acosta's list in *Las panaderías*, 221–40; Bandember owned one bakery and rented another one, and Huerta owned two bakeries.

71. AGI, *México*, leg. 2779; García Acosta, *Las panaderías*, 165, 189–92.

72. This survey also had a fiscal concern: Were the labradores, who sometimes rented hacienda land, transferring their wheat to nearby mills to avoid paying taxes (presumably the agricultural tithe)? AGI, *México*, leg. 2780.

73. That a portion of the 25,000–30,000 cargas harvested was held back for seed and tithes (see below) would help to explain part of the differential between the 12,000 cargas reported available and the total estimated harvested.

74. See Peter Gerhard, *A Guide to the Historical Geography of New Spain*, 267–70.

75. AGI, *México*, leg. 2780.

76. We would also point out that the rise in demand for flour in the capital and in other large cities during the late eighteenth century did not preclude the exportation of wheat from Mexico to Havana, Caracas, Maracaibo, and other American cities. Between 1786 and 1812 the colony shipped about 350,000 tercios, or the equivalent of 175,000 cargas. The total export, though perhaps an important step in the development of the economy, was equal to slightly more than what the capital needed in a year. Most of

Mexico's wheat was consumed at home. Miguel Lerdo de Tejada, *Comercio exterior de México desde la Conquista hasta hoy*, 15–23; and Super, "Bread and the Provisioning of Mexico City," 180–81.

77. Virginia García Acosta, "Los panos y sus precios en ciudades novohispanas," 3–16.

78. AGI, *México*, leg. 2779; García Acosta cites different figures in *Las panaderías*, 147–48, 221–41.

79. Kicza, *Colonial Entrepreneurs*, 187.

80. Ibid., 188–92.

4. Production Trends in Silver Mining

1. Garner, "Long-Term Silver Mining Trends in Spanish America," 898–935. Statistical tests appear on pp. 900, 904–5. Linear splines instead of dummy variables were used to compute the Peruvian and Mexican rates discussed in this paragraph. For the Mexican series 1559–1699 we have used tax receipts from TePaske and Klein and from 1700–1810 registrations of marks (marks converted to pesos) from Humboldt. This can introduce some distortion because the amount of silver registered in marks during the eighteenth century was higher than the amount of silver paid in taxes. If we had used tax receipts throughout the series, we would report somewhat lower growth rates for the whole colonial period and for the eighteenth century. This approach does not alter the general interpretation that Mexico's silver-mining industry had a rising curve (except for short-term lapses). It can alter the rates by a couple of tenths of a point.

2. Tax receipts from TePaske, "Economic Cycles in New Spain: The View from the Public Sector," *BA*, 198–203; mint registrations from Humboldt, *Political Essay on the Kingdom of New Spain*, 3:290–93, and Howe, *The Mining Guild of New Spain*, app. 1.

3. Borah, in *New Spain's Century of Depression*, treats mainly demographic and agricultural matters, and while his analysis emphasizes a pervasive depression, it does not focus directly on mining and mineral production. In addition, Borah suggests that the existence of a depression may more aptly describe seventeenth-century Peru (p. 29).

4. Israel, "Mexico and the 'General Crisis' of the Seventeenth Century," 33–35, 38–39, 55–57. The theme is pursued in a more extended and detailed form in his *Race, Class and Politics in Colonial Mexico, 1610–1670*, chap. 3 and pp. 267–73. We have made no attempt herein to explain the European side. One may consult Michel Morineau, *Incroyables gazettes et fabuleux métaux: Les retours des trésors américains d'après les gazettes hollandaises (XVIe–XVIIIe siècles)*, for an important study of the economic tie between the Old and New Worlds, especially during the seventeenth and eighteenth centuries.

5. TePaske and Klein, by examining treasury figures, have criticized the "general crisis" thesis as it applies to Mexico in "The Seventeenth-Century Crisis in New Spain: Myth or Reality?" Israel and Kamen responded to

TePaske and Klein's essay with a rejoinder by TePaske and Klein in "Debate: The Seventeenth-Century Crisis in New Spain: Myth or Reality?"

6.   Peter Bakewell, *Silver Mining and Society in Colonial Mexico, Zacatecas, 1546–1700*, 190–220; and TePaske and Klein, "The Seventeenth-Century Crisis in New Spain," 134. TePaske and Klein assess the mining economy in the seventeenth century as follows: "To be sure, silver production fluctuated and created cycles of moderate boom and recession, but these cycles were not marked by spectacular rises when silver production went up or catastrophic falls when . . . [it] declined."

7.   Several terminal points could be chosen for the first period. The year 1627 appears to be the last of a series of high peaks.

8.   The discussion on eighteenth-century trends is based on figures from Humboldt and Howe, *Political Essay on the Kingdom of New Spain*, 3:290–93, and *Mining Guild of New Spain*, app. 1, respectively. We have designated silver in marks instead of ounces or pesos. A mark was equal to eight ounces and was worth about eight pesos. Royal officials recorded silver at the treasury or at the mint in marks and ounces.

9.   Brading, *Miners and Merchants*, 152.

10.   Humboldt *Political Essay on the Kingdom of New Spain*, 3:251.

11.   TePaske, "Economic Cycles in New Spain," *BA*, 198–203. A revision of this essay with data in decennial rather than annual totals appears in Garner and Taylor, eds., *Iberian Colonies, New World Societies*, 141. The actual treasury accounts have now been published in TePaske and Herbert Klein, *Ingresos y egresos de la Real Hacienda de Nueva España*.

12.   We have estimated the value (in pesos) of silver production in the district under the jurisdiction of the capital because it is not clear what was mined in that district and what was reported there from other districts. We began by using mint data (in pesos) as the baseline for the total colonial output. We then summed the figures for the individual cajas presented by TePaske, but we excluded the figures for Mexico City's caja. In the final step we designated that the difference between the total for the mint and the total for the branches is an approximation of the silver registered and taxed at Mexico City's caja. In our ranking Mexico City's caja ranked second for the century, although that may be higher than it actually deserved. As more cajas were added in the eighteenth century the silver tax payments made directly in the capital by owners of silver may have fallen by the end of the century. Not all of TePaske's caja data continue to 1810. If they did, Bolaños may have ranked ahead of Sombrerete.

13.   The matter of entrepreneurship in the silver industry is dealt with only briefly in this study. Some of the major silver producers exhibited the characteristics ascribed to eighteenth-century entrepreneurs by the French economist/philosopher Jean Batiste Say; see Thomas Cochran, "Entrepreneurship." For discussions of individual entrepreneurs or of the entrepreneurial structure, see Brading, *Miners and Merchants*, part 2; Peter Bakewell, *Silver and Entrepreneurship in Seventeenth Century Potosí: The Life*

and Times of Antonio López de Quiroga; Richard Garner, "Silver Production and Entrepreneurial Structure in Eighteenth-Century Mexico"; and Richard Salvucci, "Entrepreneurial Culture and the Textile Manufactories in Eighteenth-Century Mexico."

14.   Brading, *Miners and Merchants,* 247–60, with quote from p. 250 and tables from pp. 250 and 258.

15.   Ibid., 228–30. It should not be assumed that Brading, whose figures we have used, would concur with this interpretation.

16.   Alvaro López Miramontes and Cristiana Urrutia de Stebelski, *Las minas de Nueva España en 1774,* 186–87. This average figure is less than half the total worth of the silver registrations that we have computed for Mexico City's caja in constructing table 4-1, and we emphasize again that those computations for this caja are no more than rough estimates.

17.   Ibid.

18.   Ibid, 189–93.

19.   Ibid, 93. Of the eighty-two, thirty-two were in Zacatecas and fifty in Fresnillo, a camp about fifty miles northwest of Zacatecas.

20.   1699–1725 (twenty-seven observations), $R^2 = 0.84$ and Student $t = 11.34$; 1725–63 (thirty-nine observations), $R^2 = 0.67$ and Student $t = 5.73$; and 1764–1810 (forty-seven observations), $R^2 = 0.71$ and Student $t = 3.54$ with correction for autocorrelation.

21.   Juan Lucas Lassaga and Joaquín Velásquez de León, *Representación que a nombre de la minería de la Nueva España hacen el rey nuestro señor los a poderados de ella,* 4–7. See also Brading, *Miners and Merchants,* 163–64.

22.   This in part accounts for Brading's conclusion of a diminishing creole elite; Brading, *Miners and Merchants,* chap. 9. All the data on who registered silver were copied from the ledgers kept by the treasury and were then analyzed by computer. Glenn Kreider of Penn State University's Liberal Arts Computing Center wrote the necessary computer programs. The ledgers are in the following archives: MiU-C, Zacatecas Collection, *Quinto y Diezmo,* 1700–1714, 1716–29, 1734, 1738–49, 1763–67; *Cargo y Data,* 1730–34, 1736–37, 1750–62, 1769, 1771–72, 1774, 1776–78, 1780–82, 1784–87, 1790–93, 1799, 1801–21; and Treasury Records and Correspondence, 1715. For years not in the Clements Library, consult AGI, *Guadalajara,* leg. 174, 477, 478, 480, and 482. The distinction between miner and merchant for taxing purposes disappeared in Zacatecas after the first quarter of the eighteenth century. The diezmo became the standard tax. For contemporary accounts of the city's mining industry, see José de Rivera Bernárdez, *Descripción breve de la muy noble, y leal ciudad de Zacatecas;* and Gabriel Salinas de la Torre, ed., *Testimonio de Zacatecas.*

23.   AMZ, leg. 20, exp. 22. Another camp that can be examined in terms of the occupational profile is Durango. The eighteenth-century growth in silver was modest at 0.7 percent per year: 105 observations, $R^2 = 0.18$ and Student $t = 4.90$. When the demographic data in Swann's *Tierra Adentro*

are examined for occupational shifts,the proportion of service workers to total workers rose noticeably from 1768 to 1778, but after that the shifts were relatively minor. Even Swann (pp. 89, 240, 246–47) concludes that at the end of the century Durango still had a high percentage of unskilled workers to total workers. Compare with Durango's seventeenth-century society, as described by Marcello Carmagnani, "Demografía y sociedad: la estructura social de los centros mineros del norte de México, 1600–1720."

24.   AGN, *Historia*, leg. 74, exp. 10.

25.   For a discussion of the lure of mining over farming, see José Arlegui, *Crónica de la Provencia de N.S.P.S. Francisco de Zacatecas*.

26.   The percentage is higher if we use TePaske's silver production totals and lower if we use Humboldt's.

27.   With 110 observations, zone 1, R^2 = 0.47 and Student t = 9.97; zone 2, R^2 = 0.92 and Student t = 7.81 with correction for autocorrelation; and zone 3, R^2 = 0.70 and Student t = 15.98.

28.   The mining-cost table has been assembled from different sources. From the AGI, *Guadalajara*, leg. 190, we have used figures on costs for workers, supplies, and other categories for a half-dozen mines around Zacatecas. We have also relied on Brading in *Miners and Merchants*, 152–56. A correction should be noted, however. In estimating refining costs he used a document that reported purchases of the higher-priced Austrian mercury rather than the cheaper Spanish mercury.

29.   The best modern work on refining methods remains Modesto Bargalló, *La minería y la metalurgía en la América española durante la época colonial*. See a recent discussion in Peter Bakewell, "Mining in Colonial Spanish America," 2:105–22. Humboldt presented data that showed 78 percent was amalgamated and 22 percent was smelted around 1790 (*Political Essay on the Kingdom of New Spain*, 3:251). The ratio continued to change in favor of amalgamation during the last two decades before hostilities broke out.

30.   AGI, *Guadalajara*, leg. 174 and 190.

31.   Brading, *Miners and Merchants*, 152–53.

32.   AGI, *Guadalajara*, leg. 174 and 182; MiU-C, Zacatecas Collection, Treasury Records and Correspondence, 1770–79, box B, 1780–89, box B, and 1800–1809, boxes A and B; MiU-C, Zacatecas Collection, *Cargo y Data*, 1808–21; AGI, México, leg. 1634; Carlos Berghes, *Descripción de la Serranía de Zacatecas. formada por I. M. Bustamante*, 22–23; Brading, *Miners and Merchants*, 204; and H. G. Ward, *Mexico in 1827*, 2:620–25.

33.   AGN, *Minería*, leg. 115, exp. 4.

34.   Garner, "Long-Term Silver Mining Trends in Spanish America," 914–23.

35.   Fabián de Fonseca and Carlos de Urrutia, *Historia general de Real Hacienda*, 1:383–85.

36.   MiU-C, Zacatecas Collection, Treasury Records and Correspondence, 1770–79, box B.

37. Fisher, *Silver Mines and Silver Miners, 1776–1824*, 74–75. In 1792 the region of Huantajaya, which was always faced with mercury shortages, achieved a spectacularly high ratio of 1 quintal of mercury for 316 marks of silver: that is, refiners used only 18,155 pounds of mercury to produce 57,394 marks of silver. Even as late as 1808 they reported very good ratios of 1 quintal to 121 marks. In Fisher's view, the Huantajaya refiners had learned to be efficient because their limited supplies had forced them to be.

38. This is based on Brading's treatment in *Miners and Merchants*, 284–91.

39. For the rise in costs and the decline in profits R^2's = 0.73 and 0.58 and Student t's = 7.68 and 5.43, respectively, with no apparent autocorrelation; for production as reflected in income R^2 = 0.06 and Student t = 1.46 (twenty-two observations).

40. Brading, *Miners and Merchants*, 286–87.

41. Ibid., 159–60.

42. Bakewell, *Silver Mining and Society*, 172–73.

43. Brading, *Miners and Merchants*, 153.

44. CtY, Latin American Collection, 5-E.

45. The documentation on Borda's Quebradilla venture is extensive. The major source is a large legajo, 115, with several parts at the AGN, *Minería*. Many of the same documents may be found in MiU-C, Zacatecas Collection, Treasury Records and Correspondence, 1760–69 and 1770–79. Borda's plan has been discussed in Brading, *Miners and Merchants*, 163, 198–201, and in Bernard Bobb, *The Viceregency of Antonio María Bucareli in New Spain, 1771–1779*, 181.

46. Bakewell, *Silver Mining and Society*, 132.

47. Brading, *Miners and Merchants*, 183–85.

48. AGN, *Minería, leg.* 63, exp. 2.

49. In Zacatecas, José Marcelo Anza may have received concessions for his service on the mining tribunal, although he failed to recover the mines that his father and uncle had restored at the same time that Borda began his restorations. The Quebradilla Company, Zacatecas's largest mining enterprise ever, made a substantial loan or contribution to the government in return for concessions, although the cost of repairing and maintaining the mine may have qualified the company. AGN, *Minería, leg.* 63, exps. 2 and 3; leg. 520, exp. 13.

50. Bakewell, "Mining in Colonial Spanish America," 2:111–13.

51. Doris Ladd, *The Making of a Strike: Mexican Silver Workers' Struggle in Real del Monte, 1766–1775*, 7. Also see Robert West, *The Mining Community in Northern New Spain: The Parral Mining District*.

52. See Ladd's description based on several different contemporary sources in *The Making of a Strike*, 10–14, 19–28, quote from p. 11.

53. Doris Ladd states that "There was no silver industry in New Spain. Each Real [camp] was its own industrial enterprise, controlled by its own rules and traditions" (*The Making of a Strike*, 120). This is related to the issue

of whether the economy had developed to the extent that colonial "industries" had emerged. Mining operations were not autonomous. Owners had to
import capital from outside their own camps, to buy mercury, powder, and
salt from the government, and to participate in the newly formed mining
tribunal. Colonial industries did not yet exist in the form that modern
industries have evolved with standardized procedures and consolidated
operations. Industry is a term used loosely to describe an assemblage of firms
engaged in the same general business. The term is applied to agriculture
where regional and local variations, despite the commercialization of agriculture, remained strong. In the broad sense that the term is used, a silver-
mining industry was far more visible than an agricultural industry.

    54.   Bakewell, "Mining in Colonial Spanish America," 2:119.

    55.   This paragraph draws heavily on ibid., 2:113–19.

    56.   AMZ, leg. 20, exp. 22.

    57.   Brading, *Miners and Merchants*, 152–56.

    58.   Bakewell, "Silver Mining and Society," 191.

    59.   Brading, *Miners and Merchants*, 146, 147–48.

    60.   Ladd, *The Making of a Strike*, 34.

    61.   On thievery, see ibid., 15–16.

    62.   Bakewell, "Mining in Colonial Spanish America," 2:146.

    63.   Brading, *Miners and Merchants*, 147.

    64.   Ladd believes that the strike had a deeper and wider impact than we
think the evidence supports (*The Making of a Strike*, 124 and passim, chap.
9). In addition, one can consult Instituto Nacional de Estudios Históricos de
la Revolución Mexicana, *Conflicto de trabajo con los mineros de Real del
Monte. Año de 1766*; María del Carmen Velázquez, "José Alejandro de
Bustamante, minero de Pachuca"; Robert Randall, *Real del Monte: A British
Mining Venture in Mexico*, 1; and Brading, *Miners and Merchants*, 146–49.
For a pioneering work on social unrest and its causes, see William Taylor,
Drinking, Homicide, and Rebellion in Colonial Mexican Villages.

    65.   Brading, *Miners and Merchants*, 148–49.

    66.   Ladd, *The Making of a Strike*, 15. The typical manner for estimating
purchasing power is to use constant values. We have no way of knowing if
these prices were high or low at the time that they were recorded.

    67.   AGN-AHH, *Azogue*, leg. 2309, exp. 6.

    68.   On Peru, see Garner, "Long-Term Silver Mining Trends in Spanish
America," 914–23.

    69.   Ibid., 918. The data for the second half of the eighteenth century
were provided to us by John TePaske, to whom we are most grateful. Since
Humboldt's data included both plata de azogue and plata de fuego, the
volume of silver registered generally exceeds what could be expected from
the quality of mercury known to be imported.

    70.   The documentation is not clear about how much was sold, and the
figure is an estimate based on other evidence, such as silver registrations.

    71.   AGI, *México*, leg. 1566. Reconciling these accounts and reports

either at the caja level or at the colonial level can be best described as exasperating. Examples of the numerous reviews undertaken by the various bureaucrats exist in the Zacatecas Collection, MiU-C. Often these took five to ten years to complete. At times the precision demanded (how much mercury was lost to leakage, for example) exceeded the capacity of the caja to monitor its own operations. Surely the same principle was at work in Mexico City.

72. Bobb, *The Viceregency of Bucareli*, 194.

73. MiU-C, Zacatecas Collection, *Alcabalas*, 1780; and AGN, *Historia*, leg. 204, exp. 7.

74. Howe, *Mining Guild of New Spain*, 119–21, 124–27, 254–58.

75. AGI, *Estado*, leg. 26, exp. 40 and leg. 27, exp. 34.

76. AGN, *Historía*, leg. 49, exp. 26. This was the first time in the treasury accounts at Zacatecas's caja that an entry called *azogue de rescate* (used mercury) appeared.

77. MiU-C, Zacatecas Collection, *Cargo y Data*, 1800–1804.

78. Humboldt, *Political Essay on the Kingdom of New Spain*, 3:299–304; and Howe, *Mining Guild of New Spain*, 258–60.

79. AGN-AHH, *Azogues*, leg. 205, exp. 18.

80. AGI, *México*, leg. 1566.

81. Bakewell, *Silver Mining and Society*, 171–73; CtY, Latin American Collection, 5-E; and AGI, *México*, leg. 2235.

82. Herbert Priestley, *José de Gálvez*, 242; and CtY, Latin American Collection, 5-E.

83. Bobb, *The Viceregency of Bucareli*, 188, 191–92.

84. Gamboa, *Commentarios de las ordenanzas de minas*; CtY, Latin American Collection, 6-E.

85. Bakewell, "Mining in Colonial Spanish America," 2:149–50.

86. Elinor Barrett, *The Mexican Colonial Copper Industry*, passim and 4–10, 103–9.

5. Manufacturing and International Trade

1. Richard Salvucci, *Textiles and Capitalism in Mexico: An Economic History of the Obrajes, 1539–1840*, 4.

2. Peter Kriedte, Hans Medick, and Jürgen Schlumbohm, eds., *Industrialization Before Industrialization: Rural Industry in the Genesis of Capitalism*, 6–9.

3. Kriedte, "Origins, Context and World-Market Conditions in the World Market," 34.

4. Ibid., 37.

5. Thomson, *Puebla de los Angeles*, 33.

6. For *hacienda* operations, see Kicza, *Colonial Entrepreneurs*, 187–205.

7. See Barrett's analysis of the Cortéz sugar hacienda in *The Sugar Hacienda of the Marqueses del Valle*.

8. Humboldt, *Political Essay on the Kingdom of New Spain*, 3:453.

9. Ibid., 3:457–58.

10. Kicza, *Colonial Entrepreneurs*, 187–96. Recall Salvucci's treatment of the manufacturer who differed from the processor in the sense that the former had to create a product and a market whereas the latter mainly transformed raw materials into usable products.

11. Thomson, *Puebla de los Angeles*, 33–36, 41–42, 49–51. As an indication of the state of research and the level of information, Thomson can present a much fuller picture of the manufacturing sector linked to Puebla after independence than before. For an overview of merchants as manufacturers in Europe, see Jürgen Schlumbohm, "Relations of Production—Productive Forces—Crises in Proto-Industrialization," 94–110, and "Excursus: The Political and Institutional Framework of Proto-Industrialization."

12. For a discussion of Humboldt's and Quiro's estimates, see Rosenweig Hernández, "*La economía novohispana*," esp. 491–94. Thomson's quote from *Puebla de los Angeles*, 34 n.99.

13. Salvucci, *Textiles and Capitalism*, 63–69.

14. AGN-AHH, Consulado, leg. 917, exp. 1. This is also published in Florescano and Gil Sánchez, comps., *Descripciones económicas regionales. Centro*, 109–17.

15. Eric Van Young, *Hacienda and Market in Eighteenth-Century Mexico*, 148–49; and Salvucci, *Textiles and Capitalism*, 55–56.

16. AGN-AHH, Consulado, leg. 917, exp. 1; and Florescano and Gil Sánchez, comps., *Descripciones económicas regionales. Centro*, 117, 121–22. Eric Van Young describes the industry toward the end of the eighteenth century as "apparently organized on a fairly small scale." Village output could be "substantial, with various pueblos specializing in certain types of textiles or articles of clothing" (*Hacienda and Market in Eighteenth-Century Mexico*, 149 n.40).

17. Van Young, *Hacienda and Market in Eighteenth-Century Mexico*, 149; and Salvucci, *Textiles and Capitalism*, 14–15.

18. See maps 1.1 and 1.2, which show the relative concentrations of the looms in the telares sueltos in 1781 and 1793 throughout the colony in Salvucci, *Textiles and Capitalism*, 22–23. In the early nineteenth century in five towns under the jurisdiction of Guanajuato's intendant, there were nearly 1,000 looms that produced a variety of cotton and woolen goods, including shawls, baizes, sheets, and pieces of cloth of varying size and quality. According to this survey Salamanca and Celaya had the largest number, followed by Léon, San Miguel, and Santa Cruz (AGN-AHH, Consulado, leg. 917, exp. 6). This document was published in Florescano and Gil Sánchez, comps., *Descripciones económicas regionales. Centro*, 42–43. We present a different ranking of the towns, based on the looms reported by the intendant, from what appears in Florescano and Gil Sánchez. These numbers and rankings do not necessarily coincide with the maps of the distribution of the looms in Salvucci, noted above.

19. Salvucci, *Textiles and Capitalism*, 149–160, with quotes from pp. 154–55.

20. Tobacco manufacturing may also be a good example, although it will not be discussed herein. See David Lorne McWatters, *The Royal Tobacco Monopoly in Bourbon Mexico, 1764–1810*; and Susan Deans-Smith, "The Money Plant: The Royal Tobacco Monopoly of New Spain, 1765–1821."

21. Guy Thomson, "The Cotton Textile Industry in Puebla during the Eighteenth and Early Nineteenth Centuries," esp. 36–38, 169–70, 179–82, and 189–91; and Salvucci, *Textiles and Capitalism*, 12–15, 39–45, with quote from p. 42.

22. Kicza, *Colonial Entrepreneurs*, 223–24.

23. The numbers vary from source to source and no effort has been made to try to reconcile them. It is not clear if the estimates from the sources cover both woolen and cotton operations or just woolen operations. Finally, the figures, especially for the trapiches, embraced facilities in the city proper and in the area under the government of the city. See D. A. Brading, "Noticias sobre la economía de Querétaro y de sus corregidor don Miguel Domínguez"; Florescano and Gil Sánchez, *Descripciones económicas regionales. Centro*, 47–48 n.5; Humboldt, *Political Essay on the Kingdom of New Spain*, 3:462–63; John C. Super, "Querétaro obrajes: Industry and Society in Provincial Mexico, 1600–1810," 197; and Salvucci, *Textiles and Capitalism*, 89–91, 140–41.

24. Salvucci, *Textiles and Capitalism in Mexico*, 89.

25. Ibid., 141. Trapiches rose "tenfold, from 30 to 340."

26. Super, "Querétaro obrajes," 198–205, 209–12.

27. Salvucci, "Entrepreneurial Culture and the Textile Manufactories in Eighteenth-Century Mexico," 400–401. Salvucci, distinguishing between risk and uncertainty, argues that the textile manufacturing industry around Querétaro had to learn how to convert uncertainty "into manageable risks." Historically, the economic literature has made a distinction between two forms of uncertainty: the first concerns the ability of the individual to attach probabilities to the various possible states of the world, and the second concerns the inability or reluctance of him or her to do so. The lack of certainty can be viewed as the lack of knowledge as to what the state of the world, and in particular the state of the economy, is or is going to become. The literature has referred to the first form as *risk* and the second as *uncertainty*. It is also entirely appropriate to think of a range of uncertainties, some of which are riskier than others; see Frank Knight, *Risk, Uncertainty and Profit*.

28. Salvucci, "Entrepreneurial Culture and Textile Manufactories," 402, and *Textiles and Capitalism*, 139–49.

29. Salvucci calculates that the savings in Mexico City, for example, could be as much as 15 percent, although he urges caution in accepting these findings; Salvucci, *Textiles and Capitalism*, 144 and table 5.3, p. 145. Also see price data on pp. 146–47.

30.   Ibid., 146; see chap. 3, note 6, for discussion of demand and supply curves.

31.   Salvucci's data were presented in a bar graph and were estimated for the purposes of calculating a growth rate. His main source was the alcabalas records; see ibid., 141.

32.   1686–1804 (136 observations), the rate is 0.5 percent per year; R^2 = 0.67 and Student t = 2.47; 1686–1777 (101 observations), the rate is −0.4 percent per year; R^2 = 0.60 and Student t = 1.66. Rabell Romero, *Los Diezmos de San Luis de la Paz*, 214–22.

33.   The R^2 is 0.30 and Student t 2.86. Richard Garner, "Problèmes d'une ville miniére mexicaine à la fin de l'époque coloniale," 99–103.

34.   Analysis of the labor supply in the textile industry as in other sectors suffers from the handicap of limited knowledge about demographic changes. We can assume that as the eighteenth-century colonial population grew, so too did the size of the labor force. What is harder to determine is the impact of the growth in the labor pool on relations between workers and employers. Chapter 4 in Salvucci's *Textiles and Capitalism* should be read carefully for insights on how the various labor systems—free, peon, and slave—interacted in the textile sector.

35.   Salvucci, *Textiles and Capitalism*, 124–34. Salvucci's second reason corresponds to a backward-bending supply curve. We are not entirely convinced that this applies. The backward-bending segment of labor supply curves arises from a trade off between labor and leisure. An individual worker has a finite number of hours available for work each day or each week. Total waking hours must be allocated either to work—which generates income—or to leisure. Hourly wages can be viewed as the price of leisure. As the hourly wage increases, he supplies more labor but only up to a point. When the wage becomes sufficiently high, he may choose to work less and to use more time for leisure. The extra money from the higher wage does not do him much good if he is working all the time. (For further discussion of these theoretical considerations, see William J. Baumol, *Economic Theory and Operations Analysis*, 586–89.) The point to bear in mind is that the individual must decide whether to work more hours or not. We assume that when the obrajeros offered better wages than other employers, they could attract individuals to work for them. For a backward-bending labor supply curve to come into effect, obrajeros would have to be constrained to make their current labor force work more hours. Under these circumstances workers then had to choose whether to devote more time to labor or leisure. We doubt if this situation obtained in Querétaro, where resistance to a type of employment caused workers to quit, run away, or engage in actions that caused shortages of workers among obrajes rather than to choose to work more or fewer hours. Regardless of whether a backward-bending labor supply curve applies, the larger questions of how much laborers had to work and how much they had to earn need to be examined. Salvucci is inclined to believe that they did not have to work long or earn much (pp. 122 and 127).

36. Salvucci, "Entrepreneurial Culture and Textile Manufactories," 403–4, and *Textiles and Capitalism,* 142–43.

37. Salvucci, "Entrepreneurial Culture and Textile Manufactories," 412–17.

38. Kicza, *Colonial Entrepreneurs,* 200.

39. Salvucci, *Textiles and Capitalism,* 81–83.

40. On profits in Guanajuato, see Brading, *Miners and Merchants,* 291–302.

41. Humboldt was struck by the size of the obrajes, the primitive dyeing technologies, and the unhealthy working conditions. Whites, Indians, blacks, and mixed bloods, some of whom were convicts, were compelled to work in buildings that resembled prisons rather than plants; they were often in debt to the owners and were paid in kind rather than in cash; they had few amenities or protections under the law. But Humboldt's observations were based on a visit to Querétaro, not Mexico City. Salvucci (see n. 43) was one of the first to analyze labor indebtedness in terms of whether the worker had entered the arrangement on his own volition or under coercion; if by choice, then technically peonage did not exist, and if by coercion, then it did. Further, the greater the mobility of workers to accept and leave jobs, the less effective was peonage. Both volition and mobility were more evident in Mexico City, a large urban center, than in Querétaro. Of course, volition and mobility are both conditions that derive in part from social as well as economic experiences. Humboldt, *Political Essay on the Kingdom of New Spain,* 3:463–64.

42. Kicza, *Colonial Entrepreneurs,* 201.

43. Salvucci, *Textiles and Capitalism,* chap. 4, esp. pp. 117–21 and fig. 4.1, p. 126. Our discussion is somewhat more sceptical of the mobility and opportunity facing the obraje worker than is Salvucci's. Burgeoning urban populations and narrowing job opportunities (except perhaps in more-skilled categories) would seem to argue against that. Still, the basic argument that obrajes could no longer compete is sound, although how this came about in various textile centers remains to be clarified. In addition the matter of how workers were paid is important to the point that substituting script or merchandise for money can retard economic development and change. All this tends to underscore Salvucci's principal contention that the obraje represented something less than an ideal model for creating a more manufacturing-based economic system.

44. The following discussion draws heavily from Guy Thomson, "The Cotton Textile Industry in Puebla During the Eighteenth and Early Nineteenth Centuries," 169–202. Since this 1986 publication, Thomson has also published his book on eighteenth and nineteenth-century Puebla, *Puebla de los Angeles.* With respect to woolen and cotton manufacturing they cover the same ground, although the book contains far more detail.

45. Thomson, "The Cotton Textile Industry," 177. This quote is preceded by an overview of demographic and economic changes (pp. 170–77) in Puebla during the eighteenth century.

46.   Thomson, *Puebla de los Angeles*, 40, 42–44.

47.   Thomson, "The Cotton Textile Industry," 185–86, and *Puebla de los Angeles*, 311.

48.   The Rosenbach Museum and Library (PPRF) Mexican Collection, 462/25, part 2, no. 6, and part 15, no. 3.

49.   The statistics do not inspire total confidence in the trends either for Pueblan cloth or imported cloth during the late eighteenth century. Pueblan shipments (twenty-three observations) to Mexico City increased by 2.5 percent per year: R^2 = 0.59 and Student t = 5.48. When corrected for autocorrelation the rate becomes 1.5 percent per year, with R^2 = 0.73 and Student t = 1.32. European imports declined by 3.8 percent per year: R^2 = 0.14 and Student t = 2.03. When corrected the decline is 2.6 percent per year: R^2 = 0.33 and Student t = 0.72.

50.   Thomson, "The Cotton Textile Industry," 184–85, 193.

51.   Thomson, *Puebla de los Angeles*, 62–100, with statistics from pp. 67 and 69 and quotes from p. 99.

52.   Reflecting the observations of José María Quirós, secretary of Veracruz's Consulado, Thomson writes that "merchants lacked any incentive to introduce technical innovations in spinning since they continued to profit from the almost gratuitous services of a large female urban and rural proletariat" (*Puebla de los Angeles*, 45–46).

53.   Morineau, *Incroyables gazettes et fabuleux métaux*, 474–80: and Garner, "Long-Term Silver Mining Trends in Spanish America," 900–903.

54.   TePaske and Klein, "The Seventeenth-Century Crisis in New Spain," 130–33; and for the eighteenth century, see Garner, "Exportaciones de circulante," and Pérez Herrero, *Plata y libranzas*, 159–64.

55. R^2 = 0.11 and Student t = 2.92 (sixty-four observations). This series is compiled from two sources: for the period 1717–77, from Antonio García-Baquero González, *Cádiz y el Atlántico (1717–78). El comercio colonial español bajo el monopolio gaditano*, 2:250–52; and for the period 1778–96, from John Fisher, *Commerical Relations Between Spain and Spanish America in the Era of Free Trade, 1778–1796*, 67. These figures are for shipments of coins that entered Cádiz until 1778 and Cádiz and Barcelona after 1778 in the accounts of private citizens and merchants. This money probably had many purposes, and these figures represent only an indirect measure of the level of imports from Spain to the colonies.

56.   Garner, "Long-Term Silver Mining Trends in Spanish America," 900–903.

57.   Garner, "Exportaciones de circulante," 578, and esp. fig. 4.

58.   See Fisher, *Commercial Relations Between Spain and Spanish America*, figure III, p. 50.

59.   Lerdo de Tejada, *Comercio exterior de México*, docs. 3, 4, 5, 7, 8.

60.   Wilbur Meek, *The Exchange Media of Colonial Mexico*, 62.

61.   If public-account transfers (also in coin) for the two decades were also

included, then the total currency exports would just about equal all of the silver newly minted in Mexico.

62.   Fisher, *Commercial Relations Between Spain and Spanish America*, 54.

63.   Ibid., 14–16. Fisher's book contains two chapter (3 and 4) that first appeared as articles: "Imperial 'Free Trade' and the Hispanic Economy, 1778–1796," and "The Imperial Response to 'Free Trade': Spanish Imports from Spanish America, 1778–1796." We use citations from both the book and the articles. See also Bibiano Torres Ramírez and Javier Ortiz de la Tabla Ducasse's edition of the *Reglamento*.

64.   Torres Ramírez and Ortiz de la Tabla, *Reglamento*, 34–39.

65.   Ortiz de la Tabla Ducasse, *Comercio exterior de Veracruz, 1778–1821. Crisis de dependencia*, 233–36.

66.   Fisher, *Commercial Relations Between Spain and Spanish America*, 14.

67.   1785–96, Cádiz to Spanish America, $R^2 = 0.13$ and Student t $= 1.62$; 1785–96, Cádiz to Veracruz, $R^2 = 0.09$ and Student t $= 1.45$. The Student t's do not meet our minimum, and the trends and rates should be viewed with caution.

68.   Fisher, *Commercial Relations Between Spain and Spanish America*, 46–47, 54–55.

69.   Annual growth rates for all commodities (fifteen observations), with confidence levels in brackets if less than 99 percent, are as follows: sugar, 20.4 percent; hides, 8.6 percent [93 percent]; wood, 3.2 percent [32 percent]; cacao, 16.4 percent [98 percent]; cascarilla, 15.0 percent; tobacco (Crown), 137.3 percent [98 percent]; tobacco (private), 1.3 percent [15 percent]; indigo, 22.0 percent; cotton, 20.5 percent; copper, 7.2 percent [80 percent]; cochineal, 6.6 percent [40 percent]; vicuña wool, 6.1 percent [69 percent]; and others, 14.7 percent. Fisher, "Spanish Imports," 52–53, 59, 78.

70.   Fisher, "Spanish Imports," 78. For a different approach, see Javier Cuenca-Esteban, "The Markets of Latin American Exports, 1790–1820: A Comparative Analysis of International Prices."

71.   Lerdo de Tejada, *Comercio exterior de México*, doc. 14.

72.   See also Ortiz de la Tabla, *Comercio exterior de Veracruz*, 226–40.

73.   Lerdo de Tejada, *Comercio exterior de México*, note 2a following doc. 15.

74.   These rates are only rough estimates because the statistical tests do not fall within acceptable ranges. Total commerce (exports plus imports) at Veracruz is not yet known for the period 1785–96. What we do know is that merchandise imports from Cádiz into Veracruz declined at a rate slightly above 2 percent per year, and currency exports to various ports for private transactions fell at a rate slightly below 2 percent per year. Thus we can conclude from these figures that total commerce passing through Veracruz was basically flat if not actually declining.

75. $R^2 = 0.22$ and Student t $= 2.24$ (fifteen observations).

76. $R^2 = 0.50$ (fifteen observations). The correlation between total national and foreign imports from Spain and total currency exports from Mexico is 0.79.

77. Total merchandise trade rose by 20.8 percent per year from 1796 through 1804 and by 39.6 percent (confidence level of 96 percent) between 1805 and 1810. When dummy variables of 1796/1804 and 1805/1810 are introduced, the R^2 values for many categories, not surprisingly, improve significantly.

78. Peggy Liss, *Atlantic Empires: The Network of Trade and Revolution, 1713–1826.*

79. Geoffrey Walker, *Spanish Politics and Imperial Trade, 1700–1789,* 59, 76–79, 114–18.

80. AGI, *Consulado,* leg. 796.

81. Ibid., 799.

82. Ibid., 796. Both Walker, *Spanish Politics and Imperial Trade,* chaps. 6 and 7, and Marcella Litle, "Sales Taxes and Internal Commerce in Bourbon Mexico, 1754–1821" 51–64, discuss these matters as do other authors.

83. Brading, *Miners and Merchants,* 97.

84. José Joaquín Real Díaz, "Las ferias de Jalapa," 100–101.

85. The fleet was suspended in 1740 and then was reinstituted in 1756. One fleet arrived in Veracruz in March 1757 and another one did not arrive until September 1760; Real Díaz, "Las ferias de Jalapa," 31, 34, and 111 n. 11

86. Our figures differ slightly from Real Díaz's figures. He reports (from a different document) twenty-five flotistas with merchandise worth 2,712,475 pesos compared to our 2,612,475 pesos; Real Díaz, "Las ferias de Jalapa," 112.

87. Another dozen or so flotistas had disposed of their goods and had remained in Jalapa or had been designated as temporarily absent from it (AGI, *Consulado,* leg. 799). For details on how the fair operated in the middle decades of the eighteenth century, see Litle, "Sales Taxes and Internal Commerce," 55–60.

88. AGI, *Consulado,* leg. 800.

89. Real Díaz, "Las ferias de Jalapa," 113.

90. Ibid., 34. Lerdo de Tejada reported five fleets after 1760: 1762 (which does not appear on Real Díaz's list), 1765, 1769 (which left Cádiz in 1768), 1772, and 1776; see *Comercio exterior de México,* doc. 2.

91. Lerdo de Tejada, *Comercio exterior de México,* doc. 3.

92. Consider the comment by Joseph del Mazo Calderón, superintendant of the Mexico City *Real Aduana* in 1754: to try to get the lowest prices, Consulado merchants delayed their "arrival at the fair until the last possible moment"; quoted and translated by Litle, "Sales Taxes and Internal Commerce," 53.

93. Real Díaz, "Las ferias de Jalapa," 117; and Lerdo de Tejada, *Comercio exterior de México,* doc. 11.

94. Real Díaz, "Las ferias de Jalapa," 115.

95. These products were shipped in varying units: metals in quintales (hundredweights), beeswax, spices, and olive oil in arrobas (25 pounds), and clothes in *tercios* (of varying weights).

96. Real Díaz, "Las ferias de Jalapa," fig. 3; and Garner "Exportaciones de circulante," app. 3.

97. The Consulado's estimates were given in a report written in 1805 in opposition (but not by the Consulado) to the *Consolidación de Vales Reales*, and while the contraband figures cannot be corroborated, other figures cited in the report are close to calculations that we have made; British Library, Additions, 13978, fols. 204–206.

98. Real Díaz, "Las ferias de Jalapa," fig. 3.

99. Pierre Chaunu, *Les Philippines et le Pacifique des Ibériques. xvi, xvii, xviii siècles;* and TePaske and Klein, "The Seventeenth-Century Crisis," 132–34.

100. Manuel Carrera Stampa, "Las ferias novohispanas," 203 n.4.

101. Ibid., 218; and Garner, "Exportaciones de circulante," fig. 1, pp. 558–59.

102. Carrera Stampa, "Las ferias novohispanas," 227–230. For a descriptive work on Far Eastern trade, see Vera Valdés Lakowsky, *De las minas al mar. Historia de la plata mexicana en Asia, 1565–1834.*

6. Domestic Exchange and Commercial System

1. Litle, "Sales Taxes and Internal Commerce in Bourbon Mexico, 1754–1821," 145–51.

2. Statement is based on inventories from pulperías in Zacatecas. Jay Kinsbruner in *Petty Capitalism in Spanish America: The Pulperos of Puebla, Mexico City, Caracas, and Buenos Aires* discussed inventories, which in the case of Reymundo de Moya, a Mexico City grocer, contained among other things firewood, quicksilver, bottles, spices, ham, and cloth (pp. 2–9).

3. Kicza, *Colonial Entrepreneurs*, 8.

4. For data on both the pulperías and puestos, see MiU-C, Zacatecas Collection, Treasury Records and Correspondence, 1770–90, where several boxes contain lists of pulperías, which had to pay a fee each yearly to the royal treasury in order to do business in Zacatecas. For the puestos specifically, see the cabildo ledgers in AMZ, 1750–1810. The number of puesteros can be estimated from a yearly fee that the city council charged to set up a booth in the city's main plaza. See also Kinsbruner's estimates of numbers of pulperías in Puebla and Mexico City in *Petty Capitalism*, 9–13.

5. No one can dispute the existence of an internal market. Raw materials, processed goods, and finished products from Mexico itself circulated widely through the colony. With reference to textiles, mainly in Mexico, Manuel Miño Grijalva presents the case that demand forced the creation of an internal market and the circulation of textile merchandise despite many

obstacles and high costs relating to textile production and distribution. It is entirely plausible that such a market evolved, although Miño Grijalva does not offer much empirical evidence to support his theory ("La circulación de mercancías. Una referencia al caso textil latinoamericano [1750–1810], 45–58 and esp. 45–47).

6. Kicza, *Colonial Entrepreneurs*, 101–34.

7. Richard Garner, "Reformas borbónicas y operaciones hacendarias— La real caja de Zacatecas—1750–1821," 561–71; Litle, "Sales Taxes and Internal Commerce," passim; and Juan Carlos Garavaglia and Juan Carlos Grosso, *Las alcabalas novohispanas (1776–1821)*, 11–40.

8. R^2 = 0.67 and Student t = 15.01 (109 observations). Correction for autocorrelation yields less acceptable test statistics. For the data see Te-Paske, *La Real Hacienda de Nueva España*.

9. See Litle's conclusions, "Sales Taxes and Internal Commerce," 158–60.

10. For data with growth rates from each real aduana, see ibid., 212–38, and for graphs, see 239–67. For another approach, see the work of Garavaglia and Grosso, *Las alcabalas*, 48–59.

11. Ibid., 201–2.

12. When corrected for autorcorrelation (forty-six observations), R^2 = 0.75 and Student = 10.50.

13. See also Litle, "Sales Taxes and Internal Commerce," 70; and MiU-C, Zacatecas Collection, *Alcabalas*, 1760–1821. In Mexico City each subsection under aforos may have been kept as a separate section. At times in Zacatecas the subsections were kept separately; eventually they were combined under aforos. Garavaglia and Grosso have an extended discussion of these categories in *Las alcabalas*, 28–30.

14. Viento revenues in Zacatecas exceeded 20,000 pesos per year in the 1780s, and then they dropped back to a range of 13,000–18,000 pesos from 1790 to 1810 (MiU-C, Zacatecas Collection, *Alcabalas*, 1760–1810). Those revenues in Mexico City remained above 110,000 pesos until 1785, after which they fell below 100,000 pesos until the middle 1790s, when they fluctuated between 100,000 and 120,000 pesos (Litle, "Sales Taxes and Internal Commerce," 214–15). Pursuing a different purpose, Garavaglia and Grosso found that a decline in viento income in some towns and villages near Puebla was a sign of economic distress (*Las alcabalas*, 48–60).

15. Many of the proposals and plans have been published by Enrique Florescano and Isabel Gil Sánchez in *Descripciones económicas generales de Nueva España, 1748–1817; Descripciones económicas regionales, centro;* and *Descripciones económicas regionales, norte,* three volumes published under *Fuertes para la historia económica de México* by the Instituto Nacional de Antropología e Historia, Departmento de Investigaciones Históricas, Seminario de Historia Económica.

16. Van Young writes that even after the Consulado of Guadalajara was established its members, lacking the network and the capital of the members

of the Consulado of Mexico City, had to continue "to deal through Mexico City" (*Hacienda and Market in Eighteenth-Century Mexico*, 145).

17.   Coatsworth, "Obstacles to Economic Growth in Nineteenth-Century Mexico," 91. For a description of the highway system, see Humberto Tandrón, *El comercio de Nueva España y la controversia sobre la libertad de comercio, 1796–1821*, 15–17.

18.   MiU-C, Zacatecas Collection, Treasury Records and Correspondence, 1710–19, box B; 1750–59, box A; 1770–79, box C.

19.   Coatsworth, "Obstacles to Economic Growth in Nineteenth-Century Mexico," 91.

20.   D. A. Brading, *Miners and Merchants*, 16. Also see Robert Potash, *El Banco de Avío de México. El fomento de la industria, 1821–1846*, 17, and Humboldt, *Political Essay on the Kingdom of New Spain*, 2:174–75.

21.   Enrique Florescano, *Precios del maíz*, 234.

22.   AGN-AHH, *Consulado*, leg. 1869, exp. 4.

23.   A rough comparison between overland freight rates in Mexico and the United States in the late eighteenth and early nineteenth centuries shows that these Mexican estimates are not unreasonable, even though they may be higher. For the United States a rate often is 20 cents per ton mile, about one-third lower than Mexico's rate. But that rate may have many exceptions, as is possibly true of the Mexican rate. For a sophisticated analysis of overland costs in Massachusetts, see Winifred Rothenberg "The Market and Massachusetts Farmers, 1750–1855," 295–300.

24.   There was also the cost of time. In all likelihood with small loads travel-time costs were probably as prohibitive for most small producers as the actual freight rates. This could be reduced, of course, if small producers found ways to join forces to ship their goods collectively. The maize price series were derived from data presented in chapter 1.

25.   Certificates of remissions (bullion sent by the real caja in Zacatecas to the central treasury) showed two dates: one for its departure from Zacatecas and one for its arrival in Mexico City. Those dates ranged from thirty to ninety days in the late eighteenth and early nineteenth centuries. Certificates of remissions are scattered throughout the Treasury Records and Correspondence section of the Zacatecas Collection in MiU-C.

26.   New York Public Library (NN), Rich Collection, doc. 4. Salvucci has prepared an excellent isochronic map based on this document by Pedro Gómez de la Peña, in *Textiles and Capitalism in Mexico*, 95. Our discussion hereafter is based on his map and analysis.

27.   Salvucci, *Textiles and Capitalism in Mexico*, 94–96. Salvucci concluded that the time needed for mail or freight to move between cities or between businesses was one factor that made the business community imitative and conservative in reaction to the economic circumstances rather than innovative and experimental.

28.   AGI, *Guadalajara*, leg. 527.

29.   Ibid., 528.

30. AGN, *Historia*, leg. 74, exp. 10.

31. Rendón, "Provincia de Zacatecas."

32. AMZ, leg. 17, exp 23; 17–33; 17–37; 17–41; 23–32; 25–45; 30–49; 31–26; 32–28; 33–37; 50–4.

33. Under the rules, which were not always enforced, all merchandise in transit needed a guía that showed origination, destination, value, seller, and buyer in order to pass untaxed from its origination to its destination. When the shipment with its guía arrived at its destination and the buyer paid the tax, the receiving aduana notified the sending aduana by something called a *tournaguía*. No doubt the system had many flaws and defects, but it has left a record that can be used to reconstruct overland trade. See Priestley, *José de Gálvez*, 177–80; and CtY, Latin American Collection, 5-F, for a list of rules proposed by Gálvez to govern the aduanas.

34. MiU-C, Zacatecas Collection, *Alcabalas*, 1781, 1791, 1801, 1810. To determine where the trade originated required that each entry be examined, and because that consumed so much time it was done just for the years 1781, 1791, 1801, and 1810.

35. These data on trade were gathered from the aforos. This section differed from the vientos section (discussed earlier) in that the transactions involved large quantities of luxuries or manufactures (non-foodstuffs) handled by merchants in the two cities (even when the merchant in Zacatecas was acting in behalf of a local miner, hacendado, or businessman). The total value of all merchandise shipped under aforos was recorded in the account, and although the clerks made errors, the sums, on the basis of some random checks, were essentially accurate. The strength of the series on annual total value was for the period of 1780 to 1810 (MiU-C, Zacatecas Collection, *Alcabalas*, 1766–1815). Ledgers do not exist for every year from 1766 to 1780 because in that period the Crown periodically farmed out the collection of duties and taxes and had no need to maintain any records.

36. For trade $R^2 = 0.54$ and Student t = 5.55 (26 observations), and for silver $R^2 = 0.54$ and Student t = 5.50 (26 observations).

37. For trade the Student t's are weak for short-term growth rates (twenty-three and nineteen observations).

38. MiU-C, Zacatecas Collection, *Alcabalas*, 1787 and 1788.

39. For a brief discussion of Berasueta's bakery investments, see Kicza, *Colonial Entrepreneurs*, 191–92.

40. For an older but useful essay, see Robert Smith, "The Institution of the Consulado in New Spain."

41. Brading, *Miners and Merchants*, 118.

42. Veracruz could also impose other taxes to provide water, repair docks, and strengthen fortifications. See Ortiz de la Tabla, *Comercio exterior de Veracruz*, 19, 31–36, and 80–84, for a discussion of the various port taxes and fees. Even before the new consulados were formed, interior merchants had been encouraged to buy from Veracruz merchants rather than from Mexico City's merchants because the total tax bite was smaller. Mexico City's

Consulado complained that because of the reforms it had to operate at a competitive disadvantage. See also Litle, "Sales Taxes and Internal Commerce," 145–58, 238.

43.   AGI, *México*, leg. 2989.

44.   Ortiz de la Tabla, *Comercio exterior de Veracruz*, 35–36. See also estimate by Durango merchant (ca. 1800) that his taxes on goods bought from Veracruz had a tax burden of about 40 percent (AGI, *México*, leg. 2505, and AGN-AHH, *Consulado*, leg. 1869).

45.   This was certainly the claim of Viceroy Conde de Revillagigedo in 1792 (Brading, *Miners and Merchants*, 117).

46.   There is difficulty in extrapolating the value of the trade from the Veracruz avería because the rate varied. We have used two rates—1.0 and 1.5 percent—and then compared them to total trade data published in Miguel Lerdo de Tejada. For example, in 1796 the avería yielded 50,000 pesos. At 1 percent that would make the value of trade handled by the Veracruz Consulado 5 million pesos; at 1.5 percent, 3.3 million pesos. Lerdo de Tejada reported imports and exports through Veracruz in 1796 at 17 million pesos, or a share of 19–29 percent. In 1800 using the same two rates, although a 3 percent tax was levied against some merchandise, the Consulado of Veracruz may have been responsible for as much as 40–50 percent of the port's traffic. Tandrón writes that the Veracruz Consulado collected along with *multas* the "avería, un derecho del ½% sobre todas las mercaderías importadas o exportadas a través del puerto de Veracruz" (in *El comercio de Nueva España*, 20). Contrary to this and other statements in published works on Veracruz commerce, we do not believe that all the trade that passed through the port could be taxed by the Consulado of Veracruz. Carlos Marichal and Matilde Souto of El Colegio de México will publish some important research on commerce in Veracruz.

47.   Ortiz de la Tabla discusses their activities, mainly with reference to the international market, in *Comercio exterior de Veracruz*, chap. 8.

48.   AGI, *Guadalajara*, legs. 526–31; and Brading, *Miners and Merchants*, 118–19.

49.   The value of the commerce has been extrapolated from the avería at a rate of 0.5 percent. For the year 1796 (actually 9/95–8/96), for example, income was reported by city where the trade originated: Veracruz, 15,679 pesos; San Blas, 93 pesos; and Guadalajara, 107 pesos, for a total of 15,879 pesos. At a rate of 0.5 percent the value of the trade has been estimated to be 3.2 million pesos. A year later (1797 or 9/96–8/97) avería income collected from Veracruz, Tepic, Acapulco, Chihuahua, Guadalajara, and San Juan de los Lagos (where a fair was held) equaled 11,291 pesos, for a total value of 2.3 million pesos. For the third year (1798 or 9/97–8/98) the avería yielded no more than 6,000 pesos, worth 1.2 million pesos. In all cases the avería is used to extrapolate the actual value of the merchandise shipped.

50.   See Brading's discussion on road building by the Veracruz Consulado in *Miners and Merchants*, 118–19.

51.   These places have been identified with the aid of Peter Gerhard, *The Northern Frontier of New Spain*. It is not clear how much jurisdictions overlapped (if at all) or how much the consulados competed with each other on the peripheries of their jurisdictions.

52.   The problem with this comparison is that averías concerned both imports and exports, whereas aforos only concerned imports. From the documents covering Guadalajara's averías, it cannot be determined whether the transfer of bullion figured into the receipts of the averías at all. There was a separate tax levied against any buillion exported from Mexico, and that may have overridden the Consulado's privilege to collect the avería.

53.   Christiana Borchet de Moreno, "Los miembros del Consulado de la Ciudad de México en le época de Carlos III." Brading reports (*Miners and Merchants*, 114) that eight-two members within a much larger merchant community attended elections for officers of the Consulado in 1787. However, he does not specify what the total membership was. Kinsbruner (*Petty Capitalism*, 10–11) estimates that Mexico City had 250 grocers, some of whom could have belonged to the guild.

54.   A list of merchants who paid dues (or made donations) on the basis of assets or inventories is the source for the estimate in Guadalajara around 1800. At the top of the list were merchants who paid 204 pesos and at the bottom those who only paid 8 pesos; in between were more than one-half dozen other categories (AGI, *Guadalajara*, leg. 529). On Consulado members, see José Ramírez Flores, *El Real Consulado de Guadalajara. Notas históricas*, 38–42.

55.   Van Young identifies Moreno de Tejada as an important local merchant to whom other Guadalajarans were indebted (*Hacienda and Market in Eighteenth-Century Mexico*, 163).

56.   The Veracruz merchant paid the avería that was then credited to the Consulado of Guadalajara (AGI, *Guadalajara*, leg. 529).

57.   No attempt is made here to treat all the political issues related to the Oaxacan dye trade. That is admirably done in Brian Hamnett's *Politics and Trade in Southern Mexico, 1750–1821*, esp. chaps. 1–3.

58.   Hamnett, *Politics and Trade*, 28–29.

59.   Ibid., 169–70.

60.   For volume $R^2 = 0.52$ and Student $t = 7.54$; for value $R^2 = 0.34$ and Student $t = 5.30$; and for price no verification of a trend is possible even when corrected for autocorrelation (fifty-three observations).

61.   For volume $R^2 = 0.17$ and Student $t = 2.07$; for price $R^2 = 0.55$ and Student $t = 4.55$ but when corrected for autocorrelation yields a weak Student t; and for income $R^2 = 0.60$ and Student $t = 4.96$ (seventeen observations).

62.   For volume $R^2 = 0.50$ and Student $t = 5.92$; for price $R^2 = 0.78$ and Student $t = 2.50$; and for income $R^2 = 0.19$ and Student $t = 2.98$ (thirty-six observations).

63.   We rely here on Hamnett's figures (*Politics and Trade*) from app. 1

(pp. 169–70), app. 3 (p. 172), and app. 6 (p. 175). There is a discrepancy between the figures in the appendices and those presented in the text (p. 101). For example, Lerdo de Tejada (Hamnett's source) reported 6,112 arrobas from Veracruz in 1796, and while that is the figure in Hamnett's appendix 6, it becomes 152,800 arrobas in the text. In fact, the 152,800 arrobas and subsequent figures cited in the text (p. 101) should be read as pounds and not arrobas. The argument that Hamnett is making with reference to the impact of the blockade and concessions to neutrals remains valid, however.

64.　For details see Hamnett, *Politics and Trade*, 24–32.

65.　Ibid., 100–102.

66.　Ibid., 114.

67.　Hamnett (ibid.) should be consulted for the basic plan and its numerous variations.

68.　British Library, Additions 13978, fols. 11–13; and Hamnett, *Politics and Trade*, 72–94. Hamnett cites the same bundle from the British Library but not this particular document.

69.　Based on the 1793 census as presented in Hamnett, *Politics and Trade*, 188.

70.　Hamnett's analysis is much more detailed and should be consulted for a full understanding of how a reform-minded government tried to deal with merchants, subdelegados, and others (in *Politics and Trade*, chap. 5). We have used documents from the British Library, Additions 13978, fols. 92–99, but we have not tried to duplicate Hamnett's exhaustive research in Spanish and Mexican archives. The British Library document resembles a report by Francisco Antonio Villarasa Rivera, an Oaxacan treasury official, dated 22 April 1793, found in AGI, *Mexico*, leg. 1780, and cited in *Politics and Trade*, 83–84.

71.　Correlation (Pearson's) between cochineal registrations and treasury transfers was a highly positive o.70.

72.　From data provided by Hamnett in *Politics and Trade*, app. 8 (pp. 177–82). Without knowing how complete or accurate the treasury accounts were, we offer an estimate of how merchants were distributed by city. The figures that we cite are our calculations, and not Hamnett's. Further, we should note that when the figures for individual merchants, listed in Hamnett's appendix, are summed for each year, that number may not equal the total amount for each year's transfers. Hence while the annual totals for the treasury transfers add up to 3.1 million pesos, the annual totals based on individual merchants only add up to about 2.7 million pesos. Such problems are common in work on treasury ledgers.

73.　Brading reports that Alles shifted his investments from cochineal to sugar in response to the changed structure and increased competition in the cochineal competition (*Miners and Merchants*, 116).

74.　Information from MiU-C, Zacatecas Collection, *Alcabalas*, 1788, was compared with Hamnett's list in *Politics and Trade*, app. 8.

75.   Hamnett, *Politics and Trade*, 111–15.

76.   Ibid., chap. 8 and app. 8. The impact of the European wars of the late eighteenth and early nineteenth centuries on economic development and policy is also treated in Thomson, "The Cotton Textile Industry in Puebla," 197.

77.   Hamnett, *Politics and Trade*, 128–30.

78.   Carmagnami, *El regneso de los dioses*, 107–79. There was enough in all the cajas for the government to borrow 1.5 million pesos in the late eighteenth century.

79.   See Stanley Stein's description of the merchant as lender, investor, and expeditor in "Prelude to Upheaval," 188–89.

80.   Brading, *Miners and Merchants*, 218. The role of the merchant as the administrator of lay organizations that lent money has not yet been systematically investigated. It was a point at which the activities of the colony's largest creditors overlapped. Apparently, though, Indian *cofradías* (brotherhoods) remained in the hands of the Indians themselves or of the parish priests; see William Taylor's discussion of Oaxaca and Jalisco cofradías in "Indian Pueblos of Central Jalisco on the Eve of Independence," 176–80.

81.   We are summarizing what appears in Michael Costeloe, *Church Wealth in Mexico: A Study of the 'Juzgado de Capellanías in the Archbishopric of Mexico, 1800–1856*, from the introduction, a study of the largest of the dioceses in Mexico City. Also see Asunción Lavrin, "The Role of Nunneries in the Economy of New Spain in the Eighteenth Century."

82.   Bauer, "Church in the Economy of Spanish America: *Censos* and *Depósitos* in the Eighteenth and Nineteenth Centuries," 711 and passim. Bauer is not always clear what the term *church* includes. Is he referring to just the secular church or to all branches of the church? In this brief discussion we tend to use church in a generic rather than a specific sense, but even that may not be fully satisfactory to readers.

83.   The document did not identify the archbishoprics or bishoprics. Mexico City was certainly an archbishopric, and eight bishoprics can be identified: Mérida, Oaxaca, Puebla, Guadalajara, Michoacán, Durango, Monterrey, and Arizpe. The total number of ecclesiastical jurisdictions (nine) in the protest is in agreement with the known number, but the configuration is different.

84.   The document is from the British Library, Additions 13987, fols. 204–9, and is also cited by Stein in "Prelude to Upheaval," 188–97 and tables 3 and 6. Stein's table 6 is a slight revision of table 2 by Lavrin in "The Execution of the Law of *Consolidación*," 35.

85.   Bauer, "Church in the Economy of Spanish America," 709.

86.   Asunsión Lavrin, "El capital eclesiástico y las elites sociales en Nueva España a fines del siglo xviii."

87.   Bauer, "Church in the Economy of Spanish America," 723, for references to studies by Greenow, Van Young, and others; also pp. 723–27 and 731–33.

88. Stein, "Prelude to Upheaval," 194–97. See Margaret Chowning, "The Consolidación de Vales Reales in the Bishopric of Michoacán," for a detailed study of how various classes of lenders were affected in Michoacán by Consolidación. Her general argument is that middle and small borrowers, thought by Stein and others to be adversely affected by Consolidación, may have escaped economic harm in part because the enforcement of Consolidación was limited to about two years.

89. No attempt will be made herein to reconcile the different assessments of the rents that the properties might have produced.

90. The several audits of the mayorazgo produced different figures for the revenues and the costs, so that one audit might show a balance but another would not. The aim here is to illustrate how much of the revenue of the estate was encumbered by past and current obligations.

91. NN, Poole Collection, 1. Bauer points out, and we agree, that what the church spent in the philanthropic area was crucial to a colony that devoted little tax money to such concerns. This means in effect that a large part of the private capital was transferred into the public sector.

92. Greenow, *Credit and Socioeconomic Change*, 28.

93. Ibid., 115–22.

94. Ibid., 164. Richard Lindley has written of such a network: "alliances between merchants' and hacendados' families provided the logical means to establish credit viability. . . . With the merchants' liquidity and the hacendados' security, family enterprises created by kinship alliances were in the best possible position to manipulate credit as either borrowers or lenders" (*Haciendas and Economic Development*, 37).

95. See Pérez Herrero's extended discussion of the libranza in *Plata y Libranzas*, chap. 9.

96. This certainly is the impression left by Costeloe in his analysis of Mexico City's Juzgado in *Church Wealth in Mexico*, 66–67.

97. Chowning, "Consolidación de Vales Reales," quotes from 454 and 477, data from 466 and 475–476.

98. Ibid., 456.

99. Kicza, *Colonial Entrepreneurs*, 51–61, with quotes from pp. 52 and 56. Ecclesiastical and nonecclesiastical lending practices have been examined elsewhere. Individual almaceneros like Antonio Bassoco made numerous and substantial loans, especially as other sources of credit dried up in the colonial period. Between 1800 and 1810, Bassoco granted eighteen loans worth a total of nearly 600,000 pesos. Most were for business purposes. The terms were 5 percent interest for five years, although apparently extensions were often granted. Bassoco's role as a lender was notable. More needs to be known about who borrowed the money for what purposes and to what extent the terms were complied with (García Ayluardo "El comerciante y el crédito," 34–41). In Puebla, loan volume fell sharply in the first decade of the nineteenth century mainly because private lenders could not fill the gap created by declining eccelsiastical lending (Cervantes Bello, "La iglesia y la crisis").

100.   María Cristina Torales Pacheco, "Tradicionalismo y modernidad en el comercio novohispano de la segunda mitad del siglo xviii. La Compañía de Francisco Ignacio de Yraeta."

101.   Kicza refers to María Rosa as Rosa María, but our documents refer to her as María Rosa. As noted earlier, Iraeta was involved in the Oaxaca cochineal trade (Kicza, *Colonial Entrepreneurs*, 157).

102.   NN, Poole Collection, 2 and 9.

103.   On the Icazas, see AGN-AHH, Consulado, leg. 395.

104.   Biblioteca Nacional, Madrid, leg. 544 [vol. 1, #3534], fols. 131–305. See also Gibson, *The Aztecs under Spanish Rule*, 236–43.

105.   Doris Ladd, *The Mexican Nobility at Independence, 1770–1826*, 193.

106.   Brading, *Miners and Merchants*, 127.

107.   AGN, Consulado, leg. 442, exp. 16.

7. Royal Treasury and Economic Policy

1.   Morse, "The Heritage of Latin America."

2.   When corrected for autocorrelation (twenty-nine observations) $R^2 = 0.66$ and Student $t = 3.18$.

3.   Jacques Barbier and Herbert Klein, "Las prioridades de un monarca ilustrado. El gasto público bajo el reinado de Carlos III," 492–95.

4.   For an extended discussion of how the royal treasury was organized and administered, see Andrés Lira González, "Aspecto fiscal de la Nueva España en la segunda mitad del siglo xviii." Also see Herbert Klein and Jacques Barbier, "Recent Trends in the Study of Spanish American Colonial Public Finance."

5.   John TePaske, one of the principal compilers of the treasury accounts, has offered additional guidelines in the *Latin American Economic History Newsletter* 1 (Dec. 1991): 5–8.

6.   Series C is from TePaske et al., *La Real Hacienda de Nueva España*. Although the yearly totals after 1780 appear much too high, those before 1780 appear reasonable. The post-1780 totals include some well-understood inaccuracies in the handling of year-end balances, transfers between branches, and government-mandated loans. Series A is TePaske's revision of Series C and has been published in "Economic Cycles in Eighteenth Century New Spain," *BA*, 191–92. That article was revised and later published in Garner and Taylor, eds., *Iberian Colonies, New World Colonies*, 133–135. In Series A annual revenues were lowered by eliminating categories that were counted more than once. Series B was devised by Garner in "Further Consideration of 'Facts and Figments in Bouron, Mexico,'" on the basis of criticisms offered by Brading of Series C ("Facts and Figments in Bourbon Mexico"). Until 1780 the Garner series corresponds closely to Series C and A, but after that it is best described as falling somewhere between C and A. The series treated herein are derived from the cargo (receipts) rather than

from the data (expenses) side of the ledgers. The successive revisions of series C have largely eliminated items that do not represent receipts from taxes, monopolies, and other treasury operations. One could argue that loans should be counted as a form of income. They are included in C. If they were included in A and B, they would add 1–2 million pesos to the annual totals for those two series from the middle 1780s to the end of the colonial period. But to do so would make little difference in growth rate calculations. Obviously, the inclusion of loans plus so many other large items for the late decades makes the secular growth rate as well as short-term rates noticeably higher.

7.   See discussion of royal revenue trends in chapter 1 for test statistics for each series.

8.   For a discussion and some figures, see Biblioteca Nacional, Madrid, leg. 578.

9.   Klein, "La economía de la Nueva España, 1680–1809." Klein eliminated certain categories in order to limit the distortions from double-counting and carry-over items (p. 563 n.5). Nevertheless, his estimates are still very high compared to other series.

10.   Ibid., 564 n.6 and 566–68.

11.   Klein's long-term trend is based on the variation between the data point and the mean. Since the dispersions show little change relative to the mean between 1710 and 1780, the inference is that the rise in revenue, indicated by the data themselves, is an accurate gauge of what was happening: revenue was rising at some calculable rate, although the rate, so far as we can determine, was not given. At the beginning of the century when the dispersions showed a tendency to decline and at the end of the century when they showed a tendency to rise, one might be hesitant to trust the trend lines and growth rates calculated from the data themselves. We have found that t values and R^2 values for series A, B, and C are favorable and autocorrelation can be corrected for in series C. Although Klein's graphs 1 and 2 (inserted between pp. 82 and 83) are plots of variations, they are not explained in the text or the notes ("La economía de la Nueva España").

12.   These observations are drawn from Klein, "La economía de la Nueva España," 594–98. To reach these conclusions, Klein has used a different approach in analyzing the treasury data. He has grouped the various accounts (of which there are dozens) by sectors, such as commerce, mining, consumption, and the like. The level of royal revenue from these accounts represents the level of economic activity within these sectors.

13.   In part this is due to the survival of a very large archives of reports and ledgers for the Zacatecas real caja now housed at MiU-C, and known as the Zacatecas Collection; Garner, "Reformas borbónicas y operaciones hacendarias."

14.   Statistics for remissions are $R^2 = 0.35$ and Student $t = 4.01$. According to Klein's calculations, Zacatecas's total receipts rose at the slowest rate of the entire century among the major cajas ("La economía de la Nueva España," fig. 1 on p. 566).

15.   We do not mean to imply that silver mining represented the total "domestic product" of the economy in the city and region of Zacatecas. But it certainly was the major component. The "domestic product" of Guadalajara, based on figures discussed in chapter 2, was in the range of 5 million pesos, and Zacatecas's was probably smaller because it lacked as diversified an agriculture. The data on Zacatecas's remissions except for growth rates may be found in Garner, "Reformas borbónicas y operaciones hacendarias," 550–52 and passim.

16.   For Guadalajara, see TePaske, "Economic Cycles in Eighteenth Century New Spain," 189–92, and in Garner and Taylor, eds., *Iberian Colonies, New World Societies*, 132, 136–137.

17.   Various factors could influence their respective operations, such as geographic size or population density.

18. $R^2 = 0.91$ and Student $t = 32.6$ (104 observations). Klein offers a slightly lower growth rate of 1.7 percent for a slightly longer period of 1680–1809 ("La economía de la Nueva España," fig. 1, p. 567).

19.   The survey was found in the Nettie Lee Benson Library, University of Texas (TxU), G 206–207.

20.   Garner, "Reformas borbónicas y operaciones hacendarias," 547.

21.   For a breakdown of Real Hacienda accounts for 1785–89, see Fonseca and Urrutia, *Real Hacienda*, 1:xxxix–xlii.

22.   C. H. Haring, *The Spanish Empire in America*, 263–65; and Gibson, *The Aztecs under Spanish Rule*, 205–6.

23.   Exact figures are hard to come by. These are Klein's estimates as given in "La economía de la Nueva España," 587. The amounts listed under the various tribute categories in TePaske et al., *The Real Hacienda de Nueva España*, when totaled yielded a much lower annual figure.

24.   Fonseca and Urrutia, *Real Hacienda*, 1:450.

25.   TxU, G 217. Tribute revenue was often deposited in Mexico City and not in the branches, even though some branches existed in areas with large tributary populations. A probable reason for this was that deposits were made by libranzas through a network of merchants with Mexico City merchants honoring the libranzas (Klein's "La economía de la Nueva España," 587; also Pérez Herrero, *Plata y libranzas*, 227–30).

26.   Gibson, *Aztecs under Spanish Rule*, 215.

27.   Fonseca and Urrutia, *Real Hacienda*, 1:450–51.

28.   Humboldt, *Political Essay on the Kingdom of New Spain*, 3:469–72.

29.   MiU-C, Zacatecas Collection, Treasury Records and Correspondence, 1760–69, box D, and Miscellaneous Bound Volume; and Garner, "Reformas borbónicas y operaciones hacendarias," 577–81.

30.   Bakewell, *Silver Mining and Society*, 165.

31.   Ibid., 177–78.

32.   Voluminous documentation on these debt issues survive and for nearly a decade the treasury was under pressure to make improvements;

MiU-C, Zacatecas Collection, Treasury Records and Correspondence, 1750–59, boxes A and C; 1760–69, box A.

33. Ibid., 1780–89, box C; 1790–99, boxes B, D, I.

34. Ibid., 1720–29, box A.

35. Ibid., 1770–79, box B.

36. No attempt is made here to summarize the full history of this rather controversial system during the eighteenth century and especially after 1760; see Litle, "Sales Taxes and Internal Commerce."

37. MiU-C, Zacatecas Collection, Treasury Records and Correspondence, 1750–59, box A; 1760–69, boxes A, C, E; 1770–79, box B. Also see Garner, "Reformas borbónicas y operaciones hacendarias," 561–71. On operations see Litle, "Sales Taxes and Internal Commerce," chap. 3, and Garavaglia and Grosso, *Las alcabalas*, 11–40.

38. Fonseca and Urrutia, *Real Hacienda*, 1:98–115; and Litle, "Sales Taxes and Internal Commerce," 41–47, 95–109, 120–27.

39. Garner, "Reformas borbónicas y operaciones hacendarias," 566–67; and AGN, *Historia*, leg. 76, exp. 20, in which total colonial expenses were one-fifth of the total revenues.

40. Priestley, *José de Gálvez*, 355; and CtY, Latin American Collection, 5-F. Litle describes and anlayzes both the guía and the *marchamo* (much hated customs stamp) in "Sales Taxes and Internal Commerce," 87–95, 131–32. Garavaglia and Grosso contend that by the end of the eighteenth century the guía system was widely abused (*Las alcabalas*, 32–40).

41. AGI, *México*, leg. 2096. Some of the alcabalas controversies arising from the Gálvez visita are discussed in Fonseca and Urrutia, *Real Hacienda*, 1:70–80.

42. AGN-AHH, *Alcabalas*, leg. 2166, exp. 1. A similar document exists for a shipment from Valladolid to Petatlan in leg. 2166, exp. 4.

43. MiU-C, Zacatecas Collection, Treasury Record and Correspondence, from various accounts scattered through boxes from the 1770s to 1800s.

44. These figures may be found in AGI, *México*, leg. 1554, and they have been published in *Los virreyes de Nueva España en el reinado de Carlos IV*, 1:267. When compared to the annual average for yearly alcabalas income in TePaske et al., *La Real Hacienda de Nueva España*, the two sets are close for 1765–77 (1.5 million pesos versus 1.2 for TePaske) but much farther apart for 1778–90 (3.2 vs. 1.7 for TePaske). Fonseca and Urrutia (*Real Hacienda*, 2:109) also present higher receipts than TePaske for the period 1780–89. The differences are hard to account for. The viceroy's report could be in error, but more than likely the lower figures in TePaske from 1778 through 1790 arise from the fact that the ledger entry called alcabalas may not have included alcabalas receipts from branch treasuries. Litle relies primarily on TePaske, although she compares them to Lucas Alamán's figures ("Sales Taxes and Internal Commerce," 236–37). In any event alcabalas receipts increased after 1778, although the actual amounts remain in dispute.

45.   Fonseca and Urrutia, *Real Hacienda*, 2:78–79.

46.   *Virreyes de Nueva España*, 2:268–71.

47.   MiU-C, Zacatecas Collection, *Alcabalas*, 1784–86.

48.   AGI, *México*, leg. 2505. See also *Virreyes de Nueva España*, 2:268; and Litle, "Sales Taxes and Internal Commerce," 152 n.65.

49.   Priestley, *José de Gálvez*, 142–55; see also McWatters, "The Royal Tobacco Monopoly."

50.   Priestley, *José de Gálvez*, 142–44; and Humboldt, *Political Essay of the Kingdom of New Spain*, 3:40.

51.   Priestley, *José de Gálvez*, 149–54.

52.   Humboldt, *Political Essay on the Kingdom of New Spain*, 3:42–44.

53.   Garner, "Reformas borbónicas y operaciones hacendarias," 559–61.

54.   Humboldt, *Political Essay on the Kingdom of New Spain*, 4:22.

55.   MiU-C, Zacatecas Collection, Treasury Records and Correspondence, 1810–19, box B.

56.   AGN-AHH, *Consulado*, leg. 395, exp. 1.

57.   TxU, Latin American Collection, G 206–30. Part of the purpose of the survey was to see how the towns and cities that collected the new imposts, mentioned above, planned to spend their funds.

58.   For an enlightening discussion of the motives behind and results of Gálvez's reforms, see Allan Kuethe, "Toward a Periodization of the Reforms of Charles III," 112–14.

59.   Jacques Barbier, "Toward a New Chronology for Bourbon Colonialism: the *Depositaría de Indias of Cádiz, 1722–1789*." See Chowning, "The Consolidación de Vales Reales," for a detailed study of the economic impact in the several years immediately following the enactment of the policy in Michoacán.

60.   Garner, "Exportaciones de circulante."

61.   Biblioteca Nacional, Madrid, leg. 578.

62.   Brian Hamnett, "The Appropriation of Mexican Church Wealth by the Spanish Bourbon Government—The Consolidación de Vales, 1805–1809," 100–102.

63.   Ibid., 97–100. The nonpreferential category exceeds the total (7.7) given. The 800,000-peso item was probably not included in the official total.

64.   Stein, "Prelude to Upheaval," 197–98.

65.   Morin, *Michoacán en la Nueva España*, 187.

66.   British Library, Additions 13978, fols. 204–6, 209–10. There is no way to prove these estimates, and other explanations could be advanced (devaluation and contraband) to explain why so few older coins circulated. Clearly, though, there was more to these concerns than disagreement over consolidación. If the estimate have any validity, then the change means a drop in the circulating medium of 8 pesos to 4 pesos per person in a decade.

67.   The calculations are based on several sets of figures on the impact of the consolidation in British Library, Additions 13978, fols. 204–206. See also

Hamnett, "The Appropriation of Mexican Church Wealth," 94; and Stein "Prelude to Upheaval," 197.

68. British Library, Additions 13978, fols. 204–206.

69. Pérez Herrero, *Plata y Libranzas,* 193–94.

70. Ibid., 195–253.

71. Meek, *The Exchange Media,* 34–38, 54–57.

72. AGI, *Consulado,* leg. 789. The specific complaint was in connection with sales of barrels of wine.

73. Meek, *The Exchange Media,* 59–62; and Brading *Miners and Merchants,* 143–44. Meek and Brading disagree about how these devaluations translate into the number of reales that were cut from marks. See also a document prepared by the mint director, 10 October 1776, in John Carter Brown Library, Brown University, (RPB), *Casa de Moneda,* mss. 1730–76.

74. Meek, *The Exchange Media,* 62–76. See Pérez Herrero's *Plata Y Libranzas* on goverment policies with respect not only to libranzas but also to coinage, and John McCusker, *Money and Exchange in Europe and America, 1600–1775: A Handbook,* for tables on coins circulating in the Atlantic economy.

75. Growth rates are from data in AGN-AHH, *Consulado,* leg. 395, esp. 7, and are analyzed in Garner, "Exportaciones de circulante en el siglo xviii," 556–73. These are only indicative and by no means definitive. Other figures for an earlier period, 1772–91, have been compiled by Ortiz de la Tabla in *Comercio exterior de Veracruz,* 257–58, and show an annual growth rate of 9.4 percent (90 percent confidence level). They can be compared with figures compiled by Garner that show an rise of 9.2 percent (100 percent confidence level). If currency exports from Veracruz and Acapulco are combined, the rate of increase drops only slightly to 8.6 percent per year.

76. The comparisons may be found in British Library, Additions 13978, fols. 212–214.

8. Growth and Change

1. See B. H. Slicher van Bath's discussion of construction and mining in *Real Hacienda y economía en Hispanoamérica, 1541–1820,* 137–40.

2. Eric Van Young, "Islands in the Storm: Quiet Cities and Violent Countrysides in the Mexican Independence Era," 154.

3. Van Young, "Moving Toward Revolt: Agrarian Origins of the Hidalgo Rebellion in the Guadalajara Region," 186–99, 200, 204.

4. Taylor, "Banditry and Insurrection: Rural Unrest in Central Jalisco," 244–46. Taylor makes the argument that the rise in banditry was linked to the perception as well as the experience that some village residents professed that they had been denied the fruits or benefits of the so-called economic expansion. But the magnitude of the expansion may not have actually matched the perceptions or experiences of some residents. Growth did occur in the Guadalajara region and probably resulted in the loss of land and the

transfer of labor in the outlying areas, although that growth may not have actually generated much new wealth.

5. Taylor, *Drinking, Homicide and Rebellion*, 145.

6. For comparisons with British America, one can consult John Mc-Cusker and Ronald Menard, *The Economy of British America, 1607–1789*, 51–70. In contrast, using 1980 constant dollars, McCusker and Menard estimated that the thirteen English colonies had a per capita growth of 0.3–0.6 percent per year and a total product growth of 3.5 percent per year from 1650 to 1774 (pp. 55–57). It must be emphasized that the McCusker and Menard estimates represent real growth.

7. For comparative purposes, consult George Grantham, "Agricultural Supply During the Industrial Revolution," and "Jean Meuvret and the Subsistence Problem in Early Modern France." We do not intend to propose that these two economies can be compared. Rather we are interested in Grantham's discussion of how France accomplished an increase in output in its agricultural sector between 1750 and 1850. He observed a pattern of development that he believed emerged first in the Low Countries, showed up then in southeastern England, and passed finally to northeastern France. In brief, the first phase of the agricultural revolution was mainly for farmers to respond to "market opportunities" around port and capital cities by "working harder, investing more, and . . . shifting the balance of their crop mix toward more marketable productions." More output depended on more intensive use of existing technologies: thus it was an "endogenous response to improving agricultural terms of trade along a long-run supply curve" that had been in place for many years (pp. 44–45, 68–71).

8. Arlegui, *Crónica de la Provincia*, 122–23, 132; and Rendón, "La provincia de Zacatecas," 22–34.

9. British Library, Additions 13978, fols. 116–119.

10. McCusker and Menard, *Economy of British America*, 23.

11. Much of the preceding is drawn from ibid., 17–34. Their discussion applies to British America, and because of the absence of large-scale mining there, it does not take into account the special conditions that arose from huge silver reserves. Others to be consulted on growth, exports, and development are: Richard Caves, "Export-Led Growth and the New Economic History"; James Shepherd and Gary Walton, *Shipping, Maritime Trade, and the Economic Development of Colonial North America*, 27–48; Albert Hirschman, "A Generalized Linkage Approach to Development, with Special Reference to Staples"; and Jacob Price, "Economic Function and the Growth of American Port Towns in the Eighteenth Century," 171–74.

12. Albert Hirschman, *The Strategy of Economic Development*, 100–10; and McCusker and Menard, *Economy of British America*, 26–27.

13. Numerous demographic studies of late colonial urban populations in conjunction with various viceregal reports on local urban economies may demonstrate how unspecialized the economic structures of some of the largest cities were as late as 1790 or 1820. Most of these studies, however,

have been designed to uncover more about the social structure than the economic structure. See Brading, *Miners and Merchants*, 254–60; John Chance, "The Colonial Latin American City: Preindustrial or Capitalist?" 224–26, where the observation is made that commercial capitalism must be fit between feudalism and the industrial revolution; Chance, *Race and Class*, chap. 6; and Rodney Anderson, "Race and Social Stratification: A Comparison of Working-Class Spaniards, Indians, and Castas in Guadalajara, Mexico in 1821," esp. 242–43. An important debate involved John Chance and William Taylor's "Estate and Class in a Colonial City: Oaxaca in 1792" (based on data collected by Chance and Taylor in their respective studies of Oaxaca), Robert McCaa, Stuart Schwartz, and Arturo Grubessich's "Race and Class in Colonial Latin America: A Critique," and Chance and Taylor's reply in the same journal, pp. 434–42. In the end, though, this is a debate about what constitutes a "working class," and although the working class may have reflected a less precise racial composition, it may not necessarily have reflected occupations and activities that could alter significantly the basis of these urban economies. See Anderson, "Race and Social Stratification," 210–12, in particular notes 9 and 11, for other references with respect to the working class controversy. For an overview, see Woodrow Borah, "Trends in Recent Studies of Colonial Latin American Cities."

Works Cited

Archival Materials

Archivo General de Indias, Seville (AGI). *Consulado:* (legajo) 789, 796, 799, 800.
———. *Estado:* 26, 27.
———. *Guadalajara:* 174, 182, 190, 477, 478, 480, 482, 526, 527, 528, 529, 530, 531.
———. *México:* 1554, 1566, 1634, 1780, 2096, 2235, 2505, 2779, 2780, 2989.
Archivo General de la Nación, Mexico City, (AGN). *Historia:* 49, 74, 76, 204.
———. *Minería:* 63, 115, 520.
Archivo General de la Nación, Mexico City, Archivo Histórico de Hacienda, (AGN-AHH). *Alcabalas:* 2166.
———. *Azogue:* 205, 2309.
———. *Consulado:* 395, 442, 917, 1869.
Archivo Municipal de Zacatecas (AMZ): 17, 20, 23, 24, 25, 30, 31, 32, 33, 50.
Bancroft Library, University of California, Berkeley (CU-BANC). Mexican Manuscripts, 1872.
Biblioteca Nacional, Madrid: 544 [vol. 1, #3534], 578.
British Library, London. Additions: 13978, 17561.
———. Egerton Collection: 520.
Clements Library, University of Michigan (MiU-C). Zacatecas Collection. *Alcabalas,* 1760–1821. [Scattered ledgers from 1760 to 1777, but mostly complete after that; other documents such as reports, summaries.]
———. *Cargo y Data,* 1700–1821. [General ledgers; most missing years have been found in AGI, *Guadalajara;* contain silver registrations among other ramos.]
———. Miscellaneous Bound Volume.

————. *Quinto y Diezmo,* 1700–1767. [No ledgers for some years; supplement to silver registrations recorded in *Cargo y Data* above.]

————. Treasury Records and Correspondence, 1700–1821. [Documents are separated by decade and filed in letter boxes, marked alphabetically. The documents lack other identifying numbers or letters and often lack titles.]

John Carter Brown Library, Brown University (RPB). *Casa de Moneda* mss., 1730–76.

New York Public Library (NN). Poole Collection: (box or folder number) 1, 2, 9.

————. Rich Collection: 45.

Nettie Lee Benson Library, University of Texas(TxU): (folder) G-206, G-207, G-217.

Sterling Library, Yale University (CtY). Latin American Collection: (box number and document identification) 5-E, 5-F, 6-E, 12-E.

The Rosenbach Museum and Library (PPRF), Mexican Collection, 462/25.

Printed Materials

Abad y Quiepo, Manuel. "Representación a nombre de los labradores y comerciantes de Valladolid de Michoacán." In Mora, q.v., 214–30.

Aguirre Beltrán, Gonzalo. *La población negra de México, estudio etnohistórico.* 2d ed., corrected and amended. Mexico: Fondo de Cultura Económica, 1972.

Altman, Ida, and James Lockhart, eds. *Provinces of Early Mexico: Variants of Spanish American Regional Evolution.* Los Angeles: UCLA Latin American Center Publications, 1976.

Amaral, Samuel. "Public Expenditure Financing in the Colonial Treasury: An Analysis of the Real Caja de Buenos Aires Accounts, 1789–91." *Hispanic American Historical Review* 64, no. 2 (1984): 287–95.

Anderson, J. R., J. L. Dillon, and J. B. Hardaker. *Agricultural Decision Analysis.* Ames: Iowa State University Press, 1977.

Anderson, Rodney. "Race and Social Stratification: A Comparison of Working-Class Spaniards, Indians, and Castas in Guadalajara, Mexico in 1821." *Hispanic American Historical Review* 68, no. 2 (1988): 209–44.

Anna, Timothy. *The Fall of the Royal Government in Mexico City.* Lincoln: University of Nebraska Press, 1978.

Antle, J. M. "Econometric Estimation of Producers' Risk Attitudes." *American Journal of Agricultural Economics* 69, no. 3 (1987): 509–22.

Arlegui, José. *Crónica de la Provincia de N.S.P.S. Francisco de Zacatecas.* Mexico: J. Bernardo de Hogal, 1851.

Askari, H., and J. T. Cummings. *Agricultural Supply Response: A Survey of the Econometric Evidence.* New York: Praeger, 1976.

Aubrey, Henry. "The National Income of Mexico." *I.A.S.I. Estadística* (June 1950): 185–98.

Bakewell, Peter. "Mining in Colonial Spanish America." In Bethell, ed., q.v., 105–51.

———. *Silver and Entrepreneurship in Seventeenth-Century Potosí: The Life and Times of Antonio López de Quiroga*. Albuquerque: University of New Mexico Press, 1988.

———. *Silver Mining and Society in Colonial Mexico, Zacatecas, 1546–1700*. Cambridge: Cambridge University Press, 1971.

Barbier, Jacques. "Toward a New Chronology for Bourbon Colonialism: The Depositaría de Indias of Cádiz, 1722–1789." *Ibero-Amerikanisches Archiv* 6, no. 4 (1980): 335–53.

Barbier, Jacques, and Herbert Klein. "Las prioridades de un monarca ilustrado: el gasto público bajo el reinado de Carlos III." *Revista de historia económica* 3, no. 3 (1985): 473–95.

Bargalló, Modesto. *La minería y la metalurgía en la América española durante la época colonial*. Mexico: Fondo de Cultura Económica, 1955.

Barrett, Elinor. *The Mexican Colonial Copper Industry*. Albuquerque: University of New Mexico Press, 1987.

Barrett, Ward. "The Meat Supply of Colonial Cuernavaca." *Annals of the Association of American Geographers* 64, no. 4 (1974): 525–40.

———. *The Sugar Hacienda of the Marqueses del Valle*. Minneapolis: University of Minnesota Press, 1970.

Bauer, Arnold. "The Church in the Economy of Spanish America: Censos and Depósitos in the Eighteenth and Nineteenth Centuries." *Hispanic American Historical Review*, 63, no. 4 (1983): 707–33.

Baumol, William. *Economic Theory and Operations Analysis*. 4th ed. Englewood Cliffs, N.J.: Prentice-Hall, 1977.

Berghes, Carlos. *Descripción de la Serranía de Zacatecas, formada por I. M. Bustamante*. Mexico: M. Arezalo, 1834.

Bethell, Leslie, ed. *The Cambridge History of Latin America: Colonial Latin America*. Vols. 1 and 2. Cambridge: Cambridge University Press, 1984.

Bhagwati, Jagdish, Ronald Jones, Robert Mundell, and Jaroslav Vaneh, eds. *Trade, Balance of Payments, and Growth: Papers in International Economics in Honor of Charles P. Kindleberger*. Amsterdam: North-Holland, 1971.

Bobb, Bernard. *The Viceregency of Antonio María Bucareli in New Spain, 1771–1779*. Austin: University of Texas Press, 1962.

Borah, Woodrow. *New Spain's Century of Depression*. Berkeley: University of California Press, 1951.

———. "Tithe Collection in the Bishopric of Oaxaca, 1601–1867." *Hispanic American Historical Review* 21, no. 2 (1941): 386–409.

———. "Trends in Recent Studies of Colonial Latin American Cities." *Hispanic American Historical Review* 64, no. 3 (1984): 535–54.

Borchart de Moreno, Christiana. "Los miembros del Consulado de la Cuidad de México en la época de Carlos III." *Jahrbuch für Geschichte von Staat, Wirtschaft und Gesellschaft Lateinamerikas* 14 (1977): 134–60.

Boserup, Ester. *The Conditions of Agricultural Growth: The Economics of Agrarian Change under Population Pressure*. Chicago: Aldine, 1965.

Brading, D. A. "Facts and Figments in Bourbon Mexico." *Bulletin of Latin American Research* 4, no. 1 (1985): 61–64.

———. *Haciendas and Ranchos in the Mexican Bajío: León, 1700–1860*. Cambridge: Cambridge University Press, 1978.

———. "Mexican Silver Mining in the Eighteenth Century: The Revival of Zacatecas." *Hispanic American Historical Review* 50, no. 4 (1970): 665–81.

———. *Miners and Merchants in Bourbon Mexico, 1763–1810*. Cambridge: Cambridge University Press, 1971.

———. "Noticias sobre la economía de Querétaro y de sus corregidor don Miguel Domínguez." *Boletín del Archivo General de la Nación*, 2d ser., 11 (1970):275–318.

Brading, D.A., John Coatsworth, Héctor Lindo-Fuentes, Arij Ouweneel, and Catrien C. J. H. Bijleveld. "Comments on the 'The Economic Cycle in Bourbon Central Mexico: A Critique of the Recaudación del diezmo líquido en pesos' " *Hispanic American Historical Review* 69, no. 3 (1989): 531–38.

Braudel, Fernand, and Frank Spooner. "Prices in Europe from 1450 to 1750." In *The Cambridge Economic History of Europe*, edited by E. E. Rich and C. H. Wilson, 4:378–486. 2d ed. Cambridge: Cambridge University Press, 1966–89.

Brenner, Y. S. "The Inflation of Prices in Early Sixteenth Century England." *Economic History Review*, 2d ser., 14, no. 2 (1961): 225–39.

Bronfenbrenner, M. "Inflation and Deflation." In Sills, ed., q.v., 7:289–301.

Buva, R., ed. *Haciendas in Central Mexico from the Late Colonial Times to the Revolution: Labour Conditions, Hacienda Management and Its Relation to the State*. Amsterdam: Centre for Latin American Research and Documentation, 1984.

Carmagnani, Marcello. "Demografía y sociedad: la estructura social de los centros mineros del norte de México, 1600–1720." *Historia mexicana* 21, no. 3 (1972): 419–59.

———. *El regreso de los dioses. El proceso de reconstitución de la identidad étnica en Oaxaca. Siglos XVII y XVIII*. Mexico City: Fondo de Cultura Económica, 1988.

Carrera Stampa, Manuel. "Las ferias novohispanas." In Real Díaz and Carrera Stampa, comps., q.v., 169–220.

Caves, Richard. "Export-Led Growth and the New Economic History." In Bhagwati et al., eds., q.v., 403–42.

Cervantes Bello, Francisco "La iglesia y la crisis del crédito colonial en Puebla." In Ludlow and Marichal, eds., q.v., 51–74.

Chance, John. "The Colonial Latin American City: Preindustrial or Capitalist?" *Urban Anthropology* 4, no. 3 (1975): 211–28.

———. *Race and Class in Colonial Oaxaca*. Stanford, Calif.: Stanford University Press, 1978.

Chance, John, and William Taylor. "Estate and Class: A Reply." *Comparative Studies in Society and History* 21, no. 3 (1979): 434–42.

———. "Estate and Class in a Colonial City: Oaxaca in 1792." *Comparative Studies in Society and History*. 19, no. 3 (1977): 454–87.

Charlton, Thomas. "Land Tenure and Agricultural Production in the Otumba Region, 1785–1803." In *Land and Politics in the Valley of Mexico: A Two Thousand Year Perspective*, edited by H. R. Harvey, 223–63. Albuquerque: University of New Mexico Press, 1991.

Chaunu, Pierre. *Histoire, science sociale: La durée, l'espace, et l'homme á l'époque modern*. Paris: Société d' Édition d'Enseignement Supérieur, 1974.

———. *Les Philippines et le Pacifique des Ibériques. xvi, xvii, xviii siècles*. Paris: S.E.V.P.E.N., 1960.

Chowning, Margaret. "The Consolidacíon de Vales Reales in the Bishopric of Michoacán." *Hispanic American Historical Review* 69, no. 3 (1989): 451–78.

Coatsworth, John. "Características generales de la economía mexicana en el siglo xix." In Florescano, ed., q.v., 171–86.

———. "The Decline of the Mexican Economy, 1800–1906." In Liehr, ed., q.v., 27–53, 513–40.

———. "The Economic Historiography of Mexico." Paper presented to the Committee on Mexican Studies, Conference on Latin American History, American Historical Association, December 1986.

———. "Economic History and the History of Prices in Colonial Latin America." In Johnson and Tandeter, eds., q.v., 21–34.

———. "La historiografía económica de México." *Revista de historia económica* 6, no. 2 (1988): 277–91.

———. "The Limits of Colonial Absolutism: The State of Eighteenth-Century Mexico." In Spalding, ed., q.v., 25–51.

———. "Obstacles to Economic Growth in Nineteenth-Century Mexico." *American Historical Review* 83, no. 1 (1977): 80–100.

Coatsworth, John, Héctor Lindo-Fuentes, Arij Ouweneel, Catrien C. J. H. Bijleveld, and D. A. Brading. "Comments on the 'The Economic Cycle in Bourbon Central Mexico: A Critique of the Recaudación del diezmo líquido en pesos'." *Hispanic American Historical Review* 69, no. 3 (1989): 538–45.

Cochran, Thomas. "Entrepreneurship." In Sills, ed., q.v., 5:87–91.

Cook, Sherburne, and Woodrow Borah. *Essays in Population History*. 3 vols. Berkeley: University of California Press, 1971–79.

Costeloe, Michael. *Church Wealth in Mexico: A Study of the 'Juzgado de Capellanías in the Archbishopric of Mexico, 1800–1856*. London: Cambridge University Press, 1967.

Crafts, N. F. R. "British Economic Growth, 1700–1850: Some Difficulties of Interpretation." *Explorations in Economic History* 24, no. 3 (1987): 245–68.

———. *British Economic Growth During the Industrial Revolution.* Oxford: Clarendon Press, and New York: Oxford University Press, 1985.

Cuenca-Esteban, Javier. "The Markets of Latin American Exports, 1790–1820: A Comparative Analysis of International Prices." In Johnson and Tandeter, eds., q.v., 373–99.

David, Paul. "The Growth of Real Product in the United States Before 1840: New Evidence, Controlled Conjectures." *Journal of Economic History* 27, no. 2 (1967): 151–95.

Deans-Smith, Susan. "The Money Plant: The Royal Tobacco Monopoly of New Spain, 1765–1821." In Jacobsen and Puhle, eds., q.v., 361–87.

DeVries, Jan. *European Urbanization, 1500–1800.* Cambridge, Mass.: Harvard University Press, 1984.

Fisher, John. *Commercial Relations Between Spain and Spanish America in the Era of Free Trade, 1778–1796.* Liverpool: Centre for Latin-American Studies, University of Liverpool, 1985.

———. "Imperial 'Free Trade' and the Hispanic Economy, 1778–1796." *Journal of Latin American Studies* 13, no. 1 (1981): 21–56.

———. "The Imperial Response to 'Free Trade': Spanish Imports from Spanish America, 1778–1796." *Journal of Latin American Studies* 17, no. 1 (1985): 35–78.

———. *Silver Mines and Silver Miners in Colonial Peru, 1776–1824.* Liverpool: Centre for Latin-American Studies, University of Liverpool, 1977.

Florescano, Enrique. "The Formation and Economic Structure of the Hacienda in New Spain." In Bethell, ed., q.v., 2:153–88.

Florescano, Enrique. *Origen y desarrollo de los problemas agrarios de México, 1500–1821* (originally published as *Estructuras y problemas agrarios de México (1500–1821)*). Mexico: Ediciones Era, 1976.

——— *Precios del maíz y crisis agrícolas en México (1708–1810). Ensayos sobre el movimiento de los precios y sus consecuencias económicas y sociales.* Mexico: El Colegio de México, 1969.

———, ed. *Ensayos sobre el desarrollo económico de México y América Latina, 1500–1975.* Mexico: Fondo de Cultura Económica, 1979.

———, ed. *Haciendas, latifundios y plantaciones en Américas Latinas.* Mexico: Siglo Veintiuno Editores, 1975.

Florescano, Enrique, and Isabel Gil Sánchez. *Descripciones económicas regionales de Nueva España. Provincias del Norte, 1790–1814.* Mexico: Instituto Nacional de Antropología e Historia, 1976.

———, eds. *Descripciones económicas generales de Nueva España, 1748–1817.* Mexico: Instituto Nacional de Antropología e Historia, 1973.

———, comps. *Descripciones económicas regionales de Nueva España. Provincias del Centro, Sureste y Sur, 1766–1827.* Mexico: Instituto Nacional de Antropología e Historia, 1976.

Fonseca, Fabián, and Carlos de Urrutia. *Historia general de Real Hacienda.* 6 vols. Mexico: Imprenta de Vicente García Torres, 1845–53.

Frost, Elsa Cecilia, Michael C. Meyer, and Josefina Zoraida Vásquez, comps. *El trabajo y los trabajadores en la historia de México.* Tucson: University of Arizona Press, 1979.

Galicia, Silvia. *Precios y producción en San Miguel el Grande, 1661–1803.* Mexico: Instituto Nacional de Antropología e Historia, 1975.

Gamboa, Francisco Javier. *Comentarios de las ordenanzas de minas. . . .* Madrid: J. Ibarra, 1761.

Garavaglia, Juan Carlos, and Juan Carlos Grosso. "La región de Puebla/Tlaxcala y la economía novohispana (1670–1821)." *Historia Mexicana* 35, no. 4 (1986): 549–600.

———. *Las alcabalas novohispanas (1776–1821).* Mexico: Banco Cremi, 1987.

García Acosta, Virginia. "*Los panes y sus precios en ciudades novohispanas.*" *Papeles de la Casa Chata* 1, no. 2 (1986): 3–16.

———. *Los precios del trigo en la historia colonial de México.* Mexico: Ediciones de la Casa Chata, 1988.

García Ayluardo, Clara. "El comerciante y el crédito durante la época borbónica en la Nueva España." In Ludlow and Marichal, eds., q.v., 27–50.

García-Baquero González, Antonio. *Cádiz y el Atlántico (1717–1778). El comercio colonial español bajo el monopolio gaditano.* 2 vols. Seville: Escuela de Estudios Hispano-Americanos, 1976.

Garner, Richard. "Exportaciones de circulante en el siglo xviii." *Historia mexicana* 31, no. 4 (1982): 544–98.

———. "Further Consideration of 'Facts and Figments in Bourbon Mexico.' " *Bulletin of Latin American Research* 6, no. 1 (1987): 55–63.

———. "Long-Term Silver Mining Trends in Spanish America: A Comparative Analysis of Peru and Mexico." *American Historical Review* 93, no. 4 (1988): 898–935.

———. "Price Trends in Eighteenth-Century Mexico." *Hispanic American Historical Review* 65, no. 2 (1985): 279–326.

———. "Problèmes d'une ville miniére mexicaine à la fin de l'époque coloniale: prix et salaires à Zacatecas (1760–1821)." *Cahiers des Amériques Latines* 6 (1972): 75–111.

———. "Reformas borbónicas y operaciones hacendarias—La real caja de Zacatecas—1750–1821." *Historia mexicana* 27, no. 4 (1978): 542–87.

———. "Silver Production and Entrepreneurial Structure in Eighteenth-Century Mexico." *Jahrbuch für Geschichte von Staat, Wirtschaft und Gesellschaft Lateinamerikas* 17 (1980): 157–85.

———. "Zacatecas, 1750–1821: A Study of a Late Colonial Mexican City." Ph.D. diss., University of Michigan, 1970.

Garner, Richard, and William Taylor, eds. *Iberian Colonies, New World Societies: Essays in Memory of Charles Gibson.* State College, Penn.: Privately published, 1985.

Gerhard, Peter. *A Guide to the Historical Geography of New Spain.* Cambridge: Cambridge University Press, 1972.

———. *Mexico in 1742.* Mexico: J. Porrúa, 1962.

———. *The Northern Frontier of New Spain.* Princeton, N.J.: Princeton University Press, 1982.

Gibson, Charles. *The Aztecs under Spanish Rule: A History of the Indians of the Valley of Mexico, 1519–1810.* Stanford, Calif.: Stanford University Press, 1964.

Gould, J. D. *Economic Growth in History: Survey and Analysis.* London: Methuen, 1972.

Grantham, George. "Agricultural Supply During the Industrial Revolution: French Evidence and European Implications." *Journal of Economic History* 49, no. 1 (1989): 43–72.

———. "Jean Meuvret and the Subsistence Problem in Early Modern France." *Journal of Economic History* 49, no. 1 (1989): 184–200.

Grassby, Richard. "The Rate of Profit in Seventeenth-Century England." *English Historical Review* 84, no. 333 (1969): 721–51.

Greenow, Linda. *Credit and Socioeconomic Change in Colonial Mexico: Loans and Mortgages in Guadalajara, 1720–1820.* Boulder, Colo.: Westview Press, 1983.

Grigg, David. *Dynamics of Agricultural Change: The Historical Experience.* London: Hutchinson, 1982.

———. *Population Growth and Agrarian Change: An Historical Perspective.* Cambridge: Cambridge University Press, 1980.

Hamnett, Brian. "The Appropriation of Mexican Church Wealth by the Spanish Bourbon Government—The Consolidación de Vales, 1805–1809." *Journal of Latin American Studies* 1, no. 1 (1969): 85–113.

———. *Politics and Trade in Southern Mexico, 1750–1821.* Cambridge: Cambridge University Press, 1971.

Haring, C. H. *The Spanish Empire in America.* New York: Harcourt, Brace and World, 1963.

Harris, Charles, III. *A Mexican Family Empire: The Latifundio of the Sánchez Navarros, 1765–1867.* Austin: University of Texas Press, 1975.

Hartz, Louis, ed. *The Founding of New Societies: Studies in the History of the United States, Latin America, South Africa, Canada, and Australia.* New York: Harcourt, Brace and World, 1964.

Haslip-Viera, Gabriel. "The Underclass." In Hoberman and Socolow, eds., q.v., 285–312.

Hirschman, Albert. "A Generalized Linkage Approach to Development, with Special Reference to Staples." In *Essays on Economic Development and Cultural Change in Honor of Bert F. Hoselitz,* edited by Manning Nash, 67–98. Chicago: University of Chicago Press, 1977. Published as supplement to *Economic Development and Cultural Change* 25 (1977): 67–98.

———. *The Strategy of Economic Development.* New Haven: Yale University Press, 1958.

Hoberman, Louisa, and Susan Socolow, eds. *Cities and Society in Colonial Latin America*. Albuquerque: University of New Mexico Press, 1986.

Howe, Walter. *The Mining Guild of New Spain and Its Tribunal General, 1770–1820*. Cambridge, Mass.: Harvard University Press, 1949.

Humboldt, Alexander von. *Political Essay on the Kingdom of New Spain*. 4 vols. New York: AMS Press, 1966.

Hurtado López, Flor de María. *Dolores Hidalgo, estudio económico, 1740–1790*. Mexico: Instituto Nacional de Antropología e Historia, 1974.

Israel, J. I. "Mexico and the 'General Crisis' of the Seventeenth Century." *Past and Present* 63 (1974): 33–57.

———. *Race, Class and Politics in Colonial Mexico, 1610–1670*. London: Oxford University Press, 1975.

Israel, J. I., Henry Kamen, John TePaske, and Herbert Klein. "Debate: The Seventeenth-Century Crisis in New Spain: Myth or Reality?" *Past and Present* 97 (1982): 144–61.

Instituto Nacional de Estudios Históricos de la Revolución Mexicana. *Conflicto de trabajo con los mineros de Real del Monte, Año de 1766*. Mexico: Comisión Nacional para la Celebración Sesquicentenario de la Independencia Nacional del Cincuentenario de la Revolución Mexicana, 1960.

Jacobsen, Nils, and Hans-Jürgen Puhle, eds. *The Economies of Mexico and Peru During the Colonial Period, 1760–1810*. Berlin: Colloquium Verlag, 1986.

Jiménez-Pelayo, Águeda. "El impacto del crédito en la economía rural de la Nueva Galicia." *Hispanic American Historical Review* 71, no. 3 (1991): 501–29.

Johnson, Lyman, and Enrique Tandeter, eds. *Essays on the Price History of Eighteenth-Century Latin America*. Albuquerque: University of New Mexico Press, 1990.

Johnston, J. *Econometric Methods*. 3d ed. New York: McGraw-Hill, 1984.

Jones, E. L., and S. J. Woolf, eds. *Agrarian Change and Agricultural Development: The Historical Problems*. London: Methuen, 1969.

Just, R. E. "An Investigation of the Importance of Risk in Farmers' Decisions." *American Journal of Agricultural Economics* 56, no. 1 (1974): 14–25.

Katz, Friedrich, ed. *Riot, Rebellion, and Revolution: Rural Social Conflict in Mexico*. Princeton, N.J.: Princeton University Press, 1988.

Kennedy, Peter. *A Guide to Econometrics*. 1st ed., Cambridge, Mass.: MIT Press, 1979. 2d ed., Cambridge, Mass.: MIT Press, 1985.

Kicza, John. *Colonial Entrepreneurs, Families and Businesses in Bourbon Mexico*. Albuquerque: University of New Mexico Press, 1983.

Kinsbruner, Jay. *Petty Capitalism in Spanish America: The Pulperos of Puebla, Mexico City, Caracas, and Buenos Aires*. Boulder, Colo.: Westview Press, 1987.

Klein, Herbert. "La economía de la Nueva España, 1680–1809. Un análisis a partir de las cajas reales." *Historia mexicana* 34, no. 4 (1985): 561–609.

———. "Structure and Profitability of Royal Finance in the Viceroyalty of the Río de la Plata in 1790." *Hispanic American Historical Review* 53, no. 3 (1973): 440–69.

Klein, Herbert, and Stanley Engerman. "Methods and Meanings in Price History." In Johnson and Tandeter, eds., q.v., 9–20.

Klein, Herbert, and Jacques Barbier. "Recent Trends in the Study of Spanish American Colonial Public Finance." *Latin American Research Review* 23, no. 1 (1988): 35–62.

Knight, Frank. *Risk, Uncertainty and Profit*. Boston: Houghton Mifflin, 1921.

Konrad, Herman. *A Jesuit Hacienda in Colonial Mexico: Santa Lucía 1576–1767*. Stanford, Calif.: Stanford University Press, 1980.

Kriedte, Peter. "Origins, Context and World-Market Conditions in the World Market." In Kriedte, Medick, and Schlumbohm, eds., q.v., 12–37.

Kriedte, Peter, Hans Medick, and Jürgen Schlumbohm, eds. *Industrialization Before Industrialization: Rural Industry in the Genesis of Capitalism*. Cambridge: Cambridge University Press, 1981.

Kuethe, Allan. "Toward a Periodization of the Reforms of Charles III." In Garner and Taylor, eds., q.v., 103–17.

Ladd, Doris. *The Making of a Strike: Mexican Silver Workers' Struggle in Real del Monte, 1766–1775*. Lincoln: University of Nebraska Press, 1988.

———. *The Mexican Nobility at Independence, 1770–1826*. Austin: University of Texas Press, 1976.

Lassaga, Juan Lucas, and Joaquín Velásquez de León. *Representación que a nombre de la minería de la Nueva España hacen el rey nuestro señor los a poderados de ella*. Mexico: Felipe de Zúñiga y Ontiveros, 1774.

Latin American Economic History Newsletter 1 (Dec. 1991): 5–8.

Lavrin, Asunción. "El capital eclesiástico y las elites sociales en Nueva España a fines del siglo xviii." *Estudios mexicanos* 1, no. 1 (1985): 1–28.

———. "The Execution of the Laws of Consolidación in New Spain: Economic Aims and Results." *Hispanic American Historical Review* 53, no. 1 (1973): 27–49.

———. "The Role of Nunneries in the Economy of New Spain in the Eighteenth Century." *Hispanic American Historical Review* 46, no. 4 (1966): 371–93.

Lerdo de Tejada, Miguel. *Comercio exterior de México desde la Conquista hasta hoy*. Mexico: Banco Nacional de Comercio Exterior, 1852.

Le Roy Ladurie, Emmanuel, and Joseph Goy. *Tithe and Agrarian History from the Fourteenth to the Nineteenth Centuries: An Essay in Comparative History*. Cambridge: Cambridge University Press, 1982.

Liehr, Reinhard, ed. *América Latina en la época de Simón Bolívar*. Berlin: Colloquium Verlag, 1989.

Lindley, Richard. *Haciendas and Economic Development: Guadalajara, Mexico at Independence*. Austin: University of Texas Press, 1983.

Lindo-Fuentes, Héctor. "La utilidad de los diezmos como fuentes para la historia económica." *Historia mexicana* 30, no. 2 (1980): 273–89.

Lindo-Fuentes, Héctor, Arij Ouweneel, Catrien C. J. H. Bijleveld, D. A. Brading, and John Coatsworth. "Comments on the 'The Economic Cycle in Bourbon Central Mexico: A Critique of the Recaudación del diezmo líquido en pesos.' " *Hispanic American Historical Review* 69, no. 3 (1989): 545–49.

Lira González, Andrés. "Aspecto fiscal de la Nueva España en la segunda mitad del siglo xviii." *Historia mexicana* 27, no. 3 (1968): 361–92.

Liss, Peggy. *Atlantic Empires: The Network of Trade and Revolution, 1713–1826*. Baltimore, Md.: Johns Hopkins University Press, 1983.

Litle, Marcella. "Sales Taxes and Internal Commerce in Bourbon Mexico, 1754–1821." Ph.D. diss., Duke University, 1985. Ann Arbor: University Microfilms, 1985.

Lockhart, James. "The Social History of Colonial Spanish America: Evolution and Potential," *Latin American Research Review* 7, no. 1 (1972): 6–45.

López Miramontes, Alvaro, and Cristiana Urrutia de Stebelski. *Las minas de Nueva España en 1774*. Mexico: Instituto Nacional de Antropología e Historia, 1980.

López Sarrelangue, Delfina. "Población indígena de Nueva España en el siglo xviii." *Historia mexicana* 12, no. 4 (1963): 516–30.

Ludlow, Leonor, and Carlos Marichal, eds., *Banco y poder en México (1800–1925)*. Mexico City: Grijalbo, 1985.

Luh, Y.-H., and S. E. Stefanou. "Dairy Supply and Factor Demand Response to Output Price Risk: An Econometric Assessment." *Northeastern Journal of Agricultural and Resource Economics* 18, no. 2 (1989): 103–8.

MacLeod, Murdo. Review of Trabulse et al., *Fluctuaciones económicas en Oaxaca durante el siglo xviii. Hispanic American Historical Review* 60, no. 4 (1980): 733–34.

Martin, Cheryl English. *Rural Society in Colonial Morelos*. Albuquerque: University of New Mexico Press, 1985.

McCaa, Robert, Stuart Schwartz, and Arturo Grubessich. "Race and Class in Colonial Latin America: A Critique." *Comparative Studies in Society and History* 21, no. 3 (1979): 421–33.

McCusker, John. *Money and Exchange in Europe and America, 1600–1775: A Handbook*. Chapel Hill: University of North Carolina Press, 1978.

McCusker, John, and Ronald Menard. *The Economy of British America, 1607–1789*. Chapel Hill: University of North Carolina Press, 1985.

McWatters, David Lorne. "The Royal Tobacco Monopoly in Bourbon Mexico, 1764–1810." Ph.D. diss., University of Florida, 1979. Ann Arbor: University Microfilms, 1979.

Medina Rubio, Arístides. *La iglesia y la producción agrícola en Puebla, 1540–1795*. Mexico: El Colegio de México, 1983.

Meek, Wilbur. *The Exchange Media of Colonial Mexico.* New York: King's Crown Press, 1948.

Miño Grijalva, Manuel. "La circulación de mercancías: una referencia al caso textil latinoamericano (1750–1810)." In Ouweneel and Torales Pacheco, comps., q.v., 45–58.

Mokyr, Joel. "Has the Industrial Revolution Been Crowded Out? Some Reflections on Crafts and Williamson." *Explorations in Economic History,* 24, no. 3 (1987): 293–319.

Mora, José María Luis. *Obras sueltas de José María Luis Mora, ciudadano mexicano.* 2d ed. Mexico: Editorial Porrúa, 1963.

Morin, Claude. *Michoacán en la Nueva España del siglo xviii. Crecimiento y desigualdad en una economía colonial.* Mexico: Fondo de Cultura Económica, 1979.

Morineau, Michel. *Incroyables gazettes et fabuleux métaux: Les retours des trésors américains d'après les gazettes hollandaises (XVIe-XVIIIe siècles).* Cambridge: Cambridge University Press, 1985.

Morse, Richard. "The Heritage of Latin America." In Hartz, ed., q.v., 123–77.

———. ed. *The Urban Development of Latin America, 1750–1920.* Stanford, Calif.: Center for Latin American Studies, Stanford University, 1971.

Ortiz de la Tabla Ducasse, Javier. *Comercio exterior de Veracruz, 1778–1791. Crisis de dependencia.* Seville: Escuela de Estudios Hispano-Americanos, 1978.

Ouweneel, Arij. "The Agrarian Cycle as a Catalyst of Economic Development in Eighteenth-Century Central Mexico: The Arable Estate, Indian Villages and Proto-Industrialization in the Central Highland Valleys." *Ibero-Amerikanisches Archiv* 15, no. 3 (1989): 399–417.

———. "Eighteenth-Century Tlaxcalan Agriculture: Diary 9 of the Hacienda San Antonio Palula, 1765–1766." In Buva, ed., q.v., 21–83.

———. "Growth, Stagnation, and Migration: An Explorative Analysis of the Tributario Series of Anáhuac (1720–1800)." *Hispanic American Historical Review* 71, no. 3 (1991): 531–77.

Ouweneel, Arij, and Catrien C. J. H. Bijleveld. "The Economic Cycle in Bourbon Central Mexico: A Critique of the Recaudación del diezmo líquido en pesos." *Hispanic American Historical Review* 69, no. 3 (1989): 479–530.

Ouweneel, Arij, Catrien C. J. H. Bijleveld, D. A. Brading, John Coatsworth, and Héctor Lindo-Fuentes. "Comments on the 'The Economic Cycle in Bourbon Central Mexico: A Critique of the Recaudación del diezmo líquido en pesos.'" *Hispanic American Historical Review,* 69, no. 3 (1989): 549–57.

Ouweneel, Arij, and Cristina Torales Pacheco, comps. *Empresarios, indios y estado. Perfil de la economía mexicana (Siglo XVIII).* Amsterdam: Centre for Latin American Research and Documentation, 1988.

Pansters, Wil, and Arij Ouweneel, eds. *Region, State and Capitalism in*

Mexico: Nineteenth and Twentieth Centuries. Amsterdam: Centre for Latin American Research and Documentation, 1989.

Pérez Herrero, Pedro. "El crecimiento económico novohispano durante el siglo xviii: un revisión." *Revista de historia económica* 7, no. 1 (1989): 69–110.

———. *Plata y libranza. La articulación comercial del México borbónico.* Mexico: El Colegio de México, 1988.

Pietschmann, Horst. "Agricultura e industria rural indígena en el México de la segunda mitad del siglo xviii." In Ouweneel and Torales Pacheco, comps., q.v., 71–85.

Potash, Robert. *El Banco de Avío de México: El fomento de la industria, 1821–1846.* Mexico: Fondo de Cultura Económica, 1959.

Price, Jacob. *Capitalism and Credit in British Overseas Trade: The View from the Chesapeake, 1700–1765.* Cambridge, Mass.: Harvard University Press, 1980.

———. "Economic Function and the Growth of American Port Towns in the Eighteenth Century." *Perspectives in American History* 8 (1974): 121–86.

Priestley, Herbert. *José de Gálvez, Visitor-General of New Spain, 1765–1771.* Berkeley: University of California Press, 1916.

Rabell Romero, Cecilia. *Los diezmos de San Luis de la Paz. Economía en una región del Bajío en el siglo xviii.* Mexico: Universidad Nacional Autónoma de México, 1986.

Ramírez Flores, José. *El Real Consulado de Guadalajara. Notas históricas.* Guadalajara: Banco Refaccionario de Jalisco, 1952.

Randall, Robert. *Real del Monte: A British Mining Venture in Mexico.* Austin: University of Texas Press, 1972.

Real Díaz, José Joaquín. "Las ferias de Jalapa." In Real Díaz and Carrera Stampa, comps., q.v., 1–168.

Real Díaz, José Joaquín, and Manuel Carrera Stampa, comps. *Las ferias comerciales de Nueva España.* Mexico: Instituto Mexicano de Comercio Exterior, 1959.

Reinhardt, Nola. *Our Daily Bread: The Peasant Question and Family Farming in the Colombian Andes.* Berkeley: University of California Press, 1989.

Rendón, Francisco. "La Provincia de Zacatecas en 1803." *Memoria de la Academia Nacional de Historia y Geografía* 6 (1955): 5–35.

Reynolds, Clark. *The Mexican Economy: Twentieth-Century Structure and Growth.* New Haven: Yale University Press, 1970.

Riley, James. "Landlords, Laborers and Royal Government: The Administration of Labor in Tlaxcala." In Frost, Meyer, and Vásquez, comps., q.v., 221–29.

Rivera Bernárdez, José de (Conde de Santiago de la Laguna). *Descripción breve de la muy noble, y leal ciudad de Zacatecas.* Mexico: J. B. Hogal y Cie., 1732.

Rosenzweig Hernández, Fernando. "La economía novohispana al comenzar el siglo xix." *Ciencias políticas y sociales* 9, no. 33 (1963): 455–94.

Rothenberg, Winifred. "The Market and Massachusetts Farmers, 1750–1855." *Journal of Economic History* 41, no. 2 (1981): 283–313.

Salinas de la Torre, Gabriel, ed. *Testimonio de Zacatecas.* Mexico: Impr. Universitaria, 1946.

Salvucci, Linda. "Costumbres viejas, hombres nuevos. José de Gálvez y la burocracia fiscal novohispana (1754–1800)." *Historia mexicana* 33, no. 2 (1983): 224–64.

Salvucci, Linda, and Richard Salvucci. "Crecimiento económico y cambio de la productividad en México, 1750–1895." *HISLA* 10 (1987).

Salvucci, Richard. "Entrepreneurial Culture and the Textile Manufactories in Eighteenth-Century Mexico." *Anuario de estudios americanos* 39 (1982): 397–419.

———. *Textiles and Capitalism in Mexico: An Economic History of the Obrajes, 1539–1840.* Princeton, N.J.: Princeton University Press, 1987.

Sánchez-Albornoz, Nicolás. *La población de América Latina, desde los tiempos precolombinos al año 2000.* 2d ed. Madrid: Alianza Editorial, 1977.

———. "The Population of Colonial Spanish America." In Bethell, ed., q.v., 2: 3–35.

Sandmo, A. "On the Theory of the Competitive Firm under Price Uncertainty." *American Economic Review* 61, no. 1 (1971): 65–73.

Schlumbohm, Jürgen. "Excursus: The Political and Institutional Framework of Proto-Industrialization." In Kriedte, Medick, and Schlumbohm, eds., q.v., 126–34.

Schlumbohm, Jürgen. "Relations of Production—Productive Forces Crises in Proto-Industrialization." In Kriedte, Medick, and Schlumbohm, eds., q.v., 94–125.

Schmukler, Nathan and Edward Marcus, eds. *Inflation Through the Ages: Economic, Social, Psychological and Historical Aspects.* New York: Brooklyn College Press/Columbia University Press, 1983.

Serrera de Contreras, Ramón María. "Estado económico de la Intendencia de Guadalajara a principios del siglo xix. La 'Relación de José Fernando de Abascal y Sousa de 1803.'" *Jahrbuch für Geschichte von Staat, Wirtschaft und Gesellschaft Lateinamerikas* 11 (1974): 121–48.

Shepherd, James, and Gary Walton. *Shipping, Maritime Trade, and the Economic Development of Colonial North America.* Cambridge: Cambridge University Press, 1972.

Sills, David, ed. *International Encyclopedia of the Social Sciences.* 17 vols. Reprint. New York: Macmillan and Free Press, 1972.

Slicher van Bath, Bernard. *Bevolking en Economie in Nieuw Spanje (ca. 1570–1800).* Amsterdam and New York: North-Holland, 1981.

———. "De modelos referidos a la relación entre población y economía en Nueva España y Perú durante la época colonial." In Ouweneel and Torales Pacheco, comps., q.v., 15–44.

———. "Economic Diversification in Spanish America Around 1600: Centres, Intermediate Zones, and Peripheries." *Jahrbuch für Geschichte von Staat, Wirtschaft und Gesellschaft Lateinamerikas* 16 (1979): 53–95.

————. *Real Hacienda y economía en Hispanoamericana, 1541–1820.* Amsterdam: Centre for Latin American Research and Documentation, 1989.

Smith, Robert. "The Institution of the Consulado in New Spain." *Hispanic American Historical Review* 24, no. 1 (1944): 61–83.

Spalding, Karen, ed. *Essays in the Political, Economic and Social History of Colonial Latin America.* Newark: Latin American Studies Program, University of Delaware, 1982.

Stein, Stanley. "Prelude to Upheaval in Spain and New Spain, 1800–1808: Trust Funds, Spanish Finance and Colonial Silver." In Garner and Taylor, eds., q.v., 185–202.

Suárez Argüello, Clara Elena. *La política cerealera en la economía novohispana. El caso del trigo.* Mexico: Ediciones de la Casa Chata, 1985.

Super, John. "Bread and the Provisioning of Mexico City in the Late Eighteenth Century." *Jahrbuch für Geschichte von Staat, Wirtschaft und Gesellschaft Lateinamerikas* 19 (1982): 157–82.

————. "Querétaro *obrajes*: Industry and Society in Provincial Mexico, 1600–1810." *Hispanic American Historical Review* 56, no. 2 (1976): 197–216.

Swann, Michael. *Tierra Adentro: Settlement and Society in Colonial Durango.* Boulder, Colo.: Westview Press, 1982.

Tandrón, Humberto. *El comercio de Nueva España y la controversia sobre la libertad de comercio, 1796–1821.* Mexico City: Instituto Mexicano de Comercio Exterior, 1976.

Taylor, William. "Banditry and Insurrection: Rural Unrest in Central Jalisco." In Katz, ed., q.v., 205–46.

————. "Between Global Process and Local Knowledge: An Inquiry into Early Latin American Social History, 1500–1900." In Zunz, ed., q.v., 115–90.

————. *Drinking, Homicide, and Rebellion in Colonial Mexican Villages.* Stanford, Calif.: Stanford University Press, 1979.

————. "Indian Pueblos of Central Jalisco on the Eve of Independence." In Garner and Taylor, eds., q.v., 161–84.

————. *Landlord and Peasant in Colonial Oaxaca.* Stanford, Calif.: Stanford University Press, 1972.

————. "Town and Country in the Valley of Oaxaca." In Altman and Lockhart, eds., q.v., 63–96.

TePaske, John. "Economic Cycles in New Spain in the Eighteenth Century: The View from the Public Sector." *Bibliotheca Americana* 1, no. 3 (1983): 169–203.

————. "Economic Cycles in Eighteenth-Century New Spain in the Eighteenth Century: The View from the Public Sector." In Garner and Taylor, eds., q.v., 119–42.

————. "The Fiscal Structure of Upper Peru and the Financing of Empire." In Spalding, ed., q.v., 69–94.

TePaske, John, with José and María Luz Hernández Palomo. *La Real Hacienda de Nueva España: La Real Caja de México (1576–1816)*. Mexico: Instituto Nacional de Antropología e Historia, 1976.

TePaske, John, and Herbert Klein. *Ingresos y egresos de la Real Hacienda de Nueva España*. 2 vols. Mexico: Instituto Nacional de Antropología e Historia, 1986.

———. "The Seventeenth-Century Crisis in New Spain: Myth or Reality?" *Past and Present* 90 (1981): 116–35.

TePaske, John, and Herbert Klein, with Kendall Brown. *The Royal Treasuries of the Spanish Empire in America*. 3 vols. Durham, N.C.: Duke University Press, 1982.

Thomson, Guy. "The Cotton Textile Industry in Puebla During the Eighteenth and Early Nineteenth Centuries." In Jacobsen and Puhle, eds., q.v., 169–203.

———. *Puebla de los Angeles: Industry and Society in a Mexican City, 1700–1850*. Boulder, Colo.: Westview Press, 1989.

Tilly, Charles. *Big Structures, Large Processes, Huge Comparisons*. New York: Russell Sage Foundation, 1984.

Tobin, James. "Inflation: Monetary and Structural Causes and Cures." In Schmukler and Marcus, eds., q.v., 3–16.

Torales Pacheco, María Cristina. "Tradicionalismo y modernidad en el comercio novohispano de la segunda mitad del siglo xviii: La Compañía de Francisco Ignacio de Yraeta." In Ouweneel and Torales Pacheco, comps., q.v., 59–70.

Torres Ramírez, Bibiano, and Javier Ortiz de la Table Ducasse, eds. *Reglamento y aranceles reales para el comercio libre de España a Indias de 12 de Octobre de 1778*. Seville: Escuela de Estudios Hispano-Americanos, 1978.

Tovar Pinsón, Hermes. "Elementos constitutivos de la empresa agraria jesuíta en la segunda mitad del siglo xviii en México." In Florescano, ed., q.v., 132–222.

Trabulse, Elías, T. Pastor, L. Adelson, E. Berra, F. Hurtado, J. MacGregor, and G. Zermeño. *Fluctuaciones económicas en Oaxaca durante el siglo xviii*. Mexico: El Colegio de México, 1979.

Traill, B. "Risk Variables in Econometric Supply Response Models." *Journal of Agricultural Economics* 29, no. 1 (1978): 53–61.

Tutino, John. *From Insurrection to Revolution in Mexico: Social Bases of Agrarian Violence, 1750–1940*. Princeton, N.J.: Princeton University Press, 1986.

U.S. Department of Commerce, Bureau of Economic Analysis. *GNP: An Overview of Source Data and Estimating Methods*. Washington, D.C.: Government Printing Office, September 1987.

Valdés Lakowsky, Vera. *De las minas al mar. Historia de la plata mexicana en Asia, 1564–1834*. Mexico: Fondo de Cultura Económica, 1987.

Van Young, Eric. "A modo de conclusión: el siglo paradójico." In Ouweneel and Torales Pacheco, eds., q.v., 206–31.

———. "The Age of Paradox: Mexican Agriculture at the End of the Colonial Period, 1750–1810." In Jacobsen and Puhle, eds., q.v., 64–90.

———. *Hacienda and Market in Eighteenth-Century Mexico: The Rural Economy of the Guadalajara Region, 1675–1820*. Berkeley: University of California Press, 1981.

———. "Islands in the Storm: Quiet Cities and Violent Countrysides in the Mexican Independence Era." *Past and Present* 118 (1988): 130–55.

———. "Mexican Rural History since Chevalier: The Historiography of the Colonial Hacienda." *Latin American Research Review* 18, no. 3 (1983): 5–62.

———. "Moving Toward Revolt: Agrarian Origins of the Hidalgo Rebellion in the Guadalajara Region." In Katz, ed., q.v., 176–204.

———. "Recent Anglophone Scholarship on Mexico and Central America in the Age of Revolution (1750–1850)." *Hispanic American Historical Review* 65, no. 4 (1985): 735–43.

———. "The Rich Get Richer and the Poor Get Skewed: Real Wages and Popular Living Standards in Late Colonial Mexico." Paper delivered to All-University of California Group in Economic History, Huntington Library, May 1987.

Velázquez, María del Carmen. "José Alejandro de Bustamante, minero de Pachuca." *Historia mexicana* 25, no. 3 (1976): 335–62.

Villaseñor y Sánchez, José Antonio. *Theatro americano. Descripción general de los reynos, y provincias de la Nueva España, y sus jurisdicciones*. Mexico: J. B. Hogal y Cie., 1746–48.

Los virreyes de Nueva España en el reinado de Carlos IV. 2 vols. Seville: Escuelas de Estudios Hispano-Americanos, 1972–75.

Walker, Geoffrey. *Spanish Politics and Imperial Trade, 1700–1789*. Bloomington: Indiana University Press, 1979.

Ward, H. G. *Mexico in 1827*. 2 vols. 2d ed. London: H. Colburn, 1834.

West, Robert. *The Mining Community in Northern New Spain: The Parral Mining District*. Berkeley: University of California Press, 1949.

Wilken, Gene. *Good Farmers: Traditional Agricultural Resource Management in Mexico and Central America*. Berkeley: University of California Press, 1987.

Williamson, Jeffrey. "Debating the British Industrial Revolution," *Explorations in Economic History* 24, no. 3 (1987): 269–92.

Wonnacott, Ronald, and Thomas Wonnacott. *Econometrics*. 2d ed. New York: John Wiley and Sons, 1978.

Zunz, Oliver, ed. *Reliving the Past: The Worlds of Social History*. Chapel Hill: University of North Carolina Press, 1985.

Index

Richard Garner has been a member of the Department of History at Penn State University since 1968. He received a Ph.D. in history from the University of Michigan, where he was a student of the late Charles Gibson. He has published widely in colonial economic history, with a particular interest in applying statistical techniques to historical datasets. He has conducted research in the archives of Mexico, Peru, and Spain and has taught seminars on historical statistics in Mexico.

Spiro Stefanou joined the Department of Agricultural Economics at Penn State University in 1983 after receiving his Ph.D. from the University of California at Davis. He has published numerous articles and reports on the application of econometric techniques to the study of agricultural production systems. In 1990–91 he was attached to the economic research unit of the European Community in Florence, Italy, and he serves as an economic consultant to governments in Eastern Europe.